PAPER

Also by MARK KURLANSKY

NONFICTION

Salt: A World History

Cod: A Biography of the Fish That Changed the World

International Night: A Father and Daughter Cook Their Way Around the World. Including More Than 250 Recipes

Birdseye: The Adventures of a Curious Man

Ready for a Brand New Beat: How "Dancing in the Street" Became an Anthem for a Changing America

What? Are These the 20 Most Important Questions in Human History— Or Is This a Game of 20 Questions?

Hank Greenberg: The Hero Who Didn't Want to Be One

The Big Oyster: History on the Half Shell

The Eastern Stars: How Baseball Changed the Dominican Town of San Pedro de Macorís

The Last Fish Tale: The Fate of the Atlantic and Survival in Gloucester, America's Oldest Port and Most Original Town

Non-Violence: Twenty-Five Lessons from the History of a Dangerous Idea

1968: The Year That Rocked the World

Choice Cuts: A Savory Selection of Food Writing from Around the World and Throughout History

The Basque History of the World

A Chosen Few: The Resurrection of European Jewry

A Continent of Islands: Searching for the Caribbean Destiny

The Food of a Younger Land: A Portrait of American Food— Before the National Highway System, Before Chain Restaurants, and Before Frozen Food, When the Nation's Food Was Seasonal, Regional, and Traditional—from the Lost WPA Files

FICTION

City Beasts: Fourteen Short Stories of Uninvited Wildlife

Edible Stories: A Novel in Sixteen Parts

The Belly of Paris by Emile Zola: A New Translation with an Introduction by Mark Kurlansky

Boogaloo on 2nd Avenue: A Novel of Pastry, Guilt, and Music

The White Man in the Tree and Other Stories

CHILDREN / YOUNG ADULT

Battle Fatigue

World Without Fish

The Story of Salt

The Girl Who Swam to Euskadi

The Cod's Tale

Frozen in Time: Clarence Birdseye's Outrageous Idea About Frozen Food

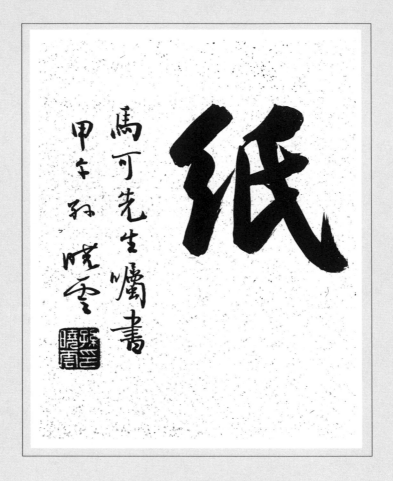

Zhi, "paper," signed by Sun Xiaoyun,
a leading contemporary Chinese calligrapher,
and dedicated to the author.

PAPER

PAGING THROUGH HISTORY

MARK KURLANSKY

W. W. NORTON & COMPANY

Independent Publishers Since 1923

NEW YORK LONDON

For information about permission to reproduce selections from this book,
write to Permissions, W. W. Norton & Company, Inc.,
500 Fifth Avenue, New York, NY 10110

For information about special discounts for bulk purchases, please contact
W. W. Norton Special Sales at specialsales@wwnorton.com or 800-233-4830

Manufacturing by Quad Graphics Fairfield
Book design by Barbara Bachman
Production manager: Julia Druskin

ISBN 978-0-393-23961-4

W. W. Norton & Company, Inc.
500 Fifth Avenue, New York, N.Y. 10110
www.wwnorton.com

W. W. Norton & Company Ltd.
Castle House, 75/76 Wells Street, London W1T 3QT

1 2 3 4 5 6 7 8 9 0

To Marian:

The human mind is often so awkward and ill-regulated in the career of invention, that it is at first diffident, and then despises itself. For it appears at first incredible that any such discovery should be made, and when it has been made, it appears incredible that it should so long have escaped men's research.

—FRANCIS BACON, *Novum Organum, 1620*

CONTENTS

PROLOGUE: THE TECHNOLOGICAL FALLACY   *xiii*

CHAPTER 1: BEING HUMAN   *1*

CHAPTER 2: THE MOTHS THAT CIRCLE A CHINESE CANDLE   *22*

CHAPTER 3: THE ISLAMIC BIRTH OF LITERACY   *48*

CHAPTER 4: AND WHERE IS XÁTIVA?   *66*

CHAPTER 5: EUROPE BETWEEN TWO FELTS   *76*

CHAPTER 6: MAKING WORDS SOAR   *98*

CHAPTER 7: THE ART OF PRINTING   *118*

CHAPTER 8: OUT FROM MAINZ   *132*

CHAPTER 9: TENOCHTITLÁN AND THE BLUE-EYED DEVIL   *147*

CHAPTER 10: THE TRUMPET CALL   *162*

CHAPTER 11: REMBRANDT'S DISCOVERY   *167*

CHAPTER 12: THE TRAITOROUS CORRUPTION OF ENGLAND   *179*

CHAPTER 13: PAPERING INDEPENDENCE   *205*

CHAPTER 14: DIDEROT'S PROMISE   *226*

CHAPTER 15: INVITATION FROM A WASP   *245*

CHAPTER 16: ADVANTAGES IN THE HEAD   *256*

CHAPTER 17: TO DIE LIKE GENTLEMEN   *275*

CHAPTER 18: RETURN TO ASIA   *293*

EPILOGUE: CHANGE   *323*

APPENDIX: TIMELINE   *337*

ACKNOWLEDGMENTS   *345*

BIBLIOGRAPHY   *347*

INDEX   *355*

PROLOGUE

|||||||||||||||||||||||||||||||||||||||||||||||||||||||||||||||

The
Technological Fallacy

PRIGHT AND PIOUS PIERRE LE VÉNÉRABLE, PETER THE venerable, a twelfth-century monk from the Cluny monastery in France, visited Spain and observed that the Arabs and Jews there, rather than using animal skins, wrote even religious texts on leaves made from old clothes—what quality stationers today call "100 percent rag paper." He recognized that this was a clear sign of a degenerate society.

Throughout history the role of technology and people's reactions to it have been remarkably consistent, and those who worry about new technology and its impact on society would do well to reflect on the history of paper.

We tend to think of "technology" as referring only to the development of physical devices, mechanical in the nineteenth century, and now electronic. But the word can also be applied, as Merriam-Webster's dictionary says, to any "practical application of knowledge."

Technological inventions have always arisen from necessity. Numerous inventions preceded paper. First came spoken language, then drawing, then pictographs, then alphabets, then phoneticism, then writing, and then paper. Paper was then followed by printing, moveable type, typewriters, machine-driven printers, and electronic word processors and the electronic printers that go with them. As needs present themselves, solutions are found. Every idea engenders a need for another. In this case, the original inventions—spoken and then written language—are not physical, man-made objects, and so are not "technology" in the traditional sense of the word. But the way they function in and influence society and history is like a technology—a founding technology. Speech was the wheel that eventually led to the cart that was paper.

Studying the history of paper exposes a number of historical misconceptions, the most important of which is this technological fallacy: the idea that technology changes society. It is exactly the reverse. Society develops technology to address the changes that are taking place within it. To use a simple example, in China in 250 BCE, Meng Tian invented a paintbrush made from camel hair. His invention did not suddenly inspire the Chinese people to start writing and painting, or to develop calligraphy. Rather, Chinese society had already established a system of writing but had a growing urge for more written documents and more elaborate calligraphy. Their previous tool—a stick dipped in ink—could not meet the rising demand. Meng Tian found a device that made both writing and calligraphy faster and of a far higher quality.

Chroniclers of the role of paper in history are given to extravagant pronouncements: Architecture would not have been possible without paper. Without paper, there would have been no Renaissance. If there had been no paper, the Industrial Revolution would not have been possible.

None of these statements is true. These developments came about because society had come to a point where they were needed. This is true of all technology, but in the case of paper, it is particularly clear.

As far as scholars can tell, the Chinese were the only people to invent papermaking, though the Mesoamericans may also have done so; because of the destruction of their culture by the Spanish, we cannot be sure. And yet paper came into use at very different times in very different cultures as societies evolved and developed a need for it and circumstances required a cheap and easy writing material.

Five centuries after paper was being used widely by the Chinese bureaucracy, Buddhist monks in Korea developed a need for paper also. They adopted the Chinese craft, and took it to Japan to spread their religion. A few centuries later, the Arabs, having become adept at mathematics, astronomy, accounting, and architecture, saw a need for paper and started making and using it throughout the Middle East, North Africa, and Spain.

The Europeans initially had no use for paper until more than a thousand years after the Chinese invented it. It was not that they had only just discovered the existence of paper, however. The Arabs had been trying to sell it to them for years. But it was not until they began learning the Arab ways of mathematics and science, and started expanding literacy, that parchment made from animal hides—their previous writing material—became too slow and expensive to make in the face of their fast-growing needs.

The growth of intellectual pursuits and government bureaucracy, along with the spread of ideas and the expansion of commerce, is what led to papermaking. But its international growth was a remarkably slow process. The use of printing presses, steam engines, automobiles, and computers spread internationally over far shorter periods of time than did paper.

Paper seems an unlikely invention—breaking wood or fabric down into its cellulose fibers, diluting them with water, and passing the resulting liquid over a screen so that it randomly weaves and forms a sheet is not an idea that would logically come to mind, especially in an age when no one knew what cellulose was. It is not an apparent next step like printing, which various societies would arrive at independently. Suppose no one had thought of paper? Other materials would have been found. Improved writing material *had* to be found, because the needs of society demanded it.

There are other important lessons to be learned from the history of technology—and other commonly held fallacies. One is that new technology eliminates old. This rarely happens. Papyrus survived for centuries in the Mediterranean world after paper was introduced. Parchment remains in use. The invention of gas and electric heaters has not meant the end of fireplaces. Printing did not end penmanship, television did not kill radio, movies did not kill theatre, and home videos did not kill movie theaters, although all these things were falsely predicted. Electronic calculators have not even ended the use of the abacus, and more than a century after Thomas Edison was awarded a patent for a commercially successful lightbulb in 1879, there are still four hundred candle manufacturers in the United States alone, employing some 7,000 workers with annual sales of more than $2 billion. In fact, the first decade of the twenty-first century showed a growth in candle sales, though the uses of candles have of course greatly changed. Something similar occurred with the manufacturing and use of parchment. New technology, rather than eliminating older technology, increases choices. Computers will no doubt change the role of paper, but it is extremely unlikely that paper will be eliminated.

The history of technology also shows that Luddites always lose. The original Luddites were artisanal workers in eighteenth- and early nineteenth-century Britain who protested the loss of their skilled jobs to machines operated by low-wage, unskilled workers. Originally, the movement was active in a wide range of fields, including printing, but by the first decade of the nineteenth century, it was largely focused on the textile industry. It is uncertain why its proponents were called Luddites, but there was a mythical anti-machine rebel of the eighteenth century named Lud who, like Robin Hood, was said to live in Sherwood Forest. The Luddites opposed such technology as power looms, and they attacked mills, smashed machinery, and fought against the British Army. One mill owner was even assassinated, which led to the Frame Breaking Act of 1812, making it a capital crime to break machines. This eventually led to mass trials that crushed the movement.

Today, the term Luddite is used to mean someone who opposes new technology. And those who rail against the use of computers today are truly heirs to the Luddites, because the machine that the Luddites originally opposed, the mechanical loom, could be programmed to weave in various patterns through the use of punch cards—an early mechanical forerunner of the computer.

In his seminal work *Das Kapital*, Karl Marx said that the Luddites failed because they opposed the machines instead of the society. He observed: "The Luddites' mistake was that they failed to distinguish between machinery and its employment by capital, and to direct their attacks, not against the material instruments of production, but against the mode in which they are used."

In other words, it is futile to denounce technology itself. Rather, you have to try to change the operation of the society for which the technology was created. For every new technology, there are detractors, those who see the new invention as destroying all that is good in the old. This happened when the written word started to replace the oral word, when paper began replacing parchment, when printing started to take work away from scribes—and it is still happening today, with electronics threatening paper. In all these cases, the arguments against the new technology were similar: the functioning of the human brain was imperiled, we would lose the power of our memories, human contact would be diminished, and the warmth of human engagement would be lost.

These early outcries against technology went largely unheeded, much the same way warnings about computers are going unheeded today. It is true that the greater the aids to memory, the less we depend on our brain. But that does not mean that our minds are being destroyed. Illiterate people have better memories than literate people. But few would see that as an argument in favor of illiteracy. The introduction of the written word demonstrated that such aids, though they make us more dependent, also make us more powerful.

You cannot warn about what a new technology will do to a society because that society has already made the shift. That was Marx's point about the Luddites. Technology is only a facilitator. Society changes, and that change creates new needs. That is why the technology is brought in. The only way to stop the technology would be to reverse the changes in the society. Printing did not create the Protestant Reformation; the ideas and the will to spread them is what created printing presses. The

Chinese bureaucrats and Buddhist monks were not created by paper. Paper was created for them.

To argue that a technology somehow changed society would entail a technology that radically changed the *direction* of society. But this simply never happens. A technology that is intended to redirect society will usually fail. In fact, most technology companies do not introduce new technology but new ways to use ideas that already exist. They spend a great deal of time and money on market research—that is, determining where society already wants to go. Only once this direction is determined do they tailor a new product to meet that need.

Not all technology is the future. Some technology succeeds in a changing society and some fails. And even when an idea is right, the machine that introduces it to the society may not be. Cai Lun did not invent paper, Gutenberg did not invent the printing press, Robert Fulton did not invent the steamboat, and Thomas Edison did not invent the lightbulb. Rather, these were people who took existing ideas or machines that were not suiting society's needs and reworked them into technologies that did. It says something about our world that we seldom remember the person who came up with an idea, but canonize the pragmatist who made it commercially viable. Already we have forgotten the people who created most of the important computer concepts and instead celebrate the people who became rich on them.

Another important lesson is that technology usually becomes less expensive over time, as well as more accessible and of lower quality. Paper is far less expensive now than it used to be, but eighteenth-century paper was of much better quality than nineteenth-century paper, which in turn was better than much of today's paper.

For more than a thousand years, papermaking was the mark of civilization: an advanced civilization was one that made paper. When the Spanish conquistador Hernán Cortés arrived in the New World in 1504, he was extremely impressed by the Aztecs. They had built the largest city in the world and were advanced in mathematics and astronomy, but it was their papermaking ability that most impressed him. To the Spaniard, a society that made paper was an advanced civilization.

Using the paper test as the mark of civilization yields a surprisingly different but not inaccurate picture of history. In this version, civilization begins in Asia in 250 BCE and spreads to the Arab world. For centuries, the Arabs were the world's dominant culture, while the Europeans were among the most backward people on Earth. They didn't read, they had no science, and they could not do simple math; even when tracking their own commerce, they had no need for paper. The "barbarians" who destroyed Rome in the fifth century were still barbarians in the eleventh century.

Most historians today emphasize that the "Dark Ages" were not nearly as dark as they were said to be. But it is irrefutable that the Europeans were far behind the Asians and Arabs in many ways. Christians had not reached the intellectual level of Muslims and Jews. This became obvious when the Christians took over Muslim Spain, destroying the civilization of Muslim al-Andalus, and when they systematically destroyed one of the most advanced civilizations in the world in Mexico, suppressing their language, religion, and culture, and burning their books.

When Europe finally began to develop, it did not do so in the geographic order that many today might assume it did. Italy developed from the south up, starting with Sicily. Ireland developed far ahead of England. Much of Europe also progressed by adopting Arab ideas, especially in the areas of mathematics, science, and accounting. Later in history, Europe's leap forward, to a position ahead of its Arab and Asian competitors, was facilitated by moveable type, a Chinese invention. The Europeans could make that invention work for them because, unlike the Asians and Arabs, they had an alphabet that was well suited for moveable type. This also meant that Europeans got to write history the way they wanted it to be read.

THE IMPORTANCE OF the written word can be seen in the number of religions that have sacred texts, and in how often it is claimed that a god wrote these texts. The Egyptians believed that the ibis-headed Thoth, the scribe of the gods, gave humanity the gift of writing. For the Assyrians, it was Nabu, the god of writing. The Maya believed that Itsama, the son of the creator, invented writing and books. Sacred texts were distributed on a variety of writing materials prior to the invention of paper, and some, such as the Jewish Torah, are still preserved hand-written on animal skin.

But it is worth remembering that despite the importance of religion and culture, and science and mathematics, one of the greatest motivators for technological inventions, then as now, is the pursuit of money. The written language, paper, and computers were all developed to facilitate the expansion of business.

In his celebrated work *The Question Concerning Technology*, Martin Heidegger asserts that technology is "a means to an end," and then goes on to assert that even more than a means to an end, "Technology is a way of revealing."

According to Heidegger, to understand this we need to ask what causes a technology to be developed. All technology starts with an original, brilliant idea that future inventions simply help to reveal. In this sense, the automobile is a further exploration of an original great idea—the wheel. And paper is also a development from a great primary invention—written language.

PAPER

Chapter 1

BEING HUMAN

||||||||||||||||||

W HAT DO HUMANS DO THAT OTHER ANIMALS DO NOT
(aside from the curious observation by Pliny the Elder in the first century CE that "only man has ears that do not move")? Much is made of our
opposable thumbs, but many animals do quite well without them, carrying, climbing, and otherwise going about their lives with teeth, claws,
or tails. Indeed, the skill with which a cat uses its claws to snatch food
from an inattentive human's plate suggests that thumbs may at times
be overrated; though it is true that paws are not much good for typing.

The ability to build and change one's environment is not a uniquely
human trait either. Beavers build dams that completely alter rivers and
their banks and surrounding life. Neither are humans uniquely violent.
Most ants spend their lives at war. Other animals, such as wolves and
cats, laugh, joke, and play, just like humans do. Their sense of humor
and play may have developed during evolution to hone certain survival
skills, but the same may be true of us. Nor is communication uniquely
human. A variety of animals—including some insects, wolves, monkeys,

porpoises, and whales—communicate with sounds, sometimes even by composing music.

But there is one truly unique human trait: people *record*. They record their deeds, their emotions, their thoughts, and their ideas . . . they have an impulse to record almost everything that enters their minds and to save it for future generations. And it is this urge that led to the invention of paper. Other recording devices such as stones, clay, boards, barks, and skins existed before paper, but once paper was developed, its advantages made it dominate.

Dard Hunter, the great American paper historian, wrote that human development could be divided into three "stepping stones": speaking, drawing, and printing. It is curious that he left out writing, but in the long stretch of human development, the few thousand years' separation between the emergence of writing and the emergence of printing seems like only an instant. Human beings have existed for between 3.5 and 5 million years, depending on what stage is recognized as human, but only started writing about 5,000 years ago. This means that humans spent 99.9 percent of their history without writing; in addition, during most of their brief literate phase, only an elite few actually knew how to read and write.

Using the general definition of technology to mean a practical application of knowledge, humankind's first technologies—basic tools and speech—seem to have developed at the same time. They came about as a result of a million-year period in the Pleistocene Age 1.8 million years ago when the human brain grew to be more than one-third larger than it had been before. During the same period, facial and throat anatomy evolved to facilitate a greater variety of sounds.

These first technological breakthroughs, just like subsequent ones, did not change society. Rather, humankind's enlarged brainpower led to a more organized society, which in turn required certain tools for building and hunting and the big breakthrough—speech. There is no way to document this, but in that early society, there were probably a few who used their new ability to warn others that their new habit of communicating through utterances was going to destroy their quality of life: There would be no more silence. People would give constant orders. Humans would lose the ability for true expression and instead rely on this easy and superficial new technology. And perhaps in some way, this was true. There is always some loss associated with a new technology.

Anthropologists suggest that humans could speak before they could draw, but by 50,000 BCE they were drawing lines. They began to make decorative objects from stone, bone, and possibly wood. They learned to grind certain minerals such as manganese to make colors. With apologies to Meng Tian, they may have also known how to bundle together animal hairs to apply colors to stone. The first drawings resembled pictographs, an early form of writing. They were drawings in which a few lines represented an object. Gradually, these drawings grew in sophistication and made more use of perspective and color. The caves at Lascaux, France, have some 2,000 drawings, most of animals, but a few of humans. The drawings date to about 15,000 BCE. More recently, drawings dated at about 13,000 BCE were found in the caves of Altamira, Spain, and even more recently, on the walls of caves in Niaux, France.

What is striking about these paintings, other than their beauty, is that they are dynamic. They depict motion. Wild horses show their delicate prance. Stags leap forcefully. Powerful aurochs charge head-down. In Lascaux, there are whole herds of fauna romping or galloping. How can we not be moved that people from 15,000 years ago made these paintings? True, it is just a moment in the millennia of human time. But for those of us who make huge distinctions between eighteenth-century enlightenment and nineteenth-century industry, this was a very long time ago.

Seeing these paintings prompts many questions: Who were these people? Did they have a fully evolved language or just minimal pragmatic phrases? Was this their only imaginative expression? Did they leave it for us? What were these drawings intended to communicate? Were the authors naturalists, storytellers, perhaps food writers? Some have suggested that the paintings are connected to religion, and others have suggested that they map the constellations.

All we know for certain is that they are beautiful. We look at them and we are moved. Communication is taking place. And all over the world, there are other remnants of communication drawn or carved on rock. The urge to communicate or to record is primal. The urge to draw is unique to humans, and is in every human. Why do people unconsciously doodle? Why do children, as soon as they begin talking, have a desire, with or without instruction, to draw?

Long before actual writing was invented, there was written communication. In the graves of the Moche, a people who lived in Peru before the Inca, pouches have been found containing beans that are carved with dots and lines. Pottery depicting couriers carrying such beans indicates that the beans contained messages. The aborigines of Australia used marked sticks in much the same way. Often, the messenger carrying a stick was instructed on the meaning of the marks, so that the stick was simply a memory aid, which is also what writing often is. The Yoruba of Nigeria sent messages with cowrie shells. To send a single cowrie meant defiance. A string of six meant that you liked someone. If a man sent a string of six shells to a woman, it meant he desired her. If she agreed to his proposition, she sent back a string of eight. In the Pacific Northwest, totem poles were carved as a record of family history.

Knots on strings and slash marks on sticks or poles were also used for counting. The poles could be split in two so that both sides in a transaction had a record. From 1100 to 1826, the British Royal Treasury accepted such notched sticks as proof of payment. Recording transactions with knots on strings dates back to the late Stone Age, but reached its highest refinement with the Incas, who recorded complicated transactions through a variety of strategically positioned knots coded by colors.

Most, but not all, scholars believe that the first writing developed in various spots in the world independently. People had a need for it and so developed a system: the Sumerians in Mesopotamia in 3300 BCE, the Egyptians in 3000 BCE, the people of the Indus valley in 2500 BCE, the people of Crete and Greece in 1400 BCE, the Chinese in 1200 BCE, the Phoenicians in 1000 BCE, the Zapotec/Mixtec of Mexico in 600 BCE, and the Mayans in 250 BCE. Missing from this list are North and South America, Africa except for Egypt, Australia, and Northern Europe except for Scandinavia, where the runic alphabet was developed, a latecomer in the second century CE. Other societies could be missing as well, but these are the earliest written languages we have found; one of the great advantages of writing is that it is left behind to be found.

Some ancient languages were slow to develop writing. Swahili, the most widely spoken of some 250 languages of the Bantu, was first written in the early eighteenth century. The Cherokee alphabet was not invented until 1821—one of numerous North American and African languages to establish alphabets in the nineteenth century. The ancient Basque language, the oldest living European language, was seldom written until the sixteenth century.

The fact that at least nine writing systems developed across the globe independently of one another shows that human development had arrived at a point when writing had become necessary. In the case of the Basque and some African and American languages, the slow development of their writing was due to the fact that other languages came into use, such as numerous European languages for Africans and North Americans, or Spanish and French for the Basques.

It is not completely clear why people started writing at all. In many cultures, people believed that writing was handed down from God. This belief was commonly held until the nineteenth century, and is still believed by fundamentalists of many religions. And consistently, wherever writing first appeared—be it in Mesopotamia, China, Egypt, or Greece—it was developed by a people who had given up the hunting and wandering life and become stationary farmers.

Historians have multiple theories regarding the origin of writing, the leading one being that it originated as an attempt to improve accounting in business transactions. Agriculture generates commerce, which in turn generates numbers. The spoken word is an effective means of communication, but mathematics taxes the memory and requires something more. The Sumerians of Mesopotamia, the first to develop writing, used it for accounting, and their development of writing corresponded with an expansion of their trade and economy. It has been hypothesized that the Inca, advanced in other ways, were slow to develop writing because they had become so efficient with *quipas*, the knotted, color-coded strings they used for accounting, that they had no need for written language.

Originally, writing was crude line drawing. These drawings then grew increasingly abstract. Some historians believe that writing was invented by an unknown genius, others suggest a group of administrators.

AS FAR AS is known, writing began among the Sumerians in Uruk on the lower Euphrates between Babylon and the Persian Gulf about 3300 BCE, but this is really just an educated guess. Uruk is referred to in the book of Genesis as Erech, and is in present-day Iraq. Sumerian writing consisted of a series of circles and other shapes initially inscribed in stone and later pressed onto clay tablets. The shapes are thought to represent commodities, and the tablets themselves are thought to be records of sales or movements of goods. The writing tool used for clay seems to have been a cut reed. Pressing straight down vertically would produce a circular impression in the soft material. Pressing down at an angle would yield a fingernail-shaped impression. These were the first two characters in written Sumerian and, along with other early characters, evolved into pictograms.

Early cuneiform, as this writing came to be called—originally by the French in the seventeenth century, from the Latin, meaning "made from wedges"—had at least 1,500 pictograms and symbols, and only experts could use them; these scribes became important men in the community. But as time went by, cuneiform was refined, and by 300 BCE, it consisted of about 800 characters. Rather than pictures, these characters were now letters representing phonetic sounds—an important breakthrough in writing because it meant that a limited number of characters in different sequences could have many meanings. For some reason, the Chinese never reached this stage, and even today most of their characters stand for ideas, not sounds.

Most cuneiform was written in wet clay, horizontally from left to right, though there is some evidence that an earlier version of cuneiform was written in columns from top to bottom and that these columns were read right to left. This change in orientation is thought to have occurred early on, when the scribes switched from writing on stone to writing on clay. The blunt reed stylus that formed a circle remained in use for inscribing numbers, but the alphabet was written with a pointed reed. This tool could not draw curves easily, and so the characters became linear and angular. It took study and practice for scribes to learn how to work a reed stylus in wet clay, which probably contributed to the move away from pictographs in the direction of abstract characters. Other, later, languages such as Phoenician were not written in wet clay, yet still adopted the simple strokes of cuneiform as a prototype for their alphabets.

Rapidly, the alphabet became more phonetic, which reduced the number of symbols needed, though the scribes remained powerful and revered experts. The Sumerian language was well suited for phoneticism. It was a monosyllabic, agglutinating language, meaning that most words were one syllable, a single sound, and that prepositions, adjectives, and adverbs could be created by adding sounds onto a root syllable. It was also a language with many homonyms—words that sound alike but have different meanings.

The Sumerians must have been both tough and creative. They tamed the wild Euphrates, a river harsher than the Nile; it changed course without warning, causing unpredictable floods and droughts. They were one of the early inventors of the wheel, used first for pottery and later for transportation. They also learned about irrigation, and developed agriculture and commerce. Constant war, the act of conquering and of being conquered, spread their written culture. The Sumerians were also one of the first societies to have professional soldiers, as opposed to sending all men off to war, and relied on slave labor to develop their agriculture.

The Sumerians were certainly not a literate people, but their scribes read what they wrote out loud to the laypeople. They left behind tablets containing not only accounting records and history but poetry. Sumerian tablets pre-date the book of Genesis by some two thousand years

Baked clay tablet with 22 lines in cuneiform writing listing barley rations for 17 gardeners for one month. Third dynasty of Ur, Mesopotamia (Iraq), 2113–2006 BCE. 6.1 x 3.9 cm. From the Dagon Agricultural Collection, Haifa, Israel.

and tell a similar story of creation, that of an Adam-esque founder who ate forbidden food and was punished, a woman made from a rib, a great flood, and two brothers similar to Cain and Abel.

The Sumerians were the world's first poets, and their poetry, like most poetry until that of the Chinese, was not descriptive. Instead, it related historical events in a manner designed for easy memorization. It was highly repetitive:

> *In those days, now it was in those days*
> *In those nights now it was in those nights*
> *In those years, now it was in those years*

Though this translation by M. I. West of the introduction to a Sumerian poem does not show it, their poetry was also heavily rhymed, another aid to memorization.

The Sumerian language lived for about three thousand years, until the arrival of Alexander the Great in 330 BCE, at which point it began to fade rapidly. For a time, Sumerian had been the language of written diplomacy in the region, and cuneiform's phoneticism would later influence the writing of the Indus valley and Egypt. Sumerian culture and writing was influential in Syria, Persia, and other parts of the region as well. Their written language, like that of the Romans, lasted longer than their civilization itself.

All this was accomplished with writing inscribed in clay or occasionally carved into stone. Once the clay tablets were fired, they became durable, and have survived until modern times. Clay tablets had the advantages of being cheap, readily available, and easy to write on. Their lack of portability, however, was an obvious drawback. Nonetheless, clay tablets were the world's primary writing material for three thousand years—a considerably longer period than the reign of paper up until now.

THE BANKS OF the Nile River are softened by thick growths of tall papyrus reeds with feathery tops that bow and sway in the breezes. According to legend, an infant who would be called Moses was found abandoned in a patch of these reeds in about 1500 BCE. At the time, the reeds themselves were already an important Egyptian product, and they would remain valuable for the next fifteen hundred years.

The papyrus plant was tall, with a bushy tuft of leaves and flowers on top. In its most favorable growing conditions, the Nile delta, it grew to sixteen feet high, with stalks as thick as two inches. In the reed's center was a soft substance that the Egyptians enjoyed eating raw or cooked. Light boats for navigating the shallow pools of the Nile were made from woven papyrus reeds caulked with resin, and the plant was also used for making ropes, sails, and baskets.

But the plants were most valued as writing material. The papyrus reed peels like an onion, and once the green outer layer is removed, there are about twenty inner layers. These would be unrolled and laid out on a hard and smooth table, with each layer slightly overlapping the next. Then a second set, turned at a 90-degree angle from the first so that the fibers were running at right angles, was placed on top. The sheets were moistened, and pressed or hammered together with weights for a few hours. Since the reed was freshly cut, its own sap served as glue; flour paste was also used as an additional adhesive. The sheets were then rubbed with a stone, a piece of ivory, or a shell until they reached the desired smoothness and a stylus could pass over the overlapping joints without hitching up. As with paper, different tasks required different surfaces. The best papyrus was white, though it yellowed with age, which is why it is depicted as yellow on tomb paintings. Individual sheets of papyrus would be joined together to make a scroll, for longer pieces of writing. Typically, a scroll was twenty sheets long, but it could be as long as thirty feet or even more depending on the document.

Using plants to make writing material was not a uniquely Egyptian idea. Incising characters on leaves is thought to be one of the oldest forms of writing—a simple method that required little preparation. Leaves were also far easier to transport than were stone or clay tablets. The practice of writing on palm leaves continued in India and Sri Lanka until almost modern times.

Other civilizations in different climates found other plants to flatten into writing surfaces. One of the most widespread was *tapa*, a Polynesian word that means "bark paper." This, and the fact that it was made by beating thin the bark of the mulberry tree, which was also one of the first paper materials, has caused tapa to be confused with paper. But it is beaten thin, not broken down and woven in a random pattern the way true paper is. The bark of other trees, including fig and breadfruit, has also been used to make writing material. A two-inch strip of tapa can be beaten into a ten-inch sheet.

Tapa is a product of tropical countries, and there is evidence of tapa being used in Southeast Asia as early as 4000 BCE and in Peru by 2100 BCE. The Chinese first mention it about 600 BCE. Some of these early dates suggest very early writing systems, perhaps far earlier than those of the Sumerians and Egyptians. Like papyrus, tapa was used for many things, such as clothing and bedding, before it was used for writing material. But unlike papyrus, tapa does not conserve well in its native environment, and only a few fragments have survived from ancient times, none with writing on them. Tapa is still being made in Africa, the Pacific, and Central and South America, but it is now usually used for clothing.

What was unique about Egyptian papyrus, however, was that it became a valuable commercial product that was exported throughout the known world.

The oldest papyrus scroll ever found dates to between 2900 and 2775 BCE, and its quality is so fine that historians believe that the Egyptians had already been making scrolls for some time before that date, probably since about 3000 BCE, only a few centuries after the Sumerians began using clay tablets for writing.

If a writing surface is at all porous, it needs a coating, otherwise known as a *sizing*, to keep the ink on the surface so that it does not soak in, which would make the lines blurry. In the case of papyrus, the plant's dried sap acted as a natural sizing that kept the pigments that were used as ink from penetrating the sheet or spreading too much. Later, the Romans would improve on papyrus by coating it with a sizing of flour and vinegar, which created a better writing surface.

The earliest Egyptian writing ever found was already completely developed, so nothing is known of the early stages of its development. It is thought to have been created independently of the Sumerian language and to have later acquired some features of cuneiform, but it is also possible that it was a spinoff of Sumerian writing.

Egyptians wrote both from left to right and from right to left. Their characters, such as the profile of a standing bird, all faced one direction, so it was easy to tell which direction the writing went. Though the Egyptians showed little interest in calligraphy, their alphabet is unusually beautiful—a complex mixture of *phonograms*, or characters that represent sounds, and *logograms*, or characters that represent objects or ideas. Some of the Egyptian pictographs faithfully represent the objects that they look like, but this is not always the case.

Papyrus grew in numerous marshes and riverbanks throughout the Middle East, but it was usually spindly. Optimum growing conditions existed only in certain parts of the Nile delta and only there did it grow to be two inches thick, making it suitable for making writing sheets. So while the demand for papyrus for writing spread throughout the Mediterranean world, its manufacture remained an Egyptian monopoly. This meant that the Egyptians controlled the price of this labor-intensive product, so that while papyrus was a more practical writing material than stone or clay, it was also expensive.

The use of papyrus as writing material seems to have existed in other countries and climates, but only a dry climate such as Egypt's allowed it to survive the millennia until modern times. The only papyrus ever found outside of Egypt was in a desert cave near the Dead Sea, part of a Hebrew collection known as the Dead Sea Scrolls.

PAPYRUS WAS MOSTLY used by scribes, who wrote with reed styluses, the ends chewed off into stiff brushes. Students studying to become scribes would begin with writing boards that were covered with a soft plaster that was erasable, just like Sumerian clay. You could simply pat the plaster down and start again. But an even more common implement that endured for centuries was the wax tablet, a board with a hollowed-out center that was filled with wax—most likely beeswax. In Assyria, such tablets have been found dating back as far as 80 BCE. They were extremely popular in ancient Greece and Rome, where the wax was black and the writing done with a metal stylus that was pointed on one end for writing and blunt on the other for erasing.

The wax tablet was an important contribution to the written culture of ancient civilizations because it was the first widely used device for *casual* writing, intended for individuals other than scribes. Before wax tablets, anything that was written down had to be considered of great and enduring importance. But once there is writing, there arises a need for temporary writing—a quick note to jot down and throw away the next day, an aid in calculating a math problem, a rough draft of a document that would later become permanent. All the other previous writing surfaces had been, for all intents and purposes, permanent. You could not bake a clay tablet to throw away the next day, or jot down something on an expensive scroll of papyrus and throw it away. And once something is literally carved in stone, it is figuratively "carved in stone." It can't be unwritten. The wax tablet, therefore, was the original Etch A Sketch for the ancient world.

Wax tablets were easier to write on and easier to erase than other writing media. Often two wax tablets would be bound together with raised edges in between so that the notations wouldn't be damaged when the tablet was closed. Such a bound and folded double tablet was known as a *diptych*. The diptych was popular among the Hebrews, and traditionally, whenever the Ten Commandments have been reimagined by film directors or artists, they have been written on a diptych made of stone, indicating that no revision was planned.

Sometimes several tablets would be bound together; in Latin this was known as a *codex*. The codex was the forerunner of the book, and while originally it referred to wax tablets, the word was later also applied to codices made of bound papyrus sheets, parchment, and eventually paper. But the codex was of limited use as long as papyrus, far better suited for scrolls, dominated.

For centuries, the kings of Babylon and other cultural centers of the Near East tried to build great libraries. In the third century BCE, Ptolemy, a Macedonian Greek, came to rule Egypt. He set out to build the world's greatest library in Alexandria, which happened to be near a papyrus production center. Every ship that called in the port of Alexandria was searched for books, and any that were found were copied for the library. Ptolemy wanted books on any subject, poetry or prose, and three centuries later, the library in Alexandria was the repository of 700,000 papyrus scrolls.

Eumenes, the ruler of the Greek city of Pergamum, also wanted to build a great library, but Ptolemy, not wanting a competitor, refused to export papyrus to him. According to Pliny, Eumenes, unwilling to abandon his grand plan, began searching for an alternative writing material, and in the next hundred years, the people of Pergamum learned how to soak animal hide in lime for ten days, scrape it, and dry it. The hides of young animals—kid, lamb, and young gazelle—were used, though the best material was that made from the skin of fetal animals. The flesh side of the hide was smoother than the fur side, and white animals produced the best quality skins. The skins were hung on a stretcher and scraped with a knife until they became smooth and hairless. After drying, they were further smoothed by rubbing with a stone.

The new product was often called pergamum, after the city in which it was invented, and is still so named in some Latin languages, but is known in English as parchment. A particularly fine parchment made from calfskin is called vellum.

Parchment was an improvement on papyrus, and though papyrus continued to be used for another thousand years, parchment, which is still in use today, outlasted it. For a few centuries, they coexisted. It was paper, not parchment, that eventually marginalized papyrus. Unlike papyrus, parchment could be made anywhere and preserved well in a wide range of climates. But like papyrus, it was labor intensive, and it was even more expensive to make—it could take as many as two hundred animals to make a single book, or codex. But the use of parchment, then as today, indicated that a document was important and meant to last.

As with all new inventions, some saw parchment as the way of the future and others disdained it. At first the Romans used it only for notebooks—very expensive ones. If it had continued to be used only for that purpose, it would have disappeared, but parchment did not fray or split when folded and so, unlike papyrus, was well suited for codices. A codex had many advantages over a scroll. It was easier to carry and worked well for any length of text. It was also easier to refer back to a page in a codex than it was to search for something in the middle of a scroll. Romans began using parchment codices in the first century BCE. The Greeks embraced the idea several centuries later.

PHONETICISM, THAT IMPORTANT innovation of the Sumerians, continued to spread, and in time alphabets were created in which every character represented a pronounceable sound, thereby greatly reducing the number of characters necessary for writing and making it much easier to learn how to write and to read. As recently as the 1960s, the ruler of China at the time, Mao Zedong, concluded that the way to spread literacy among his people was to eliminate the Chinese alphabet with its thousands of characters and replace it with about thirty phonetic symbols. His close advisers vehemently opposed the idea, and he abandoned it, but it was exactly the same process that the Sumerians and other ancient peoples had gone through. The first examples of phoneticism consisted of puns in pictograph form. The word for "owl" in Egyptian sounded like the letter *m* and so a drawing of an owl stood for the sound of letter *m*. The first letter of the name of the pharaoh Ramses is a picture of the sun, which is "re," and so a sun is also the symbol for the *r* sound.

The Phoenicians took the concept of phoneticism still further. Phoenician was written from right to left with simple characters composed mainly of straight lines. It was purely phonetic and written only in consonants. The Phoenicians were a highly commercial people, and their alphabet spread to become the language of commerce throughout the Mediterranean. Many languages were derived from it, including Hebrew, Arabic, Greek, and Latin.

Hebrew, which was also written from right to left with simple, straight-lined characters, was also phonetic, and also lacking in vowels. Most any language could be transcribed into Hebrew—the first alphabet with that degree of versatility. Jews wrote local languages in Hebrew wherever they went. In Spain, they wrote Spanish with Hebrew letters and it was called Ladino. In North Africa, they wrote Arab with Hebrew and it was called Judeo-Arab. And German written with Hebrew letters in eastern Europe was called Yiddish, while Persian written in Hebrew was Judeo-Persian.

By the eighth century BCE, the Greeks, after several centuries of commercial dealings with the Phoenicians, had developed their own variation of the language. Phoenician was problematic for the Greeks because it had no vowels, and vowels are central to the Greek language. It also had a number of consonants that represented sounds that are not voiced in Greek while it lacked other consonant sounds that are used regularly in Greek, such as the sound of *ph*. The Greeks solved the problem by taking the unused consonants and assigning them to Greek vowel sounds. This creation of a written Semitic-like language but with vowels was a pivotal moment in the development of Western writing and one that was imitated by the European languages that followed.

At first, the Greek alphabet varied depending upon the dialects spoken in its islands and city-states. But in 403 BCE, the Athenians decreed that their version, the Ionian alphabet, was to be used for all official documents and thus became the standardized Greek alphabet. The Greeks named their letters according to their Semitic names, so "aleph" became "alpha" and "bet" became "beta." In fact, *Aleph, bet* is the origin of the word "alphabet." Alphabetical order also remained more or less the same in Greek as it was in Semitic languages.

Aside from the addition of vowels, the other major change the Greeks made was that, after several centuries of writing from right to left, they decided to make theirs a left-to-right language. This change had occurred by the fifth century, when Ionian was standardized. In the process, a number of letters such as beta, epsilon, and kappa were flipped in the other direction, which is the origin of the letters *B, E,* and *K.*

The transition of writing materials from stone to papyrus to parchment meant that ever-softer writing tools, from metal stylus to brush, were developed, and this meant more curves and less blocklike letters. Nonetheless, the Etruscans adopted the Greek alphabet in its rigid block form, and the Romans subsequently took their alphabet from the Etruscans, though they flipped the orientation from right to left to left to right. The Roman alphabet was therefore also similar to Greek, but the Romans added curves to the angular letters, replacing the triangular delta with the rounded *D*, for example. The Roman alphabet eventually came to dominate the Western world, but linguists regard Greek, a language in which everything is pronounced exactly as written, to be the last great innovation in the history of Western writing, the grandparent of all modern European languages.

THE FACT THAT the Greek alphabet emerged at the time of Homer has led some to believe that the alphabet was created specifically to write Homer's work. This is unlikely, but Homer marks a critical crossroads in the history of written literature. The *Iliad* and the *Odyssey* are very odd pieces of writing, partly because they are written in a style of language that no one ever spoke—they are written in an oral language. "Oral language" is not the same thing as writing the way people naturally speak; in fact, it is almost the opposite. Before there was writing, there was an oral literature, a body of work that was never written down but that remained in the collective experience and was repeated over and over, passed from one generation to the next. For such oral literature to be effective, it had to be remembered, and the literature's rhythm, repetition, and adjectival labels were aids to memory.

This is why Homer's work is very repetitive and strongly rhythmic, written in an unyielding hexameter that is almost primitive. It never varies from six beats per line of predominantly dactyls—phrases of a hard beat followed by two light upbeats, as in "Sing, Goddess," which is the opening phrase of the *Iliad*. Wherever the meaning conflicts with the rhythm, it is the meaning that is sacrificed, never the rhythm. This leads to an enormous number of unlikely synonyms for wine and other basic words, and once a rhythmic phrase is found, it often turns up again and again. For example, characters seem to be assigned adjectives that always accompany their names, to help us remember them—*brilliant* Achilles, *tall* Hektor, *gray-eyed* Athene.

The stories of the *Iliad* and the *Odyssey* were already many centuries old before they were first written down in the eighth century BCE, though it is not completely clear how they came to be written. Little is known of Homer himself. The name Homer in the dialect of Lesbos means "blind," so he is often thought to have been blind, although he may not have been. Where and when he lived, or if he even existed at all, is unknown. Some think Homer's books are the work of several people.

Three centuries after Homer, writers such as Plato were no longer using poetry or orality to articulate abstract thought. The great philosophers and mathematicians of Greece could represent their theoretical, abstract work only in writing and only in prose; the memory devices of oral literature simply could not express what they wanted to say. A new way of thinking was emerging, and it needed to be written down in a new way.

The rise of literacy, like all new technologies, had its boosters, its detractors, and those who were both. It remained controversial. Even those who used the new technology sometimes saw its drawbacks. One of the masters of this new written thought, Plato, expressed deep reservations about written language: Was it making people less human, even mechanical?

The philosopher Socrates lived in fifth-century BCE Athens and his student, Plato, lived into the fourth century—the period when Greece was evolving from an oral to a written society. Unlike Plato, Socrates was an oral philosopher. But Plato's writing had a suggestion of orality too; it was usually presented in the form of debates, or dialogues. Socrates was one of the interlocutors in Plato's dialogues, and the question remains unresolved of how many of Socrates's words were actually his and how many were Plato putting his own ideas into the mouth of Socrates.

One of these works is *Phaedrus*, which is presented as a series of conversations between a young man and Socrates, an older man who is barefoot and slightly iconoclastic. One of its dialogues is titled "The Superiority of the Spoken Word. The Myth of the Invention of Writing." Whether Socrates once expressed the ideas contained within the dialogue, perhaps to his young student Plato, or whether they represent Plato's own reservations about the written word, or whether they are just an expression of other intellectuals' reservations isn't known.

Among the thoughts expressed in the dialogue are: Shouldn't we be exercising our memory? Are we just mechanically producing knowledge without asking important questions? Aren't we destroying our memories by not using it? Plato believed that knowledge was something accessed through memory. Tellingly, he called writing "artificial memory." In *Phaedrus,* he compares written words to figures in paintings: "The painter's product stands before us as though they were alive, but if you question them they maintain a most majestic silence."

Plato wrote, "And once a thing is put in writing, the composition, whatever it may be, drifts all over the place, getting not only in the hands of those who understand it, but equally of those who have no business with it. It doesn't know how to address the right people and not address the wrong." This may explain why he never wrote down what he considered his best ideas, his so-called unwritten doctrines, and why so much of his writing is in the form of dialogues.

Many felt as Plato did, that once something was written down, it no longer came from within a person, but was external and therefore was not sincere, not heartfelt, and thus in a sense was made less true. Aristotle said, "Memory is the scribe of the soul." Socrates, in Plato's *Phaedrus,* tells the story of the Egyptian god Thoth, said to have invented writing. Proud of his creation, Thoth asks for the pharaoh's approval. The king told Thoth, "You have invented an elixir not of memory but of reminding, and you offer your pupils the appearance of wisdom, not true wisdom, for they will read many things without instruction and will therefore seem to know many things, when they are for the most part ignorant."

Socrates makes the identical argument, warning that writing would "implant forgetfulness" and "no true wisdom." His prophecy was exactly right, but it did not dissuade anyone, including himself, from using the new technology.

Those who criticized the written word in Plato's time were no different from writers today who sit at their computers and tap out critiques, even diatribes, against computer technology. They are working with the same compromise. They recognize that the new technology is now the way to do things, but they regret it.

The debate about the written word continued for centuries. First-century Romans complained that because of the written word, the great Roman art of oratory was in decline. But Tacitus pointed out that this decline also had a positive aspect: it diminished the ability of politicians to deceive people. By the first century, writing was everywhere in Rome. There were street signs, posted city ordinances, and placards with all kinds of messages. Archaeologists digging out Pompeii, buried in the lava from the eruption of Vesuvius in 79 CE, found political posters painted on walls, along with graffiti.

The controversy over the written word was still alive even into the Middle Ages. Saint Thomas Aquinas pointed out that Christ never used the written word because great teachers never use the written word.

HOMER'S WORKS WERE sometimes referred to as songs. In an age of orality, there was little difference between a poem and a song. Similarly, one of the most ancient works of Chinese poetry is called *The Book of Songs*. And even today it is the case that many poets consider their work part of an oral tradition. In his essay on Dante's *Divine Comedy*, the Argentine poet and essayist Jorge Luis Borges insisted that his poetry was still oral:

> Truly fine poetry must be read out loud. A good poem does not allow itself to be read in a low voice or silently. If we can read it silently, it is not a valid poem: a poem demands pronunciation. Poetry always remembers that it was an oral art before it was a written art. It remembers that it was first song.

Songs belong to oral culture. Everything about the way they are written is oral, which is why they are easy to memorize. When a song gets stuck in your head, this is not by chance. That is what they were built to do; that is what all oral literature is designed to do. Since it was not written down, how else could it survive? When the fifth-century BCE Greeks of Euripides's day were taken prisoner in Sicily, they were told that they would be set free if they could recite the works of Euripides. They hadn't read him, because in those days theatre was only oral. They could recall no scenes, no dialogue. But most could recite choruses. Like the chorus of a song, the repetitious chorus of a Greek play was designed for memorization.

IQ tests are often criticized for not truly measuring intelligence. What, then, do they measure? They measure literacy, because we have grown to *associate* literacy with intelligence. Meanwhile, we can no longer imagine an oral society. What would we have thought upon visiting a preliterate civilization? Is any technological shift in human history as great as the change from the oral to the written word?

Once that shift happened, though, society could no longer get by on expensive, slow-to-produce writing materials. Something as disposable as wax, as light as leaves, as cheap as clay, and as durable as parchment was needed.

Chapter 2

THE MOTHS
THAT CIRCLE
A CHINESE
CANDLE

||||||||||||||||||

Before three emperors hatched civilization,

People ate their fill and were content.

Someone started knotting ropes, and now we're

mixed in the glue and varnish of government.

—TU FU, EIGHTH CENTURY

EOPLE WERE CREATED OUT OF THE PARASITES THAT lived on the body of the Creator, Pangu. At least, this is what Chinese legend teaches. To the Western mind, this story may seem odd, but parasites are important characters in Chinese folklore. Tales are told of parasites in the throat that escape and report to the spirits on a person's wrongdoings.

Also according to Chinese legend, writing developed in three stages under three wise emperors. The first, Emperor Fu Xi, taught the Hua people to domesticate animals, created the institution of marriage, and invented the practice of divination. Emperor Fu would randomly throw stalks of yarrow flowers on the ground and find meaning in the pattern they created, thus establishing the idea that patterns carry symbolic meanings. The second emperor, Shennong, established agriculture and trade and initiated a system of keeping accounts on string. The third Emperor, Huangdi, also known as the Yellow Emperor, frustrated by the limitations of recording everything with knotted string, ordered his officer Cangjie to come up with a better system, which led to the invention of writing.

Cangjie had four eyes and taught writing to four students. The idea of Chinese characters came to him when a hoofprint of an unknown animal was dropped from the sky by a bird. Local hunters told him that this was an unseen creature, a kind of winged lion called a *pixiu*. Cangjie decided to interpret the hoofprint in a line drawing. He then decided that studying and interpreting other special objects in nature would be the ideal written language. He created characters from the studies he made of the patterns of the stars and of nature around him, especially the tracks of animals, and from this evolved writing.

It is significant that Chinese writing was believed to have come from nature. In Chinese culture, the correlation between writing and nature has endured even into modern times. And curiously, the story of Cangjie learning writing from animal tracks parallels a Sumerian story that tells of birds that were scribes and therefore sacred; their tracks resembled cuneiform, but were a type of cuneiform that humans could not read.

The emperor Huangdi eventually turned his reign over to a sage named Shun, whose successor was his minister Yu, the founder of the Xia dynasty along the Yellow River in 2215 BCE. Yu's reign marks the beginning of verifiable Chinese history.

It is difficult to say how much truth there is to the legend of the three emperors, or if they even existed, but historical evidence shows that writing in China did indeed begin with divination and that as the society grew increasingly agricultural, writing was used for accounting. The legend of the three emperors, which all Chinese have been taught for more than 2,000 years, also defines China: it describes a society that is religious, commercial, and bureaucratic.

As had been the case in ancient Greece and elsewhere, not everyone in China embraced the new writing technology. Eighth-century Tu Fu, considered by many to be China's greatest poet, denounced the invention because it led to bureaucracy. "Now we're mixed in the glue and varnish of government," he wrote.

Tu Fu's quip may be an example of the technological fallacy that technology changes society as opposed to society inventing technology when it is needed, because, of course, writing did not create Chinese bureaucracy. Rather, bureaucracy was one of the leading factors in the creation of writing. As Chinese society evolved and became more complex, it required writing, which would eventually lead to the search for better writing material. As Tu Fu also wrote, "Everyone knows that if you light candles and lamps, moths gather in swarms."

LEGEND HAS IT that Cangjie invented Chinese writing around 2700 BCE, but the earliest Chinese writing ever found, near the Yellow River, dates from about 1300 BCE. This is two thousand years later than the first writing found in Mesopotamia and a thousand years later than the earliest writing found in Egypt. Writing was one of the few things the Chinese did not do first—though they do have the world's oldest living written language.

The Chinese writings found by the Yellow River—three thousand pieces in all, uncovered by a flood in 1899—were inscribed on tortoise shells and the shoulder blades of deer. All were written for the purpose of divination. Before an undertaking, such as a harvest or a trip, Chinese people would consult shamans, who would then make predictions. The shamans worked with a writing system of six hundred characters—enough to suppose that the writing system at that point was not new. But it was used only by shamans and only to communicate with ancestors or spirits, not by ordinary people to communicate with one another.

Later, more and more characters were added to the system. Chinese became an agglutinating language, read in vertical columns from right to left. It operated so similarly to cuneiform—albeit with different characters—that a few historians have suggested that the Chinese developed their written language through contact with Mesopotamia. Chinese historians find this heretical, and there is no evidence to support the theory other than the coincidence of similar systems.

During the Shang dynasty (circa 1763 to 1123 BCE), when the Chinese settled into an organized, agricultural way of life, they devoutly worshipped a pantheon of spirits, as well as ancestors, whom they consulted before making any important decision. Theirs was also very much a written religion. Before making an offering to the spirits, a worshipper would send a note, usually written on a tortoise shell or bone, advising the spirits of the offering. A heated bronze tool was used to cause the bones and shells to crack, and a shaman interpreted these cracks.

Some 150,000 bones with writing on them from the Shang period have been found, and instead of the 600 characters used in the Yellow River writings, they used about 3,000. This is what makes Chinese writing so different from Western writing. Rather than paring down their alphabet, the Chinese expanded it. By 100 CE, when paper started to be widely used, the language had 9,000 characters. That number rose to almost 20,000 by the fifth century and to almost 30,000 by the tenth century, which is still far fewer than are in use today. As new ideas and new subjects came up, new characters were created.

During the Zhou dynasty, which came after the Shang dynasty and lasted until 256 BCE, the religious use of writing continued, but the writing materials began to change. Bones and shells were replaced by bronze vessels, and silk and bamboo were also used. Much of the writing from this period continued to be in the form of divinations, a practice thoroughly described in the *I Ching*, or *The Book of Changes*, which was recorded between the eleventh and ninth century BCE. Most copies of the *I Ching* that have been found were written on bamboo or wood.

Even at this early time, the Chinese tendency toward bureaucracy and what later would be called paperwork could be seen. Treaties between states were written in triplicate, one copy for each party and one for the spirits. It was always assumed that the spirits could read and that they would prefer to receive written rather than oral prayers. Government started keeping archives to preserve agreements and communication between states. The archives were extensive, and disputes were often resolved by referring to documents in them.

By the Zhou dynasty, the Chinese were creating a significant written record of their life and times. Mozi, the fifth-century BCE father of Chinese philosophy, wrote, "The sources of our knowledge lie on what is written on bamboo and silk, what is engraved on metal and stone and what is cut on vessels to be handed down to posterity."

Mozi lived at a time of great change in China. The aristocracy was starting to loosen its control and the lower classes had access to education and even government positions. Literacy was increasing. Confucius, who lived from 551 to 479 BCE, believed that education should not be the exclusive privilege of the upper class and established China's first school for commoners. Also during this period, writers of philosophy and science began to emerge from humble origins.

Competing states tried to assemble the most impressive people in their court—those who could read and write. One feudal lord, Lü Buwei, in the third century BCE, was said to have gathered three thousand scholars and to have asked them to write down their knowledge. He then collected these writings in a 2-million-word book that he displayed in the market, and offered a reward to anyone who could make improvements. For him to have been able to do this suggests a degree of literacy among common people.

People had extensive collections of books, some of which they took with them when they traveled. In the twentieth century, more than 40,000 tablets of wood or bamboo from this period were discovered. They include personal correspondence, law, medical books, textbooks, calendars, literary writing, medical prescriptions, and many different kinds of records. Most of this writing was done with brushes, an improvement over the bamboo styluses that had been used earlier. The brushes would be dipped in an ink made from lampblack, the carbon from burned material—pine was best—mixed with a liquid. This was an ancient concoction.

Red and black lampblack ink had been used on the divination bones of the Shang; the ancient Egyptians had also made lampblack ink.

The invention of brushes, made from animal hair, was also a major step forward. It made writing possible on almost any surface. Other cultures may have invented the brush before the Chinese, but no other culture made it as central to its way of life or used it for as long. China is still a brush culture today.

It has never been clear to historians why Chinese tradition credits the invention of the brush to Meng Tian. He was a general from a line of generals, famous for leading an army of 100,000 or 300,000 (depending on the source) to drive back northern invaders from Mongolia, the nomadic Xiongnu, in 214 BCE, and then beginning work on the construction of the Great Wall of China to keep them out. Little remains of this original wall of tamped earth and boards, and most of today's far longer wall, which grew to more than 13,000 miles, was built centuries later. Meng Tian did go on to become a court historian who used a brush to write many documents. Modern-day historians have accused the short-lived Qin dynasty that he served of a tendency to obliterate earlier achievements and claim them for themselves. But given the iconic position of the brush in Chinese culture, it is appealing to believe that it was created by the same man who built the Great Wall.

The Chinese of the Qin period used wooden tablets for their less important writings, such as personal correspondence and official government documents, of which there were many. For more important documents, such as classic works and medical texts, they used bamboo books made from fresh-cut stalks of young green shoots cut into tubes. A tube would be split open into a strip, its outer green skin scraped off, and bound together with other strips. Bamboo books came in various sizes, and could be as short as eight inches or as long as two feet or more.

Historians often suggest that the reason why Chinese was read vertically was that it was written on these thin bamboo strips—a more likely explanation than the one ascribing the practice to Sumerian influence. But it still does not explain why the Chinese didn't hold their bamboo books horizontally. In fact, a preference for vertical orientation pre-dates bamboo; vertical inscriptions have also been found on pre-bamboo bronze writings from the Shang and Zhou periods.

Throughout the ancient world, the direction of writing varied tremendously—right to left, left to right, top to bottom, bottom to top, and from the middle outward. The Mayans and Aztecs wrote all over the page, with lines directing the reader where to go next. Some cultures, such as the Greeks, switched the direction of their writing over time. The Chinese also tried writing in a number of different directions—vertical, horizontal, and even for a time reading alternate lines and then going back to the skipped ones.

No one has successfully established the reason for these different directions, but their influence is easy to see. When you look at a Chinese painting, it becomes clear that it was created by a people who are accustomed to moving their eyes vertically from top to bottom, as that is the orientation that prevailed. In contrast, Europeans tend to move their gaze from left to right. In Western theater and film, as every director knows, the strongest part of the stage or screen is on the audience's right, because that is where the eyes go last.

Silk is generally considered to be the last writing material developed before paper. But silk is actually an ancient Chinese invention—the use of silk has been documented as far back as 3500 BCE, pre-dating written language. It was originally used for burial shrouds and for wrapping objects buried with the dead as offerings to the spirits. The earliest-found paintings on silk, from the third century BCE, are funeral banners. But only aristocrats used silk for writing. The common people still used wood and bamboo. Nevertheless, since silk was expensive, people often wrote their first drafts on bamboo or wood and their final work on silk. History, religion, maps, the teachings of the emperors, and other documents that were meant to last were all written on silk.

EXACTLY HOW PAPER was conceived of is a mystery. It bears no relation to the writing materials that came before it. Paper is made of cellulose fibers that are broken down and mixed with water until they are so diluted that they are barely visible. The liquid is then scooped up onto a screen and allowed to drain, which leaves a very thin layer of the randomly woven fibers—paper—behind.

Though the inventors of paper probably didn't know this, cellulose is one of the basic building blocks in plants made from sugar compounds produced by photosynthesis. Cellulose is therefore one of the most common organic compounds in the world, which is why so many different substances can be used to make paper: wood, bark, grasses, cotton, silk, seaweed. It wasn't until two thousand years after papermaking began that a French chemist, Anselme Payen, "discovered" cellulose, $(C_6H_{10}O_5)_n$, in 1838. Yet somehow, the Chinese discovered that these fibers could be broken down from various sources in various ways (depending on the source) and made into paper.

How did they think to do this? The first trick would have been figuring out how to separate cellulose fibers without even really knowing that they existed. The fibers have to go through a long process of chopping, beating, cooking, and soaking before they can be separated. Then something has to cause the fibers to randomly weave together. No doubt a great deal of trial and error took place before a water solution diluted enough to make a thin sheet and an appropriate mold with a screen were found. Then a papermaker would have had to learn the motions of dipping the mold in the diluted water and rocking it back and forth so that a coating of fibers with no lumps formed.

It is significant that the leading pre-paper writing materials—wood, bamboo, and silk—contain cellulose and can be broken down for papermaking. Some historians think that the idea of papermaking came from felting, a practice that pre-dated weaving and entailed beating wool until it mashed into a thick, fibrous mat. Whatever occurred, surely paper had a long evolution. It seems highly improbable that some lone genius stumbled upon the idea by him- or herself.

FOR MANY CENTURIES, every Chinese schoolchild has learned that paper was invented in 105 CE by a eunuch in the Han court named Cai

Lun. It was the first of what the Chinese call the four great inventions—paper, compass, gunpowder, and printing—and the only one that is attributed to a specific inventor.

The *Hu Han Shu*, the official history of the later Han dynasty (25 to 220 CE) states that Cai Lun, a native of the capital city of Luoyang, began serving the Han court in 75 CE, and in 89 CE was promoted to officer in charge of developing tools and weapons, an important post. Sixteen years later, the *Hu Han Shu* states, "Cai Lun reported to the emperor that he had made paper from the bark of trees, hemp, rags of cloth, and fishing nets." This launched paper into common usage, and Cai Lun was awarded the honorary title of Marquis, which came with financial rewards, including the income earned from three hundred homes. According to history, however, Cai Lun became involved in court intrigues and was accused of falsifying records. In the year 121, he bathed and dressed himself in his most beautiful robes and took his own life by drinking poison.

Some six hundred years after Cai Lun's death, a stone mortar, an ordinary tool, was placed in the Imperial Museum because it was said to have been used by Cai Lun for pounding cloth into fibers for paper-making. Temples were built to honor him, and his likeness was hung on the walls of paper shops and even people's homes, alongside images of gods and spirits.

The legend of Cai Lun was ruined by numerous pieces of paper made before 105 CE that were found in twentieth-century archaeological expeditions. Most of the older examples have been found in the dry desert of Central Asia, which suggests that more of this early paper, perhaps some that was even older, might have been found in the more humid central parts of China dating back to the second and first centuries BCE. But they could not survive the climate.

So if it's known that he didn't invent paper, why exactly is Cai Lun remembered? Given what has often happened with other inventions, it's possible that he either perfected paper in some way or commercialized it. Some historians have also thought that Cai Lun may have been the one who first realized that paper could be used for writing. Paper in its earliest form was used just for wrapping packages, especially medicine. But some of those early wrappers have writing on them. Was Cai Lun's paper better or more widely used or more inexpensive and accessible to more people? The reason for his fame is a mystery.

THE CHINESE PEOPLE call themselves Han after the Han period of their history, as if this was the era when they really began to be who they are. The Han period was one of great physical and cultural expansion for China, and because it coincides with the era of the Roman Empire, comparisons between the two cultures are inevitable. The two were world superpowers. The emperor Wudi sent an envoy to the West who traveled for twelve years and got as far as Turkestan, almost to the edges of the Roman Empire. He learned of the Romans and may even have had contact with them. Wudi's expedition led to what became known as the Silk Road, a trade route from western China across Central Asia that would dominate commerce in the region for centuries.

Once paper was somehow invented, it is easy to see how artisans would arrive at the idea of making it thinner and smoother, and coating it with wax to make it less absorbent and more suitable for ink. The demand for writing material greatly increased during the Han dynasty, which was also the period when the first official version of Confucius's classics was carved in stone. There was a burst of literary criticism and a reissuing of classics that had been destroyed by previous dynasties. There was an expansion of writing on philosophy, and the sixth-century BCE writing of Laozi, the foundation of Taoism, was revived, which in turn inspired poetry. The first comprehensive national histories were written. The first Chinese dictionary was written, in 100 CE, with 9,353 characters. By then, there were actually even more characters than this in use, but the dictionary was intended to preserve the language of the third-century BCE. Astronomy, mathematics, and botany—all were subjects of books from the Han period.

Enormous private libraries with thousands of books and scrolls were built. Bookstores sprang up. The word *shu-ssu*, meaning "bookshop," is found in documents from the final decades BCE. When the Han capital was moved from Chang'an to Luoyang, in today's Hunan Province, in 25 CE, accounts say that the emperor needed two thousand wagons to move his written records. Less than a century later, that imperial library had grown threefold.

It is not certain what portion of the Chinese population was literate at this time. All members of the large aristocracy could read and write. Along with archery and chariot driving, literacy was a basic skill that a young aristocrat was expected to learn in preparation for a position in government. Paper was intimately tied to government bureaucracy; the rulers insisted that their underlings record everything. The officer in charge of this operation was called *chih* or, in the modern spelling, *zhi* (紙), which eventually became the Chinese word for paper. The first character of the word, a vertical squiggly line, means woven. The same character is used in the word for silk and in the word for cotton; in fact, it's in the words for most woven things. The first record of the word *zhi* being used to mean paper was in the fourth century. It appears in an odd story about an incident that occurred in 93 BCE, when an imperial guard, Chiang Chung, advised the prince that the emperor was offended by his deformed nose and suggested he cover it with a piece of paper.

Once paper became widely available, the use of bamboo and wood as writing materials slowly declined, although even as late as the ninth century CE, wood was still being used in Tibet along with paper. Silk was, and is, still being used in China and elsewhere. It had the reputation of being more luxurious than paper, and it was even said that people used paper because they could not afford silk. But silk was only relatively expensive. In the fourteenth century, the explorer Ibn Battuta of Tangiers, who went on a pilgrimage to Mecca and ended up traveling for twenty-seven years, was struck by the cheapness of silk in China. In his account of his travels, he wrote:

> Silk is most plentiful among them, for the silk worm is found sticking and feeding on the trees in all their districts. And hence they make their silk, which is the clothing of the poorest among them.

IN THE SECOND century CE, paper began to change. It became stronger, thinner, and more commonly and cheaply produced. Most of the earliest kinds of paper, up to and including Cai Lun's, had been made by beating fabric scraps to a pulp with a mortar. The pulp was then poured into molds, which sat above tubs of water until the sheet set. This technique was slow, but that was not a problem at first because there was little demand for the final product. But as word of the invention spread, more people began asking for it.

Looking for a faster means of production, the Chinese came up with a new mold—a two-piece bamboo screen that could be dipped in a vat and agitated as it was pulled out. The size of the vat, the size of the mold, and the strength of the dipper were the only limitations to paper size. Once the pulp covered the mold evenly—a matter of minutes—the sheet could be pulled off and a new one made. Since then and up to modern times, better molds, better power sources, and better fiber choppers have been devised, but this basic technique for making paper is little changed. Even the mechanical and engine-driven papermakers of today imitate this handmade technique.

By the third century CE, paper was being treated, or sized, to prevent it from absorbing too much ink. At first, gypsum was used, and later a glue made of lichen, and later still starch, which was also used to make the paper harder. Over the next few centuries, the size of the molds grew and the skills of the papermakers improved. By the sixth century, a sheet of paper was usually one foot by two feet, and that size continued to grow. Scrolls remained popular, with some made up of close to thirty sheets glued end to end. The scroll was attached to a wooden roller at one end—unlike papyrus scrolls, which had no roller. Increasingly, too, specific kinds of paper for specific uses were being produced. Paper made from rattan was for official edicts. Artists preferred using mulberry bark, or bamboo, which was more absorbent, making it possible to create the soft edges and misty effects that typify Chinese landscape painting. Blends became popular; much paper was made with grass or from grass blended with other materials. In 674 CE, the Chinese government ordered papermakers to treat paper made for government documents with a poisonous substance made from the berry of a certain philodendron plant to protect it from insects.

The Chinese were becoming not only paper gourmets but paper gourmands. They were choosy about their paper and they used a lot of it. They made hats and clothes and kites and lanterns and fans with it, burned it for funerals, and used it for prayers. Red paper banners were placed on doors in celebration of the New Year, a practice that continues to this day. Kites, originally used as signals by the military, were discovered by the Chinese aristocracy to be fun to play with. Paper cups are an ancient Chinese invention, as is toilet paper, though interestingly enough it is not listed as one of the big four. Ibn Battuta, who came from a paper-using culture himself, was amazed at how much paper the Chinese used—at how they made pictures of visitors and posted them around the town and at how they used toilet paper instead of washing themselves, which seemed to him unhygienic.

Burial practices also used a considerable amount of paper. In early Chinese history, valuables had been buried with the dead as offerings to the spirits, but the problem of grave robbing soon arose. During Han times, valuables were replaced with coins, but grave robbing persisted. Then the Chinese came up with the imaginative idea of making imitation valuables and imitation money out of paper; the gesture to the spirits was still there, but nothing was of use to the thieves. The Chinese covered the paper coins with tinfoil to resemble silver or dyed them yellow with seaweed juice to resemble gold.

After paper currency started to be used in China in the ninth century, the Chinese began burning it at funerals. They quickly realized, however, that it was far better to burn fake money—so fake that it could never be passed off as counterfeit—than the real thing. Marco Polo witnessed a cremation in which money and numerous other valuables—including horses, camels, and servants—were fashioned out of paper and placed on the pyre. The practice of burning paper for the dead continued into modern times; Tsien Tsuen-Hsuin, the great Chinese scholar of writing, estimated that in the early twentieth century, the largest use of handmade paper in China was for burial ceremonies.

THE CHINESE APPROACHED writing with unusual creativity. Up until the third century BCE, a writer could make up his own characters, and one town could choose to use different characters from the next. But eventually came an effort to establish a standard set of characters; during the Han dynasty, three different sets of standardized characters evolved, and later, other newer systems were developed. But none of the simplified alphabets were put into widespread use, and the list of characters continued to expand. And that is what led to Mao's dilemma. Chairman Mao Zedong, believing that the number and complexity of characters was a cause of China's high rate of illiteracy, tried to convince his comrades to switch to a Western alphabet. Failing at that, he then promoted a "simplified" version of Chinese—characters with fewer brushstrokes— that is now in standard usage. But even in simplified Chinese, the average number of brushstrokes per character is thirteen. A really simple word like *zhi*, the word for paper, has seven strokes—far more than any of the letters in a Western alphabet.

Chairman Mao's simplified alphabet was an attempt to get all Chinese people to write in the same way. Yet even when using the new system, creative individuals have always found a way to express their own style. They would use the standard characters and follow the set rules, but add their own flair. Writing beautifully—calligraphy—was China's first graphic art form. Although elsewhere in the world people drew first and learned to write later, in China, the reverse was true. First you learned to write beautifully, and then you painted. After mastering those twin skills, you could move on to writing poetry, but many chose to remain just calligraphers, a highly appreciated art form in China.

Another huge step was the switch from silk to paper. Silk was good for calligraphy because it was soft. But only the elite could afford silk; the development of paper meant that anyone could become a calligrapher.

Calligraphy is an art of individual expression. The brush style of the characters, as well as the words used, express the personality of the calligrapher. A great calligrapher, like any other great artist, must first have something to express. And Chinese painting reflects an important concept in Chinese culture, namely that the final goal is to create a work of perfect balance. Each character executed by a great calligrapher is an abstract painting, an expression created through thick and thin curves, and straight, splashed, or swirled lines. A particularly beautiful character or sometimes a page of calligraphy is sold as art, and mounted by itself on a wall.

Just as Chinese writing supposedly sprang from forms found in nature, a good calligrapher's characters are supposed to resemble nature. There are strokes with names like "plum-tree branch" and "falling rock." Some calligraphers use very big, thick, splashy strokes, while others prefer small and delicate ones. And there are certain ideals to be achieved: a dot should look like a rapidly falling rock, and a vertical line should resemble a vine. But the characters are always abstractions, not figurative drawings. In fact, the process used by many calligraphers is similar to the process used by many modern abstract painters in the West. The Chinese calligrapher works quickly, and once his or her brush touches the paper, that stroke can never be changed, working in much the same way the abstract expressionist artist Jackson Pollock once did. To argue about which are good or bad strokes—an argument that does at times take place—is like arguing over whether a Pollock drip is good or bad.

The challenge is to be creative within a structure that has many rules. Each character is to be written with a certain number of brush strokes—as few as one and as many as fifteen. There are more than sixty basic strokes, and each one has a specific starting point.

As in painting, calligraphic styles have changed over the centuries, and along with them, the way of holding the brush, the elbow position relative to the wrist, and the type of table used for working. Sun Xiaoyun, a leading contemporary Chinese calligrapher, who has made a study of this, notes that in the thirteenth-century Song dynasty, tables and desks were generally short, making it impossible to write small, fine characters. This meant that the intellectuals of the day did not use tables and desks to write and paint on. Instead, they had their servants hold paper up for them; in order for this to work, the paper had to be thick. Xiaoyun also points out that calligraphers' posture changed over time as different styles of calligraphy and painting emerged. It is not clear if better worktables were developed when the Chinese learned how to make thinner paper, or if they made thinner paper when they developed better tables.

As time went by, calligraphers became connoisseurs of ink and brushes as well as paper. Lampblack ink sticks mixed with water on an ink stone were a major improvement over the ink made from burned tar that had been used earlier. And calligraphers and painters began to use brushes of many different sizes made of goat or other animal hair. The most responsive brushes, the ones that produced the liveliest strokes, were said to be those made from the hair of wild marten.

Paper became not only thinner but whiter, and the best kind of paper was that which contained the most bark. It was made with care, in a process that could take up to three hundred days—considerably faster than the processes used in earlier periods. Gao Lin, a scholar from the Ming dynasty, said that the best ink stones, smooth as jade, were made in Duanzhou; the best brushes were from Huzhou; the best ink sticks, from Huizhou; and the best paper, *xuan zhi*, from Xuan Straw was used to make cheap paper for wrapping or burning, and calligraphy paper was often made from bamboo. As far back as the eighth-century Tang dynasty, a cultural high point for China, the best art and calligraphy paper came from the bark of blue sandalwood, and this is still true in China today.

What we today call "handwriting analysis" became a popular pursuit in China. The Chinese believe that a great deal about a calligrapher can be known by analyzing his or her brushwork. Song dynasty emperor Huizong, who ruled in the first quarter of the twelfth century and was a calligrapher/painter/poet, had a unique style of calligraphy that he labeled "Slender Gold." It consisted of thin, light strokes. From this, the Chinese writer and art historian Chiang Yee has surmised that Emperor Huizong was a tall, thin, attractive-looking man with a somewhat feminine temperament, meticulous habits, and a slow, measured way of speaking. On civil service exams—and civil service was the traditional road to success in China—handwriting was considered as important as content. All kinds of judgments could be made by looking at someone's handwriting.

WHEREAS CALLIGRAPHERS TURNED to paper as soon as they could get it, painters, who had traditionally worked on silk, did not commonly use paper until about 300 CE. Even still, most paintings from this period were silk mounted on paper. For a long time, a painting would be sketched out on paper first and the final work done on silk. Little by little, painters came around to using paper, but painting on silk—a deluxe material— has never gone out of fashion.

Painters often used the same paper as calligraphers did, though special papers for painting were also created. In the tenth century, the last ruler of the Tang dynasty, Li Yu, was a poet who used a special paper from Anhui called Pure Heart Hall, named after his studio. Pure Heart Hall became a favorite of painters, and even today, artists have a preference for paper from Anhui Province.

Artists sometimes used very large pieces of paper, which took considerable skill and sometimes several people to mold. Some of the largest sheets involved as many as twenty people working the mold in a vat of pulp and water and agitating the frame from side to side. Some Hsien Chih paper was as big as twelve feet by eight feet, and there were even sheets fifty feet long. But the most common-sized paper for calligraphy and painting was about one and a half feet wide and slightly more than four feet long.

The first Chinese painter whose name we know is Zhang Heng, a contemporary of Cai Lun. None of his paintings have survived, and we know of him only from his writing, poetry, astronomy, and his famous observation that painters would rather depict mythical creatures than real ones. "Real objects are difficult to represent, but the realm of unreal is infinite," he wrote.

The Chinese originally used figurative art to illustrate calligraphy; sometimes only a simple line drawing was used. But later, the illustrations grew more and more elaborate. Complex paintings that included only a few lines of calligraphy began to appear, whereas some paintings contained entire poems. Calligraphy, painting, and poetry—all were often done by the same artist.

As was true in other cultures, after the written Chinese language was firmly entrenched, the popularity of oral literature stubbornly hung on. Poetry became tied to paper, yet also remained an oral art form. Chinese poetry has its roots in the fifth-century BCE *Book of Songs*, and as late as the Han dynasty, poetry was the domain of the government's Music Bureau. In the golden age of eighth-century poetry, it was both written and sung. The traditional instrument that the poet played while chanting poems was the *ch'in,* or *qin,* a slightly curved wooden box with strings that are plucked. Certain poets such as Li Po are often depicted singing.

Chinese painting and the poetry that accompanied it were deeply rooted in the spiritual beliefs of Taoism, which dates back to the fourth century BCE and extolls a love of nature and of finding the natural balance inherent in all things, as well as more abstract concepts such as embracing nothingness. Both the poetry and the painting, therefore, were largely, though not exclusively, focused on landscapes. In a famous essay, the eleventh-century master, Guo, known for the beauty of his monochromatic black ink-wash landscapes, wrote: "The din of the dusty world and the locked-in-ness of human habitation are what human nature habitually abhors; and the haunting spirits of the mountains are what human nature seeks, and yet can rarely find."

The most celebrated of the early painters, Gu Kaizhi, was a Taoist who celebrated the individual and the beauty of nature. None of his paintings have survived from the fourth century, but his writings and copies of some of his paintings have. What we know of early Chinese painting we know only because part of the later painters' training was to copy the masters, and many of these copies have survived. In one surviving passage on "How to paint the cloud terrace mountain," Gu Kaizhi wrote:

Starting with the eastern extremity and gradually rising toward the center of the picture, I would make purple rock, looking something like cumulus—five or six layers of them. Astride the hills, ascending among them, the rocks writhe and coil like dragons.

The period known as the High Tang (712 to 760 CE) was also a high point for Taoist painting and poetry. This great period in the arts blossomed against a background of political instability and social and political upheaval. The emperor Xuanzong was a passionate patron of the arts—especially the silk and paper arts of calligraphy, painting, and poetry—and the poetry created during his reign is now known as "classical Chinese poetry." It was written in a style called *shi*, which contained either five or seven characters to a line, and the style became so well established that the word *shi* eventually came to mean simply "poetry."

Early twentieth-century American and English modernists were fascinated by High Tang poetry and its style of using a limited number of characters to express complex ideas. Ezra Pound translated Li Po, one of the High Tang greats, who lived from 701 to 762, almost the exact span of the High Tang period. It is easy to understand why modernists such as Pound were attracted to classical Chinese poetry. Because of its Taoist roots there is an esthetic of "stripping away" to the simplest essence of things, which is also a key tenet of modernism.

High Tang poetry is sometimes called "mountain and river poetry" because of its subject matter; mountains and rivers reflect "the Tao," or the path of life. Once upon returning from an eastern province, the artist and poet Gu Kaizhi was asked how his trip had gone, and he replied, "A thousand mountains vie with one another in magnificence, a thousand ravines contend with rival torrents."

The moon was another important Taoist image, and one that Li Po often wrote about. Another favorite subject was wine. In a poem titled "Drinking alone below the Moon," he wrote:

> *Surely, if heaven didn't love wine,*
> *There would be no Wine Star in heaven.*

Wang Hui (ca. 1632–1717). This "mountain and river" painting is ink and watercolor on paper. It is a copy of an unnamed earlier painting from the classical period. Great Chinese painters often copied earlier masters, a practice called fanggu, *which is largely how we know of the ancient paper painting traditions since the originals have not survived.*

Appropriately enough, legend has it that Li Po's end came one night when he was on a boat, drinking wine. He tried to reach for the moon, fell over, and drowned.

Another of the seventh-century greats, Tu Fu, also a Taoist, used his poetry and painting to address social and political issues. "We have everything good government could possibly want now but good government," he wrote. Tu Fu at times could sound strikingly similar to a modern protest poet. He often denounced war, and in a poem titled "Song of the War-Carts" once wrote that because of war,

> *Even a son's birth is tragic now*
> *People prefer a daughter's birth*

These were words of incredible power in eighth-century China.

———

PAPER EVENTUALLY SPREAD from China to East Asia, along with the rest of Chinese culture. The written Chinese language was introduced to Vietnam in 186 CE, and Vietnam was among the first countries to make paper for Chinese writing. Sometimes this paper was used locally, and sometimes it was exported back to paper-hungry China. Vietnamese papermaking is thought to have begun in the third century, at a time when China ruled the northern part of Vietnam. In 284 CE, 30,000 rolls of something called *mi hsiang zhi*—a honey-scented paper, perhaps made from the bark of the garco tree—was brought to China from Vietnam. About 10,000 rolls of a very fine paper thought to have been made from either seaweed or fern were also sent to China in this period. These were considerable quantities of paper. The Vietnamese were apparently good at papermaking, however, because the Chinese continued to import both Vietnamese paper and Vietnamese paper products such as fans even after the tenth century, when Vietnam gained independence from China.

Paper also made its way to India from China, via Tibet in the seventh century. The Indians then proceeded to make paper from jute, old gunnysacks, and, at a fairly early date, recycled old paper. But the Indians were relatively late to papermaking and did not use paper extensively until the twelfth century. This is surprising, because they were the originators of Buddhism, which played an important role in the spread of paper elsewhere in Asia.

All of the Asian religions were drawn to paper, but Buddhism in particular made extensive use of it because Buddhists believe that blessings are earned by drawing or painting Buddhist images, writing down Buddhist prayers, or copying books of sermons of the Buddha, known as sutras. In China, many artists painted portraits of the Buddha or of other deities and patriarchs. In the fifth century, Chinese Buddhist monks would add pigments to pulp and made colored paper for writing—especially pink, but also sky-blue, peach blossom, gray, and yellow.

Also in the fifth century, Chinese books started to arrive on the Korean peninsula. Back in the year 109, when papermaking was still a new idea, the Chinese invaded Korea and began moving to the peninsula. By midcentury, the Koreans had regained political control, but they never reversed the now-entrenched and seemingly irresistible Chinese civilization. They started learning to write with Chinese characters and to make paper. Chinese characters were not well suited to the Korean language, a fact that the Koreans struggled with for centuries, but Chinese script was the only form of writing used in Korea until the sixth century.

Chinese Buddhist monks traveled to Korea to teach not only their religion, but also brush making, ink making, and painting, so that the Koreans could be good Buddhists and write prayers and paint deities. The Koreans wrote sutras both in their Chinese versions and by translating them directly from the original Sanskrit Indian texts.

Korean papermaking was in every respect like that of the Chinese. They made paper from rice, straw, hemp, bamboo, rattan, seaweed, and most of all, the inner bark of the paper mulberry tree. This bark was bleached in the sun, pounded, boiled, and mixed with the slime of a mucilaginous plant related to okra, which gave firmness to the sheet. The Korean paper mold, like the Chinese paper mold, was usually made of woven bamboo, but sometimes a particular Korean grass was also used.

THE JAPANESE ARCHIPELAGO, made up of mountainous islands with only small strips of arable land around the coast, was one of the poorest corners of Asia. While China had vast space in which to develop a civilization built on thriving agriculture, Japan struggled to produce enough food, and could not even produce enough salt to preserve what little food they had. This reality is still reflected in the lean, spare tastes of the modern Japanese.

By the third century BCE, when the Han dynasty began in China, Japan was still in the Stone Age. There is considerable debate, which has gone on for centuries now, over whether the Japanese had a written language before Chinese was introduced. If they did, no evidence of it has been discovered. Early in the Han dynasty, China, reaching out to all the known world and beyond, had made contact with Japan. Some Japanese people learned to read and write in Chinese, although these were only a small, elite group. There was no trade and very few relations between the two countries. But after China invaded Korea in 109 CE, some of the Chinese who had immigrated to Korea went over to the nearby archipelago and taught the Japanese rice cultivation—which became a mainstay of their diet—and helped them acquire more advanced tools, horses, and swords. In 286, Atogi, the son of the king of Korea, visited Japan and taught the Japanese people Chinese writing.

Then in 370, Japan, the once-backwards little country that now had swords, invaded Korea, and held on to Korean territory for almost the next two hundred years. This began to open up contacts among the people of China, Korea, and Japan. In 608, four Japanese students were sent to China and when they returned, they spread Chinese culture even more widely. Two years later, paper was made in Japan for the first time, perhaps under the direction of a Buddhist monk named Dancho, who was also said to be a gifted painter, skilled ink maker, and physician. Dancho presented the empress of Japan with several books of Buddhist sutras.

Japanese culture thus became increasingly Chinese, adopting Confucian concepts of government, Chinese writing, and Buddhism as their official religion. This Chinese influence dominated Japan throughout the entire Heian period (794 to 1185), which took its name from the capital city of Heian-Kyo, today known as Kyoto. Calligraphy took on tremendous social importance. People were judged by their calligraphy skills both in the professional world and in courtship. No one, it seemed, wanted someone with bad handwriting.

If the Chinese and Koreans had brought only papermaking to Japan, it might have had little long-term impact. But they brought an entire paper culture—written language, Buddhism, Confucianism, calligraphy, painting, and even bureaucracy. As in China, the government in

Japan began to demand ever more paper. Every family was required to register births, marriages, and deaths with two copies—one for the government and one for the family. This paper was of such high quality that many records have survived into modern times without yellowing, foxing, or becoming brittle. Through these documents, many Japanese can trace their family as far back as 700.

By the eighth century, paper mills were operating in nine Japanese provinces, and by the Heian period, papermaking had spread to forty provinces. By the ninth century, the Emperor's Library, which kept all of the emperors' books and paintings, established paper mills with four expert papermakers whose job it was to maintain or elevate the standards of Japanese paper. Once a year, these mills gave 20,000 sheets of their finest paper to the *kuraryo*, the curator of the emperor's storehouse. In addition, papermakers in the province of Mino sent in 4,600 sheets of colored paper.

Japanese paper has lasted because it has no acid content and so it does not yellow. A 1,200-year-old sheet looks much the same today as it did when freshly made. It was also fashioned using the same technique and from almost the same materials as is Japanese handmade paper today. The main materials were, and are, bark from mulberry trees—mitsumata and kajo (today replaced by kozo)—and another bush, gampi. Gampi, which grows wild in Japan, was probably one of the rare Japanese originals in the art of papermaking, and the Japanese began to use it around the ninth century.

The shoots were beaten with a mallet so that the bark could be stripped off. The sticks were sometimes used as firewood for the heaters and the ash made good fertilizer. The root of *tororo aie*, the same relative of okra with beautiful white edible blossoms that the Chinese used, was cooked to a slime that was added to give body to the pulp. Hemp was also used, and in 1031 we can see the first record of recycled paper—paper made from old, used paper. Since the Japanese had no way of stripping off the ink, as is done with modern recycled paper, the resulting product was gray. But it was widely used, even in the Imperial Palace.

As in China, the Japanese used paper for many things other than writing. At Shinto shrines, the one religion that originated in Japan, fortunes were, and still are, written on handmade paper and sold to be hung from trees. *Gohei* is paper cut and folded in a specific pattern, a series of angled rectangles, and hung from rice straw rope to mark a sacred area. Among these sacred areas are fermentation rooms for sake; before the Japanese learned about chemistry, they believed that there were spirits who created fermentation.

Paper was also used to build the traditional Japanese home. This was another idea imported from China, but the Japanese used it for much longer. Instead of glass windows, there were translucent paper panels called *shoji*, and instead of interior walls separating rooms, there were sliding opaque decorative panels called *karakami*. In the traditional Japanese home, art cannot be hung on paper walls. Homeowners pride themselves on owning a good collection of paintings that can be hung only one at a time and in one designated spot. The painting changes with the season, or sometimes with the month, and some families have a special painting that they put out to honor certain guests.

There is an interesting unresolved argument about technology and development in regards to the Japanese home. The Japanese were extremely late to make glass, and according to some experts, this is the reason why shoji were used. But others argue that the Japanese did not make glass because they didn't need it, because they were happy with shoji. It is much the same argument as that about the Incas and their slow development of writing, due perhaps to their skill with knotted ropes.

Shoji are very pleasant. They give a room soft and diffused warm light. In the winter, a shoji panel absorbs humidity and holds in heat. In the summer, panels can be slid open to let in a breeze. The only difficulty with shoji is that they are expensive and difficult to maintain, and need to be regularly replaced. Another difficultly, in the minds of parents at least, is that holes can easily be poked in its panels, leading to the popular boys' prank of making tiny pinholes and spying in on the neighbors.

The Japanese made paper work for them. Paper umbrellas lasted at least as long as cloth ones do today, grain was stored in durable paper bags, and paper tarpaulins protected goods in open carts from the rain.

FOR ABOUT SIX centuries, paper was an exclusively Asian product. China had outlasted the Roman Empire and was the most advanced civilization in the world. They had developed a society that needed paper and had exported it to neighboring Asian societies. But another advanced civilization was about to come along, and they, too, would need paper.

Chapter 3

THE
ISLAMIC BIRTH
OF
LITERACY

|||||||||||||||||||

*[Scheherazade] possessed courage, wit, and penetration. She
had read much, and had so admirable a memory, that she
never forgot any thing she had read.*

— One Thousand and One Nights

ANOTHER OF THE GREAT MYTHS OF PAPER HISTORY CON-
cerns Chinese prisoners. This one comes to us from Al-Thaʾilibī, a tenth-
century Arab historian who wrote a book with the dubious title *Book of
Curious and Entertaining Information*. In it, he says that after the battle of
Talas in 751, the Arab commander Ziyad ibn Salih, having defeated the
Chinese forces of Gao Xianzhi, took Chinese prisoners who then went
on to teach papermaking to artisans in Samarkand. Thereafter, according to Al-Thaʾilibī, paper was a valuable export for the city: "Its value was
universally recognized and people everywhere used it," he wrote.

The problem with this story is that paper had already been in use in Central Asia in the fourth century, as was proven in 1907 by the legendary Hungarian-born British archaeologist Marc Aurel Stein. Stein discovered a packet of undelivered letters written on paper in Central Asia dating from 313–14. An angry wife whose husband had gone off somewhere and left her with no money had written them. "I would rather be a dog's wife or a pig's wife than yours," she wrote.

According to Tsien Tsuen-Hsuin, the great Chinese scholar who died in 2015 at the age of 105, paper was first made in Central Asia no later than the early fifth century. Arab words for paper, such as *kaghid* and *qirtas*—a word that is used in the Qur'an—are thought to be of Chinese origin. Others credit papermaking in Central Asia to the Buddhist monks who were prominent in the area decades before the 741 battle with the Chinese.

In any event, it must have taken time to perfect the craft of papermaking in Central Asia. Made from beaten rags, it was different from Chinese paper. The making of paper from rags was not a Central Asian invention either (as usual, the Chinese had gotten there first), but they were the first to produce high-quality paper exclusively from rags. When rags were used in China, they were only one component in a mixed pulp. The Arabs also sized their paper differently. The Chinese often used a glue made from lichen, while the Arabs, living in a much drier climate, used a starch made from rice and wheat.

Samarkand, at the western end of the Silk Road, conquered by Alexander the Great in 329, had long been an important center of commerce. In the eighth century, linen rag paper from Samarkand, commonly known as Samarkand paper, became famous in the Islamic world, which turned the city into the first paper center outside of eastern Asia.

ORIGINALLY, THE WORD "Arab" specifically meant someone from the Arabian Peninsula. But after the Prophet Muhammad, the founder of Islam, established an Islamic theocracy in Medina in 622, the Arabs began to expand beyond their peninsula, and the word began to be applied to other peoples. In 634 the Arabs took Syria and Iraq. Eleven years later, they controlled Cyrenaica, the eastern part of what is now Libya, Egypt, and the upper Mesopotamian region.

In 660 the Umayyads, a merchant family from Mecca, gained control of the caliphate, or Islamic government, and moved their capital to Damascus. In 750 the Abbasids, direct descendants of Al-'Abbas ibn 'Abd al-Muttalib, an uncle of the Prophet Muhammad, overthrew the Umayyads and established their capital in Kufa, a city on the banks of the Euphrates. In 762 the new caliph, Al-Mansur, built a splendid new capital to the north of Kufa, a grand city of palaces and gardens named Baghdad.

Under the Abbasid caliphs, the Islamic world blossomed—it was a golden age of culture and learning. In time, they ruled an empire that stretched from the Pyrenees in the east to the Amu Darya River in the west; the Amu Darya runs through Central Asia, past Afghanistan, and into what is today Pakistan. As they expanded their reach, the Arabs took their religion, science, and culture with them—and to spread their ideas and their laws, they made paper.

The Abbasid Caliphate faced fierce resistance from the Persians, whom they finally defeated in 660, and from the Berbers of North Africa, whom they defeated at the end of the seventh century. They tried unsuccessfully to take India, controlled Sicily from 847 until the Normans conquered it in 1072, struggled to gain control of Cyprus, and, for a generation, controlled Bari and Taranto on the Italian mainland. The great Abbasid Caliphate lasted only 150 years before splintering off into smaller groups that became increasingly independent. By the late ninth century, the Turkish military controlled the caliphate and by the eleventh century, Baghdad was part of the Ottoman Empire.

As the Arabs conquered territories in the Middle East, Central Asia, and Europe, they built on and adapted aspects from all the cultures they acquired. Now a minority in the Muslim world, the Arabs were open to other cultures and peoples, though Arab blood always had special status. When Al-Mansur was building Baghdad, he consulted constantly with two non-Arab men. The first, Nawbakht, was a Persian ex-Zoroastrian, and the second, Masha'allah, was a Jew. The Muslim population was divided in many different ways—by language, by region, by culture—but the most important and long-lasting schism was between the Sunnis and Shi'as. Originally a disagreement about the succession of leadership following the Prophet Muhammad's death, this enmity became a major factor in the destruction of the Islamic Empire, and continues to be the source of much tragic strife, violence, and civil war in the Muslim world today.

THOUGH THEY LATER earned the reputation of being a highly literary and poetic people, the early Arabs had little need for writing material. They did not even develop a written language until the late fourth and fifth century, and then it was a Semitic language from the Phoenician family, written right to left with only consonants. Very few examples of pre-Islamic Arab writing have been discovered. The Arabs did have poetry, but it was oral poetry. The poet would recite his poems to his handpicked disciples, who would memorize and spread them to the general public through recitation.

The use of writing in the Arab world increased with the founding of Islam in the first half of the seventh century. The Qur'an was believed to be God's word revealed to the Prophet Muhammad, who, like most of the people on the Arabian Peninsula at the time, could not read or write. He dictated the Qur'an to scribes. As Islam spread, more and more copies of the Holy Book were needed, and each copy had to be made with painstaking accuracy. Not a syllable of God's word could be altered. The pages of the book themselves also had to be beautiful—the origin of Arab calligraphy.

During Muhammad's lifetime, only a few written copies of the Qur'an existed, as its words were largely transmitted in the same oral manner as poetry. That is why the Muslim religion has always attached a great importance to memorization. But in 633, a year after Muhammad's death, numerous *hafiz*, the men who memorized and recited the Qur'an, were killed in battles, and the Muslim leaders decided that orality was not reliable enough. More written copies of the Holy Book were needed.

Scribes were put to work, and from the time of Muhammad's death to the time of the Abbasid Caliphate 130 years later, written Arabic changed from a crude and awkward scratch to a graceful, flowing language with one of the most beautiful scripts ever created.

Muslim calligraphers were often men of high social standing, even aristocrats, and many of their names have been preserved in the histories of their day. The great calligraphers of the Qur'an were respected as holy men. In fact, it says in the Qur'an that God gave us the pen—suggesting that writing comes from God. The number of cursive styles used to write Arabic increased; by the tenth century, there were twenty—some curvy and swirling, others more angular, still others more horizontal.

IN THE COURSE of their conquests, the Muslims came into contact with many centers of learning, and every conquest advanced their knowledge. They learned papermaking and alchemy from the Chinese in Central Asia, and mathematics from the peoples of Egypt and Syria. From the Greeks, they learned hydraulic engineering, and in North Africa, Spain, and Sicily, they observed Roman civil engineering—the building of bridges, dams, aqueducts, and irrigation.

If the Arabs had encountered papermaking earlier in their history, and they may have, they would have had little use for it. But by the time they began making paper in Central Asia, they were expanding their empire and the reach of their religion, and needed it to aid that expansion. Paper was also essential for the bureaucracy that was administering their empire, for the many new things they were learning, and for their increasingly rich culture of arts and science.

Jonathan Bloom, professor of Islamic and Asian art at Boston College, defines a "literate society" as one "where a significant portion of the people regularly read and wrote," and credits the Islamic Empire as being the world's first truly literate society. The Muslims believed that the written word was a privilege not just for the elite few, but for the population at large—rich and poor, religious and secular.

When the Abbasids first came to power, everything was still being recorded on papyrus, which had become easily available after the Arab conquest of Egypt in 641. Records were kept on loose sheets or in rolls until Vizier Khalid ibn Barmak ordered that all the papyrus records be transferred to codices, which had been the Syrian practice. Papyrus does not work well for codices because the pages fray, and so like the Syrians, the Abbasids began using parchment.

In 786 Harun al-Rashid, the son of an Abbasid caliph, came to power. "Al-Rashid" was an honorific meaning "the just" and Harun's twenty-three-year reign was lavishly praised in his lifetime and throughout subsequent history. Even the nineteenth-century British poet Alfred Lord Tennyson wrote of "the good Haroun Alraschid." But in truth Harun's reign was marked by brutality, torture, and a great deal of killing. However, he was also known for spurring a rich expansion of Arab culture, and one of those achievements was that his administrator Al-Fadl al-Yahyā pushed for all government work, including that stored in libraries, to be switched from parchment to paper.

The Arabs did not give up parchment or even papyrus easily. They tried cultivating papyrus along the Euphrates, and hired Egyptian experts from the Nile delta to produce it. But in time, the Arabs came to recognize that papyrus couldn't meet their needs and that paper—inexpensive, lightweight, and durable—could. Paper also had another important advantage: it prevented fraud. Parchment and papyrus documents could be easily altered, but paper documents could not.

In order to make paper work for them, the Arabs had to make changes. The process of producing ink in the Arab world was not well organized, as each calligrapher and scribe made his own ink. Furthermore, that ink, designed for parchment, had a high acid content that ate through paper. With their switch to paper, the Arabs turned to lamp-black ink, the black carbon ink of choice for the Chinese. The new ink was called *midad*.

Handwriting changed with paper too. A new style of cursive script was adopted, with spaces between words for easier reading and comprehension by the general public.

The original Muslim scribes were men who copied the Qur'an, and even after paper was introduced, they stubbornly insisted on writing the sacred text on parchment because it would last. But as a result of the expanding empire, there were many other works to transcribe as well, and for these, the scribes did turn to paper. As the Arab Empire continued to grow, the *kutab*, the writers, became central to their bureaucracy. In theory, these men were simply bureaucrats who did the paperwork, but some became extremely powerful government aides and advisers. Government documents were expected to be not only informative but elegant in style and beautifully written. The *kutab* were expected to be knowledgeable about everything from poetry to folk tales to the Qur'an.

ONCE THE CHANGE to paper was made, a great deal of it was needed, and in the year 794 the caliphate hired Chinese workers to build a paper mill in Baghdad so that the great capital could produce its own. Baghdad was perfectly situated for a paper mill: it was situated on a river and had a large enough population to produce a sufficient supply of rags.

The Baghdad mill was water-powered. One of the important ideas that the Arabs learned from the Greeks was how to harness the force of hydraulics. Both the vertical and the horizontal waterwheel were invented in third-century BCE Greece, and a Greek engineer, Philo of Byzantium, wrote a technical book on waterwheels that the Arabs likely translated. Around 10 BCE, the Roman engineer Vitruvius had described a gear-driven water-powered undershot wheel, which is a vertical wheel with paddles that are moved by the water at the bottom to drive a horizontal axle. Only a few years later, an overshot wheel that used buckets instead of paddles was developed; the buckets were propelled by the water that was deposited by other buckets passing over the wheel.

These wheels were first utilized by the Greeks for grinding grain, and in one case, for a machine that kneaded bread. By 30 CE, waterwheels were being used in China in the iron smelting process. The Romans attached waterwheels to boats to take advantage of water movement, and later, the Arabs did the same on the Tigris and Euphrates. The Arabs combined all of these ideas in the manufacture of paper, an inventive solution born out of knowledge of two cultures. The use of a water-wheel was one of the pivotal innovations in the history of paper. From the eighth century until the nineteenth-century industrial revolution, a paper mill was a watermill built near a river or falls where the water ran swiftly.

SOME SAMPLES OF Baghdad paper have survived. Among them is a letter sent to Egypt from a member of the Babylonian Jewish academy, now housed in the Cambridge University Library. Dating from the ninth century, it is written on Baghdad paper that is thick, but smooth and even. A Qur'an from the year 1000 has also survived. Inscribed in beautiful, ornate script by the famous scribe Ibn al-Bawwab, it is written on paper that is smooth and thin, demonstrating how by that time, Baghdad was producing paper of a high-enough quality to be deemed suitable for the Qur'an.

Baghdad could not vie with the paper production in Samarkand, but otherwise, it had little competition. The Muslim world was limited in terms of its number of paper mills because mills need running water. There can be no desert paper mills. A third Muslim mill was built in Tihamah, the southeast coast of the Arabian Peninsula along the Red Sea, and a fourth farther south by the rivers below the Great Arabian Desert in what is now Yemen.

Then a more serious competitor sprang up: Damascus, Syria. The paper made there was of high quality and it became widely known, even in Europe, where it was called *charta damascena*, or Damascus paper. The Syrian town of Bambyx on the banks of the Euphrates River also began making paper, which was called *charta bambycina*, meaning "cotton paper." Because of this, the Europeans were convinced, as late as the late nineteenth century, that Arab paper was made from cotton and that paper made from rags was therefore a European innovation.

The Arab papermakers tended to live and work together in paper-making villages near the cities. Most of the paper was made out of either hemp or linen, from rags or ropes or sometimes raw material. Ropes that were untwisted and cut up were a good source of hemp. The cut-up material was then soaked in lime, washed off, and dried in the sun. Then it was ground with a mortar and pestle. The resulting pulp was highly diluted in water and the watery mix was placed in a large basin. A rectangular mold, made out of woven split reed stalks sometimes tied to each other with horsehair, was then dipped in the water. The resulting paper that formed on the mold was usually white and a bit puffy, which may be another reason why the Europeans thought it was made from cotton.

When the Arabs began making paper in Cairo in about 900, they had already been using Baghdad and Samarkand paper for a century. Yet Egypt soon proved itself to be an ideal paper producer. The Egyptians grew huge quantities of flax, which was woven into famous high-quality linen, which in turn provided ample rags for the paper industry. Cairo became not only a papermaking center, but also a market center, famous for the variety of paper sold there. By the end of the ninth century, paper was far more popular than papyrus throughout the Muslim world, and rags were becoming greatly valued. A courteous note dated between 883 and 895 ends with the apology, "Pardon the papyrus." Nonetheless, Egypt continued to make papyrus, where it was used locally and exported to other societies until the thirteenth century.

Ironically, once papyrus making did end in Egypt, it was the Arabs who kept it alive for a time. Perhaps they discovered it growing wild or perhaps they planted it in the marshes near Syracuse, Sicily, which was then under Muslim rule. At any rate, it was used briefly for local government documents, and the Sicilians exported it in small amounts. There was little market for it, however, and papyrus making soon died out.

Parchment survived, however, even in Egypt. The Muslims, Jews, and Coptic Christians all insisted on using it for sacred texts, and the Muslims and Jews used it for certain family documents such as marriage contracts and divorces. It only took about a hundred years for paper to replace parchment in the Arab world, but by the mid-ninth century, paper was the leading material used for most writing, from letters to records to books. Parchment was still used for the Qur'an until about the year 1000, when most Muslim scribes switched to writing their holy book on paper. The Jews continued to use parchment, however, and even today, Jews insist on using parchment for the Torah.

The Arabs had many uses for different papers. A special light, thin paper was also made for messages sent by carrier pigeon. And an amazed Persian traveling in Cairo about 1040 wrote, "The venders of vegetables and spices are furnished with paper in which everything they sell is wrapped." A century later, a Baghdad physician visiting Cairo caused a stir when he claimed that the paper in which the food was wrapped was made from the cloth wrappings of mummies that Bedouins had stolen and sold to paper mills.

THE ARABS, ESPECIALLY the Abbasids, were not merely open to people and learning from other cultures, they were eager for this exchange. The Qur'an says that good Muslims should seek knowledge, and they did so passionately and with a great deal of ink and paper.

Al-Mansur's vizier, Khalid Barmak, came from a family of Buddhist clergy in Balkh, a renowned Buddhist center in what is now northern Afghanistan. He and his family were also well versed in Greek culture, and it was Barmak and his family who started the movement under the Abbasids to seek out valuable manuscripts so that they could translate them into Arabic. In this way, the Arabs learned the legends of India; the history of Persia; and Greek logic, mathematics, and medicine. The Arabs also started studying astronomy and calendars, and translated the work of the seventh-century Indian mathematics and astronomy genius Brahmagupta.

Brahmagupta explained cubes and cube roots and squares and square roots, but probably his most important work was introducing the concepts of zero and negative numbers. These may seem like simple ideas to us now, but they are counterintuitive. How can there be a number for nothing? If you have five goats and you take away five goats, how many goats are left? There aren't any. But the mathematical answer is 0, a number that you can work with for further calculations. The same is true with negative numbers. These ideas advanced mathematics tremendously. Brahmagupta's simple rule, one that all schoolchildren still learn at some point, was that when zero is added to a number or subtracted from a number, the number remains unchanged. But if a number is multiplied by zero it becomes zero.

When Harun al-Rashid was only twenty-one years old, he was already a legendary general. Even at the age of fourteen he had already led successful military campaigns against the Byzantines. It was for this and not his sense of justice that he was given the title Al-Rashid, the just. Elected caliph, he built himself the grandest palace in Baghdad, and founded a library, research, and translation center, the Khizanat al-Hikma, which sought to collect and translate Greek manuscripts. Many of these had been acquired through diplomatic connections with the Byzantine emperor, and works such as Euclid's *The Elements* became extremely influential in shaping Islamic mathematical thinking. Among the other books found in the collection are translations of work by Archimedes for which no original Greek text has ever been found. The center's first chief librarian, al-Fadl, a poet and translator of Persian, was the son of Nawbakht, who had been an adviser to the caliph's grandfather in the building of Baghdad.

The next caliph, Harun al-Rashid's son, Ma'mun, came to power in 813 and wanted to go far beyond acquiring and translating Greek manuscripts, and in the beginning of the ninth century, established the Bayt al-Hikma, or House of Wisdom, in Baghdad to encourage the study of not only Greek but also Indian mathematics. An early director of the House of Wisdom was a mathematician named Muhammad ibn Mūsā al-Khwārizmī, who changed the Western world by urging the adoption of Hindu numerals—1–9—as well as the zero and the base-ten system that we use today. He recognized that using the Hindu numerals was a far more efficient means of calculation than using the Roman ones. Just compare calculating "32 + 49" to calculating "XXXII + IL."

The ninth-century mathematician Al-Khwārizmī expressed abstractions in formulas, which he called *al-jabr* (algebra), an Arab word meaning "restoration." This was one of the few true mathematical innovations made by the Arabs. The Muslim contribution to mathematics is not so much innovation as it is assimilation. The Arabs were the ones who took all the known ideas from the world around them and put them together into one system. Their skill in mathematics was applied to everything from astronomy to the making of highly accurate sundials, which were placed on the walls of mosques. The Muslim world ran their day on time-telling long before other societies. According to legend, Caliph Harun al-Rashid, who sought contacts everywhere, once sent a sundial and an elephant to Charlemagne as gifts of friendship.

Muslim learning often had a practical or even commercial side. A fascination with alchemy led to the distillation of rose water and other flower- and plant-based perfumes, which were sold abroad and along the Silk Road to China. Commercial perfume distilleries thrived in Damascus, Kufa, and Ṣabūr in Iran.

Muslims are also thought to have learned how to distill alcohol in the eighth century, though the oldest written recipe found is from the ninth century, in a tome entitled *Book of Perfume Chemistry and Distillation* by Al-Kindt. The Arabs were nevertheless among the first to distill alcohol; the Europeans didn't learn how to do so until they translated Arab writings on the subject in the twelfth century.

This is an interesting bit of trivia, given that Muslim culture ostensibly abhors drinking alcohol. But early Muslims apparently were drinkers nonetheless; the first reference to it in the Qur'an forbids attending services while intoxicated. Actually, the Qur'an never mentions alcohol per se—it probably didn't exist at the time it was written—but warns instead about "intoxicants." It is not certain when or where the absolute prohibition of alcohol consumption in the Muslim world began. The word "alcohol"—like "algebra," "algorithm," "alfalfa," and "alchemy"—is an Arabic word, as its prefix, "al," functions as a definite article, like "the" in English.

ALCHEMY, ASTRONOMY, ENGINEERING, and mathematics were only one part of what led to the flourishing of books under the Abbasids. At the time, a great European library was one that consisted of a few hundred books, such as the 400-book collection of the ninth-century Abbey of Saint Gall monastery in Switzerland, or France's twelfth-century Cluny monastery, which had 570 books. In contrast, Arab libraries of that era, even private libraries, boasted thousands or even hundreds of thousands of books.

At the center of this lively literary life were the mosques. Even works commissioned by the Abbasid leaders had to be taken to the mosque to be written. A writer would go to the mosque and find a scribe to whom he could dictate his work. This is why even the most secular of works, even a cookbook, began with a tribute to the greatness and mercy of God. Authors and scribes would sit cross-legged on the floor together creating books.

To take oral literature and write it down gave it prestige in Arab culture. It signified that a work was important and deserved to be preserved for posterity. In Arab culture, writing was everywhere, on objects and on buildings. Since Islam, like Judaism, forbids the representation of humans or animals, writing became the leading visual art.

The Islamic scholar Jonathan Bloom estimated in 2001 that 600,000 handwritten manuscripts have been found, and given the destruction of whole libraries and other mishaps with the passage of time, this is thought to be only a fraction of what was produced. Arab book production began with the Qur'an and theological books on Islamic law and Islamic schisms, creating a wealth of material that sorted out the differences between the Sunnis and Shi'as and Ibadis, the latter of whom were a sect centered in Basra. Then the government, which had previously ruled by oral decree, decided to codify those laws in books, which led to numerous other tomes on civil and religious law and the conflict between them. As the government expanded, an increasing number of books were written on administration. Next came histories, often based on the Qur'an and beginning with the creation, as well as books on the Arab language and linguistics.

Persian culture, like Arab culture, was virtually defined by poetry. The tenth-century rulers of Persia, concerned that Persian culture might disappear following the Arab conquest, commissioned Abolqasem

Ferdowsi to write the great epic poem of Persia. The sultan offered Ferdowsi a gold coin per line. Paying by the line can be dangerous; Ferdowsi wrote 50,000 long lines, making his opus, *Shahnameh*, the longest poem in history. But that was only the beginning of the expense, because scribes were also paid by the line. And then there was the cost of the paper. The sultan insisted on using Chinese paper, the best available, which may also have been an intentional snub to the Arabs. The book became the central classic of Persian literature, and while expensive copies were periodically made, sections were often read to the public by official readers. In the 1970s, a 1530 copy of the *Shahnameh*, considered the finest illustrated manuscript in Middle Eastern history, was broken apart and sold a page at a time. In 2006, a single page sold at Sotheby's in London for $1.7 million.

Even after it became traditional to write poetry on paper, poetry retained its strong oral tradition. All kinds of material, sacred and profane, highbrow and lowbrow, were publicly read, and the mosque was a favorite place for such readings. Poetry had the highest standing in the Muslim literary canon, and poems were often committed to memory. Stories, on the other hand, were regarded as literature for the masses. The readers of stories tended to be rough, working-class individuals, and in Egypt, as in Turkey, storytellers had their own guild and performed in coffeehouses. Nonetheless, the caliphs wanted everything that was publicly read, including stories, written down in books. The most famous example of this is *One Thousand and One Nights,* which is a collection of oral stories that were later written down. Each version of the collection differs somewhat from the others. The earliest version is a fragment of an opening page from the early ninth century that was found in Syria. In the late nineteenth century, Sir Richard Burton undertook to compile and translate into English as many of the stories as he could find. His work is sixteen volumes long, and contains 468 stories. An early French version is only six volumes. Scholars generally believed that there were many more stories than we have found. They were told by an unknown number of people and written down by an unknown number of authors. The Arabs say that no one can read this book through to its end—perhaps because the end has never been found.

In some of the stories, the wise Caliph Harun al-Rashid appears as a character. Some stories seem like fairy tales, others moral allegories; still others are erotic and even sometimes scatological. Pornographic literature, sex manuals, and "dirty" stories were another common Arab genre. They were called *kutub al-bah*. *One Thousand and One Nights* is essentially erotic literature. The premise is that a mythical ancient king named Shahriyar discovers his wife in flagrante delicto with a man on the kitchen staff. He has her executed and then decides that he cannot risk being betrayed again and will only make love to virgins, beheading them the next morning.

After Shahriyar spends his time deflowering and beheading numerous women, the vizier's daughter, Scheherazade, understandably against her father's will, volunteers to be his next lover. She goes ahead with the lovemaking but postpones the execution by telling a tale that she cannot finish that night. The king, wanting to hear the end of the story, allows her to live until the next night, when they again make love and she again tells him that she cannot finish the story that night. And so it goes. She tells stories within stories, so that nothing ends for 2 years and 271 days—1,001 nights. By then, she has given him several children and the king decides not to execute her.

The premise of the stories is that Scheherazade is a woman of extreme intelligence. To establish this it is stated that she not only has extensive knowledge and is well read but she also has an excellent memory. The goal of reading is memorization. A good memory is the key to enlightenment, an idea that pre-dates literate society.

FOOD WAS A favorite topic in the Arab world. Literary anthologies often contained a few pieces on culinary topics. Many poems, often commissioned by aristocrats, were written about the subject, and certain poets became celebrated food poets. Prose writing on food was also common. In fact, some intellectuals complained that there was too much of it. The eighth-century Abd al-Quddus, a rebellious thinker who was eventually executed in 783 by Caliph al-Mahdi in a campaign against heretics, once complained, "If you write about fish and vegetables, you garner much merit in [the public's] eyes, but if you expound truly scientific subjects, they find it irksome and boring."

Much of the Arab food writing, as is also true in the West today, was about food for the affluent. Like the better Arab cuisines today, the cooking was sophisticated, conversant in a wide variety of spices and seasonings, and often involved many steps. Also like fashionable food does today, it sometimes took weird turns in an attempt to be bold and new. There was "omelet in a bottle"—eggs were boiled in a bottle until hard and then the bottle was smashed open, leaving eggs shaped like a bottle behind. Or "mock brains"—liver and fat mashed up (essentially chopped liver), stuffed into a copper tubing, boiled, and shaken out onto a plate. We are told this was "similar to brains in appearance as well as in flavor."

Cookbooks were popular. These were not, however, the world's first cookbooks. In the fourth century BCE, Archestratus, a Greek in the Grecian colony of Gela on Sicily, wrote a book on food with recipes called *The Life of Luxury*. In the first century CE, a Roman named Apicius also wrote a small cookbook, and in the second century, Marcus Aurelius's physician, Galen, wrote what could be considered the first Western health-food/diet book. But the Islamic Empire was the first culture to produce an entire shelf's worth of cookbooks. Few have survived, but there are enough references to "cookbooks" in documents for historians to suppose that there were quite a few of them. In 945, Hamdani wrote, "The actual food and drink in Yemen are to be preferred to the recipes in the cook books." A 988 book gives a bibliography of books on seasoning alone, none of which have survived.

One cookbook, dated 1226, was written in Baghdad by a man named Muhammad Ibn al-Hasan ibn Muhammad ibn al-Karim al-Kātib al Baghdādi. His name provides a whole genealogical chart, complete with the names of Muhammad's ancestors and their location, but we know nothing else about him other than the fact that he loved food and quoted from the Qur'an, which does not rule out the possibility that he was a secular hedonist. As was the custom, he wrote his book, "In the name of

God, the merciful, the compassionate," and then proceeded to describe and explain the many dishes of the Abbasids:

> Pleasure may be divided into six classes, to wit, food, drink, clothed, sex, scent and sound. Of these the noblest and most consequential is food.

Muhammad ibn al-Hasan offers 164 recipes that are written, as all recipes were until late in the Industrial Revolution, in a narrative rather than formulaic style. Here is *hummādiya*, a recipe for an unspecified meat, which usually meant mutton.

> Cut fat meat into middling pieces, and leave in the saucepan with a covering of water and a little salt. Boil, then throw in the stout cotton bag containing the seasoning, namely dry coriander, ginger, pepper, and cloves ground fine: add also a few pieces of cinnamon. Now mince red meat with seasonings, and make it into cabobs: where the saucepan is boiling, throw in the cabobs, and as soon as these are cooked, remove the bag of seasonings. Now take the pulp of large citrons, seeded, and squeeze well in the hand, add about a quarter as much of grape-juice, and pour into the saucepan on top of the meat. Boil for an hour. Take sweet almonds, peel, chop up fine, soak in water, and add to the saucepan. Sweeten with sugar, or with syrup if preferred. Leave the saucepan over the fire to settle. Sprinkle with rose-water, wipe the side with a clean rag, and remove.

Here is a recipe for leftovers, *qaliya al-shiwa*, which means fried roast.

> Take cold roast of yesterday and cut into small pieces. Take fresh sesame oil, put into the frying pan, and boil: then add the roast stirring. When its fat is melted, throw in fine-brayed coriander, cumin, and cinnamon. If desired sour, sprinkle with a little vinegar colored with saffron. Garnish with poached eggs: instead of

vinegar, lemon-juice may be used, only in that case without eggs. Leave over a gentle fire an hour to settle: then remove.

Arab cuisine included dessert recipes centuries before the Europeans were eating desserts. This might have been because, also unlike the Europeans at the time, the Arabs cultivated sugarcane. Here is a recipe for *halwa*, the sweet nougat that is still made in very much the same way throughout the Arab and Mediterranean worlds:

Take sugar, dissolve in water, and boil until set: then remove from the dish, and pour onto a soft surface to cool. Take an iron stake with soft head and plant it into the mass, then pull up the sugar, stretching it with the hands and drawing it up the stake all the time, until it becomes white, then throw once more on the surface. Knead in pistachios, and cut into strips and triangles. If desired it may be colored, either with saffron or with vermilion. Sometimes it is crumbled with a little peeled almonds, sesame, or poppy.

This book bespeaks an opulent society, but only a generation after it was printed, the Mongols invaded and sacked Baghdad, burning its libraries and thereby ending the golden Abbasid age.

Chapter 4

AND WHERE IS XÁTIVA?

||||||||||||||||||

Ask Valencia what became of Murcia

And where is Xátiva, or where is Jaen?

Where is Córdoba, the seat of great learning,

And how many scholars of high repute remain there?

And where is Seville, the home of happy gatherings

On its great river, cooling and brimful with water? . . .

. . . Oh heedless one, this is Fate's warning to you:

If you slumber, Fate always stays awake

—*"Lament for the Fall of Seville,"*
ABI SHARIF AL-RUNDI, 1267

I N 670, THE UMAYYAD CALIPHATE INVADED WHAT IS NOW Morocco, a land that was home to the Berber people but had been previously controlled by Carthage, then Rome, and then the Visigoths. They called the land al-Mamlakah al-Maghribiyyah, the Western Kingdom, from which comes the word "Maghreb," which still means "Arab" in North Africa. The caliphs from Baghdad had thus extended their rule—their language, their religion, their culture—from Central Asia to the Atlantic Ocean.

But they had an uneasy hold on the region. The Berbers were more difficult to subjugate than other cultures they had conquered. They accepted Islam and even learned Arabic, but they continued to speak their own language, kept their own culture—including remnants of their ancestral religion—periodically rebelled, established their own governments, and had their own armies.

Despite the fact that he is the author of one of the most pivotal events in European history—the conquering of Iberia by Muslims—there is not much known about the leader of the conquest, Tariq ibn Ziyad. Although he had an Arab name, Tariq was almost certainly a Berber, and according to many accounts, a freed slave of Mūsá bin Nuṣayr, an Arab general credited with the subjugation of the Berbers. Shunning the brutal policies of his predecessor, Mūsá had won over Berbers with persuasion and a willingness to tolerate their customs. Some Berbers even volunteered to fight for him. Once the Arabs controlled the Berber mainland as far as the Atlantic, Mūsá attempted to conquer what is now known as Cueta, then controlled by a man named Julian, who ruled on behalf of the Visigoths. Historians are uncertain whether Julian was himself a Visigoth or a Berber, but he clearly hated the Visigoths whom he served. According to some stories, this hatred arose from Julian's daughter being raped by the king of the Visigoths, Roderic.

Julian played on Mūsá's higher and lower instincts. He told the Arab general that the Visigoths had a new king, Roderic, who was cruel and much hated. And in fact, when Roderic had come to power in 710, a breakaway group had indeed attempted to overthrow him. Julian also said that the Visigoths had a beautiful land with incredible riches. Mūsá subsequently sent a raiding party across the straits of Gibraltar to Spain, a short journey, and landed in what is now Tarifa, where he encountered no resistance at all. Then, in 711, thinking the Visigoths might be more vulnerable than he had believed, he sent a 7,000-man Berber army commanded by Tariq to head farther inland. Tariq must have had a sense of the role he was playing in history, because on the way he stopped to name the mountain island they crossed Jebel Tariq, Rock of Tariq, now known as Gibraltar.

Tariq's mission was to simply conduct raids and explore the area, but luck was with him and his army. When they landed, Roderic was in the north trying to put down a rebellion by the Basques. For three weeks, there was little sign of the Visigoth forces and the Berbers took town after town as Visigoth messengers scurried north to alert the king. Finally, the Berbers confronted the Visigoths, by then an ill-prepared, poorly armed, and worn-down army of 20,000 led by Roderic. Despite outnumbering the Berbers 3 to 1, the Visigoths were destroyed and most of their noblemen, including Roderic, were killed at the Battle of Guadalete.

Tariq then captured Toledo, the capital, and proceeded to take over the entire Visigoth Kingdom on Iberia. Mūsá then landed a second, 18,000-man army, composed of both Arabs and Berbers, and by the year 714, he had reached the Bay of Biscay and was in control of Iberia.

The Arabs ruled this enclave that they called al-Andalus for almost eight hundred years—the equivalent of the length of time from the Renaissance to today. Many Christians in the region converted to Islam, and the Jews, who had been mistreated under the Visigoths, welcomed the Muslims and prospered under them. Jews had been living in Iberia since Roman times, but when the Visigoths arrived, anti-Semitic laws were passed, barring Jews from marrying Christians, forbidding them to observe Jewish holidays, and, eventually, forcing them to convert, leave, or become enslaved.

The Christians knew nothing about the new invaders. Many thought the Muslims were a dissident sect of Christianity, as the Visigoths were. But Islam at the time was less than a century old. Islam, which recognizes Abraham, Moses, and Jesus, taught that Jews and Christians should be respected as *ahl al-kitah*—"people of the book." The Muslims' attitude toward Christians was that they were just misguided. The Muslims therefore did not force Jewish or Christian conversion, although being a Muslim meant paying less in taxes and having access to good government jobs. It took about 250 years, until the mid-tenth century, for Muslims to become the majority of the al-Andalus population.

By the ninth century, the Muslims of Iberia had a prosperous economy, though this was true of the Mediterranean world in general, and they had built a civilization and culture far beyond anything that could be found in the rest of Europe—and even, in some regards, beyond any to be found in other parts of the Arab Empire. Christendom was so focused on driving the Muslims out that it was very slow to absorb Arab learning. Yet when they eventually did, Arab culture spurred great advances in Europe.

To the Andalusians, as the people of al-Andalus were called, the Christians of the north were barbarians. While the people of al-Andalus bathed regularly in hot water and regularly washed their clothes, the Christians to the north, they said, bathed only a few times a year in cold water and never washed their clothes.

The Muslims brought with them Arab learning in mathematics, astronomy, medicine, engineering, agriculture, and literature. By the tenth century, the library in Córdoba contained 400,000 books; it took the Vatican, intent on creating the leading library of Christendom, until the year 1455 to collect just 5,000 books.

The Muslims also introduced cotton, spinach, watermelon, figs, and advanced irrigation techniques to the Iberian Peninsula, and al-Andalus was far more advanced in agriculture than was the rest of Europe. The Andalusians took the Roman system of irrigation, practiced in Syria and other Arab lands, and improved on it. They pioneered systems of water-wheels, sluices, and canals. Buckets were attached to wheels, and the wheels, turned either by the force of water or with animal power, lifted water from rivers, wells, and cisterns into irrigation canals. Their most famous and extensive irrigation project turned the marshland along the coast outside Valencia, La Huerta, into a highly productive agricultural zone administered by a "water court." The area is now celebrated as the birthplace of paella, which originally had no seafood in it—only wildlife, such as rabbits, along with rice and vegetables of La Huerta.

Philosophy and theology attained new heights in al-Andalus. Moses Maimonides challenged and examined the Jewish religion as never before by twelfth-century. At the same time, a Muslim thinker, Averroes, scrutinized Islam. In the thirteenth century, a new branch of Jewish thought was explored by the great Kabbalist Moses de León, while Islam expanded with the teachings of Ibn Arabi in a movement called Sufism.

Al-Andalus also became celebrated for its poetry and music, and its Arab and Jewish ballads are still played today. The Andalusians attempted to write down music and could indicate if a note was higher or lower than the next, but had no way of indicating the exact pitch of notes. In that respect they were no more advanced than the European monks marking Gregorian plainchants. But in al-Andalus music was written on paper.

In 912, Abd al-Rahman III became the ruler of Córdoba and during his celebrated fifty-year reign, he initiated the practice of not only commissioning poetry but commissioning an official history of his reign. Official history became an al-Andalus tradition, and it left behind a treasure trove for historians, although most of the histories are about military exploits. In the eleventh century, Samuel ibn Nagrella, a Jew who successfully led the military forces of Granada, had poetry written to record his victories; in it, he was compared to King David. He also wrote important studies of the Bible and the Talmud.

Commercial transactions and banking were carefully recorded on paper with Hindu/Arabic numerals. Bills and receipts were widespread. Mathematics was studied and written about. Mapmaking, which the Arabs had learned from the Greeks, Persians, and Indians, was an important activity always conducted on paper, though the maps themselves were not intended for the general public and were often difficult to read. Geography was of special importance in Andalusian society, because all Muslims must pray in the direction of Mecca, and all Jews toward Jerusalem. Astronomy, including the mapping of the heavens, was another important pursuit.

Architecture also reached new heights of elegance and complexity, as can still be seen in such buildings as the Great Mosque in Córdoba. Because the Andalusians had paper for sketching, new and elaborate design ideas could be planned. And because of the interdiction of figurative images, astoundingly complex geometric patterns were developed and carefully laid out. Carpet designs throughout the Arab world were sketched on paper in the same way.

THOUGH THE ANDALUSIANS clearly made extensive use of paper, the same could not be said of the North Africans, who did not embrace paper as quickly as other parts of the Arab Empire. Theirs was a sheep-herding society accustomed to using and making parchment. However, by the eleventh century, Fez, in Morocco, had become an important paper producer.

Here is a story that suggests how commonplace paper eventually became in North Africa: A mosque in Fez was adorned with elaborate carvings. But since it is against Islamic law to show representations of animals or people, the locals feared that when the ruler, Abd al-Mu'min, a strict Muslim fundamentalist, announced that he would be paying them a visit, he would destroy them. So they covered the walls with paper and then plastered them over. The mosque then temporarily appeared to have smooth bare walls.

By the twelfth century, according to one account, there were 472 paper mills in Fez. This may be an exaggeration, but it is known that around this time Fez was producing a great deal of paper and shipping it to the Mediterranean coast of Spain.

The first mention of paper being made in al-Andalus was in 1056, in the town of Xátiva, or Shatibar in Arabic, though paper may have been made in the area earlier. Xátiva was an ideal location for a paper mill. An old Roman town, it was built on a hill beside the fast-moving Albaida River. The city was surrounded by fields of flax and had been famous during its Roman days, when it was known as Saebtis, for the quality of its linen.

By some accounts, but not all, the papermakers in Xátiva were Jews. This would not have been unusual, because throughout the Arab world, paper was being made by both Jews and Muslims. There are Jewish writings on the art of papermaking that date back as early as the eighth century. By the twelfth century, the paper from Xátiva, called *shabti*, was regarded as one of the best papers in the Arab world. Western-made paper had never before been admired. Paper from the old Eastern centers such as Baghdad, Damascus, and Cairo was still considered the best. But the new Andalusian paper was thought to possibly be an improvement. In 1154 the geographer al-Idrisi wrote, "Xátiva is a pleasant town with palaces and fortifications proverbial for their beauty. Such fine paper was not made elsewhere in the civilized world and was exported to the East and the West."

A mill is a mill and, as would be discovered in the rest of Europe, most any kind of mill will do for making paper. When waterpower is harnessed by a wheel to turn a grinding stone, a mill can be used to grind many things, including paper pulp. The Andalusians converted into paper mills Roman-built mills that had once been used to grind olives to olive oil. These mills were equipped with giant stones that did the grinding, and it was these stones that made Andalusian paper smoother and better than the Arab paper of the East, where mills used smaller stones. Another important improvement were the metal wire molds used; they produced higher quality paper than did the split bamboo molds of Asia or the split reed molds of the Arab world.

Rushing water is all that is needed to turn a grinding stone, but the best-quality paper requires something more—*good* water. The water must be clear, lacking in silt, and unpolluted. Otherwise, specks will show up in the paper. In addition, water with a high iron content produces paper with a reddish or brownish cast. To produce very white paper, the presence of calcium or magnesium carbonate in the water helps, and sometimes the Andalusians would add lime, which is calcium, to the pulp. In Spain under the Arabs and the Christians, it was said that a river where trout lived had good water for papermaking.

A curious characteristic of the al-Andalus paper made between 1166 and 1360 is that when it is held up to the light, a zigzag line or sometimes a series of *x*'s or random lines coming to points, can be seen. The reason for this is not known. The lines could have been intended as an aid in folding or as an imitation of the markings sometimes left on parchment through curing and stretching. They might also have been a forerunner of the watermark, which later papermakers used to identify their work.

Colored paper, which was popular in Persia and in parts of North Africa, was also common in al-Andalus, especially Granada, which was known for its reds, purples, and pinks. A 1418 letter by Muhammad VIII found in a Catalan archive is on blood-red paper made from linen and hemp.

Only very slowly did the European Christians grow interested in the paper of al-Andalus. They tended to see it as something that Jews and Muslims produced and used. Around 1140, a monk from Cluny, Peter the Venerable, visited Benedictine monasteries in Spain, and upon his return wrote a manuscript on parchment entitled *A Tract Against Jews*. He had visited the important Christian sites, including Toledo, the seat of the cathedral for the kingdom of Castile. Known for its fine paper manufacturing, Toledo was a famously Jewish city. The Jewish quarter was the largest quarter in the city; Jews were at the center of intellectual life and, it seemed to Peter, they were everywhere. He wrote with disdain, "In heaven God reads the book of Talmud. But what kind of book? We normally read on sheepskins or goat or calf, and bark of reeds extracted from the marshes of orient (papyrus). But this is done with bits of old clothes or vilest things." Still others referred to paper as "rag parchment" and sneered at "rag scrapings."

Gradually, however, the Europeans did grow interested in paper. In time, this would have led to competition for the Andalusian papermakers, but al-Andalus did not last long enough for that. Europe was simply a good market for them. Sicily and then Italy were their first steady customers. Andalusian paper was shipped to Messina, Catania, and Syracuse, and to Genoa, Naples, and Venice. Then the Muslims expanded their sales to Bordeaux, and next, England. Soon they were also selling to the Balearic Islands, today part of Spain, and to Aigues-Mortes and Marseilles in southern France. By the fifteenth century, Egyptian and Syrian paper, which had always been expensive, were nearly priced out of the market. Andalusian paper was sold even in Egypt.

The Arabs of the Middle East were also selling to Europe, and the North Africans were selling to West Africa and the Sudan. But while the trade with Europe resulted in the establishment of European paper mills, no paper was made in black Africa until colonial times. In black Africa, paper remained an expensive imported luxury item. Neither their government administrations nor their religions, usually the two strongest motivators for the use of paper, acquired a strong need for it. Even in the seventeenth and eighteenth centuries, Africans were still not making their own paper; the small amounts of it carried by North African and Andalusian traders across the Sahara was adequate for the market.

AS IN A Greek tragedy, the flaw that undid al-Andalus was infighting—between Arabs and Berbers, between one caliphate and another, between Sunnis and Shi'as. While the Arabs and Jews of al-Andalus were living affluent, culturally rich lives, the political powers holding their society together were slowly fracturing, even as their enemies, the Christians, were growing ever more united.

While al-Andalus's trade, economy, and culture were prospering, al-Andalus was slowly disappearing. By the mid-eleventh century, infighting had splintered the enclave into more than two dozen small states, and the Christians saw their opportunity. They began chipping away at Arab lands and in 1085 took Toledo. For a time, this looked like the beginning of the end. But then the Almoravid dynasty in North Africa reinvaded the peninsula and reasserted control. They were overthrown by a more fanatical North African dynasty, the Almohad, which imposed harsh religious law, causing some Jews to flee North Africa to Córdoba and others to flee al-Andalus for Egypt. But finally in the thirteenth century, the Muslim centers of Valencia, Seville, and even the great city of Córdoba fell to the Christians one by one. "If you slumber, Fate always stays awake," the poet Abi Sharif al-Rundi warned.

Some Christians, such as Isabella of Castile, "La Catolica," the future queen of Spain, were religious fanatics, but many Christian leaders, like the Berbers before them, simply saw places they liked and decided to take them. In 1240, Jaime I, King of Aragon, wrote upon viewing Xátiva that he had "beheld the most beautiful area of irrigated farmland that we had ever seen anywhere. . . . Our hearts filled with pleasure and satisfaction at the sight; and it seemed to us that we should come to Xátiva with our army . . . in order to take the castle for Christendom." By the fifteenth century, only a small enclave of Muslims and Jews was left, and finally in 1492, starved by a blockade, the last Muslim city, Granada, surrendered. Jews and Muslims were forcibly expelled, and al-Andalus, once the greatest center of Western civilization, was gone, almost as if it had only been a dream.

Muslims had lived in Spain for eight hundred years. By contrast, Europeans have only been living in North America for five hundred years. Yet only foggy traces of the once-great al-Andalus civilization remain in Europe today. Among them are remnants of the great architecture—mosques and synagogues—now used as churches. The expelled Jews kept their Spanish dialect written in the Hebrew alphabet, the Ladino language, and they kept the keys to their homes, passing them from one generation to another; the tragedy of the 1492 expulsion is one of the calamities that Jews remember on their darkest day, a summer holiday of mourning and fasting called Tisha B'Av. The four-string oud, a musical instrument central to the Sephardic aires of the Jews and the Andalus-Arab songs of the Muslims, became the five-string lute of Europe, important in medieval and Renaissance music. (In modern Morocco, the French have gotten the Arabs to call the oud an "Arab lute"—a masterpiece act of cultural imperialism.) The Spanish language and most European languages have Arab traces, especially in the adaption of the Arab prefix "al," and Spanish includes some Arab phonemes, such as the guttural *jota*.

The Andalusians also left the Europeans another great gift: paper.

Chapter 5

EUROPE BETWEEN
TWO FELTS

||||||||||||||||||

And his nation shall be between felt and felt.

—DANTE ALIGHIERI, *Inferno*

T HE ELEVENTH, TWELFTH, AND THIRTEENTH CENTURIES were a time of tremendous creativity and change in Europe. Not that Europe hadn't had its creative thinkers and geniuses, its masterpieces, before. But that creativity was largely locked away in monasteries or offered only to the nobility for their entertainment and enlightenment. Books were hand-painted on parchment with such stunning beauty that noblemen were pleased to own them as art objects but often never read them. Even many kings and princes were illiterate. Charlemagne, an advocate of books and literacy, was read to early in his reign and only started to learn to read himself in response to his insomnia. Historians suspect that he never read well.

But then, throughout much of the world, economies started expanding. By the late Middle Ages, the average European had at least the minimal reading skills needed to conduct business or trade, and was no longer, as the Arabs had once claimed, unwashed. Business and commerce, mathematics, arts, literature, and science began to show the imposing brilliance that we have come to associate with Europe. Most of the ideas that got the Europeans started had their origins in the Arab world. Italy, which had the most exposure to Arab culture, led the way. And for centuries, it was the Italians, not the Arabs, whom the Europeans credited for ideas and inventions that had begun in the Muslim world.

Ironically, the Italians, the inventors of Roman numerals, took a great leap forward in business and mathematics when they became the first in Christian Europe to abandon the Roman system and use Hindu/Arabic numbers. In addition, their sophisticated accounting techniques, including "double-entry accounting," with columns of assets and debits, came from the Arabs, though it was known throughout Europe as "Italian accounting." Making paper from rags, an art practiced for centuries in the Arab world and before that in Asia, was dubbed an Italian invention. Of course, in a similar manner, the Arabs laid claim to other inventions, such as waterwheels and irrigation, which had originated with the Greeks or Romans.

What does it tell us about European culture when it is so often said that the Italians made the first paper in Europe? For this to be true, either Spain would not be considered part of Europe, or Muslims and Jews would not be considered European—even though they had lived on the Continent for generations. The first European papermaking outside of al-Andalus occurred in Italy. But already by then, Christians had begun making paper in al-Andalus. According to Oriol Valls i Subirà, the Catalan scholar of Spanish paper history, papermakers who had been driven out of their lands by fanatic regimes in the twelfth and thirteenth centuries moved to Christian areas, where they taught the Christians their papermaking techniques. New Christian paper mills were established in Catalonia and in the Basque country, especially in Bilbao in the twelfth century, a hundred years before Italy began making paper.

After King Jaime I of Aragon conquered Valencia in 1238, he created a huge bureaucracy. Since Xátiva was now under his control, he used its paper mills for his government, thus becoming the first Christian ruler to rely on paper documents and records.

THERE IS SOME dispute about what is the oldest example of paper made in Italy. One document written by Countess Adelaide, the third wife of Roger I of Sicily, refers to a salt mine and is dated to 1109. This is sometimes cited as the oldest paper "in Europe" (not counting Spain). However, there is no proof that the paper was made in Sicily, as a great deal of al-Andalus paper was shipped there. Furthermore, Roger I, like many Europeans at the time, found paper flimsy and generally untrustworthy, and his wife may have thought the same. During the next century, in 1145, Roger II ordered that all government documents be copied onto parchment. The official code of the Kingdom of Sicily clearly states, "Of instruments written on sheets of paper, none is to have any authority."

There is also no clear record of *where* papermaking started in Italy. Amalfi, or somewhere nearby, may have been the site of the first papermaking done on the Italian mainland. But the paper produced there appears to be Arab in the method of its manufacture, including its use of starch sizing, and so may have been imported or made in Arab-run mills. (Beautiful handmade paper is still made in Amalfi, though it is now produced on a small scale, mostly for gift shops that cater to tourists.)

The earliest verifiable papermaking site in Italy is Fabriano, a mountainous town on the west coast of the peninsula in an area known as the Marche, not far from major commercial centers such as Bologna and—farther up the coast—Venice. Tall, vertical outcroppings of rock form deep canyons along the Castellano River, so named because it ran right through Fabriano's castle. The river was renamed the Giano River in the eighteenth century, in honor of a two-faced Roman god; it was fashionable in Italy at that time to give everything Roman names. The river's clean, fresh water gathered speed and power as it ran down the hilly countryside, making Fabriano a suitable place for papermaking.

Some historians believe that the people in Fabriano learned papermaking in the eleventh century, when Arabs, attacking the nearby city of Ancona, taught it to them. Possible evidence supporting this theory is the fact that some Arab papermaking terms were used in Fabriano.

These include the Fabriano word for rag paper, *cuctunea*, which comes from an Arab word, *quothon*. That word is also the origin of the Italian word *cotone*, which means "cotton," but this is a mistranslation because the Arabs never made paper from cotton and the Italians didn't do so either until the eighteenth century. The Fabrianese were also the first Europeans to call the bundles into which they divided their paper *risma*, which comes from the Arabic *razmah*, and is translated into English as "ream." The amount contained in a ream, but not the term itself, has slightly changed over time. Today's paper is still counted in reams; a ream is five hundred sheets.

The earliest verifiable record of papermaking in Italy is a document that dates from 1264. It records a merchant's purchase of paper from Fabriano, and since it does not say anything about this being a new business or the first time this was done, it can be logically assumed that paper was produced in the city for some time prior to 1264.

The area around Fabriano was well known for its wool production and its mills, built along the rivers, to press wool into felt. Felt was not a new product; the ancient Greeks had made it. Franco Mariani, a paper historian in Fabriano, believes that merchants plying the wool trade to places such as Venice, where the Arab paper trade was prospering, came to learn about paper and started renting the felting mills out to paper-makers. This practice soon became popular—sometimes just one or two of the mill rooms were rented out—as almost no change in equipment was needed for the conversion. All that the papermakers had to do was to put metal heads on the wool-pounding hammers to turn them into suitable rag beaters. For centuries to come, many felting mills, including ones in the United States, were converted to paper mills.

Several innovations at the old felting mills of Fabriano changed the course of paper history. First, the Europeans did not use the starch siz-ing utilized by the Arabs. Earlier generations of Europeans who had chosen parchment over paper because paper wouldn't last through the centuries were right in this respect: the grain-based sizing that worked well in the arid climates of southern Spain, North Africa, and the Middle East would not work in the humid climates of Europe. Here, paper sized with grain deteriorated rapidly. The Fabriano paper, in contrast, lasted because its papermakers, working closely with the local sheep industry, sized their product with glue made from the gelatin produced by boiling sheepskin scraps.

The greatest argument in favor of the Europeans switching to paper from parchment was that paper was much cheaper. Paper historians estimate that between 210 and 225 sheep had to be slaughtered to make one Bible. Some historians believe such estimates are exaggerated, but to make one Torah scroll—which is not the entire Old Testament, just the Five Books of Moses—in the modern state of Israel today requires the skin of 60 to 80 calves and a year to write. Imported Arab paper had not been cheap either. Cheap paper was invented in Fabriano, thanks to the development of an ingenious device: a water-powered drop hammer.

With this drop hammer, the power from a waterwheel turns a shaft with carefully spaced plugs sticking out from it. As the shaft turns, the plugs catch horizontal beams that are spaced so that only one at a time gets lifted. As the shaft turns the beam farther, a metal hammer on it drops on rag mush in a box. The mush squishes out from underneath the hammer, only to be caught by the next beam and hammer. In this way, and with far less manpower and far fewer hours than had previously been needed, the mush is reduced to a fibrous pulp. The drop-hammer mill could produce so much pulp in winter, when the water was high, that the mills accumulated a surplus that could be used during the summer, when water levels were low. This method produced paper that cost far less than the imported Arab variety and far less, in fact, than any other writing material.

Another Fabriano innovation was the wire mold. This may have originally been an Arab idea, but at Fabriano, it was perfected. An extremely fine wire was used—one that came to define European papermaking. By the thirteenth century, the Italians had learned how to beat metal into thin sheets that were then cut into narrow strips; the strips were hammered until rounded. This sounds like a slow and arduous technique, but the Italians could apparently do it with impressive proficiency; molds were strung with more than a hundred feet of fine brass wire woven into a single panel.

The other pivotal innovation at Fabriano was the invention of the watermark. The oldest known watermark is from Fabriano in 1276. Many watermarks were very simple—first the initials of the makers, then easy designs such as a bell or a six-sided star. A watermark is a design made from a piece of wire woven into the mold. It imprints its pattern on the pulp, and it is possible that the first watermark was an accidentally bent wire end in a mold. A watermark makes a pattern that is seen when the paper is held up to the light. Now the papermaker could "sign" his work.

The Fabriano papermakers sold their sheets to other companies that would rub the paper surface with stones to make it smoother, and then bundle the sheets into bails. Some historians think that the smoothers and balers wanted to know who made which sheets. So did the merchants, in order to see if certain papermakers were favored by their customers, and in this way, develop a steady market for their merchandise. In modern marketing, this is known as "branding"—creating a brand name to develop a following. Or was it literally branding? The original watermarks so resembled the brands burned on livestock that it is believed that this was the origin of the idea.

The watermark belonged to the individual papermaker, not the mill, and one mill could have numerous watermarks. By the fourteenth century, many felters had become papermakers and Fabriano had at least forty paper mills, probably more, and innumerable watermarks.

It was a hard life. A papermaker in Fabriano was expected to produce between 4,000 and 5,000 sheets a day—more than 1 million sheets a year—which meant constantly being on one's feet and moving about for long hours on end. Unrelenting exposure to water led to arthritis and other ailments. And a papermaker had little hope of becoming wealthy, though papermaking did provide a steady income. And as competition increased, unscrupulous papermakers who had not garnered a following started forging the watermarks of the popular makers. False watermarks became commonplace.

EVENTUALLY, THERE WERE just too many paper mills in Fabriano, and the townspeople petitioned the municipal government to force the mills to move out. They were loud and foul-smelling. The slam of dropping hammers produced a constant thunder. In addition, since the paper was made from linen and hemp, the papermakers bought soiled clothes and underwear from rag merchants who traveled from door to door. As if the smell from that cloth weren't bad enough, ammonia was needed to break down the rags' fiber, and the best source of ammonia was human urine. Urine collectors went through the town as well. The pulp was washed so many times that the paper itself did not smell, but the mills did.

Skilled papermakers were in great demand in other parts of Italy, however, and Fabriano artisans started mills in Bologna, Amalfi, Foligno, Lucca, and Lombardy. Venice, which controlled an important paper trade with Turkey, made no paper of its own because the city was flat and lacked fresh water. But as soon as the Venetians gained control of their outlying region—Treviso, Padua, Udine—they brought in Fabriano papermakers to start mills. All the "maritime republics" also became important paper centers. These were port cities—Genoa, Venice, Pisa, and Amalfi—that became independent states grown affluent from trade, shipbuilding, and banking, as well as papermaking and paper trading.

The greatest limitation on paper production was getting enough rags. Recognizing this, rag merchants started selling outside their district in search of the best prices. In the late fourteenth century, however, the administration of Fabriano barred rag merchants from selling outside their district, and similar laws were soon passed in other parts of Italy. The Republic of Florence, the Senate in Venice, and the Signoria in Genoa all passed similar ordinances. Then in 1592, Pope Clemente VIII forbade rag merchants to sell outside their state, an ordinance that was later adopted by many European governments.

WITH ITS USE of drop hammers, animal sizing, wire molds, and watermarks, Fabriano had reinvented paper—and defined European papermaking for centuries to come. Italian papermaking was creating stiff competition for Spain, even before the Arabs and Jews were ousted. Europe became increasingly interested in paper, and Fabriano papermakers were in demand in Germany, Switzerland, Austria, and France.

In 1390, the first paper mill north of the Alps was established by the gates of Nuremberg, Germany, built by an influential businessman named Stromeyer. Other German cities followed, including Ravensburg in 1393, Chemnitz in 1408, and Strasbourg in 1445. By the mid-fifteenth century, the French had also become papermakers—in Champagne, the Vosges, Troyes, and the Auvergne. Paris had become an important market for paper, and papermakers sprang up in Saint-Cloud and elsewhere in the Paris region.

It was an auspicious moment in Europe for papermaking, occurring at a time when there was a marked rise in the cultivation of both flax and hemp, used to produce linen and ropes—and of course paper. Europeans started wearing linen underwear instead of wool. There is no record indicating that this made the Europeans less irritable, but it did make a lot more rags available. Furthermore, Italy, and subsequently Germany and France, had an advantage over Spain and the Arab lands. They had far more water and more powerful rivers to drive watermills.

But the real question is: Why had the Europeans been so resistant to paper in the first place? Why hadn't they shown any interest in the Arab-made paper, which they had known about for centuries prior to the development of the Fabriano mills? There is no evidence of an inherent cultural stigma attached to paper in the Christian religion. Indeed, Christians living in Central Asia, North Africa, and al-Andalus readily accepted it, hesitating to use it for scriptures and sacred books at first but then giving in to it much more quickly than the Muslims and Jews. A Christian text dating from the year 800 in Damascus was written on paper. So, the problem was the Europeans, not the Christians.

Dante Alighieri is an interesting case in point. Born in Florence in 1265, he was the most important European writer of his era. He lived in Italy at a time when papermaking was rapidly becoming popular and at the dawn of the new age in European learning. He wrote in Italian, is considered to be the father of Italian literature, and was one of the initiators of a change in Europe that caused the switch from parchment to paper. Before Dante, books were written in Latin, a language that only existed within the walls of monasteries. No one conversed in Latin and few laypeople read it or wanted to read it. Books were written for a very small group, most of whom were literally cloistered behind walls. With their jeweled covers and painted pages, books were a status symbol that wealthy people wanted to own even if they couldn't read Latin. Compared with the Arab and Asian worlds, there was not a lot of reading going on in Europe, and parchment therefore was perfect for its needs.

But Dante helped to change that. He wrote for everyone, in the language that they all spoke. And yet he declined to use the obvious new vehicle for this new popular writing: paper. Logically, he would have been the first great writer to use paper, but instead he was the last to use parchment. Interestingly, the word *carte*, which usually means "paper," is mentioned no fewer than nine times in *The Divine Comedy*, whereas the word in use at the time for "parchment," *vello*, is hardly mentioned. But English-language translators, including the great American poet Henry Wadsworth Longfellow, generally translate *carte* as "pages," not "paper." There are exceptions, such as in Canto XXV of *Inferno* (yes, Dante also used Roman numerals), where Dante describes paper burning—"and the white dies"—and in Canto XXII of *Paradiso* he writes of laws being *"rimasa è per danno de le carte"*: a mere waste of paper.

One phrase that frequently mystifies Dante experts is: "His nation be between felt and felt,"—*E sua nazion sarà tra feltro e feltro.* Dante scholars have innumerable explanations for this expression. *Feltro* is the Italian word for "felt." But some translators, including Longfellow and American poet Robert Pinsky, rather than translating it, put it in upper case like a proper name: "between Feltro and Feltro." In this interpretation, Dante is talking about a place between the town of Feltro in Veneto and

the region of Montefeltro in Romagna. Other scholars say it is a reference to Franciscan monks, who wore felt, or a reference to democracy,
because felt was used to line ballot boxes. Still others see it as an astrolog-
ical reference. But Italians of Dante's generation, unlike contemporary
Dante scholars, were familiar with the process of handmade paper. At
Fabriano, and almost everywhere else, once a sheet was formed, it was
peeled off the mold and stacked between layers of felt for squeezing and
drying. So, a few scholars have interpreted this passage as saying that a
nation is formed on paper, by a written text.

Dante knew something about paper, and yet in his lifetime not one of
his works was ever written on paper. In fact, the only sample of his writing we have is his signature on a document written on parchment from
Florence. All his "writing" was in fact dictated to a scribe, who wrote
it down on parchment, which was how all writers wrote until paper
was adopted. It is even possible that Dante did not know how to write.

SOME HISTORIANS HAVE suggested that the Europeans were slow
to turn to paper because of anti-Semitism and anti-Arab sentiment.
According to this theory, they saw paper as a Muslim/Jewish product
and therefore refused to use it. The argument is usually supported by
a quote from Peter the Venerable's *Tract Against Jews*. But while it is not
difficult to find examples in European literature of anti-Semitism, there
are really not many examples of that sentiment being linked to paper,
though paper may have been a more palatable idea once it could be
thought of as Italian.

The more likely truth is that the Europeans had not yet developed an
intellectual and cultural life that required a more efficient writing material. In the ninth and tenth centuries, Arabs were perplexed by the back-
wardness of Europeans. The Muslim geographer Masudi observed how
the farther north you went, "the more stupid, gross and brutish they are."

Mathematics, an Arab obsession that consumed many sheets of paper
both for calculations and for studies on the subject, had thus far made
little progress in Europe. But in the tenth century, Europe had a chance

to almost catch up. Count Borrell II, a Christian nobleman living in Barcelona, traveled to south-central France, where he stopped at a monastery in Aurillac. There he met a young man of humble origin named Gerbert. Borrell thought he had the instincts and talent of a mathematical genius. He certainly had a gift for numbers; simply by living near al-Andalus, the count had a better understanding of mathematics than most Europeans. Borrell believed that with an Arab education, young Gerbert would be capable of great things.

Despite the fact that the Muslim general Almanzor had sacked Barcelona in 985, Count Borrell and many of the Christian clergy had a cordial relationship with the Muslim rulers of al-Andalus, and Borrell arranged for the boy to study mathematics under Christian clerics in the region who had themselves studied Arab learning. Gerbert learned to count and calculate with Hindu-Arab numbers, and absorbed many other concepts as well. He also became fascinated by Arabs. When Gerbert returned to Europe, he was widely recognized as a genius for the calculations he could do in his head. He passed on his knowledge to Europeans, and they started adopting the new number system. But even a century later, the Europeans still could not accomplish the mathematical calculations that the Arabs could.

Gerbert may have been a mathematical genius, but he failed to learn the concept of zero. The European clerics under whom he studied didn't yet understand zero. European languages had no word for zero. In fact, most European languages only had words for "one," "two," and "many." You could have one potato or two potatoes or many potatoes, but if you had no potatoes, there was no number for that. It may not seem logical for there to be a number for nothing, but the concept of zero is vital for mathematical calculations—for algebra, for calculus, and even for basic accounting.

Despite this important omission, Gerbert made a considerable contribution to European learning, encouraging the study of Arab and Greek mathematics and astronomy. He not only introduced Europe to Hindu-Arab numerals but to the decimal system that these numbers made possible. He also reintroduced Europe to a number of inventions that had been lost following the fall of Rome. Among them were the armillary sphere, a model globe surrounded by metal rings that could chart the movement of the earth or of the stars and planets orbiting around the Earth, and the abacus. The Roman abacus had consisted of stones on a free board positioned for counting. Gerbert changed the stones to beads on small rods, a design similar to the Asian original, and for the next century, the abacus was the leading calculator used in Europe, though it could only calculate, not record. The Europeans were still not embracing paper.

Gerbert went on to become the first French pope, Pope Sylvester II, but died only four years later. Europe, meanwhile, went on to master mathematics two centuries later. And though Gerbert had shown the Europeans the value of Hindu-Arab numerals, the last mathematics book to use Roman numerals was published as late as 1514. The Europeans began to accept the concept of zero, but they expressed it in Roman numerals such as VoIII (503), which confused most people.

IF ELEVENTH-CENTURY EUROPE had little use for paper, thirteenth-century Europe was hungry for it. About the time that Fabriano was "inventing" European papermaking, Europe was going through its greatest period of change, and by the second half of the thirteenth century, it had become a different place. One discovery rolled in on the heels of another, which rolled in on the heels of yet another.

For one thing, Europeans began to learn about Asia. From 1253 to 1255, a Flemish Franciscan monk, William of Rubruck, traveled to Mongolia and wrote a book about his sojourn that was widely read in Europe. He discovered that the Caspian Sea was a large inland lake, and not a bay opening to the Arctic as had been previously believed; that the Mongols drank a lot of mares' milk; and that they had money made of cotton paper, though he was mistaken about the cotton. The Mongols, meanwhile, implored him to send them someone who knew how to make parchment because they wanted an alternative to paper, though it is not explained why.

William was a friend of Roger Bacon, a fellow Franciscan. He told Bacon about firecrackers, and Bacon became the first European to talk about gunpowder. Bacon also initiated the idea of experimenting for scientific inquiry, though his experimentation was still a long way from modern science; campaigned for a more accurate calendar; and introduced the idea of the leap year.

A generation after the success of William of Rubruck's book, Marco Polo left for China, in 1271. The book he wrote was an even bigger success than William's had been, though many of the popular claims about it have been exaggerated. Marco Polo did not introduce Italy to pasta, as is commonly said; pasta, particularly lasagna, existed earlier. In fact, the Italians probably learned about pasta from the Arabs. Neither does Marco Polo talk about paper, other than almost repeating William's story about paper money; unlike the monk, however, he correctly states that the money was made from mulberry bark. But his book, along with William's, made Europeans interested and aware of Asia for the first time.

The bigger problem with Marco Polo was that he had a ghostwriter. In 1295 he was taken as a prisoner of war by Genoa and, while incarcerated, met a writer of romances, Rustichello of Pisa. Polo told him of his China adventures and Rustichello assured him that, in his hands, Polo's account could be turned into a big bestseller. That did come to pass, but the problem we face is that we don't know what Polo told Rustichello and what Rustichello made up—or what Rustichello chose not to include. The omissions in the book are odd. It is strange that Polo shared nothing about printing, for example, even though his comments on paper money could have led him straight to the subject. It is also odd that he didn't have more to say about China's extensive use of paper or even mention the hot liquid made from leaves that everyone there was drinking. Tea would have been an exotic curiosity to the Europeans. These omissions have led some to wonder if Marco Polo even went to China, although he probably did.

During this period mathematics in Europe began to reach the level of the Arab world and beyond. Europe's first post-classical mathematical genius was a man from Pisa: Leonardo Pisano, or as he was commonly known, Fibonacci. Because his father was a diplomat, he grew up in what is today Algeria and was schooled in Arab mathematics and accounting. Using Hindu-Arabic numerals, he not only brought more Arab ideas to Europe, but on that foundation generated other ideas of enormous influence. His most famous theorem is built on a puzzle: if a pair of rabbits were completely enclosed by a wall on all four sides, how many rabbits would be produced in a year if every year each pair begat a new pair and each new pair became fertile after two months? This led to a numbering system known as the Fibonacci series, the foundation for numerous mathematical calculations. By the sixteenth century, Europeans were even improving on algebra, by creating plus and minus signs for concepts that had previously been expressed in words.

European engineering improved. The primary timepiece had been the water clock, a device that measured time by pouring water at an even rate into a vertical tank. For anyone who had the skill to measure a water clock against the movement of the sun, it was accurate within more or less fifteen minutes.

In 1250, a French architect, Villard de Honnecourt, had written about a device he had been working on called an escapement. An escapement ticks off gear movement in regular intervals by an unloading spring, a balance wheel, or a weighted pendulum. At the time, the Chinese had already been using escapements in mechanical clocks for five hundred years. But the Europeans didn't know this, and for them, it was an incredible new invention that they began using to make clocks of increasing accuracy. Robert Anglicus, an English astronomer, tried to build one that would complete exactly one revolution every twenty-four hours, and in the Spanish Christian court of Castile, a weight-driven clock using mercury was designed.

By 1300, mechanical clocks were everywhere in Europe—on towers, in monasteries, on government buildings. There was a growing movement to set all clocks to the same time so that everyone would be synchronized. In the fourteenth century, King Charles of France built a clock on the Île de la Cité and ordered that all the clocks in Paris be set by it. To suddenly know exactly what time it was, was an enormous change in Europe.

IN THE LATE thirteenth century, there was an increasing need for paper in a number of fields, such as law, accounting, music, and mapmaking. It became important to calculate and take measurements on paper in all of these pursuits. With paper on which to work, Europeans were becoming passionate about making calculations. Roger Bacon determined that if a man walked twenty miles a day, it would take him fourteen years, seven months, twenty-nine days, and a few hours to reach the moon.

In Medieval Europe, laws had seldom been written down; they were memorized. Writing them down was not considered necessary or desirable. But in 787, the semiliterate Charlemagne decreed that laws that were written had more force than those that were memorized. In England, however, few laws were written down until after the 1066 Norman invasion, when King William began to establish such laws and records. Most famously, he ordered a Domesday Book—the name being coined two centuries later because the book was a final reckoning—a complete survey of the land holdings and other assets of everyone living in England and Wales that could be used for taxation.

But the Domesday Book, as well as the written legal code, was referred to infrequently because there was still no custom of reading. The Normans insisted that everything be written in Latin, and documents written in Old English were translated into Latin. This brought England in line with Europe, but it discouraged the reading of these documents, as few outside of the clergy knew Latin. Whenever a decree was issued, it would still be addressed to "all those who shall hear and see this charter." In 1210, when King John signed the Magna Carta, copies were made and sent to each of the country's districts to be read out loud to the public. But historians doubt that enough copies could have been made to have one read everywhere.

The body of written law in England kept expanding. At the time of the Conquest, only about 2,000 documents existed, but by the thirteenth century, that many or more could be produced in a single year. This expansion was occurring despite a continuing widespread feeling, still lingering from the Middle Ages, that writing could not be trusted. During the Middle Ages, even a message, if it was considered truly important, was delivered orally.

Before the thirteenth century and the introduction of Hindu-Arab numerals, the Europeans conducted very little bookkeeping. Business records were not written down; Roman numerals were simply not conducive to addition and other mathematical calculations. But that began to change with the adoption of the new numeric system. Merchants began to put to paper "a bill of exchange"—one party furnished certain goods or services and the other agreed to pay a certain amount. This led to double-entry accounting, the adding and subtracting of credits and deficits.

Luca Pacioli, a fifteenth-century associate of Leonardo da Vinci, is often credited with developing accounting further. Thirteenth-century bookkeeping, even though it was a big advance, was still crude. For example, not until Pacioli's innovation was there an attempt to include fractions. Until then, numbers were rounded off, with the house getting the change. In a large transaction, those forgotten fractions could add up to a considerable amount of money.

By the start of the fifteenth century, very little could be written about the sound of a piece of music. Some advances had been made, however. For example, Guido of Arezzo, an eleventh-century Benedictine monk born in France before moving to the Italian city of Arezzo, had invented a four-line staff for musical notation (the fifth line that we are familiar with wasn't added until the eighteenth century) and had made it possible to write pitch. His system of note names, based on the first letters of a hymn, indicated the places of notes on a musical scale—ut, re, me, fa, sol, la . . . Later, "ut" would become "do," and the addition of "ti" would make it possible to express an eight-note scale. It was one thing for monks to pass on orally from one generation to the next the single line of a Gregorian chant. But even by the tenth century, European music had become more complicated, as it was often composed in two or more interacting lines—that is, harmony. And in the thirteenth century, the French composer Pérotin, who sometimes wrote with three lines of music, greatly advanced this type of composition. Clergy also began to carefully notate, or mark down, music on paper. They even wrote down some secular music in order to preserve it.

In the second half of the thirteenth century, Franco of Cologne established a system of long notes and short notes to indicate tempo. This system was not standardized until the following century, but already in the thirteenth century, music could be written that told a musician exactly what to do. This was the beginning of composing on paper— revising and redoing and then handing the completed work to a scribe who would produce a final sheet of music.

THE COMPASS WAS an ancient invention in China that dates back to the third century BCE. This fascinating lodestone that would always point in the same direction was used solely for divination at first. Not until some twelve hundred years later, during the Song dynasty, did the Chinese begin using it for navigation. The Chinese compass of that time was a needle floating in a small tank of water.

The Europeans were exceptionally fast to pick up on the compass, putting it to use only about 150 years after the Chinese started using it for navigation; the first reference to the compass in Europe was in 1190. In a change from the usual historic pattern, it appears that the Europeans started navigating by compass even before the Muslims. The oldest record of its use in the Muslim world is found in Persian writing from 1232.

In the late twelfth century, ships began to navigate the English Channel and the Mediterranean with what was called a dry compass, meaning one that did not need to float in water. Before there were compasses, navigation had been dependent on the stars and so was not possible in cloudy weather. In the Mediterranean, sailors avoided going to sea between April and October because of overcast skies. By the end of the thirteenth century, however, merchants were sailing the Mediterranean all year, which tremendously increased the economic vitality of Europe.

Once they began to use the compass, they needed navigation charts based on compass readings, and for this they needed paper. The Italians had the paper and made the first charts.

THE GREATEST SINGLE change of the twelfth and thirteenth centuries in Europe was the bursting of intellectual life coming out of the monasteries and into universities and other places accessible to the general population. This shift also meant that learning was moving from remote rural locations into urban centers.

Over the centuries, the monasteries had not changed much. From their inception in fifth-century Italy onward, they had always been places for reading. Monks, particularly in the Benedictine order, were expected to spend hours reading every day. Since reading was of necessity a daylight activity, monks were required to read only two hours a day in the winter, but three in the summer. They had to read an entire book during Lent, and smaller books were made so that a monk could fulfill his reading obligation when traveling.

In the thirteenth century, the monks were still reading and studying and dictating books in Latin to scribes, who artfully rendered them on parchment with bold and beautiful ornamentation and painting. Often, several people would work on a single medieval book. They first copied the text—not infrequently making numerous mistakes—and then passed it on to a designer, who sketched out ornaments, elaborate initial capital letters, and pictures. The text was designed as though the goal was to leave no spaces blank. Then the book was passed on, first to the painter and next to the binder, who sewed it and provided an ornate leather cover that was sometimes gilded and bejeweled. The book was usually so large and unwieldy that on the rare occasions when someone wanted to read it, they needed to prop it up on a special angled lectern. One story has it that Petrarch, the fourteenth-century Italian poet and scholar, tried to hold one of these enormous books as he read it and accidentally dropped it on his leg, injuring himself so severely that he almost needed amputation.

Scribes were among the most respected figures in monastic society, and the wealthy were still commissioning grandiose works from monasteries for their collection. But now other books and documents were being produced outside of the monasteries, for universities and libraries. Workshops were set up to create these less grand and less expensive books, with scribes who specialized in scripts that were not only faster to write, but easier to read compared to the highly ornate styles used for sacred texts. In fact, even in the monasteries during the twelfth century, a less cursive script, the precursor of today's longhand, had been developed in an attempt to write faster, because the scribes were feeling pressure to produce more. In Tang-era China (seventh to tenth century), it was written, "When customs change writing changes," and so it came to be in Europe.

Some secular literature written in vernacular languages, notably French, had emerged earlier in the twelfth century. But much of this literature had been written so that it could be read aloud to the public. The model for learning was still listening to a reader and memorizing as much as possible, which is why medieval medical science focused a good deal on the health and functioning of memory. Fat meat, vinegar or strong wine, beans, garlic, onions and leeks were all foods that were considered to be harmful to memory. If someone was thought of as brilliant or exceedingly learned, like Scheherazade in an earlier culture, their skill at memorization was always mentioned as an outstanding quality.

There were traveling performers at the time known as *joglar*, who recited from a long memorized repertoire. They were commoners and so were their audiences. There were also troubadours, who tended to be more high-born, sometimes even noblemen, and they recited higher literature. A sizeable minority of troubadours were women. Sometimes professional readers were hired to read a book aloud during a dinner party, a practice that may have come from the monasteries, where religious books were read aloud to monks while they ate.

But in the thirteenth century, copies of books were made to be read in private. This is not to say that they weren't also read aloud. Reading out loud remained a strong tradition for centuries. Even today, authors still give readings, though not to the extent that they once did. But starting in the thirteenth century, the number of readers and the practice of reading to oneself while alone increased, and the number of professional public readers started to decline. This meant more books were needed for these new readers.

The scribes who worked in the new secular shops were organized into guilds to protect their interests. They were respected as writing masters, but did not have the lofty standing of the monastic scribes. Society had become more dependent on them, however, because in the thirteenth century, a great many more people knew how to read but only a very few knew how to write. The writing masters did not have individual personal styles—instead, they mastered a number of scripts for different purposes. Book script had heavy lines; business documents required a lighter hand.

Even the artisans making illuminated manuscripts on parchment were feeling pressure to be more productive. They developed a technique to rapidly reproduce work with the help of tracing paper—now even the parchment scribes were using paper.

Literature written in vernacular languages was offering an ever-greater variety of books. Giovanni Boccaccio, a Florentine born in the early 1300s, wrote *The Decameron*, around midcentury. In this book, ten Florentines fleeing the plague leave their hometown and hole up in a country villa, where they take turns telling stories in vernacular Italian, even Florentine dialect. Some of these stories have roots in often-told oral tales. Some even bear a similarity to tales in *One Thousand and One Nights*.

Another new kind of book arrived at the end of the century, *Le Ménagier de Paris*. It was an anonymous aging husband's guidebook for his fifteen-year-old bride, whom he expected to outlive him. Published in 1293, the book seems to have been written by a member of a new class of upper-crust bourgeois, and offers advice on cooking, gardening, social and sexual comportment, even recipes. It is virtually a handbook on how the new upper middle class should behave.

BY THE FOURTEENTH century, papermaking was a common industrial activity in Europe. Wherever there was a river with a swift downhill run, clean water with low iron content, and a nearby population that could provide rags, there was a paper mill. Sometimes the mills were small family operations and sometimes they were factories employing a hundred people. Water was tested by seeing how well it dissolved soap. Hard water, which contains iron and magnesium, does not dissolve soap well and is not good for papermaking. A mill was never set up downstream of a factory of any kind.

Most mills could sell more paper than they were capable of producing. Workers did not have fixed hours, and if there was a big order, they might work all night—another reason for not living next to a paper mill. In France a shift would begin at four a.m., and in Auvergne, between midnight and one a.m. Normally the mills were closed at night and a team of "apprentice papermakers," otherwise known as children, who were small enough to crawl into the vats, scrubbed the hammers and the equipment clean. When they finished their work, according to historian Oriol Valls i Subirà, "They were quickly hauled out and rubbed dry with rough cloths. After receiving brisk spankings to take the numbness from their skin, they were given a large glass of wine and sent off to bed bundled in warm blankets."

Because of their constant exposure to cold water, the life expectancy of paper workers was less than thirty years. Tuberculosis, rheumatic fever, nervous disorders, and extreme fatigue were common, as was promiscuity and incest. In some countries such as France and Italy, paper workers attained a certain measure of power by banding into guilds. These workers were well paid and their meals were provided, so they saved most of what they earned, hoping to eventually buy their own mills. Whole families—mother, father, and children—would live and work in the mill and save toward this goal, which was attainable if they lived long enough because there was always room for a new paper mill.

By the end of the fourteenth century, there were numerous paper mills in Spain, Italy, Germany, and France. Paper mills were established in Switzerland beginning in 1411, and Flanders began making paper in the late fourteenth century. By that time, Arab papermaking was in decline, and the Europeans had begun exporting their product to Arab countries.

In fourteenth-century Europe, parchment was also still being widely used. Most of the new writing that was emerging—business accounting, mathematics, science—was done on paper. But the overwhelming majority of books in the great libraries, such as the ones in the Louvre, were written on parchment, even on particularly fine-par vellum; only a small percentage were on paper. The idea still held that if a book or document was truly valuable, something that should endure through time, it needed to be written on parchment. Time has shown that this is not necessarily true—high-quality paper made from rags has lasted through these centuries just as well as parchment.

Of the four things that the Chinese consider to be their greatest inventions, three of them—paper, gunpowder, and the compass—had been discovered by Europe in the fertile second half of the thirteenth century. But the biggest problem confronting the Europeans of the fourteenth and fifteenth centuries was the fact that the demand for books was so great that the writers could not reproduce them fast enough. It was time to adopt China's fourth "great invention."

Chapter 6

MAKING WORDS SOAR

||||||||||||||||||

The invention of printing is the greatest event in history. It is the mother of all revolution, a renewal of human means of expression from its very roots. Printed thoughts are everlasting, provided with wings, intangible and indestructible. They soar like a crowd of birds, spread in all four directions and are everywhere at the same time.

—VICTOR HUGO, *The Hunchback of Notre-Dame*

PRINTING WAS BORN OUT OF THE NEEDS OF THE BUDDHIST religion. A devout Jew reads his religious books over and over again. When antique Jewish books are found, they are usually nearly worn out. Christian books have been preserved in excellent condition because only a few people read them. A devout Muslim memorizes the entire Qur'an. But the devout Buddhist earns a blessing by copying down a prayer or, even better, making a copy of an entire sutra. So reproducing texts was central to the religion, and paper was therefore much promoted by Buddhism.

Before there was paper, there was an early form of printing: seals carved into stone or bronze, impressed into clay, then inked and printed on silk. The Chinese have always loved seals, and still do, stamping receipts, books, artwork, and any other paper they can with an official seal, usually a few characters in red ink.

In the late seventh century, perhaps earlier, the Chinese began printing wood blocks—an image carved in wood, inked, and pressed on paper. Parchment, papyrus, tapa—these other writing materials did not work well for printing. Like stamps and seals, this was reverse printing; the carved-away areas remained white and the uncut areas came out black. A skilled carver could create a black line drawing using this technique, or a lengthy text of black characters on white paper. The oldest known woodblock print is thought to have been produced, judging by the style of the calligraphy, around the year 710. It is a scroll printed on mulberry bark paper, made thick for rolling, about two and a quarter inches wide and twenty feet long. The scroll is the text of a Buddhist prayer book originally written in Sanskrit and translated into Chinese.

Though printing was a Chinese concept, the first press run we know of was executed by a Japanese royal, Empress Shōtoku, in 770 in the capital city of Nara, a city that was dominated by Buddhism. The empress ruled from 749 to 769. In 735, a smallpox epidemic had devastated Japan and the empress enlisted 116 Buddhist priests to work on the problem of driving out the disease. The solution they decided upon was to house 1 million copies of a prayer, known as a *darani*, in 1 million little three-story four-and-a-half-inch-high wooden pagodas. The prayer was in Sanskrit but was written with Chinese characters. The empress probably could have hired an unlimited number of scribes to write the prayer 1 million times, but she had a teacher, Kibi-no-mabi, who had studied in China for nineteen years, which is where the Japanese of that time went to learn. Kibi-no-mabi, who had seen Chinese block printing, came up with the idea of carving the prayer into blocks and printing it 1 million times on strips of paper. Most historians believe that the blocks were wood, but they could have been metal or even porcelain or stone. Some

Japanese historians of the eighteenth and nineteenth century believed copper was used for the printing. If it was wood, the blocks would have worn out and would have had to be re-carved perhaps one hundred times to make 1 million prints.

The printing of the prayers and building of the miniature pagodas took six years and was not completed until 770. The pagodas with the printed prayers inside were then lined up in special halls in ten temples. Historians regard this as the beginning of printing, although both Taoists and Buddhists in sixth-century China printed similar charms to drive away disease. The Taoist artist would hold his breath while making prints of suns or moons or stars.

Once printing was invented, the Buddhists did enormous print runs, though none were as large as the empress's. In the tenth century, a Buddhist monk made 140,000 copies of a picture of a pagoda in China. There are records of Buddhist printings of 20,000, 50,000, or 70,000 copies. The more copies, the greater the blessing.

THE OLDEST PRINTED book in the world that has yet been found is called the Diamond Sutra, a Chinese Buddhist prayer book printed in 868. The quality and sophistication of the printing and woodcut illustrations suggest that it was not the first such book printed but simply the oldest we have found. It was discovered along with numerous other archaeological treasures in 1907 by the famous Hungarian-born British archaeologist Marc Aurel Stein. Until the discovery, Westerners had no idea that printing in Asia had begun more than half a millennium earlier than in the West. Many thought the Asians had picked it up from the Europeans.

Sir Marc, as he was known, the prototype of the intrepid archaeologist, led four expeditions to Central Asia and lived in a tent in the Himalayas. Whether on a dig or in his mountain home, his constant companion was a dog named Dash. In his eighty-year life, he had seven Dashes.

Stein explored an area in eastern Turkestan that had been the starting

Sir Marc Aurel Stein and his dog, Dash. May 1932.

point for the Silk Road under the Han. China is far too humid a climate in which to preserve paper, and thus very little ancient paper has been found there, just as few papyrus documents have been found in Europe. But eastern Turkestan has a dry climate, and that helped to preserve treasure troves of Chinese paper artifacts. Most of the pre–Cai Lun paper has been found in this region, some of it by Stein.

The frontier town of Dunhuang in present-day Gansu Province was the military and commercial outpost for the westward expansion of the Han. In the fourth century, Buddhists carved a complex of temples into the side of a mountain overlooking the town, and in subsequent centuries, the Buddhists deposited statues, manuscripts, and wall murals in these temples. For unknown reasons, about a thousand of the temples were sealed, perhaps because of a fear of invading armies.

The temples disappeared, but the legend of Qian Fo Dong, a series of hidden deposits also known as the Caves of the Thousand Buddhas, was passed on through time. In 1900, on Stein's first expedition, he met a Taoist monk, Wang Yuanlu, who claimed to have found Qian Fo Dong. What the monk had discovered was a mural that was painted on stone. By chipping away at the bricks in a section of the mural where something had clearly been covered over, he found a hidden chamber about nine feet square piled ten feet high with rolled manuscripts. There were 1,130 bundles in all, perfectly preserved in cloth wrapping, each containing about a dozen rolls—a total of about 50,000 documents. Stein bought some of the documents and works of art from Wang and shipped them back to the British Museum. He returned in 1907 to further explore and pay, or bribe (depending on your viewpoint), the Taoists for more treasures, including manuscripts written in Sanskrit, Chinese, and Hebrew. It was then that he found the Diamond Sutra, which is still in London today. He also shipped twenty-four cases of manuscripts and four cases of artwork back to London. The British government knighted him, but the Chinese government called him a thief.

The Diamond Sutra is a perfectly preserved six pages of printed text with one elaborate woodcut showing more skill in woodcutting and in printing than Europe would demonstrate for another six centuries. Not only the illustration but also the pages of text were carved with a single block per page, a technique that came to be known in fifteenth-century Europe as a "block book." At the end of the text, also printed by woodblock, are the words "Printed on May 11, 868, by Wang Jie, for free general distribution, in order in deep reverence to perpetuate the memory of his parents." We know nothing of his parents or of Wang Jie himself, the first known book printer in history. And he might not even have been first. He might just have been the first to have a work wrapped in cloth and carefully placed in a sealed cave in the desert.

The Diamond Sutra is a popular example of Buddhist writing in which the Buddha lectures Subhuti, his aging disciple, on the nonexistence of everything. Repeatedly, the Buddha enjoins his student to make copies of this book and pass them around. Buddha says, "Whatever place constitutes a repository for this sacred scripture, there also the Lord

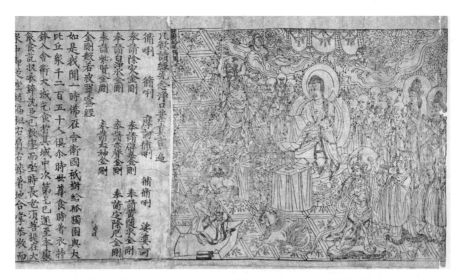

Diamond Sutra frontispiece, 868 CE. The earliest printed book ever found.
In a garden Buddha responds to questions from an aged disciple, Subhuti.
Buddha is attended by monks with shaved heads and other figures,
including an emperor and empress at the lower right corner.

Buddha may be found." Copying the Diamond Sutra therefore became a way of "gaining merit." In it, Buddha also says, "If a good disciple whether man or woman, in the morning, at noonday and at eventide, sacrificed, sacrificed lives innumerable as the sands in the Ganges, and thus without intermission throughout infinite ages; and if another disciple, hearing this scripture proclaimed, steadfastly believed it, his felicity would be appreciably greater than the other."

So, as these excerpts make clear, a Buddhist would be interested in the process of duplication and naturally drawn to printing. If there was merit in copying one edition of a sutra, how much more merit would there be in printing a hundred or a thousand copies, perhaps in less time? In fact, the Diamond Sutra became a standard text for printing by those seeking "merit," or *punya*.

Though there is almost no evidence of book printing earlier than the Diamond Sutra, but because there is so much shortly afterward that it would not be surprising if printing had begun before 868. And not all of the writing found from around the same time is Buddhist. In about

880, a man named Liu Pin wrote of finding a schoolbook in Szechuan printed from wooden blocks. In the caves of Dunhuang, several printed calendars and almanacs were found, one dating to 877. And in 932, Feng Dao, the official imperial scholar, ordered the Confucian classics to be printed.

In fact, the Koreans may have been the first to print a book. A scroll of a block-printed sutra dated to about the year 700 was discovered in 1966. It consists of twelve sheets of mulberry paper bound together, and is therefore older and longer than the Diamond Sutra.

Bi Sheng, an eleventh-century commoner, may have been the inventor of moveable type, which would make him one of the greatest inventors of all time. Yet we know nothing about him. Because of his low social status, there are no records of his life. The type Bi Sheng used was made of clay baked into porcelain. The type was laid into an iron plate with a paste of pine resin, wax, and ashes of burned paper. When the type was completely set, he heated the iron plate to melt the paste and then pressed the type with a board so that the individual types would all be of even height.

As early as the twelfth or thirteenth century, both China and Korea may have been printing with moveable type made from metal, which was an important improvement over wood and clay. The purpose of printing is defeated if the type wears out after a limited number of uses, as it would inevitably do with those earlier materials. But wooden type was still being used in the fourteenth century. Wang Zhen, a magistrate and an agronomist who wrote voluminously, ordered the cutting of 60,000 characters in wood and used them to print his work as well as a local gazette. But with those characters, he could print only about a hundred copies.

Wang Zhen arranged his type on special revolving tables that he invented, assigning each character a number. To help remember where each character was, he arranged them in accordance with traditional rhymes. Then he placed them tightly in bamboo racks and kept the type flush against each other. But for all of his inventiveness, his work illustrates the essential problem of printing Chinese with moveable type:

There are too many characters. He used 60,000, but literary Chinese can use up to 200,000. And common characters need to have duplicates made because a single page might require the same character to be used numerous times.

In 1403 King Taejong of Korea ordered that type be made from bronze. Sand was packed into a metal mold in an impression pressed from a carved wooden cube. Then a type was cast by pouring in molten bronze or sometimes lead. The Chinese greatly valued the quality of both Korean paper and ink. Korean ink, made from lampblack and glue from deer antlers, was extremely black. An oil was added to make the ink better suited for metal type, which produced a far better ink than the one the Europeans would use when they developed metal type.

Once the Koreans began printing with moveable type, they quickly moved away from the Chinese writing system and invented an extremely efficient twenty-eight-character system. It was launched in 1444 in a decree called *The Standard Sounds for the Instruction of the People*. Like all new ideas, it was disliked by some and became sneeringly known as *onmun*, or "sound writing," a pejorative that persisted until the early twentieth century when the name Hangul was devised. Koreans still write in Hangul; the system now contains only twenty-four characters.

The Chinese made bronze type, but for centuries showed a preference for Wang Zhen's wooden type and even block books. Both types of printing became commonplace in China, which greatly increased the demand for paper. More and more paper mills went into operation. But papermaking always remained difficult, low-status work for the poor and was often assigned to prisoners—a practice also adopted in India, where it persisted until the late nineteenth century, when papermakers protested about having to compete with unpaid prison labor.

The Chinese did not use printing to churn out huge editions, which may explain why the easily worn wooden type worked for them. A large printing of a Chinese book was 100 copies. By the Middle Ages, the Islamic world was producing more books than the Chinese, even

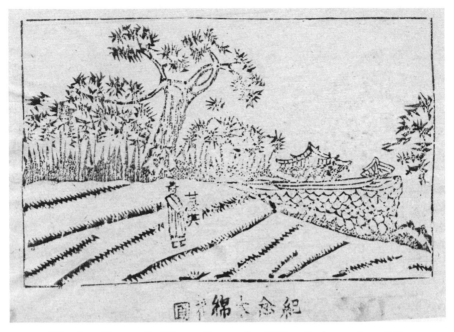

Woodcut illustration from a Korean book from the beginning of the twentieth century that is not greatly different from a Korean book five hundred years earlier. It is a biography of Moon Ik-jeom, prepared by his descendants in the early 1900s. Born in 1329, Moon Ik-jeom lived in a time when Korea was struggling to gain more independence from China. He is celebrated for stealing the Chinese secret of cotton by smuggling seeds in the hollow stem of a calligraphy brush.

though the Arabs were not printing at all; they just had extremely efficient scribes. Their graceful, swirled cursive style of writing did not adapt well to type. Both the Chinese and the Arabs, it has been postulated, loved their calligraphy too much to wholeheartedly embrace printing.

Some historians believe that it was because Europe did embrace printing, whereas Asia and the Islamic world did not, that Europe advanced and Asia and the Islamic world receded. But this is the technological fallacy at work again. Exactly the reverse occurred. Europe needed printing because it was bursting with creativity. New ideas in

Wood block from a seventeenth-century printed Chinese book. In the eight centuries since the Diamond Sutra, the style of woodcuts in printed books changed very little.

the arts and sciences, as well as in social justice and religion, desperately needed to be expressed and disseminated. The Chinese and Muslim eras of innovation were mostly behind them. They were societies in decline and didn't really need printing, which is why the Chinese, who had learned how to print, even with their impossible writing system, did not use it very much.

This is an example of another basic rule of technology. There is a tendency to imagine that technology is a Pandora's box, that once a new way is invented, it unavoidably falls into use and is unstoppable. But when a technology is invented that doesn't correspond to the needs of a society, it falls into obsolescence.

———

EUROPE HAD ARRIVED at a point by the fifteenth century where it needed a faster way of reproducing books and documents. A number of people were trying to solve this problem, without knowing that the Asians had already solved it.

Several ancient European societies had almost invented printing. The Athenians engraved maps onto smooth metal plates, and the lines they cut could have held ink. All they needed to do was ink the plate and press it onto parchment or papyrus, and they would have printed a map. And they could have printed numerous copies of that map. But instead they just used the plate as the map. If they needed a second map, they carved a second plate. And since they weren't printing, they did not need to engrave in reverse.

The Assyrians made stamps to press images onto pottery, and Roman potters copied this technique, stamping their signature on the pots they made. According to Theodore Low De Vinne, a nineteenth-century American printer who studied the history of his craft, some Roman potters made individual stamps for each letter of their name and used them to stamp their name on clay lamps. This, in a sense, was a very early use of moveable type.

The first-century BCE Roman philosopher Cicero presents a curious argument. Velleius, an atheist, insists that the world was made by chance. Balbus refutes this by saying, "From such a man I cannot understand why he should not also believe that if he threw together, pell-mell, a great number of the twenty-one letters, either of gold or some other material, the *Annals of Ennius*, could be legibly put together from the forms scattered on the ground." So even Cicero imagined moveable type, but only in his polemic as an absurd idea. He used the phrase *formae literarum*, and when moveable type was finally made some sixteen centuries later, that is the name they gave it—though it was not such an absurd idea after all.

De Vinne believed that printing went no further in the Roman world because it lacked ink suitable for the task and it also lacked paper.

Printing on papyrus would have been difficult. But the Romans might have resolved those difficulties if they had needed printing. They didn't. Their scribes were producing all the books they wanted, and most people heard rather than read them, in public readings, at dinners, and at the baths.

There is a possibility that the world's first printing with moveable type occurred in Europe, on the island of Crete by the Minoans, who had a highly developed civilization with a written language four thousand years ago. In 1908, a disk with a diameter of slightly more than six inches was found and dated to the seventeenth century BCE. Printed on both sides there are 241 impressions of forty-five different symbols on the disk in a spiral that either reads out from the center or in from the edge. Because the symbols are stamped with varying degrees of pressure, it is thought that individual types were used for each symbol—in other words, moveable type. The symbols are marked off in groupings, and it is believed that this is a text. The groupings are words. But they are written in an as-yet undeciphered language.

If the Phaistos Disc, as it is called, named after the place where it was

"Side A" of the Phaistos Disc. Fired clay. Archaeological Museum of Heraklion, Greece.

found, actually says something, and contemporary research increasingly suggests that it does, then moveable type was used in ancient Crete. But since nothing else similar to it has been found, it would have to be assumed that the civilization on Crete did not have much use for the ingenious idea and it was ignored. It is as though someone in Charlemagne's court had invented a computer. Since almost no one read or wrote, and the few who did had no sense of urgency in communication, the invention would not have jump-started civilization to the twentieth century. It would have sat in a corner of the castle gathering dust, waiting a very long time for society to catch up with technology. This may have been the fate of the Phaistos Disc.

JUST AS PLATO needed written language to work out his ideas, fifteenth-century Europe, bursting with its own ideas, required a method of disseminating them that was faster and more immediate than the slow process of dictating to scribes. Printing proved to be that method; it freed up scientists, artists, thinkers—blossoming European geniuses—from the tyranny of their dependence on scribes.

Starting in the thirteenth century with the growth of the universities, there was steadily increasing pressure for more manuscripts and more copies of each manuscript. By the fifteenth century, with the thirst for ideas that is called Humanism, the shortage of written material had become an acute problem. This was particularly true in Italy and Germany, where there was a spectacular growth in universities, greatly influenced by Italian humanism. Cicero and the Roman classics were studied, as well as Roman law, and there was demand for copies of these early works. Germany at the time was also engaged in programs to spread literacy.

Private commercial interests trying to profit from a growing market for the written word further increased the need for more books and faster production. Private bookselling had become an important international trade, and the limited number of available books was limiting the booksellers. In the early 1400s, woodblock books began to be made, apparently a solution that the Europeans thought up themselves and did not learn from Asia. Logically, block books should have been the forerunner of printed books, but block books did not become popular until after moveable-type books were printed.

JOHANNES GENSFLEISCH GUTENBERG, most historians acknowledge, changed the world. And yet we know little more about him than we do about Bi Sheng. We don't know what he looked like, as there are no portraits from his lifetime. The images we commonly see of him weren't made until after his death. We are not even sure when he was born, though it must have been between 1394 and 1399 in Mainz, Germany. Mainz had a population of 6,000, which was smaller than nearby Frankfurt and much smaller than farther-away Nuremberg, which had 20,000. But it was a comfortable, middle-class, commercial town growing affluent from charging duties on the ships passing on the nearby Rhine. Gutenberg's father was an affluent middle-class man of commerce. Nothing written by Gutenberg has survived either. But fortunately, he and his associates seem to have been of a somewhat litigious temperament, because most of what we know about him is from numerous lawsuits.

We know that Gutenberg was a goldsmith, which is significant. Many early printers were goldsmiths, because it took skill with metal to make moveable type; there were numerous high-quality goldsmiths in Mainz. It is not certain if it was because there were too many goldsmiths in Mainz or because of political upheavals but in 1428 or 1429 Johannes and his brother Friele moved to Strasbourg. There Gutenberg began experimenting with moveable type printing around 1440. We do not know if he realized he had competitors. Similar experiments were taking place at the same time in Bruges, Avignon, and Bologna. He may have suspected this, as he was very secretive about his printing experiments. His fellow goldsmiths knew only that Gutenberg had some "secret project." One, Hans Dünne, once blurted out that he thought his colleague was doing something that

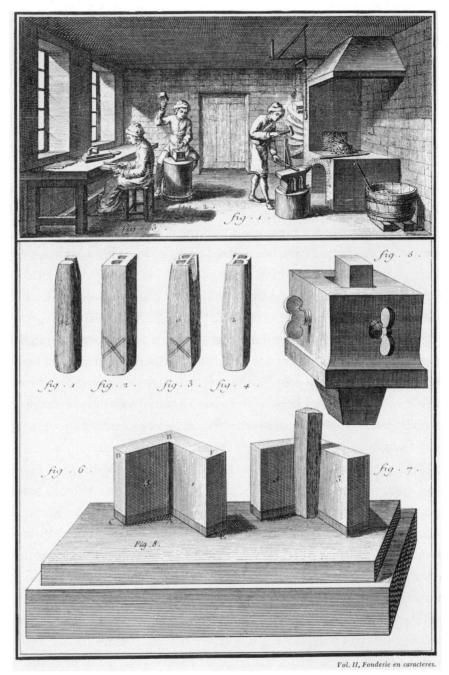

Making punches for fashioning a typeface plate. Diderot, Trade and Industry, *Volume II.*

"had to do with printing." This was a reasonable guess, as Gutenberg had acquired a press from the owner of a nearby paper mill who had died.

Gutenberg carved each individual letter into small blocks of hard metal in the same way that a goldsmith did when making an ornament. The letter was carved in reverse. Carving letters backwards into hard metal in the style of a scribe required impressive skill. This hard metal letter, called a punch, was then struck into softer copper. This was called the matrix, and Gutenberg poured molten lead into the matrix to cast a typeface. He had used the process many times before when making jewelry. He then put the letters into a rack, keeping them exactly level, tied them together with string, inked them with his own formula of gallnut shaving—bulbs formed on oak trees from wasp larva—soot, and water, and pressed them onto wet paper, whose watermark indicated that it had been made in Fabriano. The hard surface of European paper's animal-hide sizing made it perfect for printing.

Since Gutenberg had acquired his press from a paper mill, it had probably been used to press stacks of felt and wet paper sheets. Some historians say that the press was a copy of an olive-oil press, but more likely it imitated a wine press, as Gutenberg came from Mainz, the heart of the Rheingau wine country. Here, the normally south-north-flowing Rhine flows east-west, and the reflected sun heats up the slopes on its northern bank to yield some of the best wine in Germany.

Gutenberg introduced various innovations. He developed an ink for metal printing, which had not previously existed in Europe. The mold he used for casting, the matrix, was probably his own innovation, and it allowed him to make as many identical pieces of type for each character as he needed. Since every page requires a great number of letters, making multiple types allowed for printing numerous pages without ripping up the previous ones.

If the Asians had had the right religion for spreading the use of paper, the Europeans had the right alphabet—only twenty-six fairly simple characters. A complete set of type with uppercase and lowercase letters, numbers, and various signs came to about 100 pieces of type—considerably less than Wang Zhen's set of 60,000. Gutenberg used 290 pieces of type for his first book, including extra pieces for commonly used letters. The book was printed in late-medieval Latin. The typeface was carved to resemble calligraphy, and the initial letters of the individual chapters were hand-painted in red.

Many Europeans did not believe that a mechanically printed manuscript would compare with the visual standards of handwritten manuscripts. Perhaps they don't, but Gutenberg's first book, a Bible printed between 1452 and 1456, was stunningly beautiful and technically perfect, laid out in twelve hundred two-column pages, each column forty-two lines in length, in two volumes. It is commonly known as the 42-line Bible. In fact, it is so perfect that historians are convinced that Gutenberg must have experimented on a considerable number of pages before producing the Bible, though no such pages have ever been found. There is a decade-long gap between the time he moved to Strasbourg and the printing of his first book in which he may have been working on his idea.

Usually the person credited with an invention, the one who makes it work and makes it profitable, is a savvy businessman. This was probably true of Cai Lun, but it was not true of Gutenberg. He never became wealthy. A businessman, Johann Fust, had financed Gutenberg's years of experimentation, and Gutenberg was not able to keep up with the interest payments on Fust's loan. Fust took him to court and gained control of Gutenberg's equipment and his ideas.

In 1588, 120 years after Gutenberg—who may have gone blind—died a near pauper, Hadrianus Junius, a Dutch poet, physician, historian, and jack-of-many-trades, published a book on another inventor of printing, Laurens Janszoon Coster of Haarlem. Coster enjoyed teaching, reading, and writing to his grandchildren. To this end, he cut letters into wood blocks and printed them. Then he started printing whole pages with the wooden type. Next he decided that type made out of lead and tin would be better. And that is how Coster came to be known as the inventor of moveable type.

According to Junius, on Christmas night 1440, a student from Mainz stole all of Coster's type. Junius's source for this claim was the older people of Haarlem—apparently it was well known in the town that moveable type had been invented there. Junius's leading source was a bookseller named Cornelius, who said that he had slept in the same bed as the thief from Mainz. Unfortunately, however, Cornelius appears to have been born one or two years after the incident occurred. In any event, Coster was a well-respected citizen of Haarlem during his life-time. And Haarlem was known for a certain type of block book. Coster may have been engaged in that craft.

Another early printer was Johannes Brito of Bruges, but the evidence seems to show that Gutenberg was first in his invention. Also, in the Italian town of Feltre, which Dante may or may not have mentioned in *Paradiso*, a statue was erected in 1868 to Panfilo Castaldi, physician, poet, and . . . the inventor of moveable type. He may have invented the type independently, but there is no evidence of him printing with it until 1470.

Then there was a goldsmith in Avignon, Prokop Waldvogel from Prague, who certainly had the skill to make moveable type. He was said to have been engaged in "artificial writing." But he was secretive, and was well paid by a watchmaker in Trier on the condition that he told no one what he was working on. Waldvogel also made Hebrew letters for an Avignon Jew named David of Caderousse, who also pledged secrecy.

Historians and, especially, the local people of Haarlem, Bruges, Avignon, and Feltre enjoy entertaining the possibilities of who was really the inventor of moveable type. But the truth is that none of them, Gutenberg included, was the original inventor. Gutenberg, like Thomas Edison and probably Cai Lun, took an idea and executed it so well, proving it to be workable, that he caused the world to adopt it. He is thought to have printed two hundred Bibles, though only forty have been found. Once Gutenberg started printing, most Europeans saw it as the way of the future. After Gutenberg, there were no significant changes in print-ing until the nineteenth century.

MOVEABLE TYPE DID not eliminate handwritten books. Many people who could afford them still preferred them. And following Gutenberg's lead, most printed books imitated the look of the old manuscripts. A style of lettering resembling the work of scribes was used, and a blank space was left at the opening of every section for a woodcut of an ornate first letter. Sometimes that letter was painted by hand. Gutenberg had preferred using carved wood blocks for these, and on occasion he would print the letter in two colors by using two blocks. Eventually, printers maintained a collection of blocks of letters, sometimes loaning them out to other printers. Often the blocks included figures hanging playfully or resting on the letters. One book of sermons has a chapter opening with the letter *Q*; on it are figures of lovers in an embrace under attack by a pious multitude.

Hans Holbein the Younger, the most well known painter and portrait artist from a distinguished family of painters in Augsburg, Germany, also created famous sets of wood blocks for the initial capitals of three books—*Alphabet of Children, Peasant Alphabet,* and *The Dance of Death.* The workmanship was so fine that it was very difficult to print.

Of course, not everyone loved printing. As with every other new technology, there were those who were disdainful—some who thought it was barbarism, some who thought it was the end of civilization, and some who thought it was a threat to their jobs. The scribes and copyists felt threatened, though in reality their jobs continued. Many of the aristocrats who employed scribes and maintained libraries of handwritten books were contemptuous of what they saw as sleazy imitations, which in a sense the printed books were. Federico of Urbino, a wealthy fifteenth-century arts patron whose entire library, said to be second in size to the Vatican's, was entirely handwritten on parchment, usually by his own scribes, and bound in red velvet with silver clasps—as were all the books in the Vatican Library—said that he would never stoop to having a printed book in his collection and that he "would have been ashamed to own a printed book."

Books had been rare, and their power had been well appreciated. So these newfangled printers with their strange ability to produce books for sale by the hundreds were regarded in some quarters with great suspicion. Was there a dangerous political agenda? Were they in league with the devil? When Johann Fust, Gutenberg's ex-partner, went to Paris with cases full of books to sell, he had to flee, accused of being sent by the devil.

The powerful block printers' guild, which included card makers, block book makers, painters, artists, scribes, illuminators, and wood engravers, would not let typographers—the printers who used moveable type—join their guild. A certain human touch was missing in the way the letters and the words all had exactly the same spacing, they said. It was rigid and uncreative. Even twentieth-century anthropologist Marshall McLuhan, dividing history into pre-Gutenberg and post-Gutenberg, believed that the latter was more "constricted" in its thinking.

Moveable-type printing ended the competition between parchment and paper. Gutenberg printed thirty-five of his two hundred Bibles on parchment, which served to show that paper worked better for printing. Parchment was for handwritten documents and manuscripts, and printing was to be done exclusively on paper, which considerably increased the demand for it. The idea remained fixed that anything meant to be permanent, which is to say anything of great importance, should be written on parchment. But paper was no longer regarded as a low-quality material to be used only for inconsequential jottings. Printing gave paper standing; it too was enduring and important, a sentiment that has itself endured. In 1831 sentiments had changed, and Victor Hugo wrote that printing bestowed a greater permanence and durability to the written word: "The book of stone, so solid and enduring, was to give way to the book of paper, more solid and enduring still."

By the end of the fifteenth century, Europe, with its paper and printing presses, had for the first time in history become the most advanced civilization in the world. In science, music, art, mathematics, architecture, literature, geography, philosophy—in fact, in most any field imaginable—Europe was producing the leading thinkers and printing their ideas on paper.

Chapter 7

THE ART OF PRINTING

||||||||||||||||

The science of design, or of line drawing, if you like to use this term, is the source and very essence of painting, sculpture, architecture.

—ATTRIBUTED TO MICHELANGELO IN
"Dialogues sur la Peinture dans la Ville de Rome"
BY FRANCIS OF HOLLAND,
ARCHITECT AND ILLUMINATOR, 1538

APER CREATED A MONUMENTAL SHIFT IN EUROPEAN art. Printing changed it even more.

Drawing is a primal urge. Almost everyone throughout history has had the urge to draw. But drawing only became a standard art form when paper became available. In the case of Europe, this occurred during the Renaissance, when paper was still a new idea on the Continent. Previously, there had been very little informal use of parchment for art because it was too expensive and too difficult to erase. At first, European paper was also too expensive to be used to dash off a quick sketch and had too low a standing to be used for serious art. But by the late fifteenth century, this had all changed. Paper opened up the possibility of the sketch. Renaissance artists sketched out their work before they drew, painted, or sculpted it—or, in the case of Albrecht Dürer's woodcuts, carved it. This new ability to not only plan but toy with ideas raised their art to a level not known in the Middle Ages.

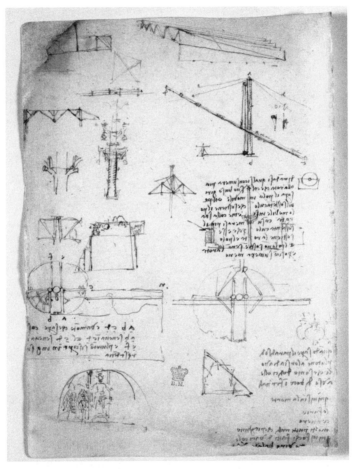

By the sixteenth century paper had become essential for mathematical, engineering, and scientific calculations. This is Leonardo da Vinci's sketch on the mechanical powers and forces—percussion, gravity, motion, optics, and astronomy— with various arithmetical and geometrical propositions, courtesy of the British Library.

Artists drew and sketched with varying degrees of skill. Leonardo da Vinci was legendary for his skills as a draftsman. Michelangelo, known for his frescoes and sculptures, was equally brilliant as a draftsman—many art historians consider him to have been the greatest draftsman who ever lived—though most of his drawing was scribbled chaotically on sheets of paper not intended for public view. Both artists used Fabriano paper at least some of the time.

Sixteenth-century artist and historian Giorgio Vasari, whose *Lives of the Most Eminent Painters, Sculptors, and Architects* is the leading source of biographical information on the Italian Renaissance artists, tells the story of a sketch by Michelangelo that was displayed in the Palazzo Medici for art students to copy. Since the sheet, like most of Michelangelo's sheets, had a variety of sketches on it, students started tearing off pieces of it, and they became "scattered over many places." According to Vasari, those fortunate students who ended up with a remnant treasured it and regarded it as something "more divine than human."

Michelangelo used a great deal of paper, in part because he considered himself as much a poet as an artist. Between five hundred and six hundred sheets of Michelangelo's drawings have survived, and written on many are poems, personal letters, notes, and details about finances. Almost any piece of paper he used contained a few sketches. A few are finished drawings. A stunning drawing of the resurrection of Christ is also marked with a shopping list. Masterful drawings were folded up, with notes about the banal ephemera of everyday life jotted on the reverse side. Rarely is there a single drawing on a sheet. He also wrote some three hundred poems, invented dialogues, theoretical essays, proposals, and outlines for essays on art theory, including a response to Dürer's *Four Books on Human Proportion*. But most of this paper was not intended for anyone else to see, and before his death he attempted to destroy as much of it as he could.

Michelangelo may have been among the first to jot down quick ideas for himself. Some 2,000 letters from and to Michelangelo have also been collected. Letter writing is another practice that blossomed with the widespread use of paper.

Leonardo da Vinci was notorious in his lifetime for his inability to complete projects. He would accept a commission for some grand undertaking and would never get beyond the start. As a government official in Florence said in 1506 about a mural the artist had only begun, "He made a very small beginning of a very large thing." Leonardo's problem was well summed up by Pope Leo X, who once saw him engrossed in trying to create the perfect formula for varnish instead of painting: "This man will never do anything, for he begins by thinking about the end before the beginning of his work."

*Leonardo da Vinci. This drawing, originally in red chalk
on brown paper, is generally recognized as being by Leonardo
and is thought to be a self-portrait, although this is not certain.*

Fortunately, there was paper, on which Leonardo could capture his genius. Though he is usually thought of as a painter, only fifteen paintings, some unfinished, have been found, along with two damaged murals. He also attempted some sculpture, though he never finished one piece. But he left behind thirty bound notebooks. Unlike Michelangelo, he did want people to see this work on paper, including the notes he made in his mirror-image script—a curious response to being left-handed. He left drawings depicting all kind of inventions, and notes on literature, arts, mythology, anatomy, engineering, and, most of all nature. He also left instructions on how his drawings should be printed; printing was still a fairly new development in Italy and France at the time of his death in 1519. But somehow none of this work was published or shown to the public until 1880.

Leonardo also left behind four thousand sheets of drawings of staggering beauty.

He was the first artist to be recognized for his drawings on paper. Leonardo's work became the standard for art in Renaissance Florence. Studying art now meant working on paper, learning to draw. Leonardo had learned art that way himself, in the workshop taught by Andrea del Verrocchio. Artists have been trained on paper ever since.

ONE OF THE major products of fifteenth-century Cologne—known for its religious printing—was a Dutch Bible printed by Heinrich Quentell in 1479. This Bible was particularly influential because it contained a high-quality woodcut illustration, which others eagerly imitated. Quentell was also one of the first to include title pages in his books; these presented the opportunity to create woodcut borders as decorations.

German papermaking had begun in Nuremberg, and by the fifteenth century, the city was the largest printing center in Germany. One of the biggest presses there was run by Anton Koberger, a goldsmith, who had given up his craft in 1470 at the age of thirty to open a print shop. The following year, he started putting out books. With twenty-four presses and one hundred employees, he became the first industrial printer—subcontracting and making arrangements all over Germany for printing and selling his volumes, even running a book bindery.

One of the trademarks of Koberger's books was their use of numerous woodcuts. Sometimes these were colored in with watercolors, which meant that each book was different from the next. His more successful books sold hundreds of copies. *Nuremberg Chronicle*, a history of the world, known in German as *Die Schedelsche Weltchronik* (Schedel's world history, after the author, Hartmann Schedel), sold between 1,400 and 1,500 copies in Latin and as many as 1,000 in German. The book contained 654 woodcuts, hand-painted in watercolor in some editions. Among the illustrations is one of the Ulman Stromer paper mill—the first depiction of a paper mill in a European book.

The woodcuts from Koberger's books were not only integrated into the texts but were also printed to be sold separately. A few were done by Koberger's young godson, Albrecht Dürer. More were done by Wilhelm Pleyden and Michael Wohlgemut, artists best remembered today as Dürer's teachers.

Dürer was a paper artist of the same generation as Michelangelo; Leonardo was a generation older. But because Dürer was German and had a great printer for a godfather, he was much more influenced by printing. Although Dürer made more than seventy-five paintings, he always struggled with them, whereas his paper work seemed to pour out of him. In the age of woodcuts, he was the single greatest woodcut artist, and, in fact, was an important reason for their popularity.

THANKS TO PAPER and then printing, one of the greatest changes in the history of art occurred in the fifteenth and sixteenth centuries: the birth of affordable art.

Woodcuts were the first cheap art form, art for the lower classes, first made popular in the fourteenth century, when many Christians went on pilgrimages. Woodcut illustrations of saints were for sale at shrines and along pilgrimage paths. Wealthy pilgrims might have a medallion of a saint or some other figure made by a jeweler; Gutenberg had made many of them when he was a goldsmith. But for the commoner, there were woodcuts.

Even before that, wooden blocks had been used for printing playing cards. Card playing is believed to have started in ancient China as a form of divination, and only later became a game. Europeans may have learned about cards from the Arabs during the Crusades, and cards seem to have followed a similar historical path as paper, which is needed to make them. When paper came to Europe, so did cards. Cards became popular in fourteenth-century France, Germany, Italy, and Spain—the papermaking countries of fourteenth-century Europe—and were printed with wood blocks. By the fifteenth century, there was a card-printing industry, sometimes illegal but always popular. In the sixteenth century, when Lyon, France, became a major printing center, the woodcutters who illustrated the books came from the playing-card industry.

The craft of printing from carved blocks of wood had probably started much earlier, as a textile craft. Roger of Sicily, for example, had a shop in Palermo for printing cloth as far back as the twelfth century. Fifteenth-century block books were often about religious themes and usually involved storytelling. They looked a bit like modern graphic novels, often with several illustrations to a page, marked off in boxed sections that divided them up. Some even had dialogue bubbles. Their market was people who were caught up in the contemporary trend toward books but had not yet mastered reading.

Yet from the beginning, printed books with text often included a few woodcuts as well. Their ornate capital letters were usually printed from woodcuts. In 1462, the early books of Gutenberg's former colleagues Fust and Peter Schöffer carried woodcuts of their two coats of arms, and after that, many of the leading book printers copied this practice, using woodcuts to "sign" their books. Printed books often had a few woodcut illustrations too. Woodcuts are a logical companion to printing because, like type, they are carved in relief and can be inked and pressed. A woodcut is, in effect, a large, complicated piece of type. As with type, the uncut parts are printed and the cut-away parts remain white spaces.

The printer has only to set the woodcut in a rack and print it with the same press as the type. Sometimes a small woodcut would be set on a page with a moveable-type text.

Woodcuts were part of printing almost from the beginning. An early print shop in Bamberg, Germany, started by Albrecht Pfister in 1460, copied Gutenberg type and was the first moveable-type shop to incorporate woodcuts in their books. The woodcuts were very simple line figures and were supposed to be filled in with watercolors. Johann Zainer, meanwhile, published a number of books in Ulm in the 1470s with woodcuts, and by the late fifteenth century, they were growing in popularity. From an artist's point of view, they had an advantage in that the prints could both be used in books and sold separately as popular art. But block books, where every page was cut from wood in its entirety, died out in the sixteenth century. They were far more difficult to produce than printed books. The market of illiterate book buyers may also have been shrinking.

When creating a woodcut, an artist would design the block on a piece of paper and then turn it over to a *Formschneider*, a wood-block carver. A good *Formschneider*, such as Hieronymus Andreä, who sometimes called himself Hieronymus Formschneider, could become famous in his own right. Andreä worked in Nuremberg and executed some of Dürer's most famous work.

Formschneiders joined the ranks of scribes and others who opposed printing. This was somewhat surprising because, unlike scribes, *Formschneiders* got work from printers. But once block books started to decline, the artisans feared that printing would reduce their work to just a few blocks in a book of words. *Formschneiders* had a well-organized guild, and in 1466, the guild tried to prevent Günter Zainer of Strasbourg, probably the brother of Johann Zainer who was printing in Ulm, from opening a print shop in the Bavarian town of Augsburg. The *Formschneiders* were successful at first. But then a local abbot, a great admirer of the new printing who would later set up his own print shop at his monastery, negotiated a settlement wherein Zainer could open his shop if he agreed to regularly use an ample number of woodcuts.

DÜRER'S FATHER WAS not a particularly affluent goldsmith. Originally from Hungary, he had immigrated to Nuremberg and trained his son to work in the craft. Young Dürer, like Gutenberg, became a skilled carver as a result of that training and was one of the rare artists who, though his designs were very complicated, could carve them himself. As he grew older, more famous, and more in demand, however, he carved less and less. After 1515, Andreä did almost all of Dürer's cutting.

The quality of woodcuts and book illustration was already on the rise when Dürer was still a young man. In 1486 in Mainz, the birthplace of printing, the first known woodcut art book was published. The author was a skilled writer, Bernhard von Breydenbach, an aristocrat who undertook a trip to Jerusalem, and took with him a well-known Dutch artist and printer who lived in Mainz, Erhard Reuwich. Von Breydenbach then published an account of his trip with Reuwich's woodcuts. The result, *Sanctae Peregrinationes*, was the first illustrated travel book ever printed.

The book included five foldout woodcuts, something never before seen in Europe. A panoramic view of Venice, which von Breydenbach and Reuwich passed along the way, was five feet long. Other illustrations were double spreads. Some blocks were in black and white, and others colored. The text was well printed in an ornate typeface with wood-block prints of elaborate capital letters starting off each page. The book also featured an Arabic alphabet—the first time Arabic was printed. In addition, Reuwich did woodcuts of the exotic animals that the two men supposedly saw, such as a camel, a crocodile, and what he claimed was a unicorn.

The book contained another important first—the colophon, the seal at the end of a book that provides information about the publisher. This first colophon included a woodcut of the coat of arms of the archbishop of Mainz, which featured the first cross-hatching to create gray tones ever used in a woodcut. Originally published in Latin, then German, and then French, Spanish and Dutch, *Sanctae Peregrinationes* was successful in much of Europe and had an influence on future publishing. It probably influenced Dürer as well.

Dürer most likely worked in his godfather's print shop, where he must have quickly shown extraordinary ability. His woodcuts do not look anything like anyone else's. At the time, most woodcuts were simple line illustrations awaiting a watercolorist to fill in all the blank spaces. But with Dürer, there were no blank spaces. The entire block was a rich picture full of characters and action; and through such techniques as cross-hatching, there were shades of gray and areas of light and shadow.

Albrecht Dürer, The Four Horsemen of the Apocalypse, *woodcut, 1498, from* The Revelation of Saint John.

Worked out first on paper, the compositions were complete tableaus, like Renaissance oil paintings on canvas.

Only a nobleman or the church could afford an oil painting, but a woodcut, whether in a book or sold separately, could be bought by most people. In addition, an almost limitless number of copies of a single block could be printed. That Dürer himself saw these individual paper prints as works of art to be sold is indicated by the fact that he was one of the very first artists to sign and date his prints. On the one hand, Dürer was lifting woodcuts from low to high art, and on the other, he was inventing art for the masses.

A great patron of woodcuts and the idea of art printed on paper was the Holy Roman Emperor Maximilian I, who commissioned histories, musical dramas, architecture, paintings, and sculptures. When the woodcut reached new heights of popularity in Germany, he commissioned at least 1,000 woodcuts, including three huge projects. Maximilian commissioned much of his work from Hans Burgkmair, the other great genius of woodcuts. The first artist to print a woodcut with color, he was also the first to use three separate blocks for several colors. This technique, later made famous by such modernists as Pablo Picasso, is called chiaroscuro, which despite the Italian name and the Italian claim to having invented it, was done in Germany a decade earlier, in 1508, by Lucas Cranach the Elder while working with two blocks. The leading chiaroscuro cutter and printer, one of the top *Formschneiders* of this golden age, was Jost de Negker, who was Flemish-born, but worked in Augsburg at the time.

Maximilian wrote an autobiography, *Weisskunig* (White king), for which Burgkmair made 117 of the 211 woodcuts used to illustrate it. He also made 14 of the 118 woodcuts that illustrate *Theuerdank,* Maximilian's account of his courtship of Mary of Burgundy. Most of the other woodcuts were done by Hans Schäufelein, Dürer's former assistant. *Theuerdank* was not a romantic story but rather the history of the intense negotiation undertaken by Maximilian to acquire Burgundy, one of the wealthiest countries in Europe. That acquisition led to fifteen years of warfare, which Maximilian paid for with the dowry from his second

The opening of The Triumph of Maximilian I.
Woodcut by Hans Burgkmair, circa 1512.

wife, after Mary. Mary had died only a few years after they were married, in a horse-riding accident.

The first of Maximilian's grand woodcut commissions was a series of ninety-two woodcuts based on Caesar Augustus's arch in Rome, but highly ornamented with Renaissance details. It was followed by the equally grand *Triumphal Arch*, designed, cut, and printed from 1512 to 1515. Fully displayed on a wall, the work measures nine feet high and ten and a half feet wide. It is telling that Maximilian also commissioned a series of paintings on vellum for his own private collection; the woodcuts were for "the people." Painting was for the rich; paper art was for everyone else. Maximilian's first two commissions were drawn by Dürer and cut by Andreä.

For the third commission, *The Triumph of Maximilian*, at least 137 blocks were carved by a team of *Formschneiders*, including Andreä. The leading artists in Germany designed these blocks. Dürer was among them, but many more blocks were designed by Albrecht Altdorfer—an artist of the Danube school, which depicted biblical stories in Romantic European landscapes—and Dürer's woodcutting student, Hans Spring-inklee. *The Triumph of Maximilian* depicted an imaginary march led by a naked herald mounted on a griffin, followed by horses, exotic animals, musicians, jesters, fencers, drummers, falconers, and jousters. It was 177 feet long and designed so that copies could be made and hung along the walls of public buildings.

There are two important things to be learned from these works. The first is that Maximilian took the Holy Roman Emperor idea very seriously. The first Holy Roman Emperor was Charlemagne, who reigned in 800, three hundred years after the end of the Roman Empire. Parts of Italy were included in the Holy Roman Empire, as was Burgundy, thanks to Maximilian. The Holy Roman Emperor, who was supposed to embody the Roman emperors of old, was elected by noblemen and crowned by the pope. It has been popular among high school history teachers for many years to point out that the Holy Roman Empire was neither holy nor Roman nor an empire. But Maximilian wanted to be a true Roman Emperor. Roman or not, he was a great promoter of woodcuts and printed paper art. Had a Medici of Florence or Rome commissioned a depiction of a triumphal march measuring 177 feet long, it would have been a frieze, a mural, or a fresco. But this Roman Emperor was German, and he wanted woodcuts printed on paper.

IN 1515, WHEN Dürer stopped cutting wood and farmed his drawings out to Andreä the *Formschneider*, he started, not coincidentally, to learn of a new way of making prints: etching.

The idea is thought to have originated with Daniel Hopfer, an armor decorator and sometime woodcutter. Etchings are made with a metal plate—Hopfer used iron, but copper was soon substituted—that is covered by a soft, waxlike, acid-resistant ground. Originally the ground was made of wax, mastic, and amber. The plate was heated so that the ground could be rolled out evenly, and a blunt instrument called a burin could be used to draw lines into the substance down to the metal. The plate was then dipped in acid and cleaned off. Those parts of the metal plate covered by the waxy ground remained unaltered, but the lines where the metal plate had been exposed were eaten away by the acid. How deeply the lines were etched was determined by how long the plate was left in its acid bath.

Dürer probably took so quickly to this new technique—he was producing it within two years of learning about it—because the burin was a tool that he knew well. It was used by goldsmiths to engrave metal. But ordinarily, a burin scratched into metal makes all the lines the same. With this new technique, the lines could be thinner or thicker depending on how you applied the tool. Also, even darker lines could be made by leaving the plate in the acid for a time, pulling it from the bath, varnishing over the lines that were to remain lighter, and putting the plate back in the acid for further "biting." Compared to carving wood, it was a very fast and precise process, making it easier to create the fine lines and rich detail that Dürer loved.

Intaglio printing also emerged in this age. A print idea involving inked metal on paper, it is the reverse of moveable type and woodcuts. The difference is that the parts that are cut away get the ink and the parts that are not cut away remain white. After the plate is inked and rubbed, it is put in a printing press. Dürer was one of the pioneers of intaglio printing as well, though he only did it from 1515 to 1518. Since then, it has become one of the most popular techniques for printmaking on paper, partly because it only requires drawing skills, not carving ones.

Chapter 8

OUT FROM MAINZ

||||||||||||||||||

*He became so absorbed in his books that he spent his nights
from sunset to sunrise, and his days from dawn to dark, por-
ing over them; and with little sleep and much reading his
brains got so dry that he lost his wits.*

—MIGUEL DE CERVANTES,
The Ingenious Gentleman Don Quixote of La Mancha

ORE BOOKS WERE MADE IN EUROPE IN THE SECOND
half of the fifteenth century—some 8 million is a conservative estimate—than in all of previous European history. From Gutenberg on,
printing overtook Europe, step by step. Johann Fust, the businessman
who had gained control of Gutenberg's operation, not only possessed his
press and process but had also taken on his assistant, Peter Schöffer, a
talented man with an eye on the future, a former scribe turned printer.
Under Fust, the Gutenberg press, which had failed to earn money for its
creator, became a profitable house selling books throughout Germany

and France. Another member of Gutenberg's team established a print shop in Bamberg in Bavaria, while others stayed and plied their craft in Mainz.

Printing might not have spread as quickly as it did if Bishop Adolf von Nassau had not lost his perch as archbishop of Mainz and decided, with the pope's backing, to take it by force. This sacking of Mainz in 1462, a virtual destruction of the city, caused many residents, printers included, to flee. A remarkable group of Germans, starting with those who had studied under Gutenberg or Fust and Schöffer, then took some of their equipment and, more important, their skills and knowledge, and traveled throughout Europe. They would establish print shops in one town, teach apprentices there, and then move on to the next town.

A print shop was not portable. The large oak press was heavy, as was a complete set of lead type. So the printers took with them only their punches, used to make type molds. They followed the Rhine to cities that had book markets—cities with universities, such as Cologne and Strasbourg. Universities were hungry for more books, and printing could now provide them. Between 1348 in Prague and 1508 in Frankfurt, fifteen German cities successfully established universities; in addition, Ulm, Lünenburg, and Breslau started universities that failed. Upon arriving in a university town, the printer would simply find a carpenter who made wine presses and instruct him on how to build a printing press. Then, using his punches, he would make new molds and type.

Ulrich Zell was one of those who had learned printing from Fust and Schöffer, and who fled Mainz in 1462. By 1463 he was printing in Cologne, producing mostly books for the university with a typeface very similar to that of Fust and Schöffer. He seemed to prosper as a printer, as he lived grandly in a palatial estate, though his marriage to a wealthy woman undoubtedly helped as well. But whatever the case, people believed that printing was the source of his wealth, which led to many imitators and competitors.

By the time Zell died in 1503, there were more than twenty other printers in Cologne and the city had become a printing center. The

Cologne printers had also spread printing north to Northern Germany and Holland.

They then took their printing south to Italy and Spain, and west to France. There was even interest to the east, in Russia under Tsar Ivan V, though his printing press, started in 1563, was soon destroyed in a riot. Russia did not even have a paper mill until 1576; like England and Holland, it did not start papermaking until it needed paper for its own printing industry.

Italy took an early lead in printing because it was very quick to welcome German printers. The Subiaco monastery, a Benedictine monastery near Rome, invited German Benedictines who knew how to print to come to teach them, despite the fact that the principal activity of the Subiaco monks was copying manuscripts. But they were interested in a more efficient way to copy, and the Subiaco monastery became the first printing house in Italy, producing printed books as early as 1464. By the late fifteenth century, there were also numerous German printers in Rome, both religious and secular. A few prospered, many struggled, and some failed.

One of the great German successes in Rome was Ulrich Hahn, who started printing there in 1468 and was probably the first in Italy to print a book illustrated with wood blocks. But by the turn of the century, these were commonplace, with illustrated Italian books being printed in Rome, Verona, and Naples, to be followed soon thereafter by Florence and Venice. In Naples in 1485, Sextus Riessinger, a German, printed a much-admired edition of the Greek classic *Aesop's Fables*, illustrated with thirty-seven woodcuts for Italian publisher Francesco Del Tuppo.

Venice, one of Europe's most important paper trading centers, quickly became the printing capital of Italy. By the beginning of the sixteenth century, when Naples had 67 printers, Rome 41, and Florence only 37 despite its dominance in art, Venice had 268.

The first Venetian printer was a goldsmith from Mainz, Johannes de Spira. The chief magistrate of Venice, known as the doge, granted him an exclusive five-year contract to print books in Venice, but shortly after producing his first book in 1469, he died. His brother Wendelin tried to continue the exclusive arrangement, but the doge would not recognize an heir to the contract and this left the field open for many competitors, including a number of Germans.

Venetian books became renowned for their beauty. In 1490 the Venetian printers Giovanni Ragazzo and Lucantonio Giunta published Niccolo de Mallermi's Italian translation of the Bible. The pages have a two-column format and, unusual for the time, four hundred small woodcuts one-column wide that run throughout the book. The book also has a woodcut border of architectural design. Later, small woodcuts and decoratively bordered title pages came to typify the celebrated Venetian book.

The most celebrated name in Venetian books was Aldus Manutius. Before becoming a printer, Aldus had been a scholar in Rome specializing in ancient Greek writing. He lived in the household of the wealthy nobleman and noted philosopher and author Giovanni Pico, Count of Mirandula. Aldus was instructor to the count's sister, the princess of Capri, but struggled to teach her because he could find few useful textbooks—no doubt the plight of many teachers at the time.

Aldus moved to Venice, where he gave lectures, though his greater aspiration was to print books, including textbooks. But something else was on his mind as well. He believed that the world was changing and that printed paper would take over. Anything that was not printed would disappear, or at least be doomed to obscurity. Almost none of the great Greek classics had been printed—it became his mission to save these works through printing.

He opened a shop, but he may not have had a shopkeeper's temperament. A sign on the front of his shop, the Aldine Press, read, "State your business briefly, and then immediately go away." His success was not based on his personality, however, but on the beauty and innovation of his books.

True to his original plan, his first book, in 1494, was a Greek grammar textbook. Five years later, he printed the fictional *Hypnerotomachia* by Francesco de Colonna, a book that garnered more attention. It was

Opening page of Gregorius, *printed in Venice in 1498. It is often considered one of the finest pieces of ornamental book printing from the Renaissance.*

an erotic romance, not at all shocking for the time; pornography was a popular genre in the emerging printing trade. The book was illustrated with 168 woodcuts, many of them erotic.

Aldus believed that the times called for smaller and more portable books. To facilitate these little books, he invented a new typeface supposedly based on Petrarch's handwriting. His first book in the new type, which he called *italics*, was published in 1501. Italics was subsequently copied all over Europe, even though Aldus jealously guarded his invention and was angered when other publishers printed in italics.

In point of fact, italics was not Aldus's invention but his punch cutter's, a dubious character named Francesco Griffo who eventually had a falling-out with Aldus and returned to his native Bologna, where he was arrested for beating his son-in-law to death with an iron bar. According to some accounts, he was subsequently hanged for his crime. Griffo was probably also the punch cutter for Bembo, a very readable Roman typeface designed by the poet and Greek scholar Pietro Bembo in 1496 for one of his books published by the Aldine Press. Bembo, like italics, is still in common use. And the Aldine symbol, a dolphin coiled around an anchor, is today the symbol of the American publisher Doubleday.

By the time of his death in 1515, Aldus Manutius, the man who had sought to revive the classics; the first to print Aristotle, Sophocles, Herodotus, Euripides, Aristophanes, Plato, and Thucydides; and the first to consult several texts to find the most accurate classical scribe, had completely revolutionized book printing. The Aldine Press was continued by Aldus's family until 1579.

Tens of thousands of Aldus's books, known as Aldines, have survived. Not only are they still perfect, beautiful small books, but their pages have survived half a millennium remarkably well. Historians have written much about the unreliability of paper in the sixteenth century, but these pages remind us of the quality of rag paper. They are flat and smooth and pearly white, with no discoloration and no spots. These small, portable books, which Aldus called *libelli portatiles*, are credited with changing people's reading habits. This, of course, is the technological fallacy at work once again. Aldus did not change reading habits. Rather, a change in reading habits prompted him to produce a different kind of book. He could see that books were too big for the way the new readers wanted to use them. Books were no longer read only by learned monks and scholars at stands in monasteries and castles but by a broad

Aldus in His Printing Establishment in Venice Showing Grolier
Some Book Bindings. *Etching by Léopold Flameng, 1891. Jean Grolier
de Servières (1489–1565) was a French treasurer general, an avid book
collector, and an enthusiastic fan of the Aldine Press.*

range of people, especially in Italy and France. People wanted to read
while lounging in chairs or at a café; they wanted to take books to work
to read on breaks or on trips. And another small point, or two actually;
Aldus was the first to use the modern semicolon.

WITH ITS LARGE and growing university, Paris was Europe's leading
intellectual center and therefore a leading destination for German printers selling their wares. But no printing was done in Paris until 1470, when
two professors from the Sorbonne, the German-born Johann Heynlin

and the Frenchman Guillaume Fichet, sent for three printers from Germany: Ulrich Gering, Michael Friburger, and Martin Crantz.

Heynlin and Fichet's first book, the first book printed in France, in 1470, was *Epistolae Gasparini*, a student's guide to writing Latin by Gasparinus de Bergamo. Over the next two years, they printed about thirty more books, many aimed at an academic audience. Then they moved their operation to the nearby rue Saint-Jacques, a major street in Paris. One of their apprentices, Pierre de Kaysere, went into business for himself and established a competing press, the Soufflet-Vert, on the same street. And soon the rue Saint-Jacques became the publishing and bookselling center of Paris.

Being one of the longer streets in Paris and a major thoroughfare until the nineteenth-century redesign of the city, the rue Saint-Jacques was an ideal location for the delivery of bulky paper supplies and the shipping of books. The street was lined with booksellers, while printers and bookbinders set up shop in the adjacent narrow streets. By the seventeenth century, several thousand workers and their families lived off the thoroughfare's book business. The bookstalls along the Seine today are what remain of that trade.

THE GERMAN PRINTERS also went to other French cities, most notably Lyon. Lyon had a strong Italian connection because, like Italy, they had a silk industry; the Italian silk was said to be of higher quality, but the Lyonnais silk was more affordable. The city also had commercial ties to Germany.

Silk manufacturing in Lyon was a competitive and demanding industry. Because Lyon was located just above the meeting of the Rhône and Saône Rivers, it was often said that Lyon had three rivers: the Rhône, the Saône, and the tears of the silk workers. Living beside the hard-pressed working class, however, was a very affluent silk merchant class that stimulated banking and commerce, and sponsored fifteen-day international trade fairs four times a year. In the fifteenth century, Lyon was still, for the most part, an oral society. Certainly the silk workers and other workers could neither read nor write, and the merchant class could only do so to the extent needed for their business. Yet among the population also lived an educated elite that had heard of, and yearned for, the new printed books.

Lyon printing began with Bathélemy Buyer, who was born in Lyon in 1433 to a prominent family—lawyers on his father's side and garment makers on his mother's. He probably met the Paris publishers Heynlin and Fichet while he was studying at the Sorbonne, and in 1472 returned home with a passion for the new German printing devices. He brought to Lyon an experienced printer named Guillaume Le Roy, who was from Liège but probably learned his craft in Germany. Le Roy in turn brought with him four German workers. It is believed that the group then set up shop on the rue Mercière on the left bank of the Saône—the location of the city's flourishing print trade for centuries to come.

Lyonnais books were not known for their elegance or beauty. The printers there had little interest in competing with the work of scribes or with the finer books being published in Germany, Italy, and Paris. Instead, their books tended to be printed on smooth and white, albeit thick, paper. The print they used was dark and clear but difficult to read due to their fondness for Gothic typeface.

The Lyonnais sold their books throughout Europe. And, taking advantage of their close commercial relationship with Venice, they were infamous for copying Venetian books. Aldus Manutius denounced the Lyonnais printers and listed the many errors in their books, but the Lyonnais, rather than apologizing or denying the theft, simply used his denunciations to make corrections.

The Lyonnais printers thought of themselves as popular publishers, as opposed to the academic presses of Paris. Their readers were not scholars or intellectuals. One of their important markets was doctors, and they published numerous books on diseases and remedies. But the core of their market were the booksellers from around Europe who attended their fairs and bought hundreds of books to sell elsewhere. The Lyonnais publishers tried to produce editions in print runs of five hundred; sales of five hundred gave a book bestselling status.

The Lyonnais produced the first books ever printed in the French language (the first Paris-published books were in other languages), starting with *Livre des merveilles du monde* (The book of wonders of the world) in 1475 or 1476. Martin Husz, a German printer in Lyon, printed the first French books with woodcuts embedded in them. The Lyonnais books were often printed from blocks made in Germany, but local woodcutters who had developed their craft in the playing-card industry also contributed.

By the end of the fifteenth century, Lyon was printing more books than any other city except for Venice, Frankfurt, and Paris. Germans went to other French cities, including Bordeaux in 1486, to start printing operations, and by the end of the century, Parisians too were bringing printing to southwest France, including Périgueux in 1498. Many of the fifteenth-century printers, especially the Germans, continued to live a traveling life. They spent a few years in one town, a few in another, and then moved on.

SPANISH PRINTING BEGAN with Germans as well. Jakob Vizlant, a representative of the German trading company Ravensburg-Constance, started up printing shops in Valencia that produced their first book in 1475. Another German, Paulus Hurus, began a printing press in Zaragoza that was unusual for the time; rather than reprinting classics or other existing books, he commissioned new works. Barcelona was also a site for an early Spanish printing shop, founded by German printer Johann Rosenbach.

To induce Spain to develop a paper industry, the Spanish Crown exempted papermakers from military service. This had also occurred in some parts of Italy, where papermakers were not only exempted from military service, but from some taxes. This was not to say that Spanish paper workers were well treated. The paper mill was a closed community. Catalan paper historian Oriol Valls i Subirà described it as "a sort of convent, but with very hard living conditions."

Another way of putting it might be a labor camp. The paper mill was the home of the owner, along with the workers and their families. Even married men and women were required to sleep separately. There were no set working hours. The mill operated around the clock, as paper mills still do today. This meant that the workers and their families seldom knew quiet, for the loud stampers that pounded rags into pulp never stopped. The workers' only respite from the noise occurred during the weekly cleaning of the vats and stampers—the most arduous work in the mill.

In sixteenth-century Spain, as in much of Europe, the average life expectancy of a paper worker was less than thirty years. Tuberculosis was rampant. But by the standards of the time, paper workers were not considered poor. Their working conditions were no worse than the working conditions in the lesser-paying cloth, iron, and flour industries. Conditions were no harsher than in France and Italy. But French and Italian workers did gain some rights, such as holidays, by organizing in guilds; there was no such organizing in the Spanish mills.

As had occurred in earlier centuries in Italy, the growth of paper mills in Spain created a tremendous need for rags, and in the early 1600s, the Spanish king Philip IV banned the export of rags from the region along the Huécar River near Cuenca, the site of a very large and high-quality paper mill. The late-sixteenth-century Spanish author Francisco de Quevedo wrote:

> *Those that were rags yesterday,*
> *and thrown away by the cook,*
> *are today documents that govern two worlds*
> *and threaten three others.*

AT FIRST, THE paper produced by the Spanish mills after the Reconquista, the centuries-long period when the Christians fought to regain control of the Iberian Peninsula from the Muslims, was not as high quality as the paper produced elsewhere in Europe, and Spain imported paper from France and Italy. But in time, that began to change. By the year 1500, there were printers in the Spanish cities of Valencia, Barcelona, Cuenca, Zaragoza, Seville, Lleida, Tortosa, Salamanca, Valladolid, Zamora,

Toledo, Tarragona, Palma de Mallorca, Burgos, Murcia, Pamplona, and Granada—seventeen in all—and Spanish books became known for a certain style and beauty, with rounded gothic lettering and ornate title pages.

It was in 1605 that Spanish publishing hit its famous low and high point. Francisco de Robles decided to publish the latest work of Miguel de Cervantes, a fifty-eight-year-old struggling writer. His stories had been mostly ignored, though his poetry had garnered a few awards and a little attention. He had written a very long work—but it was only Part One. Part Two was coming later, the author said. It was called *El Ingenioso Hidalgo Don Quixote de La Mancha*, which today we recognize as the world's first novel. In 1605, however, it wasn't clear what to call it.

Robles was taking a risk. Cervantes had given readings from the book before it was published, leading the playwright Lope de Vega, the most illustrious writer in Spain at the time, to say, "There is none so foolish as to praise Don Quixote."

For his printer, Cervantes chose Juan de la Cuesta, whose shop on Calle Atocha is a museum today. He had published some of Cervantes's earlier work, and more important at the time, was the publisher of Lope de Vega—no small feat since de Vega wrote, or was soon to write, 1,800 plays, three book-length poems, thousands of sonnets, and three novels. That was a lot of paper.

Machine-made books and handmade paper were a tough combination. From the fifteenth century, when printing was invented, until the nineteenth century, when machine-made paper was developed, purchasing enough paper was the greatest problem confronting the book-publishing industry. De la Cuesta obtained his paper from a paper mill at the monastery of El Paular in Segovia—not one of the better paper mills in Spain. For the mill to produce, and Robles to pay for, enough paper to publish a significant edition of Cervantes's very large book took four years. The total purchase came to 1,100 reams of paper, some 550,000 sheets, each folded down to eight printed pages, which was called a quarto.

Robles may have used low-grade paper because he expected the

Cover of Don Quixote. *First edition printed in Madrid by Juan de la Cuesta in 1605. Courtesy of the Biblioteca Nacional de España, Madrid.*

book to be a hit and could not afford huge quantities of good paper. Or he may have intended to put out a cheap edition because he expected it to sell to a lower class of readers. Still another possibility is that he chose low-quality paper out of habit; he had used the same El Paular paper to print Cervantes's other works. But whatever the case, the book was an immediate hit—and has continued to be so for more than four hundred years. According to some historians, it is the most-sold secular book in the history of publishing. Its ideas are incredibly durable, and throughout all of the shifts in history the book has always remained relevant. When Fidel Castro came to power in Cuba in 1959, this was the first book his government published; they used it for a mass literacy campaign.

Many handsome editions of *Don Quixote* have been printed over the centuries, but the first edition was not pretty. Its paper, made from a very low grade of cloth, was lumpy and marked with impurities and wrinkles. It was also extremely brittle. Juan de la Cuesta's work was inferior as well. The printing wasn't crisp and was extremely difficult to read, especially because the type from the reverse side tended to bleed through.

DON QUIXOTE, LIKE all great works of literature, has many layers of meaning, but fundamentally it is the story of an old-fashioned man who lives in a fast-changing world in which he cannot find his place. The instant enthusiasm of the Spanish public for the book is testimony to the fact that this is what Europe was like at the beginning of the seventeenth century. Don Quixote, wanting to be a chivalrous medieval knight, is confronted with an emerging middle class that is pragmatic, not romantic. They are stirred not by idealism but by the notion that if they work hard they can get ahead. Most everyone in the book except Don Quixote—even his faithful "squire," Sancho Panza—belongs to this emerging class.

But there is a twist. The book *Don Quixote* was being published for this very same emerging class. And the problem with Don Quixote—the reason why he seems mad and fails to grasp the world around him—is that he reads too much. In particular, he reads medieval romances, one of the most popular genres of the time. There is clearly an intended irony here, because Cervantes himself loved reading. Known to be an uncontrollable reader, he would even pick up scraps of paper from the street to see what was written on them.

Don Quixote's niece, distraught by the bizarre behavior of her uncle, takes a clergyman to her uncle's library to show him the source of the problem. The curate examines the books, some large and finely bound, and others smaller. The niece suggests that he sprinkle them all with holy water, but the priest laughs at her naïveté. Clearly the only way to save her uncle, he says, is to burn his books. The pair even contemplate burning a book by a certain Cervantes called *Don Quixote*, but decide that since it is only Part One, they will wait to see if Part Two is any better.

To return the Old World to the way it was, all books would have to be burned.

Chapter 9

TENOCHTITLÁN
AND THE
BLUE-EYED DEVIL

||||||||||||||||||

They had counted eighty horses and eight hundred men and ten or twelve guns, all of which they had represented on a piece of their paper.

—HERNÁN CORTÉS,
Letter to Emperor Charles V,
OCTOBER 30, 1520

WHEN CERVANTES WAS A SMALL CHILD, SPANISH PRIESTS really were trying to save people by burning their books. Shortly after the death of Aldus Manutius in 1515, while Albrecht Dürer was perfecting his craft in Nuremberg and Michelangelo had just finished the ceiling of the Sistine Chapel, one of the great tragedies of history began to unfold in Mexico.

Dard Hunter, the indefatigable paper historian, once observed that what is fascinating about pre-Columbian Mesoamerica is that, like other cultures, "regardless of the isolation or distance of one continent from another, or the remote origins of peoples, the pattern of man's progress developed everywhere in the same way; the steps involved in the growth of civilization were almost identical."

Before the Europeans arrived in the Americas at the end of the fifteenth century, the Mesoamericans already had written languages and paper and were recording their own history. Many aspects of their civilization were as advanced as the Europeans' except for two decisive things: the Europeans could use gunpowder, an invention they had imported from China; and they could ride horses, a skill they had learned from the people of Central Asia, who had domesticated horses long before the rest of the world.

There is some debate over whether the Mesoamericans made true paper. If they did, they were the only civilization to invent paper besides China. The reason for the uncertainty stems from the fact that the Mesoamerican civilization was so thoroughly destroyed by the Spanish that we are still struggling to learn about it. One thing we do know: They had libraries filled with books, of which only three Mayan codices and fifteen Aztec works have survived.

Until 1986 it had been believed that the first written language of the Americas was Mayan, from a people who lived in Guatemala and southern Mexico. But a monument uncovered that year showed that an early Olmec people also had a written language. In fact the Olmecs, who lived mostly in the lowlands of southwest Mexico, in today's states of Tabasco and Vera Cruz, were the originators of many things that we once attributed to the Mayans and Aztecs. In 2006, an entire Olmec city was unearthed not far from Mexico City, and it is now thought that several writing systems were in use before the Mayans', which is why the Mayan system is so complicated.

The earlier languages of the American peoples were largely written on stone, but the later Aztec language was mostly written on animal skin, bark, or paper. The earlier languages were all written before 900 CE, whereas Aztec writing did not begin until 1100 CE. Early Mayan script was written on stone or pottery from 600 BCE into the first century CE, but after that paper codices were used.

The fact that the Mayans were already writing on paper made from mulberry bark early in the Christian era is one piece of evidence used to support the theory that the American peoples originally came from Asia, over a Siberian land bridge that is now gone. There are other remarkable similarities between the Asian and the Mesoamerican use of paper as well. These include the utilization of folded paper fans, the burning of paper for religious ritual, and the decorating of temples with paper.

Writing in Mesoamerica reached its full development in what is called the classical Mayan period, from 250 CE to 900 CE. Mayan writing used several different types of characters. Some were a kind of phonetic pun—a picture of one thing that happened to sound like another. Some characters were purely phonetic and had to be placed together to make a word. Others were purely pictographic—a representational drawing of something. About 800 characters from Mayan have been translated. Their entire spoken language could be written in the glyphs.

The Mayans, like the Europeans of the same period, wrote through scribes. Mayan scribes belonged to a royal caste and, like the scribes of ancient Egypt, were considered leading figures in the society. Scribes could choose between using phonetic symbols or pictographs, which left much room for personal flair.

Very knowledgeable about astronomy, the Mayans developed sophisticated calendar systems. They were also far more advanced in mathematics than Europeans at that time. They grasped the concept of zero and wrote their entire number system with just three characters—a shell meant zero, a dot meant one, and a bar meant five. From both Spanish and Mayan accounts we know that Mayan libraries were full of thousands of codices about astronomy, history, genealogy, and religious rituals, written on deerskin or tree bark. All were destroyed by the Spanish except for the three mentioned above, which came from a later Mayan period and were about astronomy and ritual.

The material that the Mayans used for writing, starting in the fifth century, came from the inner bark of the wild fig tree, cut and stretched thin. Whitish in color, and called *huun*, it was like papyrus, but more durable. It was not made of randomly woven fibers; in other words, it was not true paper. The Mayan works were written in codex form, the same format used by the Romans, but their and later the Aztecs' codices differed from the Romans' in that their pages were bound accordion-style so that they could be completely opened into one long strip.

One of the surviving Mayan codices, the two-volume *Codex Troano-Cortés*, was found in two parts in Spain in 1860; one part was discovered in Extremadura, the native region of Conquistador Hernán Cortés and many of his men, so it is probable that one of them brought it back to Spain. Another Mayan codex, the *Codex Dresdensis*, or Dresden Codex, dates from the eleventh or twelfth century, but is thought to be a copy of a codex written three or four centuries earlier. It was nearly lost to water damage during the fire-bombing of Dresden during World War II, but was dried and saved. The third codex, the *Codex Peresianus*, is currently housed in the Bibliothèque Nationale in Paris, where it was found in 1859 in a basket of discarded papers.

When the Mayan civilization waned, the Toltecs rose to power. Great architects and builders of cities, they created elaborate urban centers in Teotihuacan, Tula, and Cholula. Each of these urban cultures had its own writing and made its own paper. The Toltec word for "book" was *amoxtli*, and in the year 660 the Toltecs of Tula, under the astrologer Huematzin, wrote the *Teoamoxtli*—the Divine Book—which claimed to be "a History of Heaven and Earth," with details on the constellations, a plan for the division of time, and records of the historic migrations of people. But like the Mayan civilization, the Toltec civilization declined; it was replaced by the Aztec.

All of these rising and falling civilizations had certain things in common—they all wrote, they all made paper, and they all improved their writing and papermaking techniques as time went by. In addition, they were all knowledgeable about astronomy and fascinated by time; they all produced calendars and histories.

WHEN THE SPANISH arrived in the Americas, the Aztecs were the region's greatest power, but they had been dominant for less than two hundred years. By the Aztecs' own account, they had come down from a northern location to consolidate power in central Mexico in 1320 CE. They began building their capital, Tenochtitlán, on a muddy island in the middle of a lake starting in 1325. They settled on several other islands as well, created produce gardens on the lake, and constructed four causeways connecting the islands to the mainland. By the time the Spanish arrived in 1519, marching in on one of the causeways, Tenochtitlán was probably the largest city any of the conquistadors had ever seen. Its population was 200,000. The population of Madrid and Seville at the time was only 150,000 each. Tenochtitlán boasted not only works of ingenious architecture but also a highly developed legal code and exceptionally capable administrators. Runners were spaced every five miles throughout the Aztec empire to relay messages written on slips of paper.

Historians argue over what percentage of Aztecs could actually read and—certainly an even lower percentage—write. They did, however, have a highly evolved writing system, perhaps adopted from the Mayan, though it was completely different, with a great deal more phoneticism and even more pictographs. For example, the character used for *amatl*, the Aztec word for "paper," was a simple line drawing of a roll of paper tied around the middle with rope. Spanish missionaries tried to use the phonetic characters of the Aztecs to teach them Christianity in Latin. Not surprisingly, the endeavor was not entirely successful. Aztec scribes wrote in color using mineral pigments—red, blue, green, yellow, brown, orange, and purple—and always outlined their figures in black. This made their manuscripts appealing and fanciful to look at, and gave scribes creative choices.

Working directly with the priests, the Aztec scribes were among the most powerful people in their society. They kept track of all legal and commercial activities, including the tributes paid to the Aztecs by those they had conquered, the foundation of their state revenue; these tributes did not go entirely to the Aztec king but were distributed to various community representatives within the nation. The scribes also wrote down Aztec history, rituals, and holiday traditions. Their most important task was to follow the calendar and make sure that the end of each cycle was properly observed, in order to avoid the end of the world. Fear of such an apocalypse was very real.

ACCORDING TO ONE surviving Aztec book, the *Codex Mendoza*, 480,000 sheets of paper were brought in tribute to Tenochtitlán every year. The *Codex Mendoza* was named for the viceroy of New Spain, and it is not clear whether he ordered it, commissioned it, or just received it. It was written in 1535, fourteen years after the Spanish Conquest, and it is apparent that the economic rules of colonialism were firmly in place by then because rather than using local paper, the Aztecs wrote the work on imported Spanish paper. A record of Aztec history from the founding of Tenochtitlán to the Spanish Conquest, with tales of Aztec victories and tributes included, it was intended for the king of Spain. But the ship carrying it was seized at sea by the French, to somehow land, in 1659, in the Bodleian Library at Oxford University, where it lay unnoticed until scholars discovered it in the nineteenth century.

In the *Codex Mendoza* is an illustration of a building collapsing in flames, and next to it is a scroll tied with rope. Under the list of tributes, there is another scroll tied with rope, and next to it, a pouch with three tassels. According to J. J. Valentini, a scholar of Aztec civilization who presented his findings to the American Antiquarian Society in 1880—findings that have gained wide acceptance ever since—what all this means is that the town of Yzamatitlan, "Paper City" in Aztec, was conquered by the Aztecs and forced to pay tribute to Tenochtitlán to the tune of 24,000 reams of paper every year. A pouch is the symbol for 8,000, and the three tassels indicate a multiplier of three. This is an enormous amount of paper, and the tribute shows that, on the one hand, paper was a highly valued commodity, and on the other, it was being abundantly produced.

Aztec arithmetic was based on the number 20, a number that they thought had been prescribed by the gods. Why else would humans all have exactly twenty digits? Numbers less than 20 were indicated by a dot or small circle. A flag represented 20; an upright feather meant 400; and a pouch was 8,000.

The Aztecs used paper for writing, for decorating altars and temples, and for religious rituals. Masks worn during religious dances were made of paper. Paper was also burned as a sacrifice, and the priests adorned themselves with paper for ceremonies. Some deities were symbolized by elaborate paper crowns. And for certain human sacrifices, the victims, who were to be burned alive, wore strips of paperlike hair.

The Franciscan monk Bernardino de Ribeira, usually called Father Sahagún because he was born in Sahagún, Spain, lived for most of the sixteenth century in Mexico, where he chronicled the traditions and customs of the Aztecs. His most famous book, *General History of the Things of New Spain*, has earned him the title "first American ethnographer." Interestingly, at a time when modern bound books were being printed and published widely in Europe, Father Sahagún wrote his history in a codex edition of twelve books with a total of 2,400 pages. The work was bilingual, written in both Nahuatl (the Aztec language) and Spanish, with 2,500 illustrations by Aztec artists—a masterwork of book publishing for its day.

In his book, Sahagún describes many ritualistic uses of paper. In one chapter entitled "The Gods which Ancient Mexicans Adored," he discusses the god of merchants, Yacatecuhtli, whom Aztec merchant guilds honored with offerings of paper, often covering his statue entirely with it. Clearly paper was thought of as an important commercial commodity.

BUT THERE IS a problem with this narrative. Much of this Aztec paper, like the Mayan paper before it, was not really paper, the random weaving of cellulose fibers, but the inner bark of the wild fig tree that had been beaten and stretched and dried like its forerunner, tapa.

Tapa was made in South America for almost as long as there is evidence of human inhabitants in the region. Tapa from 2400 BCE has been found in Peru, along with stone tapa beaters that are almost 10,000 years old. To make tapa, the outer bark of the fig tree was scraped off and beaten with mallets until the inner bark was ready to come free. The inner bark was then peeled off in one piece, washed in a stream to remove its latex content, hung up, and carefully stretched. After it was dry, it was stretched a little more.

The Aztecs' variation on tapa, *amate*, was named after the Aztec word for the fig tree, which was also the Aztec word for writing material. Very similar to tapa, though often thinner and finer, it was made by cooking the fig tree's inner bark in a lye powder made from soaking corn. It is highly skilled work, but was mastered by many in pre-Columbian Mexico. Amate made for excellent writing material—but it was not paper.

Some historians are convinced that the Aztecs never used true paper, just amate. They argue that the Europeans mistook amate for paper, which is quite possible, as amate looks very much like paper, though without the telltale screen marks that are made by a mold. This argument rests on the fact that no pre-European paper has been found in Mexico. However, most of the amate from that era has not survived either.

The central highlands of Mexico have a humid climate, with a rainy season, and neither paper nor amate age well there. Furthermore, the Aztecs tried to hide or burn all their ritual papers, to keep them out of the hands of the Spanish, who themselves were burning all the Aztec books they could find, claiming them to be heretical. Of the few remaining books found, none seem to be written on true paper. But to conclude from this that the Aztecs did not make paper would be like examining thirteenth-century European culture with nothing more to work with than a few surviving manuscripts and concluding that the Europeans used only parchment.

A close examination of the Mayan Dresden Codex, generally agreed to be written on *huun*, the Mayan variation of amate, reveals the presence of agave fibers. This is significant because there are numerous reports that the Aztecs made paper from agave, whose fibers contain cellulose, as well as many other things, such as a fermented juice called pulque, a distilled alcohol known today as tequila; roof thatching; food; clothing; and rope.

Bernal Díaz del Castillo, an adventurer who served with Cortés in Mexico and later became the chief chronicler of the Spanish Conquest, asserted that true paper was made from agave. Francisco López de Gómara, a Spanish historian who never went to the Americas but interviewed Cortés and other returning conquistadores, told a similar story, although Díaz del Castillo insisted that López de Gómara was an inaccurate historian. Toribio de Benavente, a Franciscan monk and one of the original twelve missionaries sent in 1524 to convert the "Indians" also reported that they made paper from agave. According to these Europeans' reports, agave paper was coarse and bumpy, probably ill-suited for writing; indeed, it may have been reserved for other uses. There are records of paper fans made from agave.

ON APRIL 22, 1519, Hernán Cortés, a soldier on his first command, with an army of a few hundred men, most of whom had never seen combat, sailed from Cuba and landed on the Caribbean coast of Mexico in what is now the state of Vera Cruz. Cortés had largely financed the operation himself, and had no idea what he would find or even who his enemy might be. But on Easter Sunday, he met with Totonac, the chief of a people called the Tentlil, who told him that somewhere in the center of the country was a great king called Montecuçoma, ruler of all the lands even to the Vera Cruz coast.

Instantly, Cortés became singularly focused on overthrowing this Montecuçoma, better known to most North Americans as Montezuma. Mounted on horseback, Cortés's forces rode into the central highlands looking for the king and a place called Tenochtitlán. Apparently, Cortés had great powers of persuasion. He talked to local people and formed alliances with groups whom the Aztecs had fought against but failed to conquer. Chief among them were the Tlaxcalteca, a Nahuatl-speaking group that Cortés called the Tascalteca; later, during Cortes's siege of Tenochtitlán, the Tlaxcalteca provided him with "more than 25,000 warriors," he wrote. Along the way, Cortés had his men shoot muskets to impress the Aztecs with his great firepower. But when the actual siege began, the Spaniards' chief weapon was the crossbow, an old-fashioned weapon then being quickly replaced in Europe with firearms.

In one town near present-day Tabasco, Cortés was offered slaves, among them a woman named Malinche. An unusual woman, especially for a slave, she was well educated and spoke Nahuatl and several dialects of Mayan. She came from an aristocratic background and it is not clear how she become a slave. Since Cortés's only translator spoke Mayan but not Nahuatl, Malinche became his translator's translator and an invaluable source of information. She also became Cortes's mistress. Malinche is remembered today as a villain of Mexican history, and her name became the word *malinchiste*, which means "traitor" or "sellout"— which is perhaps unfair.

Meanwhile, in the great city, even before word arrived of the Spanish landing, Montezuma had a vision of being destroyed by strange men who rode on the backs of deer. A mystic for whom premonitions and visions were very important, the king had seen other bad omens—of weather phenomena and other disasters—in his dreams.

On or about November 8, Cortés and his men marched down the causeway to Tenochtitlán. He wrote, "I left the camp with fifteen or twenty horsemen and three hundred Spaniards and all our Indian allies of whom there was an infinite number." By November 14, they had taken Tenochtitlán. Montezuma had "voluntarily" donated his kingdom to the crown of Castile. This brief adventure, known as the Conquest of Mexico, is reenacted in masked dances in small villages in central Mexico even today. By legend, Cortés had blue eyes; the dancer who plays him wears the mask of the blue-eyed devil.

After taking Tenochtitlán, Cortés wrote five letters to King Carlos, also known as Charles V, the Holy Roman Emperor. In them, Cortés expressed admiration for the Aztecs' administrative skills and their skill in papermaking. He understood the correlation between papermaking and a developed civilization. Cortés also wrote to the king about the Aztecs' system of collecting tributes, saying, "They kept an account of what each one was obliged to give in characters and drawings on paper, which they make, which is their writing."

Cortés was impressed that Montezuma had been informed of the Spaniards' arrival via a message written on paper stating how many men, weapons, and horses they had. He was even more impressed that Montezuma was able to rule a large empire through orders written on paper and delivered back and forth by an elaborate system of messengers.

THE LAST AREA to fall to the Christians during the Reconquista was the south of Spain, the most Arab part, and it was this region that became the center for activities in the Americas. Its ports were the ports of New Spain; the conquistadors hailed from the southern provinces of Extremadura or Andalusia. Later, the architecture of Mexico and Spanish America would be built in an Andalusian style, which is to say Moorish, with patterned tiles and arched doorways.

Architecture aside, the Spanish were determined that their newly claimed land was to be entirely Christian. The Inquisition, originally started not in Spain but in France by Pope Gregory IX in 1231, came to Mexico. Its purpose was to stop all heresy, any deviation from traditional Catholic practice, by rooting it out and punishing the heretics. But the Inquisition really had little effect in Spain until the end of the Reconquista, when King Ferdinand of Aragon and Queen Isabella of Castille, a Catholic fanatic, had to figure out how to unite the various kingdoms now under their control. Their answer: the ruthless enforcement of a common Catholic faith. They became determined to root out all Jews and Muslims who had pretended to convert rather than leave but were secretly keeping their old practices; the Spanish called these Jews *Marranos* and the Muslims, *Moriscos*.

In 1478, while there were still pockets of Spain under Muslim control, Pope Sixtus IV had given Isabella the right to establish a Spanish Inquisition that could operate independently. So in Spain the Inquisition was run by the Spanish Crown; even the Inquisitor General was appointed by the Crown, though he had to be confirmed by the pope. The Spanish Inquisition conducted lengthy investigations of anyone who wanted to

go to the New World, in order to make sure that no "impure blood"—
that is, Jews or Muslims—settled there.

But New Spain also had its own heretics, the Mesoamericans, and
so the main task of the Mexican Inquisition was to extinguish all native
practices. The first clergy, who arrived with Cortés, had Inquisitional
powers, and in 1522, the Mexican Inquisition conducted its first trial, of
an Indian accused of concubinage. Unfortunately, the records of this
trial have vanished, but it was clear from that early date that the Indians
were to be the Jews and Muslims of Mexico. They had to abandon all of
their practices or face torture and death.

From 1536 to 1542, the Inquisitor of Mexico was Juan de Zumárraga,
a Basque Franciscan. Zumárraga is a difficult figure to understand. He
considered himself a friend of the Indians and bitterly denounced their
mistreatment by the Spanish authorities. He also encouraged crafts and
agriculture and tried to bring flaxseed from Spain to Mexico to start a
linen industry. Mulberry trees and silkworms were imported under his
direction and he even brought over some Moriscos, impure blood and
all, to teach Indians how to make silk. Still more surprising, given that
he had burned Jews at the stake, he also brought over a converted Jew
to start the first Mexican press. It seems that he had the establishment of
a paper industry in mind, but it never came to fruition, perhaps because
he wasn't in Mexico long enough.

Zumárraga was also determined to root out and end all heresy,
which is to say, all practice of the Aztec religion. To be fair, some of
these practices were horrifying—human sacrifice especially. Motolinía,
one of the first Spanish clergy to arrive in Mexico, described in appalling
detail how huge numbers of prisoners of war, sometimes fifty or more,
were given up to the gods, their blood and various body parts—ears,
lips, arms, hearts—ripped off while they were still alive as offerings.

Zumárraga sought out Aztec idols and other religious objects and
destroyed them. In reaction, Motolinía wrote in his book *Historia de
Los Indios de la Nueva España* how the Indians would hide their idols "at
the foot of the crosses or beneath the altar steps, pretending they were
venerating the cross whereas they were actually adoring the demon."

Zumárraga sent his men throughout the countryside in search of Aztec books and religious objects. Using bribery and torture, they located all of the best collections and destroyed them, including almost every book. This particular act of barbarism was not without precedent. At almost the same time, in 1526, the Ottomans took Budapest and, wishing to annihilate the conquered culture, burned down their science library.

Zumárraga was eventually removed from office for excessive cruelty after he burned an Aztec leader at the stake, but his book-burning campaign was one of the most successful in history. Generally, cultures have recovered from book burning, but in the case of the Aztecs, much of their culture remains lost. Their language lives on in rural Mexico, as do some religious practices, passed on from generation to generation, but much of their learning is gone. A culture that had been literate at a time when Europe had neither writing nor books has become largely an oral culture dependent on memory.

The Mayans suffered the same fate as the Aztecs; their entire library, except the three overlooked codices sent abroad, was burned by a Spanish missionary, Diego de Landa Calderón, in 1549. A Franciscan from Spain sent to the Yucatan to convert the local Mayan population, Calderón wrote his own book on Mayan culture and traditions years after destroying all their books.

THE SPANISH PRINTED the first books in Mexico, on imported Spanish paper, at a time when printing was still a fairly new craft in Europe. They wanted to provide the indigenous people with small-format primers, catechisms, and books of grammar in order to teach them how to be good Christians. To help in this endeavor, the Spanish church contracted Juan Cromberger, a leading printer from Seville, himself the son of a German printer, who in turn enlisted Italian printer Giovanni Paoli to establish a press in Mexico. Paoli and his wife were to labor without salary, with only the barest of living expenses and only two helpers, and produce three thousand sheets of paper daily. After ten years, they were to return to Spain, where they would receive one-fifth of whatever profits their enterprise had generated.

But then a stroke of good luck befell the Paolis. After only a year, Cromberger died. They Hispanicized their name to the Pablos, inherited the equipment Cromberger had lent them, and turned their operation into a profitable business, acquiring land and living well. In 1550 they hired a well-regarded punch cutter, Antonio de Espinosa, and a type founder, Diego de Montoya. The Pablos included woodcut illustrations in their books and, starting in 1554, italic type. In 1559 Espinosa broke away and started his own print shop.

Tenochtitlán became Mexico City. The Europeans who lived there intermarried with the local people, and they and their children, a new mestizo population of mixed blood, wanted European paper. French and Spanish papermakers became interested in selling to the market in New Spain and, typical of a colonial economy, rags from New Spain were shipped to Spain to make paper to be sold back in the Americas. Paper was needed in Mexico for accounting, books, and government documents.

The Mexican printers all used imported Spanish paper—that was the rule of colonialism. But finally the Spanish recognized that the system was not practical and built their first paper mill in Mexico in 1575. Papermakers Hernán Sánchez de Muñón and Juan Cornejo were granted a twenty-year exclusive contract to make paper in the village of Culhuácan just south of Mexico City. Printing caught on in the Spanish colonies much faster than did papermaking. The second printing press in the New World was built in Lima, Peru, in 1584, and it used paper imported from Spain.

TODAY, AMATE IS still made in Mexico by the Otomi people, who live in the mountains in the central highlands of the Puebla state. The village of San Pablito is famous for its "paper making." But the Otomi did not move to San Pablito and start their industry until after the Spanish Conquest, which had destroyed many amate operations elsewhere.

Before the Spanish Conquest, forty-two Aztec villages produced amate. Now, none of those villages continue that tradition.

In San Pablito, the villagers cannot make enough amate to satisfy a booming market, mostly composed of tourists and artists. The amate is made by women and children, because there, as in many Mexican villages, many of the men have left for better-paying work in Mexican or American cities. But the biggest problem the villagers face in keeping up with the demand for amate is the lack of trees. The fig and mulberry species there are in danger of extinction.

To make amate, Otomi women pound the bark against boards, dry it in the sun, and peel off its inner layer. The stones they use for pounding are identical to the ones archaeologists have found in Aztec digs. The Otomi amate has the feel of true paper. It is vanilla-colored, but is highly textured and so not well-suited for writing or printing. Many Otomi and other indigenous people in the area use amate primarily for a feast that is held to honor the spirit of Montezuma, believed to be living in the mountains. The people present the spirit with dolls and other objects made from amate because they believe that Montezuma will return one day to resume his rule. If so, he will want his paper tribute.

Chapter 10

THE TRUMPET CALL

|||||||||||||||||

The art of printing is a commendable one,
as it were the final trumpet call of the world.

—MARTIN LUTHER

O NE CLASSIC EXAMPLE OF THE TECHNOLOGICAL FALLACY at work is the Protestant Reformation of the early sixteenth century. Many historians claim that without printing, it wouldn't have happened. However, just as many believe that this is not true. For example, French historians Lucien Febvre and Henri-Jean Martin wrote in *L'Apparition du livre*, "It is not part of our intention to revive the ridiculous thesis that the Reformation was the child of the printing press."

It would be closer to the truth to say that the printing press was the child of the Reformation. The Reformation was the first movement to use printing to spread its propaganda and was a major reason why printing was invented where and when it was. After all, Europeans had known for a long time how to build a press, how to carve metal, how to cast lead, how to ink and print a carved image, and they might have started printing with moveable type at any time. It is not a coincidence that Germany, seething with unrest and new ideas and an appetite for change, was the place where printing was invented. The activists of the Protestant Reformation seemed to intuitively understand the potential of this new technology and used the printing press so well that it served as a kind of organizing model for every movement since then, until the rise of the Internet.

Traditionally, before the printing press, ideas were spread through oratory, especially sermons. But once people could read, there was a more effective method of dissemination. The seventeenth-century novelist and rebel Daniel Defoe, who was once literally pilloried for his pamphlets, said, "The preaching of sermons is speaking to a few of mankind, printing books is talking to the whole world."

Among the writers of the Northern Renaissance, there was none more influential and emblematic of the new age and new way of thinking than Gerrit Gerritszoon, who renamed himself Desiderius Erasmus. Born in Rotterdam in 1466, he was the illegitimate son of a doctor's daughter and a man who ran away to become a monk. Though he wrote in classical Latin, he was one of the important new voices of reform in the Church, and his thinking deeply influenced the Reformation. Nonetheless, he himself refused to join the Reformation movement or ally himself with Martin Luther. He remained a loyal Catholic all his life.

Like Defoe, Erasmus believed that the only way to effectively spread ideas to large numbers of people was through books. For his publisher, he chose Johann Froben of Basel, Switzerland, who with his son would soon help turn Basel into a leading printing center. Erasmus's work was illustrated by the famed artist Hans Holbein, and his metal plates were cut by a former Parisian named Jakob Faber, né Jacques Lefèvre.

In 1508, a printer named Johann Rhau-Grunenberg moved to Wittenberg, Germany, attracted by its newly founded university. Eight years later, in 1516, he printed Martin Luther's first works. The following year, Luther, himself an Augustinian monk, printed "The Ninety-Five Theses on the Power and Efficacy of Indulgences," a critique of Church venality and corruption. According to legend, Luther posted his manifesto on the door of the Castle Church of Wittenberg. Many historians now doubt this story of the church door, but Luther did print the document, and even though the original had been in Latin, a version printed in German was widely circulated and launched the Reformation as a popular movement.

After that, the demand for printed material from Luther erupted. Part of the excitement was the fact that the printed material was in vernacular German—something rarely seen before. Other Wittenberg printers started publishing Luther's tracts, and a Bible as well. Among them was Melchior Lotther, originally from Leipzig, who printed Luther's Bible in both Low and High German on three printing presses working simultaneously. It was the first good translation of a Bible into spoken language. Over the next two years, the book sold out fourteen editions in Wittenberg alone. It was then reprinted all over Germany and sold 410 editions between 1522 and 1546. Historian Henri-Jean Martin estimated that between 1518 and 1523, one-third of all publications in Germany were produced by the Reformation.

Between 1517 and 1520, Martin Luther issued thirty publications. According to historian Elizabeth L. Eisenstein, he sold 300,000 copies of these publications in all, a conservative estimate, which would be a good sales record even today. Considering that there were only between 13 and 14 million Germans at the time, that sales number is even more impressive. Luther's Reformation marked the first written revolution; that is, the first movement to be spread through the use of paper—and not just words, for the publications included satirical woodcuts, such as images of clergymen with the heads of wolves. From the 1520s on, German printing was at the service of political and social movements, with inexpensively printed pamphlets in vernacular German sold by street peddlers doing especially well.

In a quotation that was often repeated, Martin Luther said that the printing press was a gift from God—"God's highest and extremist act of grace." The idea he espoused was that God gave man the printing press to open people's eyes. This was an updated version of the ancient belief that God provided written language.

Both sides of the Reformation, Protestant and Catholic, recognized the power of the printed word. The sixteenth-century British Protestant historian John Foxe wrote in his hugely popular 1563 *Book of Martyrs*, "Either the pope must abolish knowledge and printing or printing must at length root him out."

From Germany, the Protestant cause spread to France, and new French printers emerged in Protestant strongholds such as La Rochelle. Much printing work was still done in Lyon, but once the Catholics gained control of the city, many of the printers who were involved in the Reformation moved to Geneva. Protestant printing turned Geneva into a major publishing center, especially after 1541, when French Protestant leader John Calvin established his ministry in the city. The Protestant movement also led to the growth of printing back home in Frankfurt, which thanks to its newly established book fairs, became the hub of European publishing. The Frankfurt book fair is still a major event in the book-publishing world today.

The Reformation led to a new way of spreading information, through printing not only books but also tracts, posters, and pamphlets written in simple, vernacular language. A poster was printed to announce every event of the movement. The stances that Luther was noted for, and is remembered for today, were not great sermons or speeches, but posters and tracts that he allegedly affixed to church doors. Only two weeks after such a poster was created, it would arrive in every town in Germany. Posters attacking the pope would show up overnight. Luther himself was surprised at the extent of public interest in his printed material, and their response prompted him to produce even more. The printers were happy to comply. Sometimes the Church fought back with posters of its own.

At times, it seemed as though the printing presses could not keep up with the demand for Luther's work, especially pamphlets, known as *Flugschriften*, or "quick writing." One pamphlet titled "To the Christian Nobility of the German Nation" was printed on August 18, 1520, and had to be reprinted one week later. In three weeks, 4,000 copies were given out. In two years, thirteen editions and about 50,000 copies were printed.

The printers themselves belonged to a new bourgeoisie that had little fondness for the established Church; much of their clientele consisted of secular humanists. They devoted themselves to printing for the Protestants, and many refused to print for the Church. In a sense, it was the beginning of modern publishing, because the Reformation printers, rather than finding a wealthy patron to support them, would often finance their own publishing. And publishing could be profitable.

FLUGSCHRIFTEN DISTRIBUTED THROUGHOUT the German countryside led to a broad peasant uprising in 1524 and 1525, the so-called German Peasant War. But the peasants had few arms, and the aristocracy and their armies massacred them. An estimated 100,000 peasants were killed.

In France, the night of October 17, 1534, is remembered as the Affaire des Placards, the poster affair. On that night posters were mysteriously placed in the most conspicuous public places of Paris, Blois, Tours, Orléans, and Rouen. One was even hung on the bedroom door of King François I, who was asleep in his Loire valley castle in Amboise. The Protestant posters denounced Roman Catholicism and bore the provocative title "Genuine articles on the horrific, great and unbearable abuses of the papal mass, invented directly contrary to the Holy Supper of our Lord, sole mediator and sole savior Jesus Christ."

Although the posters were printed anonymously, it later came out that their author was Antoine de Marcourt, a pastor from the northern region of Picardy. Marcourt had already printed a number of anti-Catholic works, some published by Pierre de Vingle, who in 1535 had issued the first Bible in French.

The Affaire des Placards only provoked King François into implementing harsher anti-Protestant measures. But printed paper was now firmly established in France as a way to organize a dissident movement. In the future, it would be used with greater success.

Chapter 11

REMBRANDT'S
DISCOVERY

||||||||||||||||||

LEARLY THERE ARE CERTAIN PREREQUISITES FOR PAPER-
making. The Dutch had three of the most important: a population with
a need and desire for paper (that is, a growing commercial class, engineers, scientists, mathematicians, and artists); a large enough population
to produce enough rags to make paper (Dutch linen was plentiful and
famous throughout Europe); and waterways on which to build paper
mills (there are few countries with more waterways than Holland; all
Dutch live near water).

And yet for a very long time, the Dutch made no paper of their own.
Their printers depended on the Germans, French, and Swiss. This was
due in part to Holland's struggle for nationhood. From 1384 until 1581 the
Hapsburgs, first from Burgundy and then from Spain, ruled the country,
and France and Spain served as their source for paper. The Dutch started
one of the earliest printing industries in Europe without ever developing
a papermaking industry. The first mention of Dutch-made paper is from
1586, when their printing industry was already more than one hundred

years old. It appears in a government decree authorizing Hans van Aelst and Jan Luipart to establish a paper mill near Dordrecht.

The only drawback to making paper in Holland is the fact that, with the exception of a small hook of land in the south, it is completely flat. Its ubiquitous waterways do not generate enough power to drive a waterwheel. But by the time the Dutch finally developed a papermaking industry, they had already solved that problem with an ingenious machine that they used to grind grain and spices—a high-mounted wheel with sails on the tips of its spokes and powered by the wind.

Windmills have become associated more with Holland than with any other country, but they were not a Dutch invention. They date back to ancient Persia and China, and first appeared in northern Europe in the village of Weedley, Yorkshire, England in 1185. Historians believe that the English, who apparently had no knowledge of Persia or China at the time, took the idea from somewhere in continental Europe, but no record of this has been found.

Watermills generated about 20 horsepower of energy, and windmills only 14. Neither was wind power as reliable as waterpower; some days, a mill could not operate at all. But in a flat, windswept area with no downhill rushes of water, wind power was an important alternative. Windmills were introduced to Holland in the thirteenth century, possibly earlier.

Zaanland is a peaty area just north of Amsterdam. Well suited for windmills, it became an important milling center in the fourteenth century. Nearby Amsterdam was becoming an international port, and Zaanland had a water connection for moving bulky products to the city. First, the Zaanland region milled grain, then cut lumber, and finally, became one of the most famous papermaking centers in Europe.

Zaanland papermaking had begun with two men, Jan Simonz Honig and Pieter Janz van der Ley. Their two families intermarried and became wealthy. Their most famous mill was De Bijkorf, which means "beehive" and is a reference to Jan Simonz's surname, Honig, which means honey.

Some historians believe that De Oude Ganse (the old goose) or

DeWitte Ganse (the white goose) was the first paper mill to be established in Zaan, in 1605. Other historians believe that the first was De Kauwer (the chewer), in 1616. Whatever the case, the first mills made gray, blue, and brown paper, most of it very thick, some of it cardboard. Much of the paper was used for wrapping and packaging, though artists also used it. They drew in black and white chalk, sometimes adding gray pastel, on blue-gray paper. Pieter Van der Faes, a seventeenth-century Dutch artist who made his career while living in England, where he was known as Sir Peter Lely, was the first to use this technique, and it became popular.

ONE OF THE few significant changes in the technology of papermaking was developed by the Dutch between 1630 and 1665. Used in Zaanland mills beginning in the early 1670s, it was a device for rendering rags into pulp. Known throughout Europe as "the Hollander beater," it could produce more pulp in a day than a stamper could produce in a week. Despite its nickname, it used metal blades to *chop* rags into pulp, whereas the stamper beat rags into pulp.

As so often happens when a cheaper and more efficient technology is introduced, some claimed that the Hollander beater produced an inferior product. Chopping the rags in the beater produced much shorter fibers than those produced by the stampers, and long fibers make for stronger, more flexible paper. The Hollander beater paper required more sizing to make it stronger and this made it less favorable for printing at first. But the Hollander beater could be adjusted, its blades raised to avoid short fibers when desired, and soon the Dutch were producing excellent paper. Within a year of installing the beaters, Holland became a white-paper exporter and a major international competitor.

The Hollander beater was also more efficient at removing dirt from rags, because it utilized continuous washing. One of the first books ever written about papermaking, *The Art of Paper Making*, published by the French Royal Academy of Sciences in 1761 and written by Jérôme de Lalande, a leading early astronomer who has a moon crater named after him, discussed the advantages of the Hollander beater. De Lalande observed that during the Hollander's beating and washing process, you could see the pulp gradually becoming whiter.

The Hollander simplified rag sorting as well, because it could beat different grades of rags together. When the stampers mixed different grades together, coarse, inferior paper was produced. Different rags required different beating times. Rag sorting, almost always done by women, was a skilled job. It was also a very unpleasant one. The rags were filthy and often reeked. Sometimes they carried diseases, including a noxious dust that could settle in the lungs. De Lalande wrote that the eighteenth-century French sorters could rapidly divide rags into fine, medium, and coarse grades. Sometimes, he said, they even sorted them into seven grades, the coarsest of which they discarded.

Because the Hollander beater was faster, it produced cheaper paper. The French, British, and other papermakers found it very difficult to compete with Dutch paper until they acquired Hollander beaters too.

As the Dutch gained a reputation for fine paper, their paper workers, including their rag sorters, became in demand. In the eighteenth

Women sorting rags for paper. Diderot, Trade and Industry, *Volume II.*

century, when the Swedish wanted to build up their paper industry by hiring Dutch workers, one of the first that they took was a Dutch rag sorter. The Swedes also used Zaanland papermakers to help them produce higher-quality currency. And in the early eighteenth century, Zaanland papermakers went as far as Russia to help them build their paper industry.

The Dutch also became expert at a process for preparing rags called "souring." Buttermilk or sour milk was added to the rags; later, fermented bran or rye was used instead. The rags were soaked for five or six days, and then taken out and washed. The process was repeated, and then the rags were left out in a field until dry and fairly white. The process could take six to eight months, and was an important and extremely lucrative industry in Haarlem. Its workers were exclusively women. Not all Dutch paper was made from soured rags, but the finest paper was. Souring ended after 1799 when a Scottish chemist, Charles Tenant, discovered bleach by passing chlorine through lime.

Jérôme de Lalande devoted several pages of his book to comparing French and Dutch paper. He highlighted several points in favor of the French: their paper was thinner and stronger and didn't tear as easily. But he finally concluded that Dutch paper was superior, for a variety of reasons: the Dutch weren't as obsessed with whiteness; they were more frugal and less obsessed with money; and they made their paper "more slowly, more carefully, and with more precautions."

PRINTING IN WHAT was called the Lowlands, now the Netherlands and Belgium, coincided with their Renaissance, which took place somewhat later than the Italian Renaissance and earlier than the English. This is more than a coincidence. The ideas, literature, and art that were being created in the Lowlands required a more efficient writing system than the old one of scribes writing on parchment could provide.

Lowlands books of the fifteenth century, like those in Germany, were heavily illustrated with woodcuts. These early illustrations, with their shaded, draped fabrics and wooded backgrounds, were clearly an attempt to imitate the great painting that was flowering at the time. But they were not great woodcuts—nothing near the standards of Dürer. Some of the first Lowlands books published, by Colard Mansion of Bruges, were in Flemish. A calligrapher and a scribe, Mansion saw how the world was changing. He started printing in 1476, and his first book was Ovid's *Metamorphoses*, for which he did the woodcuts himself.

Holland's woodcutting centers were Delft and Haarlem, the latter being home to the leading printer Jacob Bellaert, who produced seventeen books between 1483 and 1486. His principal illustrator was called the "Master of Jacob Bellaert"; his real name is not known, but his woodcuts are very painterly and he is thought to have been either a master painter or the student of a master painter. The popular books of Delft and Haarlem centered on stories from the Bible or classical mythology, and could have as many as seventy-five woodcuts apiece. One of the most popular of these early books was *Dialogus creaturarum moralizatus*, on the subject of animals and minerals, published by Gerard Leeu in Gouda in 1480. It had 121 woodcuts.

As in Germany, several of the great Dutch and Flemish painters became book illustrators. In Antwerp, a center for woodcuts, a leading shop was owned by a man named Jerôme Cock, who happened to be both the engraver and father-in-law of the great Flemish painter Pieter Bruegel. Bruegel was an unusual artist for his day in that his subject matter was almost exclusively the lives of peasants. And woodcuts and drawings were not a sideline occupation for Bruegel. He was deeply interested in producing quality art on paper—and not only drawings in their own right, but also drawings designed to be woodcuts.

Christophe Plantin was a French businessman who opened a bindery in Antwerp in 1540. Binderies were good business, as the prolific printing presses sold their books unbound. Six years later, the entrepreneurial Plantin went into the printer/publisher trade and became famous for his so-called Polyglot Bible, commissioned by Philip II of Spain. It was composed of eight volumes in Aramaic, Greek, Hebrew, Latin, and Syriac.

He published thirteen sets for the king, printed on vellum, and 1,200 for the public, printed on paper. Vellum was still considered the finest of all writing materials. Plantin liked to have his illustrations done by recognized artists and on copper plates rather than wood. Copper-plate etching involved a different printing process, and in Antwerp, much of it was done by Bruegel's printer, Jerôme Cock. Plantin used many etchings by the Flemish master painter Peter Paul Rubens, who was considered to be the greatest painter of his age.

Rubens demanded to be paid well for his illustrations, and he may have been somewhat disdainful of the work, since he would do illustrations only on Sundays—as if to say it was not part of his real work. Rubens did his best book illustration early on. By 1637, he was passing

Portrait of Christophe Plantin by Hendrick Goltzius, circa 1590.

it on to others in his studio and allowing them to sign his name to it. Nevertheless, books circulated far more than art, and Rubens's illustrations greatly enhanced his fame and reputation in much of Europe.

Partly due to the influence of Plantin, etching and other copperplate printing techniques completely took over book publishing, first in the Lowlands but eventually in all of Europe. Woodcuts would almost completely disappear until the nineteenth century, when they would become popular again.

WOODCUTS AND ETCHINGS are essentially black-and-white. Colors can be painted in or created by printing with several blocks in different-colored ink, and drawing techniques such as crosshatching can be used for shadows, but woodcuts and etchings do not have true shading.

The first printmaking technique to make grays, or halftones, possible was called mezzotint, and was invented in 1642 by Ludwig von Siegen, a German. The technique, which spread quickly to Holland and England, involved spiky rollers that "roughed up the plate" to grab ink; those areas could then be smoothed down to varying degrees to achieve the desired lightness.

About ten years after mezzotint was invented, Jan van de Velde in Amsterdam introduced a technique known as aquatint. Aquatint is a method of etching with a heated resin that is applied by a brush, followed by an acid bath, and then more resin painting so that there are different gradations from black to gray to white. The great master of this technique was the eighteenth-century Spanish artist Francisco Goya, who combined aquatint with the crisp lines of conventional etching.

The greatest paper artist of Holland, however, was Rembrandt Harmenszoon van Rijn. He was to etching what Dürer was to woodcut, the master who set the standard for all who followed. But unlike Dürer, who was brilliant in paper but struggled with painting, Rembrandt was good at almost everything. In his lifetime, he produced approximately

Rembrandt Harmenszoon van Rijn. Self-Portrait Leaning on a Stone Sill. *Etching, 1639.*

600 paintings, 300 etchings, and 1400 drawings, and is best known today as one of the greatest painters of all time.

The only thing at which Rembrandt did not excel was book illustration. His etchings were too fine to hold up to constant reproduction, and in some of the books he illustrated, his work was replaced with that of other artists in later editions. Only a few books with Rembrandt's illustrations have survived, one being *La Piedra Gloriosa o de la Estatua de Nebuchadnesar,* published in 1654 by his friend Samuel Menasseh Ben Israel, the first to print in Hebrew in Holland. The book, which relates a set of mystical tales, is credited with persuading Oliver Cromwell to let Jews back into England.

Rembrandt had his own press and an important collection of master etchings from around Europe. He did his own printing so that he could control the final image, and sometimes did several acid bitings of different periods of time to create lighter and heavier lines. Sometimes he left ink on part of the plate for a shadowy area. Toward the end of his life, for reasons that remain mysterious, he produced very little. Depression is sometimes cited, but some historians believe that he was simply trying to move on to a new idea that he never found. Because of a lack of work, and an absence of income, he was forced to sell both his press and print collection.

LEARNING TO USE the Chinese compass made the Dutch the great international traders of the seventeenth century. Dutch skill in using maps and nautical charts had also been steadily improving since the sixteenth century, thanks largely to the master works of the Flemish cartographer Gerardus Mercator, who coined the word "atlas." Mercator is famous for his 1569 world map, printed from twenty-four large copper plates, with ingenious projections that account for the curvature of the Earth while still keeping sailing courses in straight lines. One year later, his friend Abraham Ortelius, noted for the brilliant colors in his wooden engravings, produced *Theatrum orbis terrarium*, a book of fifty-three maps that is considered to be the first truly modern atlas.

In 1602 the Dutch East India Company was established to enable trade with Asia, and in the years that followed, Amsterdam became the port from which Europe finally began to learn about China and its neighbors. Up until then, most Europeans still knew almost nothing about the Far East and still believed that they—or, as some more generously suggested, the Arabs—had invented paper. Paper was thought to have evolved from Egyptian papyrus, which is why the word for paper in most European languages either stems from the word "papyrus" or the Greek word *khartes*, which means papyrus.

In the seventeenth century, however, when European traders started frequenting China and Japan, they were surprised to learn that its peoples were using paper. Their immediate assumption was that the Asians had somehow picked up—but not perfected—the European art of papermaking. The Asians wrote with a brush rather than a quill like the Europeans, which meant that Asian paper required a different finish; the quill worked poorly on this finish. The European traders in Asia would resort to using the local paper when their own supplies ran out, but complained about its "inferiority" and pleaded with their home offices to send them more "good paper."

The traders almost never bothered to ship the Asians' so-called inferior paper back to Europe—clearly no one there would want it. But the Dutch, who enjoyed a virtual monopoly on trade with Japan from 1639 until 1854, twice brought some Japanese paper to Amsterdam, in 1643 and 1644. Rembrandt, who would scour the city in search of the best paper for his drawings and etchings, found some of this Japanese paper and purchased it. Thin and yet strong and supple with its long fibers, the paper had a way of grabbing the ink. Plates could be inked more lightly, yielding very delicate images. Rembrandt started doing many of his etchings on Japanese paper. He also found good Indian paper and printed etchings on that as well.

In the seventeenth and eighteenth century, Jesuit missionaries went to Asia, where they learned and brought back the legend of Cai Lun, the man whom the Chinese believe invented paper. In the 1730s, Jean-Baptiste du Halde, a Jesuit priest, wrote *The General History of China*, the definitive book on the subject, by interviewing seventeen Jesuits who had been there—he himself never left Paris. A popular book, it was republished in English in London in 1736. "A great mandarin," du Halde wrote, "made use of the bark of different trees, and of old worn out pieces of silk and hemp cloth, by constant boiling of which matter he brought it to a liquid consistence and reduced it to a sort of thin paste, of which he made different sorts of thin paper." Still, Europeans remained convinced that making paper from rags was a thirteenth-century Italian or German invention.

It took centuries for the rest of the art world to catch on to Rembrandt's discovery about the quality of Japanese paper. But in the nineteenth century, Japanese paper started being shipped to London and Paris, and artists such as J.A.M. Whistler, Edgar Degas, Paul Gauguin, and Édouard Manet all made prints with Japanese paper. And another century later, following the archaeological expeditions of the late 1800s and early 1900s, the Europeans finally came to understand that paper was indeed a Chinese invention.

In seventeenth-century Europe, however, Japanese paper remained Rembrandt's special material.

Chapter 12

THE
TRAITOROUS
CORRUPTION OF
ENGLAND

||||||||||||||||||||

Thou hast most traitorously corrupted the youth of the realm in erecting a grammar school, and whereas, before, our fore-fathers had no other books but the score and the tally, thou has caused printing to be used; and contrary to the King, his crown, and dignity, thou has built a paper-mill. It will be proved to thy face that thou hast men about thee that usually talk of a noun and a verb, and such abominable words as no Christian ear can endure to hear.

—WILLIAM SHAKESPEARE,
Henry VI Part 2, ACT 4, SCENE 7

THE BRITISH ISLES DID NOT HAVE A PRINTER UNTIL WIL-
liam Caxton set up shop in Westminster in 1476. More surprising, he printed on paper imported from the Lowlands because there was no British papermaker until John Tate established the Sele Mill in Hert-fordshire in 1495. There are a number of countries that have this kind of reverse history—first printing and then papermaking. A printing press was easier to set up than a paper mill. Printing presses needed neither water nor power.

Caxton was born in Kent about 1422 but later spent thirty years in the Lowlands, as a merchant and British consul-general. While he was there, in the 1470s, printing began in the town of Louvain in what is now Belgium. Like many commercial people of his generation, Caxton was a man of letters. In 1469 he began translating Raoul Lefèvre's *Recuyell of the Historyes of Troye*, a somewhat fanciful history in which ancient Troy resembles a European walled city with red-tile roofs. Caxton put the project aside, but his patron, Margaret, duchess of Burgundy, sister of Edward IV, urged him to finish. According to the often-repeated, though hard-to-believe story, the English colony in Bruges loved his book and he was wearing himself out writing copies for them—there is a record of him complaining about it—so he went to Cologne in 1471 and learned to print. There he is believed to have studied under Ulrich Zell, the priest from Mainz who started Cologne's first print shop. In 1473, he returned to Bruges, built a print shop of his own, and in 1474 published his translation of *Recuyell of the Historyes of Troye*.

In the fall of 1476, Caxton returned to England, rented space in Westminster, and established a press. In 1477 he produced the first book ever printed in England, *Dictes and Sayings of the Philosophers*, a compendium of passages of wisdom that Anthony Woodville, 2nd Earl Rivers, had translated from the French while on a pilgrimage to Santiago de Compostela in northwest Spain. Woodville was the brother-in-law of King Edward, and after the death of Edward in 1483, the duke of Gloucester had Woodville beheaded—an unseemly ending for England's first printed author.

Woodville's book had a complicated origin. It was based on a French translation of a Latin book interpreted by a French aristocrat, Guillaume de Thionville, which itself was derived from an Arab text, *Mukhtar al-hikam wa mahasin al-kalim* (Choice maxims and finest sayings), written in the eleventh century by al-Mubashshir ibn Fatiq, an Egyptian emir. Caxton's only revision to the book was to ask Woodville to add some of Socrates's comments on women; Socrates, at least according to Plato, had argued for equal rights for women and was against ascribing gender roles.

England was the only European country besides Germany to have printing introduced by a native. Caxton printed thirty books in his first three years. None of them are known for their beauty or the quality of the type, but his historic significance is inarguable. He was the first printer of Chaucer. Among the 103 known editions of Chaucer that he printed, twenty are Caxton's own reworking. The fact that Chaucer wrote in the Midlands dialect, one of four prevailing dialects of English at the time, had an enormous influence on the future of English. One of the consequences of printing is that it tends to standardize language. Caxton and subsequent London printers published in a local variation on Chaucer's Midlands dialect, and so gave the London way of speaking dominance in England.

By 1480, Caxton already had competition. John Lettou, who is thought to have come from the Baltics, set up a print shop in London. Caxton then sent for a colleague from Bruges, a Dutchman named Wynkyn de Worde, to help him produce more. After Caxton's death in 1491, Wynkyn de Worde took over his business.

De Worde was a considerably different kind of publisher from the sort that Caxton had been. Caxton started English printing; de Worde popularized it. He published inexpensive books with mass appeal. Caxton had rarely used illustrations, but most of de Worde's four hundred books were heavily illustrated. He stopped buying expensive foreign paper and purchased his paper from John Tate. In his translation, the first in English, of Bartholomaeus's *De proprietatibus rerum* (On the properties of things), a thirteenth-century forerunner of an encyclopedia by a French Franciscan, are the lines:

> *And John Tate the younger Ioye mote he broke*
> *Whiche late hathe in Englande doo make this paper thynne*
> *That now in our Englysh this book is printed Inne*

De Worde's publications were mostly religious in nature, but he also published romantic novels and poetry, including the work of John Skelton, a popular poet in Tudor England and the favorite teacher of the future Henry VIII. De Worde became wealthier from printing than any other early British printer.

One of 140 European towns that began printing in the last quarter of the fifteenth century, London was considered to be an important printing center by 1500. William de Machlinia from the Lowlands became a major printer in London, while Richard Pynson from Rouen was the first printer in England to use Roman type, later also used by most other British and American printers. Pynson too influenced the standardization of the English language, following Caxton, in the use of what is called Chancery Standard, which is largely London English but also borrows from the Midlands dialect. Pynson published five hundred books and was the official printer for Henry VIII.

The English learned other things from the Protestant Reformation in Germany besides printing. Catherine of Aragon was only twenty-four when she married Henry VIII, but they did not have a suitable heir—that is to say, a son—and once she was in her forties it seemed she never would. Henry asked the pope to sanction a divorce, but since the Roman Catholic Church does not recognize divorce, the pope refused. Henry then asked the leading cleric in England, the archbishop of Canterbury, to recognize a divorce. He agreed, and so Henry decided that England would leave the Roman Catholic Church and establish its own Church of England. This was a delicate public-relations problem. A Church of England would need popular support, and the argument that Rome should not be allowed to dictate English affairs could resonate with the population. But it needed to be sold. Thomas Cromwell, the king's chief minister, both negotiated the move with Parliament and, like the German Protestants, turned to the printers to garner popular support. Cromwell published a series of tracts arguing the anti-papist cause in vernacular English, and the pamphlets and their ideas were well received. This was the new way of doing things in the sixteenth century.

DESPITE THE EXISTENCE of John Tate's mill and others, printing developed more rapidly in England than did papermaking, and printers continued to buy their paper from the Continent. Yet, thickly veined with rivers and brooks that swiftly fell through chutes and falls, England was an ideal place for papermaking. Watermills were common, and there were even windmills. The mills were most commonly used to grind grain, but all it took to turn a grain mill into a paper mill was a shaft and wheel driving a few stamping hammers, a vat or tub, and some molds. Mills near London also had easy access to rags and a short shipping time to presses.

Most of the early paper mills failed. Tate's Sele Mill operated for only a few years. The British papermakers could not get enough rags, and they could not compete with imported French paper, which dominated the British market. And, as so often happened in English history, the French were to blame, or so the British claimed: The French bought up all the rags and shipped them to France. They sold their white paper for less than it cost the British to make it. The French authorities relentlessly harassed French papermakers who attempted to work in England.

German papermakers saw opportunities farther afield than London. They built a mill near Cambridge in 1550, and one in Scotland in 1590 in Darly Near Edinburgh on the Water of Leith River. By the nineteenth century, the Water of Leith would be a major paper center with as many as ninety mills in operation. Some historians believe that Tate's mill also employed Germans. John Spilman, a goldsmith to the queen, was one of the most successful German papermakers in England. In 1588 the Crown granted him a lease of two grain mills at the royal manor of Bicknores, Dartford, on the River Darent in Kent, and he converted them into paper mills.

Spilman was a man who knew how to use his royal connections. His watermark, for example, was a crown with the letters "E. R.," for Elizabeth Regina, the queen. One year after opening his mill, he persuaded the Crown to grant him exclusive rights to making white writing paper, control over the manufacture of other types of paper, and most important, a monopoly on rag collection in the kingdom. But paper was also important to Elizabeth personally. No British monarch before her had ever used so much paper. She wrote speeches, translations, prayers, poems, and essays on paper. She also wanted Spilman's mill to succeed because she was troubled by the extent to which England relied on imports from France. When James I later became king, he visited the mill and awarded Spilman a knighthood.

Historians suspect that Spilman knew nothing about papermaking, though as a German he probably had more general knowledge of the trade than did the average Englishman. He brought papermakers from Germany to work his mills, and it was probably their knowledge that led the mills to produce such high-quality white paper. Mills making lesser-quality paper coveted his German workers, but the Crown forbade them from switching employers. Spilman's exclusive rights lasted for eight years, and were then renewed for another fourteen.

Over the course of the next one hundred years, papermaking became an established trade near London, especially in Kent, Buckinghamshire, Middlesex, and Worcestershire. Between 1601 and 1650, forty-one paper mills began operations in England, twenty-three of them within thirty miles of London. There were also a few mills farther west in Exeter and farther north in Shropshire, Lancashire, and Yorkshire. Like Spilman's mill, many of the paper mills were converted grain mills. Others were converted "fulling mills" from a declining textile trade; fulling was a process of cleaning and thickening wool by beating it, similar to felting.

But the British had entered the game late and had not developed enough skilled workers. They could make brown paper that was good enough for wrapping or even taking notes on, but not enough smooth, white paper suitable for printing. The Reformation in France gave England a new source of papermakers, however. On September 10, 1627, royal French troops fired on La Rochelle, the stronghold of the Huguenots, a French Protestant denomination, and the Church's highest-ranking authority, Cardinal Richelieu, had the city blockaded for fourteen months until it surrendered. Subsequently, the Huguenots were persecuted for many years. Then Louis XIV came to the throne. He expelled three hundred Protestant families from La Rochelle in November 1661, and life for the Huguenots who remained grew even worse. In 1685 Louis XIV revoked the 1598 Edict of Nantes, which had guaranteed rights to French Protestants. A large number of Huguenots fled France, some to found the town of New Rochelle in New York, others to a variety of destinations, including England.

Among the Huguenots who settled in England were many highly skilled papermakers. The French Crown that had tried so rigorously to stop their papermakers from working in England ended up driving them there. Britain received many highly skilled rag-sorting women, vatmen, and businessmen; the latter helped finance and establish a paper industry in Scotland and the Irish Paper Company in Ireland. The French war on Protestants also caused some French paper mills to shut down, reducing their output of the valuable export. Realizing their mistake, the French government attempted to win back some of their papermakers. Numerous French papermakers in England were taken into custody and legal action ensued; others were persuaded to return home, their travel expenses paid for.

PAPERMAKING AND EVEN printing was not always popular in England. As was the case everywhere that paper mills sprang up in Europe, those who lived near the mills complained of the smell and the incessant noise. They also complained that the farmers now had to take their grain farther away to be milled, that the waterwheels were killing the fish, that rags were spreading the plague, and even that they were endangering the royal family, who lived near mills in Windsor. During an attack of plague in 1536, paper mills in Middlesex were closed down, and when the government asked the public to help support the out-of-work papermakers, the locals complained that they had earned better salaries than most artisans and should have saved their money.

The controversy over paper is touched on in Shakespeare's *Henry VI Part 2*. Part of Shakespeare's celebrated War of the Roses cycle, this history play is regarded by many as the worst play Shakespeare ever wrote. However, it is largely remembered among paper and printing history buffs because of Jack Cade and his tirade.

In act 4, scene 7, Jack Cade has come to power and declares that the country will be returning to the old system of oral codes. Henceforth, no laws are to be written down and all existing written laws are to be burned. Saye, from the former regime, is brought before Cade and accused of losing Normandy to the French, undermining English society, corrupting youth by teaching them grammar, and encouraging papermaking and printing. Cade also accuses Saye of surrounding himself with unbearable people who constantly discuss nouns and verbs, and even charges Saye with imprisoning people for illiteracy. Saye meanwhile defends knowledge and proclaims that ignorance is a curse. Cade orders him beheaded, and the next time we see Saye, his head appears on a pike. Shakespeare, like Cervantes a decade later, exposes a contemporary belief that no doubt he did not share. Although theatre is an oral art form, Shakespeare arranged to have both his poetry and his plays printed beginning in 1593, early in his career.

When Cade accuses Saye of erecting a paper mill, it is believed that Shakespeare was referring to Spilman's mill. The events of the play take place in 1450, when there were no paper mills in England. But in Shakespeare's time, there were, and not everyone was happy about it. Shakespeare is clearly castigating Cade for his willful ignorance and for standing in the way of progress. As the scribes of old were keenly aware, literacy is empowering and a threat to despotic rule. Saye's great crime, according to Cade, was not losing Normandy but sending children to school.

Spilman turns up again in English literature in a poem by Thomas Churchyard, an occasional poet and full-time mercenary who fought in Ireland, Scotland, the Lowlands, and France. He fled to Scotland after displeasing Queen Elizabeth, was forgiven in 1583, and returned to England where, in an attempt to stay in the queen's good graces, he penned a 353-line tribute to Spilman and papermaking. The poem was dedicated to Sir Walter Raleigh, just back from fighting for England in Ireland and a favorite of the queen. Printed in 1584 in a large-format fifteen-page book with a lengthy, unmusical title—"A Description and playne discourse of paper, and the whole benefits that Paper brings, with rehersall, and setting foorth in verse a Paper myll built nere Dartford, by a High Germaine, called Master Spilman, Jeweler to the Queen Majestie"—it shows that the parchment-versus-paper debate was still very much alive. The poem also suggests that Churchyard might have been more skilled as a soldier than a poet:

> I prayse the man, that first did Paper make,
> The onely thing that set all virtues forth:
> It shoes new books, and keeps old works awake,
> Much more of price than all the world is worth;
> Though parchment duer, a greater time and space,
> Yet can it not put paper out of place:
> For paper still from man to man doth go,
> When parchment comes to few men's hands you knowe.

FLAX, FROM WHICH linen was made, was the British papermakers' first choice for making paper. When linen was pounded, the fibers frayed, and the frayed threads, known as febrils, interwove to make strong white paper. Cotton, their second choice, did not fray, but flattened, and this gave paper an opaqueness and a softness that was valued for making copper-plate prints such as etchings. Lime was sometimes added to the cotton pulp for whitening. Hemp from cloth or rope was also used, usually for lower grades of brown paper.

The paper was formed on a mold in a vat that contained a mixture of about 2 percent pulp, called *stuff*, and 98 percent warm water. The percentage of the pulp varied slightly depending on the thickness of paper desired, and the water was warmed for the comfort of the vatman, the most skilled tradesman in the operation, whose hands were in the vat the entire day. The vatman held to the mold a wooden frame, known as a *deckle*, from the German or Dutch, which created a slightly uneven edge around the paper sheet as it was formed. After machine-made paper was invented, the deckle edge, as it was called, became a distinguishing and valued characteristic of handmade paper.

The vatman held the mold and deckle firmly but not stiffly, dipped them vertically in the water-pulp mixture, and brought them up again

Jost Amman (1539–1591). Der Papyrer *(the papermaker).*
Zürich-born Amman became one of the leading woodcut artists
in Nuremberg in that city's golden age of woodcut book illustra-
tion. He usually drew the image and let a Formschneider *cut it.*
Among the 1,500 woodcuts for which he is responsible, some of
the most famous, like this one of a vatman, were for the 144
woodcuts he drew from the 1568 Das Ständebuch *(the book of*
trades), featuring poems by Hans Sachs, a Nuremberg native,
shoemaker, and celebrated author of both songs and poems.

with an easy scooping motion—just as the Chinese papermakers had
done more than a millennium earlier. Then he held the mold horizontally and shook it gently until all the water had passed through and an
even layer of fiber remained. Next, the vatman handed the mold to the
coucher next to him. The coucher, whose job title was taken from the
French verb *coucher*, to lay down, turned the mold over onto a layer of

felt and the newly formed sheet of paper dropped out. A sheet of hand-made paper (and this is sometimes true of machine-made paper as well) has two distinct sides, a wire side with a pattern and a felt side that is smooth. An artist can chose to work on either side.

A vatman and a coucher were expected to make a sheet of paper in thirty seconds, and could make between two and four reams of paper a day. Afterward, there was still pressing, drying, sizing, and finishing—usually hand-rubbing with a polished stone—to be done, but the type and quality of the paper had already been determined by the selection of rags, the making of the pulp, and the thirty critical seconds that had passed between the vatman and coucher.

The wet paper, known as a waterleaf, was pressed in felt and dried, hung over horsehair ropes that left a mark known as the back mark. Various techniques were used to rid the sheets of back marks until the nineteenth century, when the papermakers realized that paper should be dried lying flat—"flat-dried." As customers, especially artists, became more demanding, the sizing used to make paper became an important issue too. Paper for different tasks needed different types of sizing.

THE ENGLISH MANUFACTURED paper for many purposes. White paper was for printing, and industrial paper, usually brown or blue, for wrapping, packaging, and encasing firearm cartridges. Brown paper was popular with artists, such as the eighteenth-century painter Thomas Gainsborough, for sketches and works done in charcoal, chalk, and pastels.

Until the eighteenth century, England lacked the craftsmen needed to meet the country's demand for white paper and thus supplemented their small production with imports. Most English paper was brown, though this was more a classification than a color: "brown" paper was just off-color, which sometimes meant gray. Brown wrapping paper was so popular in sixteenth-century England that the British mills couldn't make enough of it, and some brown wrapping paper was imported as well.

Pasteboard, made of several sheets of paper laminated together, was another popular packaging material; it was also used for making playing cards and, occasionally, book covers. Blue paper was in demand as well, perhaps because there was a lot of blue clothing and hence blue rags. It was used as wrapping paper, most famously for wrapping sugar, and books left the printers wrapped in blue paper to be taken to the bindery. Blue paper was also popular with artists.

Papier-mâché, a craft learned from the Japanese despite its French name, which means "chewed paper," became an important industry in eighteenth-century England. It was made from scraps of paper mixed with glue. The English learned how to waterproof papier-mâché, and it became an important element in creating architectural details, such as molding. Everything from coach doors to lightweight canoes to snuff boxes was made of it, and papier-mâché was also found to be more effective than paper in stuffing firearm chambers. Gunpowder needs a well-sealed chamber separate from the bullet in order to explode and effectively propel the bullet forward; plugs made of papier-mâché, called sabots, suited this purpose well. Paper was also rolled into tubes to make gun cartridges containing both powder and balls. The paper used for this purpose was coarse and heavily sized.

Wallpaper became extremely popular in seventeenth-century Europe. The Asians had made the first wallpaper, sometimes hand-painting it and sometimes printing it with wood blocks, and the Europeans started producing wallpaper when they, too, started producing wood blocks. In fact, Albrecht Dürer had designed wallpaper; some of the huge pieces commissioned to him by Emperor Maximilian were essentially wallpaper. But paper as wall decoration did not achieve true popularity until the seventeenth century. By the eighteenth century, England was Europe's leading wallpaper maker, and it was mostly made from English paper. This paper was also used to line boxes and trunks.

By the late eighteenth century, paper of all sorts had become extremely fashionable in England. Decorative paper adorned tea caddies and picture frames, and elaborate paper fans were everywhere. Designing flowers or other objects with colored or gilded paper was a widespread hobby. The English had fallen in love with paper.

Paper was also used as roof covering. Brown paper was coated with rosin, sand, and oil. Later, pitch and tar were used as a coating instead, and both "tar paper" and "rosin paper" are still in use today. In 1776, Henry Cook of the Stoke Holy Cross paper mill in Norfolk developed a paper that was both fireproof and waterproof. Unfortunately, however, he either neglected to use it himself or it didn't work as promised because he lost his mill in an accidental fire.

In 1788, Charles-Louis Ducrest invented a paperboard for use in the construction of buildings, bridges, and even ships. Ironically, its strength was based on the addition of steel filings, which in time were destroyed by corrosion, causing the paperboard to deteriorate.

MARBLING BECAME A British paper specialty. Marbled paper had first been invented in twelfth-century Turkey or Persia, by mixing dyes into liquids that refused to blend, such as olive oil and turpentine, to create a marble-like pattern. Soon it was discovered that more colors and even more intricate patterns—swirls and zigzags, stripes and crests, drops and tears—could also be created, depending on the elements mixed. The process became a closely guarded secret, yet somehow crossed over to Europe, either through the Persians or the Crusaders who had learned about it in the Middle East.

For centuries, the French, Germans, and Dutch were the great marblers of Europe, and so when the secret finally crossed the Channel, the English imitated the Continental work. Marbled paper was primarily used for books, either for endpapers or, as leather became more scarce and expensive, covers. Then an impressive array of seventeenth-century men of science took an interest in the secret. Francis Bacon mentioned it in his writings, and John Evelyn, whose family had made a fortune in gunpowder, introduced it to the Royal Society in London. The Royal Society had been founded by Robert Boyle, the father of chemistry, in order to enable the discussion of the new scientific approach to learning about the world—experimentation. Boyle also took an interest in the secret of marbling.

But English marbling did not come into its own until the

mid-eighteenth century. It is not certain exactly when, because early British marbling is indistinguishable from that of the Germans, French, and Dutch. The first example of marbling that is definitely British-made is in a 1766 pamphlet by Richard Dymott entitled *An Examination of the Rights of the Colonies upon Principles of Law.*

Benjamin Franklin, who was deeply involved in papermaking and printing most of his life, lived in England from 1757 to 1774, representing the colony of Pennsylvania and enjoying the sophistication of London; in fact, he became somewhat of an Anglophile. He was active in the Royal Society for the Arts and through them tried to promote British marbling. But ultimately, realizing that his efforts to reconcile the American colonies and the British mother country that he admired were in vain, he set sail for America and the American cause.

In 1775, Franklin was involved in the printing of American currency. He believed that marbling would be impossible to duplicate and therefore an ideal safeguard against counterfeiters. The British planned to wreak havoc with the colonial economy by flooding it with counterfeit bills. A 1775 $20 bill of colonial money, called Continental currency, featured a thin band of marbling that could not be duplicated.

Two years later Franklin was in Paris, one of three commissioners attempting to secure French support for the American cause. He settled in Passy, on the route to the court in Versailles, and established a printing press for American publications (by then rebels were printers). He managed to get top-quality British paper, a typeface for his press, and apparently something else. Once loans were secured from the French government, Franklin printed promissory notes that somehow featured British marbling, despite the vaunted secrecy of British marblers. It is not known who did this clearly British marbling.

How many British marblers existed in Franklin's time cannot be said because they did their work in absolute secrecy. They often worked at night in laboratories at secret locations, toiling behind locked doors and covered windows. Rooms were even examined for peepholes. It was nearly impossible to learn marbling at that time unless you were born into a marbling family. Even apprentices, who were always relatives, were not entrusted with complete formulas until they were older and deemed trustworthy. Marblers had their own secretive guild, and though they worked with book binderies, kept themselves absolutely separate from the bookbinders' guild. Meanwhile, the bookbinders' guild frequently sent spies into the marblers' guild, attempting to discover their secrets.

A CHANCE DISCOVERY in sixteenth-century England had a huge impact on scientists, mathematicians, storekeepers, writers, artists—in fact, on most everyone who wanted to jot something down on paper. In 1565, as the story goes, a large oak tree was uprooted in a storm in Cumberland and an odd black mineral was discovered clinging to its roots. This led to the digging of England's first graphite mine and the development of the pencil—a cheap, portable, erasable writing tool.

Pencils in Europe are older than paper. The word comes from the Latin name of a type of fine-tipped writing brush, a *penicillum*. The Greeks and Romans also sometimes used metallic lead to write or draw on papyrus, which is the origin of the modern expression "lead pencil"—despite the fact that a modern pencil contains no lead. But technology is only embraced when it answers a society's needs, and only after a society began to write constantly and casually did the pencil become a commonplace tool. According to Henry Petroski's history of the pencil, the first person known to use a graphite pencil was a sixteenth-century Zürich writer named Konrad Gesner. He mentions and even supplies an illustration of a graphite pencil in his 1565 book on fossils.

It was at about this same time that graphite was discovered in Cumberland. Soon afterward, graphite was inserted into a wooden tube and use of the new writing implement spread. By 1600, wooden cases and sticks of graphite were being sold, separately, on the streets of London. Pencils were initially most popular with scientists, but artists and writers used them too. In 1610 one artist recommended that books be marked with a pencil and later the markings erased. Gesner had used his pencil for sketching when researching in the countryside. Others noted that the pencil was a good tool for writing notes when on horseback. By the eighteenth century, artists such as J. M. W. Turner always began a painting by first making a pencil sketch.

AMONG THE EARLIEST books printed in the West were books about science and medicine. In 1483, *Herbal*, a book written in 400 CE by Apuleius Barbarus, was printed in Rome. In 1485, *Gart der Gesundheit* (The garden of health), about medieval herbal medicine, was printed by Peter Schöffer, Gutenberg's former apprentice, in Germany. In seventeenth-century England, the field of modern science was still in its earliest stages, but it was already a pursuit that demanded paper. Scientists took notes and published their findings.

What had previously been thought of as science had been rooted in Aristotle and had dictated a system of debating and reasoning to arrive at what were perceived to be truths. But that method of inquiry was beginning to be questioned. Francis Bacon wrote, "Our present sciences are nothing more than peculiar arrangements of matters already discovered, and not methods for discovery or plans for new operations." He insisted that ideas had to be tested through experiments—and that this process had to involve careful notations and record keeping at every step. "We cannot, however, approve of any mode of discovery without writing, and when that comes into more general use, we may have further hopes," he predicted correctly.

A generation later, Robert Boyle, founder of the Royal Society in London, introduced the use of a scientific methodology that would lay the foundation for modern chemistry. And another generation later, Isaac Newton, the first modern theoretical physicist, used mathematical calculation and physical observation to lay the foundation for both physics and calculus. He developed theories on gravity and the laws of motion, and built the first true telescope, from which he could observe his theories at work in space.

When Newton was twenty-three, sequestered in his room to avoid the plague, he started conducting a series of experiments with a prism, bending a beam of sunlight to pierce through a small hole in a window shade. With the prism and mirrors, he studied the color of light and observed that it broke down into red, green, and blue. He called these primary colors. Then he remixed them, to find that together they formed white light. The three primary colors were separated from one another by other colors made from them—yellow, cyan, and magenta. This is not how artists see color or mix paint, but it is how light mixes, and his experiments led the way to color printing and color photography.

The findings of these early scientists became known because their books were published. Much of modern science is based on works by Boyle, such as the *Sceptical Chemist* and *The General History of Air*, as well as the ten books that Newton published in the late seventeenth century.

As for Bacon, himself the author of numerous books, he made no significant scientific discoveries. However, he is credited with leading the way for Boyle, Newton, and others. As the man who urged experimentation and the necessity of writing down results, Bacon was also less than perfect in his own methodology. In 1626, he was riding in a coach with a doctor, on their way to visit the king, when snow started to fall. The two men began discussing how snow resembled salt and speculated on whether it might have the same preserving qualities with food. Suddenly, infused with enthusiasm, Bacon wanted to conduct a scientific experiment. Stop the coach! he shouted, or so the story goes. He ran to a peasant woman and bought a chicken, which the woman killed and cleaned for them. Then the two scientists, on their hands and knees in the snow, stuffed the chicken with snow and packed snow all around it. The experiment was a success. It did seem to preserve the chicken. But poor Bacon had no time left in which to discover that freezing and salting preserved food in two completely different ways. He died in a matter of days from pneumonia, the first—perhaps the only—martyr to frozen food.

SCRIBES SURVIVED THE age of printing. But they were forced to endure a major demotion—from revered writer to ordinary calligrapher. Some scribes, hoping to regain their status, became printers; but most continued as scribes. There was always some deluxe item that called for the work of a calligrapher. But in the age of printing, the author and not the scribe became the star of literature.

The sixteenth-century writer Robert Greene is sometimes considered to be the first English author; that is, the first Englishman to earn a living from what he published. Greene wrote numerous book-length romances that enjoyed great popularity in the 1580s, though today he is chiefly remembered by Shakespeare scholars for having berated the Bard for being an upstart actor pretending he could write.

Some literary historians consider *Don Quixote* to be the first true novel, certainly the first enduring one. Others consider the novel to have been an English art form that did not come to full fruition until Daniel Defoe's work of the early eighteenth century. But no matter what book was first, such works as Defoe's *Robinson Crusoe* in 1719 and *Moll Flanders* in 1722, along with Jonathan Swift's *Gulliver's Travels* in 1726, firmly established novels as cultural artifacts that could be appreciated by a popular audience—and provide their creators with the means of making a living.

Printing had a similar impact on music. Throughout Europe, composers were at last able to free themselves from the demands of wealthy patrons, who had previously subsidized their art. Composers could now earn a following and their own livelihood by publishing their music. In earlier eras, composers had written their music down any way they pleased. Music was written on four-, five-, or six-line staffs. But once music started to be published, in the seventeenth century, notation became standardized, with a five-line staff, measures of equal beats, and key signatures for a choice of twelve major and twelve minor scales. Compare this with the Middle Ages, when there had been only two keys, C and F. Publishing also preserved the composers' music. We don't really know the exact sound of the original Gregorian chants, but, with a few unwritten exceptions, we do know exactly what Bach performed in his church.

IN EIGHTEENTH-CENTURY ENGLAND, papermakers and artists started working together to develop new papers for new art forms. In 1740, England's most celebrated papermaker, James Whatman, started Turkey Mill, where among the innovations for artists was "wove paper."

The traditional papermaking mold had horizontal wires braided into the vertical wires every inch or so, which left a ribbed pattern on paper—this was called laid paper. Whatman thought that some art and possibly some printing might look better on paper without this pattern. So in 1754 he bought brass wire cloth, a newly manufactured product, and experimented with this fine mesh, to produce the first wove paper—smooth paper with no mold marks—in 1759.

Wove paper immediately came to the attention of John Baskerville, a leading printer whose work was so admired by Benjamin Franklin that he adopted his type for the first printing done by the US government. Baskerville printed his 1755 edition of *Virgil* on wove paper. Papermakers began to think that with their new, smooth paper, they could at last dethrone parchment from its perch in the luxury market. Wove paper was sometimes called vellum paper or wove vellum because it was considered to be as fine and smooth as vellum. When the French started producing wove paper in the late 1770s, they too called it *papier vélin*, vellum paper.

Soon the British began to produce a thicker, hand-sized wove paper that came to be called drawing paper. It was actually designed not so much for drawing as for watercolors. Just enough sizing was used to allow paint to remain on the surface and dry brilliantly before sinking into the paper. The paper was also thick enough for techniques such as scraping, rubbing, and wiping—to remove excess paint—to be used without wearing a hole in the paper.

Watercolors, beloved in East Asia for centuries, had never been regarded as a serious art form in the West before. But suddenly there was a growing public embrace of all forms of paper art, and though the times were not easy—Britain was at war with France for more than twenty years in the late 1700s—there was an expanding market for it in England. With England cut off from French imports because of the war, British papermakers also had an unexpected opportunity. Previously, France had been Britain's source of art paper; but the native papermakers could now fill the void.

Stationers and other shops that sold etchings, watercolors, papier-mâché objects, paper, and books conducted a brisk business, especially in London. They also became social meeting places, part of the intellectual life that Benjamin Franklin had so loved about London.

One of the most popular stationers was Ackermann's Repository of Arts. Rudolph Ackermann was a German who had moved to London, where he published books. His first was a book on watercolors, and he gave lessons in the popular new art form in his store. He sold paper and art and his own brand of watercolor in dried, compressed cakes—a new invention from another London art supply company, Thomas Reeves. In 1813 Ackermann added a tearoom and a library. Ackermann claimed, though it has been disputed, to have invented a popular fad of the time, transparencies. These were prints with certain areas varnished so that if held to the light, those parts of the picture were translucent, luminescent, to great dramatic effect.

For the first time artists, like writers and composers, could earn a living from their creative work. How-to books by watercolorists sold well, and such artists were in great demand for watercolor lessons. But the man who established English watercolors as a true art form more than anyone else was Joseph Mallard William Turner. Born in 1775 in London's Covent Garden, a market district that had fallen into disrepair and was known for prostitution at the time, Turner was the son of a barber and a butcher's daughter.

Before Turner, watercolorists were not called artists but draftsmen. Yet the power and luminosity of Turner's work, the richness of the color and freedom of his brushstrokes, raised forever the status of the watercolor. He was called "a painter of light," although with watercolors you do not so much paint light as paint shadows. But Turner could create the illusion that the light itself was the primary subject of his paintings. He earned a reputation for his oil paintings as well, though art historians point out that his oil paintings exhibit watercolor techniques. The converse could also be argued. His watercolors show an oil painter's sensibility.

Artist Mary Lloyd once asked Turner's advice about watercolors, and he said, "First of all, respect your paper." Turner grew up and developed as an artist at a time when British papermakers were first beginning to develop papers for specific arts—copper-plate paper, watercolor paper . . . Papermakers and artists had a dialogue, and papermakers competed to attract artists. Turner experimented with everything he could find—different surfaces, different sizings—and his work was always shaped by the paper he was working on. He scraped gray paper white in places to create highlights, used colors differently depending on the paper's sizing, and sometimes washed paper to bring out its nap or texture.

Turner's interest in working on paper coincided with his discovery of papers specifically made for art, and in 1798, he began a period of great experimentation. For a time, he would paint only on the wire side of paper. Then for a time he would paint only on the felt side. Later he would go back to the wire side. But as papermaking became more sophisticated, he tended to gravitate toward smoother surfaces and hard sizing.

Much of Turner's paper came from Whatman's mill, in part because Whatman offered a wide variety of papers and paid careful attention to sizing. But there were other quality British papermakers of interest to Turner as well. From August 1819 to January 1820, he traveled in Italy and filled twenty-three sketchbooks, made of British paper from eight different papermakers. Some of Turner's most celebrated work was created on blue paper made by George Steart at the Bally, Ellen and Steart paper mill. It specialized in white writing paper, but also made colored wrapping paper, which many artists liked to use, especially the blue.

In 1805, for the first time in history, London held a series of exhibitions devoted exclusively to watercolors—Turner's work among them—and they changed the British art world. Yet even with Turner at the height of his career, it took some time for other countries to recognize watercolor as a legitimate art. This was partly a result of the war, during which France ruled out any admiration of things British. It was not until an 1824 exhibition of British watercolorists in Paris that the art form gained international acceptance.

Turner was also famous for his etchings and mezzotints of landscapes. While they were a mainstay of East Asian art, landscapes had low standing in Europe at the time. Rembrandt had helped to popularize the genre with his etchings and drawings, but in Europe, high art meant portraits and historic and biblical scenes, done in oils, preferably on large canvases. But because of the genius of Turner, both landscapes and watercolors done on paper, the highest art forms in China for more than a thousand years, started to be taken seriously in Europe.

ANOTHER SIGNIFICANT BRITISH contribution to paper art was wood engraving, a craft similar to woodcuts that had similarly evolved from textile printing. Whereas a woodcut is carved along the grain of the wood, an engraving is carved at the end of a block. The preferred material for engraving is boxwood, a slow-growing evergreen that is more of a shrub than a tree. It is an unusually dense, tight-grained hardwood; its one limitation is that you cannot get a very large block from a boxwood bush. The end of the block is smoothed and then carved with a burin, the metal tool used for etchings, which is pushed away from the carver. Because of the tightness of the wood, very fine-lined images can be carved into it—much more delicate and detailed ones than can be carved on a woodcut. The boxwood block would be cut down to the height of the type, about seven-eighths of an inch, so that it could be set into a page of type.

The great pioneer and undisputed master of wood engraving was Thomas Bewick, born in 1753 in a farming village near Newcastle. His father owned a small coal pit. From an early age, Thomas was a great draftsman, but at that time he had no paper and so his drawings would turn up on the sides of the church, on gravestones, or on the stones of his family's fireplace. Finally he was given a pen and some paper, and while still a small boy, earned a reputation in the area for his drawings of birds and hunting scenes.

At age fourteen, Bewick was apprenticed to Ralph Beilby, a copper engraver in Newcastle. At first, Beilby had him doing coarse work, such as doorplates and sword blades, and the boy complained that his hands were becoming like "those of a blacksmith." But then Beilby noticed that the boy excelled at wood carving and tried to give him wood projects. Not long thereafter, Bewick won a medal from the Royal Society for a woodcut illustration for a new edition of *Aesop's Fables*. Beilby eventually made him a partner in his firm; and through such famous works as the 1790 *A General History of Quadrupeds*, for which Beilby wrote the text, Bewick became the most sought-after illustrator in England.

Like Turner, Bewick had the good fortune to live at a time when paper-makers were making special paper for different types of work. There was an explosion of printmaking in England—etchings, mezzotints—in

Thomas Bewick, Waiting for Death, *1828. This is the largest wood engraving ever made by Bewick. It is printed from four blocks. Intended as a protest against the mistreatment of old horses, it was Bewick's last work. He died before completing the final touches.*

the early eighteenth century, and papermakers responded. Whatman's wove paper was only one example. Another was soft-sized paper for copper printing.

In an age of printmaking, Bewick did for wood engraving what Turner did for watercolor: he gave it legitimacy and standing as a major art form. Woodcut illustration virtually disappeared and engraving became the leading form of illustration. Bewick had not invented the technique, but he perfected it, drawing by what was called white lines. In this technique, the spaces between the black lines were as fine as the black lines themselves, and light and shadow could be created by the thickness of the white lines instead of by crosshatching. Bewick supervised the printing of his engravings, instructing printers to wipe off ink in those places he wanted to be grayer.

THE TIMES WERE right for Bewick and wood engraving because of two emerging uses of paper. One was children's books. There had long been books for the education of children, but the modern children's book for the child's enjoyment, usually with brightly colored illustrations, was an eighteenth-century English invention. John Newberry is often credited with starting the genre, with a stream of books starting in 1744.

The other was journalism. Journalism came out of pamphleteering, which first became important during the Reformation, but continued to grow in stature in the seventeenth and eighteenth centuries. In France, there were writers such as François-Marie Arouet, who wrote under the name Voltaire—and who once said, "To hold a pen is to be at war"—and Jean-Jacques Rousseau, whose *The Social Contract* is possibly the most influential political pamphlet ever written. It begins, "Man is born free and everywhere he is in chains." The ideas of Voltaire and Rousseau were the underpinnings of both the American and French Revolutions, and the echo of *The Social Contract* is heard in the American Declaration of Independence, itself written in the manner of an eighteenth-century pamphlet.

The English writer Thomas Paine became known for a fifty-page pamphlet he published in January 1776 while visiting America. He called it *Common Sense*, and the arguments it presented led many Americans and a few British to conclude that America ought to be independent. Paine wrote other pamphlets while in America too, one excoriating the slave trade. Then he returned to England, where he made an industry of pamphleteering. His best-known work, *The Rights of Man*, has been reported to have sold 100,000 or even 200,000 copies, though historian William St. Clair, who tried to document its sales record, could find evidence for only tens of thousands of sales—still a significant number. The typical successful pamphlet of the time found five hundred readers. *The Rights of Man* was probably the bestselling pamphlet of the late eighteenth century, at least until the British government banned it.

Among other eighteenth-century pamphleteers whose work is still remembered are Jonathan Swift and Daniel Defoe. The British abolitionist movement was built on pamphlets as well. The British public had no idea, for example, that a British slave ship left for Africa every other day until 1791, when William Fox published a pamphlet entitled "An address to the People of Great Britain on the propriety of abstaining from West India Sugar and Rum." In 1792, more than 500 petitions with more than 700,000 signatures demanding the abolition of the slave trade were sent to Parliament. By 1823 the Anti-Slavery Society was publishing 200,000 copies of anti-slavery pamphlets a year, a figure that would more than double in the years to come.

It is more difficult to measure the influence of Mary Wollstonecraft's *A Vindication of the Rights of Woman*. This pioneering declaration, published first as a pamphlet and then as a book, drew to it a fair number of admirers and a huge number of detractors. As was becoming clear in this new world of print, women were not content with their traditional roles, a fact that many decried. One frequent response to the pamphlets was to suggest, with no intended irony, that it would be best if women did not read.

THE WORLD'S FIRST newspaper, *Avisa Relation oder Zeitung*, was published in Strasbourg in 1609. Almost a century later, in 1702, the world's first true daily newspaper, *The Daily Courant*, was published in England. By 1757, the total circulation of British newspapers grew to eight times the number it had been in 1712. And this despite the efforts of government, starting in 1712, to suppress the growth of newspapers by taxing them.

In 1771, under pressure, Parliament finally granted the press the right to report on parliamentary debate. Newspapers continued to grow, spurred on by the burning debate over American independence. In 1785, a Scot named John Walker started a daily of a different kind from those that had existed before—it would attempt to be independent of all political parties and movements. It was called *The Daily Universal Register*, but after three years changed its name to *The Times*. Another Scot, James Perry, started *The Morning Chronicle*, which supported the Whigs (liberals), while still another Scot, Daniel Stuart, started *The Morning Post* in support of the Tories (conservatives).

As newspapers grew more numerous and more competitive, they consumed ever-increasing quantities of relatively low-grade paper. In 1760, more than 9 million British newspapers were sold. In 1811, more than 24 million were sold, and by 1820, newspaper circulation exceeded 29 million. Demand for paper was exceeding supply. A small newspaper with a circulation of 3,000 required twelve hours of printing with experienced printers moving as quickly as they could. A large newspaper needed four presses, two for each side of a sheet. New technology was needed.

Newspapers tried to expand their reach to working-class readers by keeping their prices low, while government levied taxes to try to keep those papers out of the hands of the working class. Reading was dangerous. There were important issues at stake, and these issues were being disseminated, consumed, and debated on paper.

Chapter 13

PAPERING
INDEPENDENCE

||||||||||||||||||

*New York, July 11: On Wednesday last, the declaration of
independence was read at the head of each brigade of the
continental army, posted at and near New York, and every
where received with loud huzzas, and the utmost demonstra-
tions of joy.*

—*London Chronicle,*
SEPTEMBER 26, 1776

HE FIRST PERMANENT BRITISH SETTLERS IN NORTH
America, arriving in what is now Massachusetts on the *Mayflower* in
1620, brought no papermaker, printer, or printing press with them. That
oversight was probably not regretted nearly as much as their lack of
farmers, skilled fishermen, and salt makers, who might have produced
and preserved enough food to get the settlers through the harshest winters they had ever experienced.

Immediately, the settlers sent for those who could provide their small
community with the sorely needed skills. But while it took only fifteen

years to begin to organize a university, Harvard, it took twenty years to get a printer in the new colony.

John Glover was a minister in England who was shunned by the Church of England for his extreme Puritan views. In 1634 he decided to see if the Puritan colony in America would suit him. A wealthy man, he had his own ship, the *Planter*, on which he sailed to America. He found it to his liking, bought land, had a house built, and returned to England to bring his wife over. He was interested in the colony's plan for a new university. Some historians believe that he was hoping to be its president.

In any event, it seemed to Glover that the colonists were going to need a printing press. He purchased printing equipment at his own expense, and type, which was paid for by supporters. In Cambridge, England, he found a locksmith, Stephen Daye, whose two sons were apprentices at a print shop. He convinced the Dayes to come with him to America to set up the first American print shop.

In the summer of 1638, Glover; his wife, Elizabeth; and the Dayes set sail for Massachusetts. Along with the press and type, they may also have brought paper, as none was being made in the colony. On the voyage, Glover died of smallpox. The rest of the party arrived safely, and the Dayes established a print shop, to be run by then nineteen-year-old Matthew, who changed the spelling of his last name to "Day." The first piece of printing done in America was a half-sheet entitled "The Freeman's Oath"; the first book was *An Almanack for 1639, calculated for New England by Mr. William Pierce, mariner.*

No examples of these first two efforts survive, however, and so what is remembered instead as "the first book printed in America" is *The Bay Psalm Book*, originally entitled *The Whole Booke of Psalmes Faithfully Translated into English Metre*. As the title suggests, the book is a metrical translation of the Psalms from Hebrew into English with a discussion of the use of the Psalms in public worship. The editor, Richard Mather, was one of thirty religious leaders in New England who worked on many of the translations. The book was widely used not only in New England but in England and Scotland, and the translations were criticized for being more concerned with meter and rhyme than with faithful translation.

Like Glover, Mather was an English clergyman who had run afoul of the Church of England for his Puritan beliefs and had emigrated to New England. He became minister of a Congregationalist church in Dorchester, Massachusetts, and four of his sons became ministers. One son, named Increase, also became president of Harvard, but Increase's son Cotton Mather was denied the post because of his prominent role in the scandalous Salem witch trials.

Eleven copies of *The Bay Psalm Book*, some whole and others incomplete, have survived. In 2013, Sotheby's sold one of them for $14,165,000, making it the most expensive book in the world at the time. *The Bay Psalm Book* has a history of record-breaking prices; the previous time a copy went to auction, in 1947, it fetched $150,000, then the world's highest price for a book.

Like the Spanish Catholics in Mexico, the New England Puritans thought the printing press could be a great tool for converting the American Indians in order to save their souls. It was for this reason that some of the first books printed in America were printed in indigenous Indian languages. John Eliot, a Puritan minister, born in 1604 in Hertfordshire, where English papermaking had begun 110 years earlier, arrived in Boston in 1631. A well-educated man, he was one of the translators for *The Bay Psalm Book*. But his primary interest lay in converting Indians, and to this end he learned their language, Massachusetts, which was a dialect of Algonquin. But when he first began preaching to the Indians in Massachusetts, he was met with blank stares. He therefore decided that preaching would not be enough and so turned Massachusetts into a written language, using the Roman alphabet. He then had to teach the Massachusetts how to read his invention of their language.

Puritan ministers in New England were having an easier time taking on ambitious projects at this time because Oliver Cromwell and the Puritans had come to power in England. Cromwell's government had even financed an agency called A Corporation for Promoting and Propagating the Gospel of Jesus Christ in New England. By this point, Matthew Day had died and Samuel Green was running what was still the only printing press in the colony. Green was not a trained printer;

he learned with each task given to him. Eliot had translated the Bible into Massachusetts, but when he gave it to Green to publish, the project seemed overwhelming to him, and the two men wrote to the Corporation for Promoting and Propagating the Gospel of Jesus Christ in New England for a more experienced printer to help him. In 1660 a skilled London printer named Marmaduke Johnson was sent over. Working with two hand presses, Johnson and Green then printed fifteen 1,200-page copies of the Old and New Testament, completing the project by 1663. It was the first Bible ever printed in America, and it was printed in Algonquin. The second Bible printed in America was printed nearly a century later, during the Revolutionary War, in English.

ALL OF THESE early New England books were printed on European paper that had been brought over. There was no American paper until the end of the seventeenth century, and none made in the Massachusetts colony until 1728, when the Liberty Paper Mill was started on the Neponset River, eight miles from Boston, by a group of investors. Among them was wealthy merchant Thomas Hancock, uncle and benefactor to founding father John Hancock. It took several years for the Liberty mill to achieve full-scale production—they could not find skilled papermakers and produced a fairly low-grade paper. The mill was never profitable.

The first paper mill in the American colonies, established in 1690—thirty-eight years before the Liberty mill—was built in Pennsylvania by William Rittenhouse. Born Wilhelm Rittinghausen in 1644 in the German village of Broich on the Ruhr River, he may have first learned his trade in Germany; several of his family members may also have been papermakers. When he took the oath of citizenship in Amsterdam in 1678, he described himself as "paper maker." He changed nationalities again and settled in Germantown, Pennsylvania, after taking up the Mennonite faith.

In fact, Rittenhouse was the first Mennonite bishop in America. He built his paper mill on Wissahickon Creek, a tributary of the Schuylkill

River, and the area soon became known as Paper-mill Run. He made paper from linen rag and produced about 250 pounds of paper daily. The colonies grew flax and made their own linen, making it a relatively plentiful cloth. Flax was produced in the area of Germantown and that, combined with a clean, rushing river, made it an ideal location for paper mills.

Rittenhouse's first mill was financed by a group of businessmen that included a linen draper, Robert Turner; an ironmonger, Thomas Tresse; and the first printer in Pennsylvania, William Bradford, who needed paper for his press. Not surprisingly, Bradford took the most active interest in the mill, helping to build it and buying most of the paper it produced.

It was also Bradford who gave a young Benjamin Franklin his first printing job in Philadelphia. But Bradford alienated powerful people in that town by printing a 1681 charter that created the Pennsylvania colony without their permission, and then, even worse, printing a pamphlet by George Keith, a Quaker who denounced slavery. In 1697 Bradford moved to New York City, where he opened that city's first printing shop. He rented his one-quarter interest in the Germantown paper mill to Rittenhouse in exchange for an annual payment of seven reams of printing paper, two reams of writing paper, and two reams of blue paper, the latter of which he probably used for wrapping.

In 1710, Rittenhouse's son Claus and Claus's brother-in-law, William de Wees, started another mill in Germantown, also on the Wissahickon Creek. A third Rittenhouse mill was built by William's grandson. And in 1729, Thomas Wilcox, an Englishman in partnership with Thomas Brown, started another paper mill on Chester Creek, twenty miles from Philadelphia. Wilcox was friendly with Benjamin Franklin, and during the Revolution made the paper for the Continental currency. Philadelphia was British America's first printing center, and Pennsylvania its first papermaking region. In the years that followed, paper and printing in the colony continued to expand, thanks in large part to Benjamin Franklin, who is credited with starting eighteen mills.

In New York City, Bradford was still buying all the Rittenhouse paper he could get, but it was not enough for his busy printing press, still the only one in the city. In 1724 he petitioned the New York Assembly for the right to start a paper mill with an exclusive monopoly in New York for fifteen years. This kind of arrangement was how paper mills had been started in England, and some in the assembly favored the idea. But the New York governor, William Burnet, an aristocratic intellectual who was tutored as a child by Isaac Newton, was a staunch believer in the economics of colonialism—that is, he believed colonies were supposed to enrich the merchants of the mother country, as stated in the Navigation Act of 1663. If Americans wanted paper, he believed, they should buy it from British papermakers, not make it themselves. Burnet had a long career, serving as colonial governor in New York, New Jersey, Massachusetts, and New Hampshire, and though admired by farmers, was loathed by merchants for his colonialist views. He was also a favorite of the royal family; in fact, King William II was his godfather.

In another fifty years, the issue of colonialism would explode, but it was 1724 and Bradford, his proposal rejected by New York, turned to New Jersey. He wanted to start New York's first newspaper, to be called *The New York Gazette*, but could not get enough paper. Yet somehow, in 1725, he did start publishing the *Gazette*, probably with the paper he made at his own mill in Elizabethtown, New Jersey, though when that mill was founded is unknown.

The first paper mill in the New York colony was not started until 1768, when another printer, Hugh Caine, helped Hendrick Onderdonk and Henry Remsen start a mill in Hempstead, Long Island.

A LACK OF silver and gold created one of the early demands for paper. What little money the Massachusetts colony had was quickly exhausted, and they purchased what they needed from England by barter, trading salt cod and other products. But the English would not send over coins to America because there was a scarcity of them in England.

When the colonists needed money locally, they used the Indian currency called wampum. Wampum was a successful currency. In fact, when the first Europeans arrived in North America, wampum may have already been in use for a long as four thousand years. It came in two colors—white, from whelk shells; and purple, from quahogs—usually carved into disks, but sometimes into other shapes, and often strung together in set amounts. *Wampum* is a Narragansett word meaning "white shell beads."

In 1652 the Boston government authorized two colonists, John Hull and Robert Sanderson, to start a mint and strike coins—from Spanish silver coins they had gathered in the Caribbean, according to one story. The two men minted threepence and sixpence coins and their famous "pine tree shilling." The coin had a pine tree on one side, because New England pines with tall, very straight trunks were a major export to England, used for ship masts.

All of the coins from the mint were dated 1652, though many were minted far later. Many of the pine-tree shillings were made around 1670. Minting coins was a royal prerogative and therefore illegal. But from 1642 until 1660, there was no monarchy in England—the Puritans had overthrown it—meaning that minting coins during that period was legal. The colonists therefore kept the 1652 date, the date their mint was founded, on all their coins. By 1682, however, the monarchy was firmly back in power and it forced the Massachusetts mint to shut down, despite a desperate attempt to convince King Charles II that the pine tree was actually a royal oak.

Eight years later, in 1690, the British wanted colonists to arm themselves and march north to attack the French in what is now Canada. The colony of Massachusetts financed the expedition by printing paper money, the first paper money in America. By 1711, New Hampshire, Rhode Island, Connecticut, New York, and New Jersey had all issued paper money as well. Given the amount of paper being made in the colonies at that time, it is likely that all this money was printed on Dutch or English paper imported by the British.

THE YEAR 1690 was not only the year of the first paper money in America, and the first paper mill, it was also the year of the first newspaper,

Publick Occurences Both Foreign and Domestic, published in Boston by Benjamin Harris. It had a small format, only 6 inches by 9½ inches when folded, and was four pages long. The third page was blank; here, the reader was encouraged to add a news item of his or her own and then pass the paper on. This may have been the world's first interactive news media. But it didn't last for long. Only one issue of the newspaper was published before the Massachusetts governor and his council declared that the paper had not been authorized and forced it to close.

In 1704 a newspaper sanctioned and financed, at least in part, by the colonial government, *The Boston News-Letter*, was printed by Bartholomew Green. The editor, John Campbell, had been postmaster, and in that capacity, had learned a great deal about the news. He started his editing career by producing a newsletter for colonial administrations and then decided that he should provide this service for the general public. His newspaper was also small format—6¼ by 10½ inches—and was printed on both sides. A weekly, except for a brief inactive period, it published until 1776. When it started out, whenever the paper attracted 300 subscribers annually, it was considered to have been a good year, but as discord with England grew, the circulation rose as high as 3,600.

Soon most of the other colonies also had newspapers with growing readerships, and newspapers became central to the livelihood of printers. One of the great entrepreneurs of this first newspaper boom, really America's first press baron, was Benjamin Franklin. Franklin started up, or had a partial interest in, many newspapers throughout the thirteen colonies. He was owner, editor, and publisher of his first newspaper, *The Pennsylvania Gazette,* when he was twenty-four years old. And he not only published newspapers but had an interest in thirteen paper mills and was in the rag business.

Colonial newspapers were badly printed and difficult to read; Franklin once complained that he nearly went blind trying to read Boston newspapers. They were printed on four relatively small pages with four very crowded columns. There were no editorials, few headlines, and almost no illustrations. What little copper engraving they had was done by artisans, including Paul Revere, the famed Boston silversmith, but most lacked the sophisticated artistry of Thomas Bewick and other European illustrators of the time. In addition, most presses were capable of printing only 200 pages in a hardworking hour.

HUNDREDS OF PAPER mills were established in North America in the eighteenth century. Most were small operations, usually using only one vat. Sometimes paper was made in mills that also ground grain or that were used as sawmills. Papermaking was done during only part of the year, in accordance with agricultural needs and the demands of boat traffic and competition with other mills for use of the river.

It required considerable capital to build even a simple one- or two-vat mill. Many mills did not last long because of either a lack of linen and cotton rags or a shortage of skilled workers. Generally, if a mill produced paper, it could sell it. Isaiah Thompson, a well-known printer in Worcester, Massachusetts, tried to compile a complete list of American paper mills at the beginning of the nineteenth century, but found that so many small, one-vat operations were forever starting up or closing down that the task was impossible. In 1810, he published his best estimates:

New Hampshire, 7; Massachusetts, 38; Rhode Island, 4; Connecticut, 17; Vermont, 9; New York, 12; Delaware, 4; Maryland, 3; Virginia, 4; South Carolina, 1; Kentucky, 6; Tennessee, 4; Pennsylvania , about 60—in all other states and territories, say 16.— Total 185.

As had been the case from the very beginning, Pennsylvania remained the heart of American papermaking. In the 1740s alone, the number of paper mills in Eastern Pennsylvania more than doubled. And Boston, despite its lack of paper, became the American print center. By midcentury, two out of every three books and pamphlets printed in the colonies were printed in Boston, along with four out of seven colonial newspapers. Boston, or rather nearby Milton, was also the country's card-making center.

Some American book and newspaper printers, like their European counterparts, probably published cards, but Jazaniah Ford, born in 1757, was the first American to call himself a "card maker," and his Milton shop turned card-making into a major Massachusetts industry. In the late eighteenth century, French soldiers played a card game called "Boston," which they said they learned while in America fighting the Continental Army. According to an unproven legend, Paul Revere also engraved plates for playing cards. James Franklin, Benjamin's older brother, was a Boston printer who produced cards with jingles about Blackbeard the pirate written by his little brother. Benjamin later characterized these jingles as "miserable ditties."

Linen was the favored material for papermaking in America, and cotton, hemp, and jute were also used. But rags were difficult to come by in the sparsely populated colonies with their poor and rugged populations that did not easily discard old clothes. A common watermark of the time read: "save rags." Whenever a new paper mill opened, it would immediately advertise for rags, and newspapers, desperate for paper, ran advertisements urging people to save rags.

The American mills used stampers, sometimes manually, with workers hand-beating the heavy hammers in mortars due to the lack of a water-powered system. Hollander beaters were not introduced in the colonies until 1760, and were not commonly used until after the Revolution. It is believed that even Rittenhouse, who trained in Holland, used stampers. Until the nineteenth century there were no "knotters," or screens that filtered out debris, either. American paper had lumps, twigs, hairs, and even bugs enmeshed in it. Often, the American papermakers did not separate white and colored rags, which resulted in tan to brownish-colored paper. Sometimes a bluish coloring was added. Newspapers were often printed on light-blue paper.

By the early eighteenth century, demand for paper started to get ahead of production. To finish and properly dry a sheet of paper took several days. The quality of American paper was further diminished because it was always being rushed and so not sufficiently pressed or properly dried. Many seventeenth-century American books do not lie flat because of the improper drying of their paper. Yet the books were being printed on long-lasting rag paper, and by the mid-eighteenth century, Americans were producing books that are still in good condition today.

THE COLONIES WERE slow to build paper mills, because for most of the seventeenth century, they had little need for paper. They had no newspapers and their few presses did not produce many books. In the sixty-two years between the launching of John Glover's press in 1639 and the end of the seventeenth century, fewer than 1,000 works, counting both books and pamphlets, were printed. There does not even appear to have been a great deal of letter writing, other than the colonial administration's correspondence with London.

In 1753, shortly before moving to London, Benjamin Franklin, then owner of *The Pennsylvania Gazette*, and his colleague William Hunter of *The Virginia Gazette*, were jointly named deputy postmaster general. In that capacity, they greatly improved mail service, and inter-colony correspondence increased. Postal roads were enlarged, improved, and expanded. By 1764, service between New York and Philadelphia was so quick that with luck a New Yorker could get an answer from a letter sent to Philadelphia the next day.

The demand for American paper probably rose during this early period because of the almanac, or "almanack" as it was spelled at the time. In all likelihood the first almanac was printed by Matthew Day—even before the psalm book—which would have made it the first American book, though no copy has survived. Almanacs were a bit like annual magazines. They came out once a year, with calendar information, weather forecasts, stories, recipes, poetry, historical anecdotes, political commentary, and inane little aphorisms. They were inexpensive—a few cents—and most everyone had one in their home. As with newspapers, their cost was kept down by printing them on low-quality paper. One of the most successful almanacs, Benjamin Franklin's *Poor Richard's Almanack*, sold more than ten thousand copies every year from 1732 to 1757.

As anti-British sentiment grew in the colonies, the almanacs became politically edgier. *Ames' Almanack*, from Boston, which claimed 60,000 subscribers in 1764, offered a recipe for making gunpowder in 1775, and commented, "Patriotism and America for Americans beams from every syllable of this year's production."

Printers, especially in the seventeenth century, had a very limited amount of type available to them, and so had to set up a few pages, print them, tear up the type tray, and reset it for the next few pages. This may have been one of the reasons for the growing fashion of what were called broadsides. These one-page anonymous handbills, distributed in secret in the eighteenth century, became a favorite tool of political dissidents wishing to denounce the British colonial administration. Broadsides infuriated the British government, but they were unable to stop them.

One famous broadside, printed on December 16, 1769, was entitled "The Betrayed Inhabitants of the City and Colony of New York" and was signed by "A Son of Liberty." The broadside denounced the New York Assembly's decision to increase funding for the British troops in New York. Several days later, a second broadside, this one signed by "legion," appeared on the streets arguing the same thing. The assembly was infuriated and offered a reward to anyone who exposed the author. A worker in a print shop revealed that his boss, Alexander McDougall, known for his radical views, was the printer, and McDougall was taken to court. The authorities failed to make their case and it was dismissed, but McDougall was jailed for "high contempt" anyway because he refused to say whether he was the author. He became a cause célèbre, and supporters of the idea of freedom of the press rallied behind him. According to historian Arthur M. Schlesinger, the case "deterred other provincial administrations from creating like martyrs to freedom of the press." After that, even more anti-British broadsides began to appear.

Pamphlets, longer and more reflective than broadsides, were also increasingly popular. Unlike broadsides, pamphlets had traditionally been aimed at the intelligentsia, but Thomas Paine's *Common Sense*, clearly aimed at common citizens, changed that. In an age of flowery prose, his language was clear, direct, and unadorned. Published in 1778, *Common Sense* argued for American independence from England and the establishment of a republic, and is credited with pushing many Americans off the fence and into the independence camp. Since the pamphlet was anonymous, many at first believed John Adams to be the author. He vehemently denied authorship, however, and complained that the pamphlet had gone too far—it referred to King George III as "The Royal Brute of Great Britain."

THE HISTORY OF paper offers insight into why the colonists wanted independence from Britain. A coin, a paper mill, a newspaper—whatever it was that the colonists wanted, the Crown often prohibited it. And then the British tried to earn revenue by taxing the goods the colonists were forced to import from England because local production was stifled.

In 1764, the British, looking for revenues in an economic recession that had hit both England and the colonies, proposed the Stamp Act. This required all American colonists to pay a tax on every piece of printed paper, including shipping documents, legal documents, books, pamphlets, newspapers, broadsides, and even playing cards. The tax did not cost the average colonist a great deal, but they objected to the principle of the new legislation. The Stamp Act went beyond the normal practice of regulating commerce: It was a fund-raising measure, and one that was being done without the consent of local legislatures.

But for newspaper publishers, the Stamp Act was a true hardship. It assessed a halfpenny on each copy of a newspaper printed on what was termed "half a sheet." If a newspaper used a larger format, it was assessed a penny per copy. The act also charged two cents for an advertisement—and some of these ads only earned three cents—and a halfpenny for each copy of a pamphlet. An additional tax on publishing in foreign languages killed a thriving German-language press in Pennsylvania. Lawyers, whose documents were also taxed, were harmed by the Stamp Act as well, and together, newspaper publishers and lawyers led a successful campaign to repeal the act. The experience also pushed the newspaper publishers into taking a pro-independence stance, which was critical in winning over public opinion for the revolution.

The Stamp Act was repealed before it did any real harm. The British were sensitive to the Americans' political objections to it, but not to the economic hardship that it would have created. They then reasoned that since the Americans objected to internal taxes levied from England, they would raise money via port levies instead. In 1767, the British Chancellor of the Exchequer, Charles Townshend, promoted a piece of legislation that placed added taxes on various British goods that the Americans imported, including glass, lead, painters' pigments, tea—and paper. Townshend's legislation passed into law, and the British established a bureau in Boston to enforce the new duties. Newspapers vociferously protested.

One American response to the Townshend Act, first suggested in 1767 and broadly promoted by newspapers the following year, was to boycott British goods. The movement started in the North and quickly caught on in the South. New York newspapers declared that those who bought British goods were "enemies to their Country." In Philadelphia, newspapers preferred the phrase "an Enemy to the Liberties of America." In the process, newspapers themselves became committed, for the first time, to printing on American-made paper.

Newspapers had already started buying American paper in the mid-1760s, but with the Townshend Act, more and more of them were printed on American stock. They would boast of this fact. People also considered it an act of patriotism to bring their rags to paper mills. In 1769 the first type made in America was cut and cast in Killingworth, Connecticut, by Abel Buell. That same year, the first American-made printing presses went on sale, manufactured in New Haven by Isaac Doolittle.

Americans vowed to content themselves with inferior American paper, even if, due to the competition created by the Townshend Act boycott, it cost more. But in truth, the thirty-four paper mills operating in the thirteen colonies in the 1760s did not have the capacity to meet America's paper needs. The higher price of paper did encourage new mills to start up, and local government provided further inducements in subsidies and interest-free loans; between 1775 and 1783, twenty-six new paper mills were opened. But it was not enough.

Once the Revolution began and British imports cut off, American paper mills, by this time numbering eighty, still could not meet the demand for paper. In 1775, Gen. Philip Schuyler in Albany apologized in a letter to Gen. George Washington: "Excuse these scraps of paper; necessity oblige me to use them, having no other fit to write on." In 1776, John Adams, who wrote faithfully to his wife, Abigail, penned the words, "I send you, now and then, a few sheets of paper; but this article is scarce here as with you."

Obtaining enough rags to keep the mills in operation became a more and more serious issue. It took about twenty tons of rags to keep one vat operating full time for a year. In February 1776 the Massachusetts House of Representatives declared:

Whereas this Colony cannot be supplied with a sufficient quantity of Paper for its own consumption, without the particular care of its Inhabitants in saving Rags for the Paper-Mills:

Therefore *Resolved* that the Committees of Correspondence, Inspection and Safety, in the several towns in this Colony, be, and they hereby are required immediately, to appoint some suitable person, in their respective towns, (where it is not already done) to receive in Rags for the Paper-Mills; and the Inhabitants of this Colony are hereby desired to be very careful in saving even the smallest quantity of Rags proper for making Paper, which will be a further evidence of their disposition to promote the public good.

It is interesting that the writer of this resolution assumed that the average citizen knew what kinds of rags were useful for papermaking. Other appeals were more specific. In Sutton, Massachusetts, a key paper mill made this political appeal:

It is earnestly requested that the fair daughters of Liberty in this extensive country would not neglect to serve their country by saving, for the Paper Mill in Sutton, all Linen and Cotton-and-Linen

Rags, be they ever so small, as they are equally good for the purpose of making paper as those that are larger. A bag hung up at one corner of a room would be the means of saving many which would be otherwise lost. If the ladies should not make a fortune from that bit of economy, they will at least have the satisfaction of knowing that they are doing an essential service to the community, which with eight pence per pound, the price now given for clean white rags, they must be sensible will be a sufficient reward.

Similar pleas were made in other colonies. A North Carolina mill suggested that if young women would sell off to the paper mill an old handkerchief "no longer fit to cover their snowy breasts," they might get it back someday in the form of a love letter.

Newspapers, meanwhile, were forced to skip issues due to a lack of paper and ran apologies saying that they wanted to include more articles but did not have the paper to do so. In 1781, the New York Assembly did not print an account of their second session because they couldn't find the paper. Nonetheless, thanks to the huge demand for news during the Revolution, newspapers survived. A few did close and a few more were started up, but the colonies consistently maintained about thirty-two newspapers throughout the war.

DETERMINED TO KEEP the paper mills open during the Revolution, the colonists exempted papermakers from military service. The Council of Public Safety of Pennsylvania went as far as to stop papermakers from volunteering to join a force planning to march on the British in New Jersey.

Paper was a strategic commodity, not because of newspapers or the need for writing material but because paper plugs were needed to seal the black powder in the muskets' firing chambers, to keep it separate from bullets, and paper cartridges were required to encase the powder and bullets. Sometimes, that paper was scarce. In 1776, according to historian William St. Clair, most of the 3,000-copy press run of Saur's 1776 German Bible was used to fire American muskets. In 1777, two wagonloads of unbound copies of John Foxe's *Book of Martyrs*, on their way to the bindery, were seized by Continental troops and used in the Battle of Brandywine. Paper was integral to the war effort. William Hoffman started the first paper mill in Maryland expressly for the purpose of making cartridge paper in 1775–1776. He built it on the west bank of what came to be known as Great Gunpowder Falls in the town of Bradshaw.

In June 1778, George Washington's troops, at last resupplied after the deprivation of the winter at Valley Forge, prepared for the Battle of Monmouth. They still lacked paper for their muskets, so the Continental Army sent soldiers foraging. They found a house where Benjamin Franklin had once lived and had a printing office. There, he had printed a sermon by Rev. Gilbert Tenant, entitled "Defensive War," but had not delivered it, apparently because he had not received payment. The soldiers found 2,500 copies of the sermon and sent it off to Monmouth, where it was used to plug the muskets of the men fighting the British to a draw in a famously tough battle—later renowned as the one instance in which George Washington was said to have cursed.

PAPER HISTORIAN DARD Hunter wrote, "The mold has always been the most important tool of the papermaker." Part of the reason why American paper was so crudely made was that its mills were using roughly fashioned molds. There was not a good mold maker in the Colonies until 1776, when twenty-five-year-old Nathan Sellers, a fourth-generation American, set up shop in Upper Darby, Pennsylvania. His great-grandfather, who had emigrated from England with William Penn, had been a weaver; his father was an engineer who developed techniques for weaving wire.

Sellers was also interested in weaving, and had invented several textile machines. As a young man, he had been involved in wire-weaving projects. When the American Revolution began, he joined the Pennsylvania militia. But once his skill with wire came to the attention of the Continental Congress, he was pulled out of the ranks; the country needed a mold maker if they were to expand their paper industry. Once armed hostilities began and imports stopped, there was no source for paper molds. One of the first projects that the Continental Congress assigned to Sellers was to work on making molds for paper money.

In 1775, Benjamin Franklin had turned to the Ivy mill outside of Philadelphia when printing American currency. Sellers's molds were satisfactory, yet that currency had not been a great success. The money was supposed to finance the war, but as economists always point out, printing money is a dangerous enterprise. As the money supply increases, its value declines. A British plot to flood the colonies with counterfeit money was also a worry, as it could potentially aggravate the problem of inflation. The Ivy mill used colored threads, mica flakes, and complicated watermarks to make counterfeiting difficult, but even without counterfeit, the money supply increased too rapidly. By 1780, $241,552,780 in Continental bills, in denominations ranging from one-sixth of a dollar to $80, had been printed, but it was barely worth more than the British paper it was printed on. The money had to be withdrawn from circulation. After independence, bearers could redeem the bills for US bonds at the rate of a penny for every dollar.

Between 1776 and 1820, Nathan Sellers made molds with watermarks for hundreds of American paper mills. Other craftsmen fabricated the wooden frames; Sellers specialized only in the wiring of molds. He made his own wire equipment, including a wood block with rows of metal pins, which was used for straightening wire. He could not buy wire thin enough for his needs and so would redraw it to make it thinner.

After the war, Sellers helped popularize wove paper. Paper-mill owner Joshua Gilpin of Delaware had traveled to England, where he learned about wove paper from the Whatman mill, and upon his return, commissioned two wove molds from Sellers. The earliest American book printed on wove paper was Charlotte Smith's 1795 *Sonnets and Other Poems*, printed by Isaiah Thomas.

GIVEN THE PATRIOTIC movement to boycott the use of British products, the printing of the Declaration of Independence—a purely symbolic act, as it did not have the power of law—is difficult to understand. Instead of printing it on American-made paper, the founding fathers (two of them, Franklin and Hancock, in the paper business themselves) embraced the European notion, by then almost a thousand years old, that for a document to truly last, it had to be published on parchment. The Congress commissioning the declaration ordered the congressional clerk, Timothy Matlock, to make "an engrossed copy"—that is, a handwritten manuscript on parchment.

Matlock was a master calligrapher and a colorful man, an excommunicated Quaker known for cockfighting and street fighting. He was also an active patriot who had fought in New Jersey, an author of the Pennsylvania constitution, and is said to have had input into the Declaration of Independence itself. Unfortunately, there is no record of where Matlock's parchment was bought and whether it was American. He produced the declaration slowly, between July 19 and August 2, and then it had to be signed by each member of Congress, which took a number of months.

However, Congress also wanted their declaration to be read by as many people as possible, as quickly as possible. In 1776, the best way to disseminate a political tract was to print a broadside. The manuscript was immediately taken to Congress's preferred printer, John Dunlap, who quickly—haste is evident in the broadside—printed at least 200 copies, though the exact number is not known. He also made a copy to be reprinted in newspapers, and stayed up all night working. The broadside and newspaper version of the declaration bore no signatures, only the printed name of John Hancock and the congressional secretary, Charles Thomson, as witness.

It is indicative of the cultural and political differences between John Adams, the New England pragmatist, and Thomas Jefferson, the Virginia aristocrat, that Adams oversaw Dunlap's printing and Jefferson looked after Matlock's parchment manuscript. Dunlap, a twenty-nine-year-old

Irish immigrant, was a patriot and loyal supporter of the independence cause, but he had not boycotted British goods. The first copies of the Declaration of Independence, the one sent to the British and the one read by General Washington to his troops, were printed with English-designed type on imported paper.

The paper used to print the original Declaration of Independence—at least twenty-six copies of which have been found, with others still to be discovered—have three different watermarks, none of them American. They are all Dutch laid paper. Some have the mark of L. V. Gerrevinck, thought to be the mill where Whatman first learned his craft. Paper with this same watermark was also used by Thomas Jefferson for his notes on the 1776 Virginia Constitution, which was in progress at the same time, and his rough draft of the Declaration of Independence. Another watermark was that of Dirk and Cornelius Blauw, the largest papermakers in Zaanland. The third was the watermark of the old Zaanland family the Honigs. This Dutch paper had been made specifically for Britain to sell in America; some of it even had British royal watermarks to indicate its destination.

Even after the revolution, printers continued to use imported English paper. *The Federalist Papers*, a 1788 collection of essays by Alexander Hamilton, James Madison, and John Jay arguing for the ratification of the American Constitution, was printed on English paper. Some of that paper came from Whatman's mill and had the British royal seal in its watermark. The public also complained that US senators were using stationery with the British royal seal.

It was never easy for the British colonies to get out from under British commercial rule. Mohandas Gandhi, in his fight for Indian independence in the twentieth century, wanted Indians to use only paper made in India and started a school of papermaking. On July 17, 1937, he proudly announced in the first edition of his magazine, *Harijan*, that it was entirely printed on Indian-made paper. But that was the only edition of *Harijan* to use Indian paper. After that they resorted to English paper just like the American rebels had.

In 1789 the new US government enacted protective tariffs on

imported paper, and in 1791, Alexander Hamilton's *Report on Manufac-turers* optimistically asserted that with those tariffs in place, the future of American paper was secured. In 1819 two competing reproductions of the Declaration of Independence were published, one by Benjamin Owen Tyler and one by John Binns. Tyler used Gilpin's paper from Brandywine Creek, and Binns used Thomas Aimes's paper from Phila-delphia. For the first time, the Declaration of Independence was truly American.

Chapter 14

DIDEROT'S PROMISE

||||||||||||||||||

Indeed, the purpose of an encyclopedia is to collect knowledge disseminated around the globe; to set forth its general system to the men with whom we live, and transmit it to those who will come after us, so that the work of preceding centuries will not become useless to the centuries to come; and so that our offspring, becoming better instructed, will at the same time become more virtuous and happy, and that we should not die without having rendered a service to the human race.

—DENIS DIDEROT, *Encyclopédie*, 1755

B Y THE END OF THE EIGHTEENTH CENTURY, THERE WAS more demand for paper in the Western world than ever before in history. The public was reading books at an unprecedented rate, and volatile politics had made newspapers and broadsides extremely popular. Papermakers and printers could barely keep up.

Parchment and vellum were still in common use for fine publishing. In 1801, for example, the Didots, one of France's leading publishing and printing families, released a luxury edition of the works of

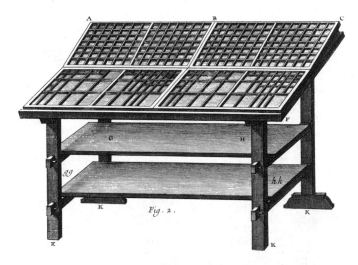

*A case for holding a typeface. The larger and nearer sections
were for the most used letters. With a well-arranged case,
a skilled printer could set up 1,500 letters an hour.*
Diderot, Trade and Industry, *Volume II.*

Racine in three large volumes on vellum with illustrations by leading artists.

Printing was still being done on wooden presses that were not substantially different from the one Gutenberg had built three and a half centuries earlier. If Gutenberg had walked into a late-eighteenth-century print shop, he would have felt at home. In fact, print shops were often located in a printer's home. The large wooden turn-screw press dominated. Nearby would be the type cases. There would be a stock room for storing paper, a vat for soaking the paper before printing, and a store, as most printers also sold their books.

But there were a few new trends: having a separate room for typesetting and the use of "stereotyped printing," a French innovation developed by François-Ignace-Joseph Hoffmann. Traditionally, while a page was being printed, type would not be available for composing the next page—type was scarce and expensive. But Hoffmann cast a single metal block of the set page—a matrix. This matrix could then be used for printing

Stamping mill for tearing rags into fiber.
Diderot, Trade and Industry, *Volume II.*

while the type was torn apart and set up for the next page. Hoffmann busied himself with this new technique, printing an inordinate number of pamphlets and broadsides denouncing the French monarchy, until his shop was shut down in 1787.

Aside from the Hollander beater and the medieval innovations of waterwheels and wire molds, papermaking in late-eighteenth-century Europe was not that different from what it had been like in ancient China. A French paper mill on the eve of the French Revolution still involved women sorting rags, a pulper—usually old water-powered stampers—a vat, a vatman, a coucher, waterleaves pressed between felt by sturdy men, a presser with a big bar to compress the felt, women hanging paper to dry, a sizeman cooking up sizing, women examining sheets and removing the flawed ones, and a loftman wrapping the sheets into reams. These workers all had very specific skills, and there were strict rules about which jobs were for women and which for men.

According to a survey conducted by the French monarchy, eighteenth-century France had about 750 paper mills, distributed around the country so that every region had its own local paper supply. From these surveys, French historian Henri-Jean Martin calculated that the 750 mills represented about 1,000 vats and that each vat produced about 2,000 reams of paper annually. He estimated that France had 10,000 workers producing 2,500,000 reams of paper, 500 sheets each, which would be about 100 sheets per capita. An important and ever-increasing share of this was used for government work.

In prerevolutionary France, paper workers had more power and were more assertive than most other workers because they were few in number and highly skilled. They were known to walk off the job and spend an afternoon in a nearby tavern, returning only at mealtime. They had a reputation for being independent and unruly, and they ignored government regulations. Their unique skills, the source of their power, were carefully preserved, seldom shared, and usually passed on to a son or daughter. They had their own rituals and festivals, known as *modes*, and to be in the profession meant to know these modes. Apprentices were expected to learn the modes, which included recognizing when to slip someone a coin and when to buy a round of drinks. A marriage or death or birth required some coins. Eating fat on a holy day resulted in a fine.

Certain food was expected on certain dates. The foods varied in different regions. Management had to know the rules too, and failure to comply with one would result in an angry workforce demanding the mill master's resignation. According to historian Leonard N. Rosenband, the mill at Dauphiné was required to provide both a regular meal and a coq d'Inde, an Indian rooster otherwise known as a turkey—an "exotic" bird from the Americas—on New Year's. A pig's ear was required for Mardi Gras, doughnuts for Palm Sunday, and a carp for Good Friday.

Nonetheless, papermaking was a hard and often itinerant life. It was frequently seasonal and demanded long hours when the mill was in operation. Everything would stop whenever the water level in the river got too low, or there were not enough rags, or the mill was needed for an agricultural purpose. Then the papermakers would wander the French countryside in search of another mill that needed them.

The percentage of a publisher's expenses that went toward paper was high by modern standards; the cost of the paper comprised more than half the price of a book. And this despite the fact that the publisher did not have the expense of binding. He sold sewn pages, which the buyer, after carefully inspecting the quality of the paper used, took to a book-binder. Real connoisseurs, those who demanded the highest quality of paper, took their books to binders who could tool covers of Moroccan leather and add elaborate, possibly marbled, endpapers.

The French monarchy felt threatened by all the reading going on in France. An estimated 40 percent of the prisoners in the infamous Bastille were involved in the business of books. Reading was becoming a major pastime—and not just of books, but also of pamphlets and magazines. By 1750, 150 periodicals were being read. Book lending and even book renting were popular in France, and reading rooms and libraries were fashionable meeting places. Historian Raymond Birn, who studied eighteenth-century French book ownership, concluded that in 1700, 23 percent of salaried workers and 30 percent of servants in France owned at least one book. By 1780, those figures had increased to 30 percent of workers and 40 percent of servants. In eastern France just before the Revolution, a third of death notices listed books among the deceased's property.

Everything in France seemed to require paper. Even the lengthy list of books banned by the monarchy was itself printed on paper by the book guild and distributed to all booksellers so that no one would accidentally sell contraband.

DENIS DIDEROT WAS one of the more unusual rebels in a revolutionary age. He wanted to change the world with an encyclopedia. He said that a good one should have "the character of changing the general way of thinking." He also wanted to catalogue crafts, the manufacturing of the age. He wrote:

> Let us at last give artisans their due. We need a man to rise up in the academies and go down to the workshops and gather material about the arts to be set out in a book, which will persuade artisans

to read, philosophers to think on useful lines, and the great to make
at least some worthwhile use of their authority and their wealth.

Greatly influenced by Francis Bacon, Diderot believed that science
and technology would free society from the shackles of an outmoded
order. His beliefs were a distillation of what at the time was modern
thinking, a merging of Bacon and Newton with Rousseau and Voltaire. "No man has received from nature the right to rule others," he
asserted. "Liberty is a gift from heaven and every individual of the
race has the right to enjoy it as soon as he attains the enjoyment of his
reason." His promise for the future was that technology would replace
the oppression of religion and the reigning aristocracy, to help build
a democratic society.

Diderot's encyclopedia was the first book of the industrial revolution.
Technology had not yet changed; manufacturing was still done largely
by hand—papermaking being a case in point—and in shops, not factories. But his book announced that the social order was in the process of
changing and would give birth to a technology that had not yet been
seen, a technology that would set them free.

The *Encyclopédie* was composed of twenty-eight volumes, with 71,818
articles written by 100 contributors—all members of the encyclopedia
movement who shared Diderot's beliefs—along with 3,129 illustrations.
It included a lengthy, well-illustrated and detailed explanation of papermaking, which is not surprising given that paper had long been ranked
as one of France's top industries. The first volume was published in 1751,
and the project continued for nearly thirty years. Ironically, in 1777 there
was a crisis in paper supply, and the publisher, Neuchâtel in Switzerland,
struggled to procure 36 million sheets of fine, thick, white paper; the
project nearly stopped.

The challenge to papermakers in France, as in America, was how
to keep up with the demand for their product. French papermakers
were also preoccupied by their Dutch competitors, who seemed able
to produce more and sell more—and even made inroads into the most
traditional of French paper markets. The Dutch began selling French

candy makers the violet paper that they traditionally rolled into cones for selling sugar. The Dutch were also starting to outsell the French, both in France and internationally, in fine paper for artists, which was a long-standing French specialty. The Dutch reputation was so favorable that some French mills used watermarks such as *"armes d'Amsterdam"* to imply that they were Dutch.

Dutch paper was a bluish-white color with a velvety finish created by a unique finishing process called échange; the process involved gentle pressing in the drying room and a reshuffling of the stack of paper after each small pressing so that a sheet was always touching a different one than it had touched on the previous pressing. This left a very soft grain to the paper. Not being privy to the Dutch technique, the French tried to get a similar finish by burnishing their paper with smooth stones. But French paper never had the soft luster of the Dutch product.

French mill owners sent industrial spies to Holland to steal Dutch papermaking ideas. More openly, in 1768, the French government sent its manufacturing inspector for papermaking, Nicolas Demarest, at his own request, to observe papermaking in Zaanland. On his way back, he stopped in Flanders to see water-driven Hollander beaters. But when he returned and presented his findings, they were greeted with considerable resistance. The British and the Dutch were much more open to new ideas than were the French, who in general tended to cling to old ways. While some French papermakers did seek out and buy Hollander beaters, many others insisted that the beaters cut fibers too short and made inferior paper.

THE MEN AND women of the French Revolution knew that their cause was going to require a lot of paper. Like the American Revolution and the Protestant Reformation, this movement had to be "sold" to the general public, and that would take books, newspapers, pamphlets, broadsides, posters, satirical drawings, sheet music, and even playing cards. One set of cards printed in 1792 featured the king card with a red cap (a symbol of the Revolution) instead of a crown, the queen labeled *"Liberté,"* and the jack *"Égalité."*

But when the Revolution first erupted in 1789, it was books that were needed the most. In 1785, only 900 book titles had been published in France, but in 1789, 1,500 titles were published—a record number that France did not reach again until 1825. The great social change that Diderot had predicted burst forth in 1789, a year of astounding events in France. Crudely armed crowds stormed government buildings, a new constitution was written under siege in a tennis court, and a violent peasant revolt tore apart the countryside. Hundreds of posters, flyers, and pamphlets circulated, and 185 new daily newspapers started up. The following year, another 335 papers were launched.

Since the old French monarchy had only one newspaper, the French Revolution was the true birth of the French press. Most of the new newspapers did not have a huge circulation, or at least not a huge press run, but that was simply because the presses were not capable of it. A few printers had larger shops. Charles-Joseph Panckoucke, publisher of the two leading papers, *Mercure de France* and the *Moniteur*, had twenty-seven presses and ninety-one workers, and also published books. *The Gazette Universelle* put out 11,000 copies on ten presses. Historians estimate that all the revolutionary newspapers combined did not produce a half million newspapers on any given day.

Pornographic attacks on the regime, both in words and pictures, were also well circulated. An especially popular subject was the alleged lasciviousness of the queen, who was frequently depicted in various erotic acts, the illustrations accompanied by reports of her probably fictitious orgies. It began a tradition of outrageous, off-color political satire that has continued in France till this day. The satirical weekly magazine *Charlie Hebdo*, which became famous as the victim of a January 2015 terrorist attack, followed in this same tradition. Broadsides were particularly important in popularizing the revolution as well. More than half the French population was still either illiterate or barely literate. Heavily illustrated and written in spare, simple language, the broadsides targeted the lower classes.

The French government, which had previously always controlled what was printed, was helpless in the face of this flood of printed matter.

Even when they closed down a few known print shops, dozens of others sprang up in the back streets. Those opposed to the revolution, however, resisted in kind, with their own posters, pamphlets, and newspapers. The more the revolutionaries printed, the more their opponents printed. A bishop made a speech, and two thousand copies of that speech would appear on the street that week. Michel Vernus, a French historian who specializes in the Franche-Comté region in central France, found that between January and May 1789, during the great debates of the Estates-General, whose dissolution began the Revolution in May, 200 booklets and pamphlets were printed in Franche-Comté alone, with an average press run of 1,000.

And yet, in this age of paper, printing, and reading, oral culture had still not vanished. The revolutionaries presented public readings, announced with the pounding of drums, and the general population was pressured to prove their loyalty to the cause by attending. Oral culture met printed culture in the phenomenon of revolutionary songs. It started with the song now known as "La Marseillaise," which was composed by a French Army officer, Claude Joseph Rouget de Lisle, in 1792.

The lyrics, first printed in two newspapers and later performed, did not elicit a strong reaction at first; they are almost bizarrely violent calls for watering the French countryside with the "impure blood" of tyrants. But the song was not written for the revolutionaries, and neither was it meant to be a national anthem. It was written as a marching song for French troops going off to fight Austria, against whom war had just been declared. The song's title was "Chant de guerre pour l'Armée du Rhin" (War song for the army of the Rhine).

But on July 30, 1792, troops from Marseilles marched into Paris singing a stirring rendition of the new song. Parisians loved it. The troops fanned out in the capital and taught people how to sing it. It was printed and distributed throughout the country. This was the birth of printed songs in France. Other "revolutionary songs" followed. Soon, for any song to become popular, it had to be distributed first in print.

This eruption of paper and printing—books, pamphlets, broadsides, posters, and flyers on the street—was a phenomenon associated with all

the great political upheavals of France. It was seen during the revolutions of 1848, and again during the student and labor uprisings of 1968.

AS DIDEROT HAD predicted, huge social changes pushed technology
forward. One of the first technological innovations, one that completely
altered paper art and illustration, was developed, probably by accident,
by a young writer in Bavaria named Alois Senefelder. Born in 1771, the
son of a Munich actor, his ambition was to be a playwright. But he failed
to find a publisher for his plays. He decided to publish them himself, and
built a makeshift press for printing copperplates. Copper was expensive,
however, and so he started experimenting with a limestone slate known
as Solnhofen stone. The stone was inexpensive and commonplace in
Bavaria. Using nitric acid, Senefelder was able to produce a slightly raised
image on the stone that he could ink and print.

But it was difficult to keep the ink off of the lower cut-away parts
that were intended to be white space. He experimented with various
solutions, and eventually came to realize that he did not need raised and
lowered areas with stone as did etchings and woodcuts. The trick was to
use substances that would attract or reject ink. Since ink was oil-based,
water would reject it. He could use a dampened stone and draw with a
greasy, water-resistant crayon. When inked, the crayon part would be
printed and the wet areas around it wouldn't. Senefelder had invented
the first chemical printing process.

He further developed the technique—by using a range of crayons, a
soluble but greasy ink known as *touche*, and various pens and brushes. He
found talented artists to work with him and wrote a manual that became
the standard textbook for this type of print, which became known as a
lithograph. Lithographs were less expensive than copper printing, and
did not require the skill of wood engraving. In 1801, Senefelder took his
invention to London to be patented. Lithography became a new popular
form, a very affordable kind of art, especially because the stones would
not wear out and could be washed off and reused. Even today, lithographs
are one of the least expensive art forms. By the 1820s major artists were

embracing lithographs, especially for book illustration; French painter
Eugène Delacroix, for example, illustrated an 1828 edition of *Faust*.

Lithography also led to another important invention in this age of
discovery. As early as 1793, Frenchman Joseph Nicéphore Niépce and
his brother Claude had become interested in the idea that light could
be used to create permanent images—somewhat like a fixed shadow. In
1813 they began experimenting with lithography and the possibility of
applying their ideas about light imagery to Senefelder's invention. These
experiments took time. The brothers' primary interest was in the idea
that if a volatile fuel were exploded in a controlled chamber, it would
release energy that could be harnessed, an invention that they called a
pyreolophore, but that we now call an internal combustion engine. They
built one that powered a model boat on rivers. It was the prototype of
the engine that still powers boats and automobiles today.

Starting in 1816, the Niépce brothers also worked sporadically on
their idea of fixing a shadow image. They found that a certain asphalt
compound was light-sensitive, and in the 1820s they produced the first
photographs, which they called heliographs. The oldest-known permanent photograph, an image of a man leading a horse, dates from 1825.
The heliograph was an image fixed on polished pewter coated with a
thin layer of bitumen, or asphalt, dissolved in lavender oil. The image
had to be exposed in the camera for at least eight hours, the brothers
said, but it may have taken days.

Nicéphore Niépce took his invention to the Royal Society in London,
whose members were not impressed. He then partnered with Louis-
Jacques-Mandé Daguerre, who developed a technique for capturing
images on silver-coated copper sheets. Silver salts were extremely light-
sensitive. Daguerre's copper images—daguerreotypes—along with
lithography, enjoyed tremendous popularity, whereas heliographs were
completely ignored.

Then in 1840, an Englishman, William Henry Fox Talbot, learned
to capture light images on paper coated with silver salts, a process
attempted unsuccessfully by the potter Thomas Wedgwood in 1800.
From then on, photography on paper developed. But Joseph Niépce was

forgotten. He had the distinction of authoring two of the most important inventions of the nineteenth century, the internal combustion engine and the photograph, without ever becoming famous. Once again, history shows that creating important inventions and becoming a "famous inventor" involve very different skills.

A LITHOGRAPH REQUIRED a stiffer ink than other types of prints, as well as a printing press that applied the image to the paper with greater pressure. By the early nineteenth century, the old Gutenberg press was finally changing.

In a notable example of the technological fallacy, numerous historians credit the dramatic increase in reading at the beginning of the nineteenth century with the improved capacity of the printing press, along with the dramatic increase in the capacity of nineteenth-century paper mills. But others, not succumbing to the fallacy, correctly point out that this dramatic growth in reading began before any of these advances in technology. Cambridge professor William St. Clair observed, "The technological changes, the evidence suggests, came after the expansion of reading was already well under way, and were more a result than a cause."

The expansion in reading was not simply a by-product of the revolutions in France and America, but a widespread phenomenon. It could even be argued, as Diderot did, that the spread of reading and its accompanying spread of knowledge led to rebellion against the old order. This was why that old order, the aristocracies and clergy of Europe, were tremendously fearful of this increasing popularity of books and newspapers and reading in general. In the late eighteenth century, people of all economic classes, rural and urban, the well educated and the little educated, men and women, young and old—everyone started reading more. People were also reading more for entertainment and much less for instruction. People were no longer reading just one book but reading one book after another. More and more newspapers were being published.

As with all changes, there was considerable discussion about their repercussions. Not everyone believed, as did Diderot, that reading was a positive and liberating experience. Some believed, as Cervantes had noted with irony, that too much reading could ruin a person. This fear of reading was connected with the desire to oppress, as is evident in the many arguments over time claiming that reading was not good for the working class or for women or for slaves.

Books were being produced at an unprecedented rate. More books were being published than people wanted, though publishers naturally tried to avoid this. Some books didn't sell at all, including some by famous poets. Percy Bysshe Shelley, like many poets today, was never published by a commercial publisher in his lifetime. William Blake, revered today as both a poet and an illustrator, had only a few hundred copies of his books published in his lifetime, many of which never sold. The phenomenon of the remainder book—excess stock sold at deep discounts—emerged, a particularly ignominious development for authors. In England, old books started turning up at groceries and cheese shops, where their pages were used for wrapping. Book pages also proved useful for lighting pipes, fireplaces, and lamps. At worst, they supplied toilets.

A NUMBER OF eighteenth-century discoveries were emblematic of the nineteenth century. The use of coke—baked carbon with sulfur removed—improved metal and eventually led to steel. The steam engine was first invented in 1698 by Thomas Savery in England to pump water out of mines. In 1712 a blacksmith, Thomas Newcomen, designed a steam-powered piston-driven engine for the same purpose. The steam engine was greatly improved in 1765 by James Watt, who created a revolution in powering machines. Then in 1804, the British Royal Navy built a steam-powered conveyor belt for the production of a type of crackers called ship's biscuits. It is impossible to say when the "Industrial Revolution" began, but once steam-powered conveyor belts were in use, it was well under way.

One of the first steps forward in printing technology was the building of presses out of iron instead of wood. In 1800, Lord Charles Stanhope built an all-cast-iron printing press and placed it in the printing shop of William Bulmer, a close friend of Thomas Bewick, the famed wood engraver. Because it was made of unyielding metal, it only required 10 percent of the force used in old wooden presses. Also, it could print 480 pages in an hour, about double the production of the old wooden press.

Soon afterward, in 1804, a German inventor named Friedrich Koenig moved to London and began working on an even more efficient press. In 1810 he produced a printing press powered by a steam engine, which could print 1,100 pages an hour; four years later, *The Times* of London began using it. Later models of the press could print on both sides of a sheet of paper at the same time. In 1843, Richard M. Hoe, a New Yorker and the son of a manufacturer of steam-powered presses, designed a press with a rotary type cylinder. It was far faster than the flatbed type press used earlier—millions of copies of a page could be printed in a day.

NOW THERE WAS both the demand and the capacity for much more printing, but where could additional paper be found?

In the first two decades of the nineteenth century, steam engines made their way into paper mills, replacing waterpower. This meant that paper mills could operate at the same pace year-round regardless of the water level in the rivers. But since steam engines were coal fired, it also meant that papermaking was dependent on the price of coal.

The problem of the demand for rags outstripping the supply had not been resolved, but was slightly eased when German chemist Carl Scheele, working in Sweden, discovered chlorine in 1774. Chlorine is a gas that when mixed with lime becomes bleach. This meant that while rags were in higher demand than ever for paper production, papermakers were no longer restricted to using white rags to make white paper. They could bleach colored rags. The ever-resourceful American papermaker Joshua Gilpin, returned from his fact-finding travels in Europe and set up a bleaching house in 1804 at the Brandywine Mill, thereby introducing bleaching to the United States.

But what really changed the production capacity and economics of papermaking in the early nineteenth century began in France in 1798. A Parisian, Nicolas-Louis Robert, had tried to volunteer in the French Army to fight for the American Revolution, but he was rejected as being too frail. He didn't go to America, but with persistence he managed, after four years, to be accepted into the French Army. Sometime between 1790 and 1794, he left the military and began working for the most famous Parisian printer, Pierre-François Didot. The Didots—sons and grandsons, brothers and cousins—were inventive printers and papermakers well known, among other things, for the Didot typeface. A handsome font of contrasting thick verticals and thin connecting lines, it is still in use today. The Didots sent Robert to Essonne, an area just south of Paris, where they had a paper mill dating back to the fourteenth century; it made high-quality paper used for printing money.

Robert had an idea for a machine that, rather than producing one sheet of paper at a time, would produce a continuous roll of paper. This was the same concept as that of the conveyor belt, though Robert had been experimenting with the idea a few years before the first conveyor belt was developed. His belt was not just a belt for moving an assembly, it was a screen with a "wet end" and a "dry end." As the belt passed under a vat, a watery pulp was poured onto it. The belt then did a side-to-side shake, similar to the motion that a vatman performed, to evenly distribute the fibers on the screen. Farther down the belt, water was sucked out of the pulp, and the waterleaf moved on to a series of felt-covered drums called couch rolls for preliminary drying. From there, it traveled to a series of heated drums on which it dried further and then rolled off the belt. The screen belt was made of a fine mesh, so the paper resembled wove. Later, a roller called a dandy roll was added to the process; it left a watermark every foot or so on the strip of waterleaf.

Long rolls of paper would prove to be invaluable to the new, fast printers as they developed, because the printers would no longer be hampered by the need to feed in sheet after sheet of handmade paper. Pierre-François Didot rejected Robert's first two attempts at such a machine, but he took the third one to his British brother-in-law John Gamble, who had it patented in London.

For fans of Denis Diderot, it would be nice to imagine that Robert came up with his machine so that more books and newspapers could be printed to enlighten and free the masses. But the truth was almost the opposite. He disliked the papermakers' guild and the papermakers, with all their rights and privileges—as did many on the management side of papermaking—and was candid about his goal of finding a way to unseat them from their perch. This was one of the first signs to the careful observer that Diderot's promised century was not going to unfold the way he imagined. Soon weavers would be in a death struggle with Joseph-Marie Jacquard's automatic punch-card-operated looms, another French invention put into operation in Britain. The weavers, like the paper workers, were a highly skilled and well-organized group who had won many rights.

The continuous-paper-machine patent caught the interest of the Fourdrinier brothers, Henry and Sealy, papermakers who built several prototypes of the huge and complicated machine, and went bankrupt in the process. Then industrialist Bryan Donkin became interested in what he called the "Fourdrinier" machine. Donkin did not play a role in the technological revolution as imagined by Diderot. It was one thing to talk of using technology to topple the authority of the aristocracy and the Church, but who or what would replace them? Diderot and the French revolutionaries had assumed it would be "the people." But as the nineteenth-century French historian Jules Michelet once wryly observed, "The people, in its highest ideal, is difficult to find in the people."

As the nineteenth century progressed, the old order was replaced by the Bryan Donkins of the world. His talent lay in identifying good ideas developed by other people and translating them into commercial practices, making a great deal of money in the process. Building the first industrial paper machine in 1804 and a better one the following year was but one example of Donkin's business acumen. Another was seizing on the ideas of another Frenchman, Nicolas Appert. Appert had written a book in 1809 called *The Art of Preserving All Kinds of Animal and Vegetable Substances for Several Years*, which had been translated into

English. He had learned how to preserve food by sealing it in a jar with a tight lid and then heating it. Only months after the book's publication, a Londoner named Peter Durand, giving no credit to Appert, patented the idea. Durand listed a number of containers besides jars, including metal, that could be used for the process, and from that patent, Bryan Donkin built the first canned-food factory across the Thames from London. Among the other ideas that Donkin developed and made a fortune on were gas valves, a machine for measuring the speed of rotating engines (that is, in terms of revolutions per minute, or rpm), and an engine that could count.

1809 A LONDON stationer named John Dickinson, celebrated for developing a type of paper to use in cannons that would not catch fire, and for making artillery safer (for the person firing it anyway) and more efficient, patented his own idea for a continuous paper machine. Known as a cylinder machine, it consisted of a cylinder of fine wire mesh revolving in a vat of pulp. The motion caused the pulp to rise to the top in a thin film, which a layer of felt then carried off to the rest of the machine. Changes in the cylinder could facilitate the production of a variety of industrial papers such as heavy wrapping paper, building paper, boxes, and roofing paper. More and more cylinders—up to eight—were later added to the machine, allowing it to produce enormous quantities of paperboard, which is made from several layers of paper. At his paper mill in Hertfordshire, Dickinson also developed silk-thread paper. This was used for postage stamps and envelopes, including the first self-sticking envelope.

It was an age when it seemed as if machines were being built to do most everything. Thomas Cobb in Banbury, Oxfordshire, worked on a paper machine from 1807 to 1812 in his North Newington Mill by the Soar River. It was based on the new idea of conveyor belts. Mechanically operated molds drained pulp and made sheets. Once the sheets were deposited on the felts, the molds were washed and mechanically returned to the vat end of the belt. A Scot, Robert Cameron, developed a similar idea in 1816. There might be a market for such machines today because there is an interest in paper that looks handmade, but they did not catch on back then because they were designed to produce individual sheets; continuous rolls were what new industry wanted.

In search of an improved paper machine, the forward-thinking American papermaker Joshua Gilpin had traveled to Europe once again in 1811. There, he had tried to negotiate with Henry Fourdrinier for one of his machines, but Fourdrinier had greeted him with seeming distrust (in truth, he had already lost control of his company and was bankrupt). Gilpin would have done better to have approached Donkin, who had already placed eighteen working Fourdrinier machines in mills around the country. While in Europe, Gilpin also became aware of Dickinson's cylinder machine, which was smaller, simpler, and easier to install than the Fourdrinier. But the problem that Gilpin encountered was that the Fourdrinier brothers, before going bankrupt, had realized the competitive advantages of the cylinder machine and had bought off Dickinson. They now had rights to that machine too, and they weren't interested in doing business with Gilpin.

And so the resourceful Gilpin decided that he would *steal* the ideas for the cylinder machine. He could never have done this with a Fourdrinier, which was much more complicated, and he did not think any Philadelphia metalworkers would understand how to build it anyway. But he studied the cylinder machine, watched it work, drew sketches, found knowledgeable people with whom he could discuss the machine's working parts, and studied the considerable amount of information that had been filed with its patent. Gilpin visited Dickinson to get a look at a working machine, but was unable to get close enough. Yet by an incredible coincidence, Gilpin's foreman, Lawrence Greatrake happened to be in London on family business. The son of an English paper-mill owner in Hertfordshire, Greatrake visited Dickinson and the two seemed to enjoy each other's company. Dickinson invited him to stay for several days and observe the machine. He would not let him take measurements, but Greatrake did manage to pace off basic dimensions. Back home at the Brandywine Mill, Greatrake and Gilpin's brother, Thomas, then built and patented their own cylinder machine in 1816; that machine did not turn out satisfactory paper until 1818.

The era of machine-made paper in America had begun. In 1827, Peter Adams in Saugerties, New York, installed the first Fourdrinier in the United States. It made what was then considered among the best writing paper in the country.

IN THE EARLY part of the Industrial Revolution, France was the land of ideas and Britain was the land of manufacturing. There was no papermaking machine in France until 1811, and in 1827, there were only four. In the 1830s, papermaking machines were commonly used in France, but most were British-built. By 1819, the Germans were also importing British machines.

British paper workers were no happier about papermaking machines than textile workers were about automatic looms. In 1816 the papermakers of Maidstone petitioned the House of Commons to stop the building of Fourdriniers. In 1830 there were riots in High Wycombe, just north of London. Workers occupied mills and destroyed some equipment. Troops were called in.

With machine-made paper, production increased tremendously and the price of paper dropped. Owning a mill became far more profitable than it had ever been before, while working in one became considerably less so. The power of the papermaking guild and other workers' organizations was considerably weakened.

On the eve of the French Revolution, Diderot had predicted that enormous changes were coming to society, that those changes would bring with them technology, and that technology, in turn, would make people freer. This is partly because he thought that technology would make information more readily available. But the dissemination of information alone does not set people free, and a new information technology creates a new ruling class. Technology by itself does not change the nature of society.

Chapter 15

INVITATION FROM
A WASP

||||||||||||||||||

The wasp seems to teach us a means of
overcoming these difficulties.

—RENÉ ANTOINE FERCHAULT DE RÉAUMUR

T WAS A MACABRE SCENE ON THE DESERTED, WINDSWEPT
killing fields of the Napoleonic Wars before the burial details went to
work. Ragmen picked through the dead, stripping off their bloodstained
uniforms and selling the cloth to papermakers.

This was not a uniquely European practice. In the summer of 1863
in the United States, after the Battle of Gettysburg, in which 51,000 men
were killed in three days, ragmen and other "scavengers of mixed nationalities," as one contemporary observer put it, traveled by wagon from
Spring Forge, more than twenty miles away, to gather rags. Others were
also looking for souvenirs, especially guns and swords, from the corpses
that were starting to fester. Three ragmen loaded their wagons with the
clothing they had stolen and sold it to the Jacob Hauer paper mill on
nearby Codorus Creek.

Hauer had died eight years earlier, and his heirs in Philadelphia
owned the mill. It produced 1,500 pounds of paper every day on one
Fourdrinier machine. The paper was made from rags bought from

wandering ragmen. But once the Civil War had begun, it had become more difficult to obtain rags and the mill was starving for them—until they received the wagonloads of uniforms, bandages, and slings from the Gettysburg battlefield.

The local people were deeply offended by the scavengers, especially the ragmen, some of whom, they said, went as far as to dig up shallow graves. The army sent in cavalry and infantry troops to stop the stealing, and the 21st Pennsylvania Cavalry apprehended the three ragmen as they were taking a wagonload back to the paper mill. The three men were given the dirtiest post-battle job—clearing 5,000 dead horses from the battlegrounds. Most were put in piles and burned. The stench, spreading out for miles, was overwhelming.

But once again, the mill had no source of rags. They could not even buy clean scraps, because these were sent to a nearby military hospital for bandaging. The mill went out of business and its 101-acre facility was sold at a bargain price by the Orphan Court. It was subsequently purchased by a twenty-one-year-old local, Philip Henry Glatfelter, for $14,000. The Glatfelter Company still makes paper on the site today.

WITH PEOPLE READING more than ever and presses printing more than ever, on paper that the mills could produce faster than ever, there was only one part of the equation missing. Nothing had been done to increase the rag supply. The problem was becoming desperate.

Even at the height of the Industrial Revolution, nothing had changed in the rag-collection process. The ragmen wandered the streets and took what they gathered to the rag merchants. In the United States, ragmen went from house to house looking for rags until near the end of the nineteenth century. The American people still had ingrained in them from Revolutionary times that they needed to save rags so that paper could be made. The advertising line "Ladies Save Your Rags" was ubiquitous.

John Clark & Company, which opened in 1807 in Black River, Wisconsin, even tried poetry to acquire more rags:

Sweet ladies pray be not offended,
Nor mind the jest of sneering wags
No harm, believe us, is intended,
When humbly we request your rags.
The scraps, which you reject, unfit
To clothe the tenant of a hovel,
May shine in sentiment and wit,
And help to make a charming novel . . .

Incredibly, there are three more stanzas like this.

The United States did not have nearly enough rags to supply its paper mills, and so it imported rags from Europe. Foreign rag imports to New York, mostly from Italy, rose three and a half times between 1845 and 1859. In Europe, automated textile mills were producing more cloth, but that was not translating into useful rags. Wool had become increasingly fashionable, often replacing cotton and linen. In 1825, the United States imported $79,639 worth of rags. The following year, the figure had risen to $122,624. By 1832, it had reached $707,011. These rises reflected both an increase in the amount of rags imported and an increase in price; the scarcity of rags had made prices climb. By the 1850s, rags represented half the cost of making paper.

Meanwhile, the demand for paper, especially inexpensive paper, was soaring. Newspapers in particular, with their growing number of subscribers, operated on a commercial model that required cheaper and faster product. Once the telegraph was launched in the 1840s, news could arrive with great rapidity and newspapers were expected to keep up, especially with news from the trade and commodity markets. In 1852 the *New York Tribune* installed six-cylinder presses that could print 15,000 sheets per hour. This seemed nearly miraculous until other papers started installing ten-cylinder presses that could print 25,000 sheets an hour. And that output more or less doubled after the 1860s, when presses could print both sides of a sheet at the same time. As transportation improved, notably through railroads, circulation areas also expanded. It all seemed limitless—if newspapers could only get enough low-priced paper.

In both Europe and America, papermakers needed to find a material for making paper that was both cheaper and more readily available than rags. In ancient times, the Asians had found numerous alternatives, such as bamboo and tree bark, but the nineteenth-century Europeans and Americans struggled to find one. In Britain, the first written suggestion of an alternative paper source appeared in a slim booklet published in 1716 with the unwieldy title *Essay for the month of December 1716 to be continued Monthly, by a Society of Gentlemen, For the benefit of the People of England*. Aside from the not-entirely-impractical suggestion that paper mills be set up on barges in the Thames and other large rivers, which the authors said was already being done on the Elbe and the Danube, the society suggested that instead of making paper from rags and hemp products such as rope, raw hemp could be used. That was similar to what the Aztecs might have done with agave. The society also suggested that mills could grow their own supplies by planting hemp on the mill grounds.

But the real forefather of modern paper, the man who solved the rag problem, though it took over a century for his ideas to be implemented, was a Frenchman born in the late 1600s, René Antoine Ferchault de Réaumur. Réaumur, who has a major street in Paris named after him, was a restless genius who studied everything from geometry to birds' nests. He is most famous for creating a temperature scale in which zero is the temperature at which water freezes. It is the basis of the Celsius thermometer used by most of the world today, though, foolishly, not by the United States.

Réaumur was fascinated with insects. He studied wasps and found that they built nests from wood fibers—nests that very much resembled paper. Wasps gathered wood particles from weathered old barns or fenceposts and built ingeniously designed waterproof homes with dome-shaped roofs of thin, light, overlapping paper. It occurred to Réaumur that these remarkable natural engineers had a better way of making paper than people did. When in 1719 he presented his study of wasps to the French Royal Academy, he stated:

> The American Wasps form very fine paper, like ours; they extract the fiber of common wood of the countries where they live. They teach us that paper can be made from the fiber of plants without the use of rags and linen. And seem to invite us to try whether we cannot make fine and good paper from the use of certain woods. If we had woods similar to those used by the American wasps for their paper, we could make the whitest paper, for this material is very white. By a further beating and breaking of the fibers that the wasps make and using the thin paste that comes from them, a very fine paper can be composed.

He went on to say how important it was to study wasps, because rags were becoming scarce and expensive. He warned, "While the consumption of paper increases every day, the production of linen stays the same." But neither he nor anyone else took up the wasps' invitation.

The Europeans did start looking for other materials with which to make paper, however. In 1727, Franz Ernst Brückmann, a German mineralogist, published a book about geology printed on asbestos paper, a toxic idea that fortunately did not catch on. A Flemish eighteenth-century naturalist, Albertus Seba, came up with other ideas that had more of a future. He suggested making paper either from trees or seaweed, both of which are done today. Others suggested using various bushes or swamp moss. In 1771, a German clergyman and aspiring naturalist, Jacob Christian Schäffer, published a six-volume investigation of alternative sources for making paper; included in the volumes were sample sheets that he had made. The formulas' main ingredient was vegetable fibers, to which about 20 percent cotton fiber was added. He made paper from raw hemp, bark, and straw, all three of which were familiar in ancient China. He also made paper from wasp nests, vines, moss, cabbage stalks, pinecones, asbestos, thistles, turf, corn husks, potatoes, old shingles, reeds, and the leaves of horse chestnut, walnut, tulip, and linden trees. He experimented with several types of wood. For his paper made from potatoes, which he called earth apples after the French *pommes de terre*, he had to first explain what potatoes were, as they were then unknown in most of Europe.

After Schäffer's investigations, it was understood that there were any number of materials that might be used to make paper. In the United States, there was even an attempt to make paper from okra. In 1800, the Marquis of Salisbury presented King George III with a book whose pages were made entirely from straw. That same year, Matthias Koops published *Historical Account of the Substances which Have Been Used to Describe Events, and to Convey Ideas from the Earliest Date to the Invention of Paper*. More significant than its text was the yellowish paper on which it was printed—it too was made entirely from straw. Koops even started calling his Millbank paper mill the Straw Paper Manufactory. There were other experimental features to Koops's book. The second edition contained an appendix that was printed on paper made of wood; according to historian Dard Hunter, this was the first use of bleached wood paper in an English book. Koops also experimented with recycled paper.

By the middle of the nineteenth century, the British were making small amounts of paper from mill sweepings. Irish mills made paper from the waste flax found in linen mills. Cotton mills started selling their waste to paper mills rather than discarding it. Early nineteenth-century paper mills in Lancashire became dependent on the scrap from cotton and linen mills. Straw produced an unattractive off-white paper that was used for newspapers but little else. A more successful alternative to rags, used in Britain, was esparto grass, which is a perennial grass that grows in Spain and North Africa. Even with import costs, the grass was cheaper than rags, and by midcentury, the British were making significant amounts of paper with it. Esparto grass was a British specialty adopted by no other country.

Esparto may be why Britain was slower than the Continent to turn to wood pulp. There were patents registered in Britain for making paper from wood pulp in the 1840s and 1850s, but the idea was not taken up by paper mills. On the Continent, the wood-pulp industry was inaugurated in 1840 when a German, F. G. Keller, patented a very workable method of making paper from the pulp produced by grinding wood. By 1850, paper based on the Keller patent was being commercially manufactured. German techniques for producing ground wood pulp were then readily adopted in North America, a land where forests were plentiful.

MAKING PAPER OUT of wood, though it may seem natural enough today, did not strike most people as a sensible thing to do. In Germany in 1765, paper was made experimentally from wood pulp, but outside of a few eccentric circles and a patent or two filed in London, the idea did not catch on—not even after machine-made paper had generally replaced handmade. The first wood-based paper in America was not made until 1863; papermakers hesitated giving up scrounging for old, dirty clothes and replacing them with a natural product made principally of cellulose.

Cellulose is the fiber from which paper is made, and wood is about half cellulose. The exact amount varies slightly. European spruce is exactly 50 percent cellulose, but American white spruce is 56.48 percent. American aspen or poplar is 57.25 percent cellulose, and American hemlock is only 48.7 percent. The percentage of cellulose can vary by as much as 4 percent on different parts of the same tree.

Traditional paper sources such as flax and hemp have a higher percentage of cellulose than wood, and cotton is 90 percent cellulose. If those statistics had been known in the mid-1800s, they could have been a good reason for papermakers to hesitate about using wood for paper, especially since it was obvious that very little needed to be done to cotton to turn it into paper, whereas a great deal needed to be done to wood. Making paper from wood is counterintuitive; wood is hard. In contrast, grass, flax, cotton, hemp rags, and other materials are soft, like paper, though they require a long process of soaking, fermenting, and beating before they can be reduced to the fibers necessary for papermaking.

Nobody even knew about cellulose until 1838, however, when French chemist Anselme Payen discovered it. Cellulose is a carbohydrate made of glucose. It is what chemists call "a straight chain polymer," which means that while other starches tend to coil or spread out, cellulose fibers remain in stiff rods with hard outer walls that are not soluble in water.

The first attempt in the United States to commercially produce wood pulp for paper mills was by a Massachusetts company, Platner & Smith in 1857. The effort failed, however, because the process was too expensive and yielded poor-quality paper. The first commercially successful wood pulp did not appear until 1867, when it was made in Curtisville, Massachusetts, by two German brothers, Albrecht and Rudolf Pagenstecher, who had brought over two German Keller-Voelter wood grinders. They sold their pulp to the Smith Paper Company, which used it to produce one of the fastest-growing commercial products of the day, newsprint. Seventeen years later, in 1884, turning wood into paper became truly efficient thanks to Peter Jensen in Maasbüll, Germany. He started producing wood chippers, machines that rapidly cut wood blocks into pieces no more than one inch long and 1/8 to 3/16 of an inch thick.

In the 1860s, an American chemist named Benjamin Chew Tilghman experimented with breaking down wood by cooking it in a sulfur dioxide and water bath placed in a long rotating cylinder that he called a digester—the name by which it is still known. At first the pulp came out very dark and wouldn't bleach, but he solved the problem by adding a base, lime, to neutralize the acid. His digester was fifty feet long and three feet wide. In 1867 Tilghman patented his invention in London, *the* place for industrial patents at the time. His patent included environmental measures such as instructions on how to use water to absorb the sulfur-dioxide gas fumes the process produced and how to turn that water and sulfur-dioxide solution into fertilizer. But the paper industry was mainly interested in the first part of his patent.

Tilghman's "sulphite" process ultimately became the mainstay of

North American paper production. By 1920, the United States and Canada, rich in forestland, were producing more than 2 million tons of sulphite pulp annually. The sulphite process gave off horrendous odors, but fortunately many paper mills, no longer needing to be situated near population centers for rags, were now located deep in the countryside, near forests. And though the mills were no longer water-powered, they were still located near a water source. A tremendous amount of water was needed to move and spread the wood fibers thinly on the screens; the solution had to be only 2 to 4 percent wood fibers and 96 to 98 percent water, making the pulp look like slightly cloudy water. All paper mills today are still located by a water source.

To the Europeans, wood pulp seemed to be the answer too, but since they had far fewer forests than the North Americans did, they often had to import the pulp. By the end of the nineteenth century, Britain was importing almost 500,000 tons of wood pulp annually. By the 1950s, they were importing four times that much. Paper demand and paper production had caught up with each other, making it much easier to produce more. Between 1870 and 1880, Britain doubled the amount of paper it produced; in the last forty years of the nineteenth century, an average of two new paper mills started up there every year. This led to price wars, which was hard on the paper mills, making it difficult for some to survive, but it was good for newspapers, which thrived on making their product as cheap as possible. In 1869, the cost of *The Times* of London went from 4 pence per paper to 3.

According to the US census, there were 169 paper mills in the United States in 1820; by 1870, that number had grown to 669. And in the 1870s, it became fashionable to make inexpensive paper versions of everything. A paper petticoat went on the market and, whatever its drawbacks, cost only 15 cents. An invention was patented for making coffins from paper pulp. Men's paper shirt collars were a $75 million a year industry in Boston. A Troy, New York, company started making boats out of varnished paper. In 1874, Nathaniel Bishop shoved off from Quebec on a 2,500-mile voyage in one of their fifty-eight-pound paper canoes. Eight months later, he arrived in the Gulf of Mexico.

WHEN THE SECOND edition of Matthias Koops's book came out, the appendix in the back printed on wood-based paper was white, but over time, it turned brown. So have most of the books printed between the 1860s and the early twentieth century. The culprit is lignin, the substance that holds cellulose fibers together. Where there is cellulose, there is lignin. Hemp has less than 4 percent lignin, but wood can be as much as 30 percent lignin. That is what makes wood the only really solid vegetable fiber that is sturdy enough for construction.

Paper that turned brown with time was acceptable for newsprint. The basic assumption about newspapers, though not always correct, was that they were inexpensive and intended to be thrown away. That assumption was true for certain other types of paper as well, including what used to be called "math paper," cheap paper for schoolchildren to use to work out math problems. But books and stationery and official documents could not be allowed to turn color after a year or two.

In 1879 Carl F. Dahl invented a process in Danzig, then part of Prussia, called *kraft*. Kraft is a German word for "strong," and Dahl's process made paper stronger. Wood chips were treated with sodium hydroxide and sodium sulfide, sometimes called white liquor. This broke down the bond that holds cellulose to lignin, and the lignin could then be washed away. In 1895, the Glatfelter mill near the Gettysburg battlefield installed the kraft process and only then did they completely abandon rag for wood. Both in Europe and the United States the kraft process was embraced by some, but did not completely take over the old sulfite process until the 1940s.

A 150-year-old book made from wood paper will not hold up as well as the 500-year-old books of Aldus Manutius made from rag paper. Even today, the finest paper, used for quality stationery, artwork, or currency, is often made from linen or cotton, not wood. Some mills, such as Crane in Dalton, Massachusetts, always stuck with linen and cotton and never switched to wood. But they could do so because their mainstay business was the high-grade paper used to print US dollars and other currencies.

When papermakers turned to wood, they used acidic water to soak pulp. It was logical to think that acid would break the pulp down to fibers, and it did. The problem was that the acid continued breaking down the paper, and so now more than a century's worth of books are falling apart. It was not until 1970 that the concept of acid-free paper was widely embraced. Although it is counterintuitive, alkaline, the exact opposite of acid, breaks down pulp just as well as acid. Now in the Library of Congress and the New York Public Library they are deacidifying books published from 1840 to 1970 with a gas or alkaline solution.

A huge number of books were produced during this period, often with paper made on the originally French-designed Fourdrinier machines, grown so large that they had to be housed in huge airplane hangar–like buildings. An American Fourdrinier in 1867 produced 100 feet of paper a minute. By 1872, it had sped up to 175 feet a minute. In 1880, Glatfelter installed a Fourdrinier that turned out 200 feet of paper per minute. By the end of the century, a roll of paper that came off a Fourdrinier was more than 13 feet wide.

Already by 1873, the United States, a land of forests and industry, had overtaken Europe as the largest papermaker in the world. Germany and Britain competed for second place.

Chapter 16

ADVANTAGES IN THE HEAD

||||||||||||||||||

The advantage of hand-press work does not, then, after all, lie in the hand but in the head, which is here allowed to direct each step of the work, humoring the refractory sheets of hand-made paper in a thousand ways, which are impossible when printed by other means.

—CLARKE CONWELL, *Catalogue for the Elston Press*

THE PAPER WORLD GREW INCREASINGLY MECHANIZED, both in papermaking and printing, and as with all new technology, there was a strong reaction against it by those who saw it as a degradation of culture and society. In Britain, a movement arose in the late nineteenth century called Arts and Crafts. It was led by art critic John Ruskin, designer William Morris, and artist Walter Crane. They wanted to return to Diderot's ideal of artisans crafting with pride at their workbenches; they believed that factory workers lived an inhumane existence. They also wanted to bring art to the lives of working-class people, but there was an inherent contradiction in that goal: the old-fashioned craftsmanship that they embraced made objects that the working class could not afford.

William Morris wanted to make art for the masses based on designs from the medieval age, hardly an art-for-the-masses period of history. He founded his own press, the Kelmscott Press, and used an old-fashioned type setting, producing stunningly beautiful books. He had an extremely skilled punch cutter, Edward Prince. Morris, who designed the two facing pages of an open book as a single work, printed on an 1823 hand press, and his 1896 Chaucer is considered to be one of the most beautiful books ever made. These books were published in very small editions for high prices, however, and it is doubtful that any factory worker ever had one at home. The Kelmscott Press was extremely influential, however, and marked the beginning of a movement of small private presses printing high-quality books. There is always a small but avid market for expensive, limited-edition books. Today there are still small presses making beautiful books on hand presses, sometimes even using handmade paper as well.

The foremost private press in France in the early twentieth century was run by Ambroise Vollard, who produced books on a hand press with illustrations by Pierre Bonnard, Raoul Dufy, Pablo Picasso, and Georges Rouault, among others. Vollard was a perfectionist, and some of his books took years to produce.

The Arts and Crafts movement had a huge influence in America as well, beginning with Boston and at Harvard. Charles Eliot Norton, a Harvard fine-arts professor, founded the Boston Society of Arts and Crafts. Lectures on typography were given at the Boston Public Library. Several small presses were started.

Thomas Bird Mosher of Portland, Maine, the son of a Yankee sea captain, did not consider himself to be part of the Arts and Crafts movement. From 1891 to 1923, he produced books that were small and inexpensive. Nevertheless, they were handmade. His type came from the Dickinson foundry in Boston or William Caslon's foundry in England, the same British type used for the Declaration of Independence. He relied on handmade paper, usually from Holland, but sometimes from Japan. The Elston Press of New Rochelle, New York, also used the old British Caslon type, hand pressed on handmade paper. The publisher, Clarke Conwell—his wife, Helen M. O'Kane, often the illustrator for his books—said that the advantage of printing handmade lay not so much in the material as in the way you could control every step.

The Kelmscott Press also influenced commercial publishers in Britain, on the Continent, and in the United States. While working within the confines of industrialization, publishers pushed to produce high-quality products. Sometimes they even imitated handmade paper—for example, manufacturing fake, machine-made "deckle edge" sheets.

BY THE MID-NINETEENTH century, newspapers and magazines were trying to use photography in their publications. The Crimean War and the American Civil War were the first wars covered by photographers. If people could see what war actually looked like, the thinking went, perhaps it would no longer seem romantic. In fact, war photography of that era was particularly grizzly because a camera's shutter had to be kept open on an unmoving object for a long period. Even blinking would give the subject spooky, blank, gray eyes. The only soldiers who could stay still long enough to be photographed were dead. And so photographers shot frame after frame of dead soldiers, lying where they fell on the battlefield.

Newspapers and magazines needed other pictures too—especially illustrated magazines, which had become fashionable. This led to a revival of Thomas Bewick's style of wood engraving. Frank Leslie's *Illustrated Newspaper*, founded in 1852, was one of the first publications to use what could be called photojournalism, although, recognizing photography's limitations, he relied mainly on wood engravings. The Harper & Brothers publishing company founded *Harper's Weekly* magazine in 1857. The company's four brothers—James, John, Wesley, and Fletcher—had founded a monthly seven years earlier, publishing British authors such as Charles Dickens and William Makepeace Thackeray, and it had proven to be so successful that they started the weekly. Its leading competitor, *The Atlantic*, distinguished itself by publishing abolitionist writers, but *Harper's* wanted to be a national magazine read in the North and the South and so avoided issues such as slavery. Abolitionists sneeringly called it *Harper's Weakly*. But once hostilities broke out, *Harper's* built a strong following with their well-illustrated war coverage. One of their illustrators was Thomas Nast, the most famous cartoonist of the nineteenth century, who made engravings of battleground scenes in the Border States. Nast is also credited with creating the symbol of the elephant for the Republican Party and with an image of Santa Claus that has dominated American Christmases ever since.

Harper's also had wood carvers, modern American *Formschneiders*, at the ready to make engravings. The magazine hired major American artists such as Winslow Homer, who drew battle scenes and camp scenes during the war, and afterward, provided the magazine with images of his native New England.

Seesaw—Gloucester, Massachusetts, *wood engraving from a drawing by Winslow Homer,* Harper's Weekly, *September 12, 1874.*

ILLUSTRATED MAGAZINES AND satirical cartoons were popular in Europe too. In 1841 a wood engraver who had worked with Thomas Bewick, Ebenezer Landells, founded *Punch*, a heavily illustrated satirical magazine influenced by the radical French magazine *Le Charivari*. *Le Charivari* was illustrated by Honoré Daumier, the nineteenth-century French artist most famous during his lifetime for his caricatures. When he and the art of lithography were both young, he was one of the first to master the new print form. In his lifetime he made about 4,000 lithographs, 1,000 wood engravings, and 1,000 drawings. He also produced 500 paintings and 100 sculptures. Daumier's many fine paintings and sculptures were not recognized by the art world until after his death in 1879 at age seventy.

Punch drew notable writers, among them William Makepeace

Honoré Daumier lithograph, 1854, from a series titled "Tenants and Landlords." The caption reads, "There you go, the only place still available to rent. See if you can put your things there. And I should warn you that the last tenant was thrown out for a lack of cleanliness."

Thackeray. Their chief political cartoonist was John Tenniel, who drew 2,000 cartoons for the magazine though he is best remembered today as the original illustrator of *Alice in Wonderland*. He was succeeded by Ernest Shepard, who became known as the illustrator of A. A. Milne's *Winnie the Pooh*.

Some British magazines grew popular through the authors they serialized. In 1837, Richard Bentley began *Bentley's Miscellany*, which published the enormously successful serialization of Charles Dickens's *Oliver Twist*, illustrated by George Cruikshank. Cruikshank came from a family of illustrators and, like Daumier, became celebrated for his satirical caricatures. He became close friends with Dickens during the serialization of *Oliver Twist*, but that friendship ended when he started to claim that he was the true author of the novel.

WITH INDUSTRIALIZATION CAME new commercial ideas. In the United States, playing cards, now easier to produce, took on new subjects. In the 1880s, two different sets of cards with pictures of seventy-two leading baseball players were produced, one in Boston and one in New York—the first appearance of baseball cards.

In midcentury, a huge change took place in typesetting with the introduction of the keyboard. A popular curiosity at the Great Exhibition of 1851 in London, considered to be the first World's Fair, the keyboard was part of a new writing machine being marketed to individuals, not presses. However, the first typewriter did not go into commercial production until 1873, when it was manufactured by the arms maker Remington. Author Mark Twain used a Remington, and it is sometimes claimed that he was the first author to turn in a typewritten manuscript, though the claim of first is uncertain. Numerous typewriter models followed, some with letters arranged on a curve, some printing on a flat surface, some printing on a cylinder. Once separate keys and bars for each letter were established, it was discovered that frequently used letters, if next to each other, would jam during rapid typing; one key would fail to retract in time for the other. The configuration of the keyboard was then changed, based on letter usage in the English language, to avoid jams. That is why *a* is below *q* and above *z*, and why *c* is straddled by *x* and *v*. Despite writing in different languages, the Europeans adopted the American keyboard with only a few changes.

The keyboard was also used for the new linotype machines invented in 1886. The name was derived from the fact that a mold, known as a matrix, for an entire "line of type" could be composed on a keyboard and cast, which was far faster than setting type letter by letter. Linotype machines were used by newspapers into the 1970s.

Along with the new technology, a new occupation was invented, that of the typist-secretary. It was widely believed that women had more nimble fingers than men. They had supposedly demonstrated that skill while working in the garment industry, and soon the secretary—previously a man's position—became a woman's job.

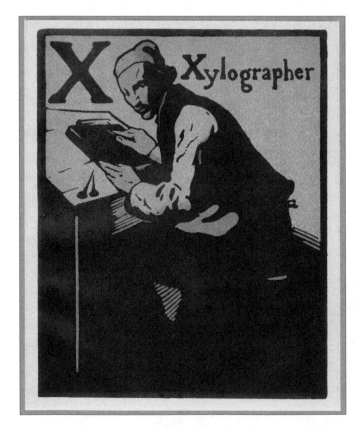

Xylographer.
*A lithograph
by William
Nicolson from
An Alphabet,
1898. The series
was originally
woodcuts, but
then lithographs
of the woodcuts
were made to
facilitate greater
reproduction.*

In 1868, Hippolyte Marinoni, a French printing machine maker, invented the flexible zinc lithographic plate, which could curve around the printing cylinder. The invention was steadily refined and evolved into what is called offset printing, first used in 1904.

Offset printing made it much easier to merge printed text and illustrations on the same page, as had been done with block books in the fifteenth century. The new process also facilitated the publishing of cartoons.

According to the French, the artist Rodolphe Töpffer, a German, had invented cartoons, *bandes dessinées,* in the 1820s by publishing stories that were largely advanced through illustrations with only a few lines of text. Gustave Doré, the great French book illustrator, also told stories in this way, creating the first of his popular *Travaux d'Hercule* (Labors of Hercules) series in 1847 when he was only fifteen years old. By the 1890s, cartoon books had become very popular in France. At about the same time, American newspapers started featuring cartoons in their Sunday papers. *The Yellow Kid*, tales of a waif in a bright-yellow robe, was a beloved newspaper feature in the United States at the end of the century.

EVEN IN THE faster world of an industrialized society, fine art was not vanishing. In fact, it was flourishing. Old forms were being revived. The late nineteenth century became a golden age of printmaking.

In the 1860s, Alfred Cadart formed the Société des Aquafortistes, the etchers' society, to restore the importance of that art. Soon major artists were making etchings. Cadart then tried to do the same for lithography and gave stones to Édouard Manet, Henri Fantin-Latour, Félix Bracquemond, Alphonse Legros, and Théodule-Armand Ribot—five of the leading French artists of the day. But those lithographs were never published; there seemed to be little public interest in lithography as fine art. Lithography had become associated with book illustration, advertising, and other commercial endeavors.

Some artists did have more success with lithographs a decade later, however. In the 1870s, the artist Jean-Baptiste-Camille Corot created interesting lithographs at the end of his life. Manet's lithographs for an edition of Poe's "The Raven"—a commercial failure—made a strong impression on artists. Edgar Degas and Odilon Redon also worked with lithographs. But the man who revived lithography—along with wood-cuts, an art form that had died out centuries earlier—was artist Paul Gauguin. Raised in luxury in Peru, and not as "a wild Inca" as he liked to claim, Gauguin was then living penniless in France. A rebel and an outsider, he didn't really fit in anywhere and yet was enormously influential. An artist's artist who earned little from his work, he was taken in by Impressionists such as Camille Pissarro and Paul Cézanne, but didn't really belong to the Impressionist movement.

Gauguin painted not what he saw, but what he felt about what he saw. Symbolism, Expressionism, and Fauvism all owe a debt to Gauguin. Because he was so influential and did so much work on paper, paper became important to the era's modern art movement. And because he went back to carving woodcuts, that too became part of modern art.

Gauguin was already over forty when he produced his first prints on paper in a series of eleven zincographs for the 1889 Exposition Universelle, a government-sponsored centennial celebration of the French Revolution. The event drew huge crowds and was a place where French art "totally triumphed," in the words of one of the organizers. A zincograph was a crayon drawing done on a Hippolyte Marinoni zinc plate rather than on a stone. The ability of the plate to bend and fit into the printer was its chief advantage from a printer's point of view. But the artist was much more interested in the delicate images that the plates could produce. Zinc-plate images were difficult to print well, but in those difficulties lay great possibilities. Gauguin's eleven zincographs are still regarded as a high point in lithography.

When creating art on paper, Gauguin understood from the outset that the paper itself made a statement. At the time, many artists were drawing and creating prints on colored paper—usually pale blue or greenish blue. The colors were soft and understated. But for his zincographs, Gauguin chose a bright canary-yellow wove paper. The Cleveland Museum, which owns a set of the zincographs, commissioned London paper historian Peter Bower to analyze and identify the paper on which they are printed. He found it to be machine-made paper of cotton and linen rag, with a small amount of soda-treated soft wood pulp added. This was a fairly typical blend for quality machine-made paper in the late nineteenth century. However, Bower could find no French, German, Dutch, or English papermaker from that time who made bright-yellow paper and wondered if it was specially commissioned from a small mill. The color came from a chemical pigment, chrome yellow, made from chromium, mixed in the pulp. Chrome yellow was a common pigment used by nineteenth-century painters, including Gauguin. Gauguin loved yellow, as did his friend Vincent van Gogh, whom he visited in Arles just before starting his zincographs. The two artists considered it to be the color of modernism.

During Gauguin's time, machine-made art paper that imitated hand-made paper was starting to be produced. A leader in this area was, and still is, the French company Arches, whose machine-made paper some-times has deckle edges and is made from cotton with the occasional addition of flax or esparto. The Arches company began making paper in 1492 in the Vosges, and their paper was used by artists from Albrecht Dürer to Henri Matisse as their company seamlessly transitioned from handmade to machine-made "handmade" paper.

TO CARVE WOODCUTS, the artist must in essence work in reverse, because printing the inked block on a piece of paper produces a mirror image. But Gauguin carved his blocks with the images facing in the same direction as they did in the final print. He even carved his name, "P. Gauguin" in the normal way. His trick lay in using handmade Japanese paper. It is thin as tissue, but because it is composed of extremely long fibers, it is strong enough to survive the fairly violent rubbing needed to transfer the ink to the paper. Gauguin could display the print bled through to the flip side of the thin paper, where it had a slightly diffused, softer look.

Woodcuts had never gone out of fashion in Japan, and Gauguin was a great admirer of Japanese art. In the 1670s, Hishikawa Moronobu popularized a style of woodcuts called *ukiyo-e*, which cryptically means "picture of the floating world." His woodcuts were characterized by fine lines and a dynamic placement of figures. The pictures always seemed to be in motion, as though in midstory. But Moronobu's popularity also came from his subject matter—beautiful women in vaguely erotic poses.

Moronobu hand-colored his blocks occasionally, but his work was mostly black-and-white, and his style of woodcarving continued to be popular after his death in 1694. In the eighteenth century, artist Okumura Masanobu began making colored wood-block prints in the ukiyo-e style by using several blocks in different colors. Ukiyo-e reached its highest development in the nineteenth century, shortly before Gauguin was born, with the landscape prints of Katsushika Hokusai. His 1831 wood-block series, "Thirty-Six Views of Mount Fuji," is the world's most famous work of ukiyo-e, and one of these prints in particular, *The Great Wave of Kanagawa*, is one of the most famous works of Japanese art.

Gauguin, who admired Japanese art in general, was particularly drawn to ukiyo-e. In his studio in Le Pouldu, a little port on the tip of Brittany, he kept many prints by Kitagawa Utamaro, an eighteenth-century ukiyo-e master known for his color prints of beautiful women. Gauguin took ukiyo-e prints with him to the South Seas, where he produced his famous Tahitian paintings, many featuring beautiful women not unlike the women in Utamaro's prints. Forty-five Japanese prints were found stuck on the walls of the hut where Gauguin died, in the French Polynesian town of Atuona in the remote Marquesas Islands. Gauguin produced about eighty different works on paper. He thought of them as an inexpensive way of spreading his reputation, in the hopes that people would buy his paintings. But his paper work was so original that it set off a passion for works on paper that lasted all the way through the twentieth century and into the twenty-first.

In the early twentieth century, the German Expressionists rebelled against society by rejecting the use of any kind of natural realism in either color or form. It was inevitable that they would turn to woodcuts, as the movement held both Dürer and Gauguin in high esteem. Their woodcuts were dark in color, and dramatized white spaces with large swathes of pure black. Although Norwegian, Edvard Munch, born in Oslo in 1863, was one of the early figures in German Expressionism. He was strongly influenced by Gauguin while in Paris, and in 1894, moved to Berlin, which was to become the center of the new movement. Munch showed virtuosity in lithography, woodcuts, mezzotints, and etchings, and invented a technique of inking different areas of the same block with different colors.

Another leading German Expressionist, Emil Nolde, was from a German peasant family. As a young man, he worked as a furniture carver, but he did not start carving wood blocks until 1906, when he was almost

Käthe Kollwitz,
Old Man with
Noose, *1923.*

forty years old. His wood blocks flaunt a crude simplicity. He carved very quickly, welcoming oddly turned lines, and relished aberrations in his printing—no two prints of his are the same. He had faith in the fortuitous little accidents of weak ink transfers or heavy blotched lines.

After the horrors of World War I, the German Expressionist prints became dark in subject matter as well as color. Käthe Kollwitz, the wife of a doctor in working-class Berlin whose son had died in the war, created chillingly morbid prints of widows. Another of her prints depicts an old man hanging himself. Kollwitz would probably be better known today if most of her work had not been destroyed in a 1943 Allied bombing.

BY THE TWENTIETH century, art on paper had become an essential part of the work of most artists. In his long and creatively restless life, Pablo Picasso produced 2,400 prints. When he died in 1973, a mountain of unknown plates and proofs was found in his studio. Picasso did his first prints, a series of etchings of acrobats, *saltimbanques*, in 1904–1905. He sent the plates off to a printer in the hopes of making some money, but they did not sell well. Nevertheless, he became increasingly serious about creating art on paper and in 1907 bought a small printing press for his studio.

Like Dürer, Picasso realized the tremendous potential of paper to reach a broad segment of the population. He also used printmaking for political causes, such as raising money for the Spanish Republic during the Spanish Civil War. At the 1937 Paris World's Fair, for which Picasso did his famous painting *Guernica*, he put on sale an edition of 850 copies of a portfolio of two prints and a poem he wrote himself entitled *Sueño y Mentira de Franco* (The dream and lie of Franco).

Initially through the efforts of the dealer Daniel-Henry Kahnweiler, who started his own press because he wanted to see books illustrated by major artists rather than professional illustrators, Picasso illustrated numerous works. Joan Miró, who became as well known for his etchings and lithographs as for his painting, did the same. It was the way of the modern artist.

Picasso went through phases in almost everything. But paper was apparently never far from his thoughts. In the 1930s, when he became an avid sculptor, he did a series of forty etchings on the same themes as his sculptures. An artist can sell many etchings, but only a few buyers can afford sculptures. For a while, Picasso turned to lithography. Then in the 1950s, he was one of the first to popularize linoleum cuts, which are like wood, but softer and more receptive to ink. He used linoleum cuts for posters at first and then for more serious work.

Twentieth-century paper didn't have nearly as many variations and imperfections as the paper made in previous centuries, when every mill produced a different paper, some with little translucent circles caused by accidental water drops. But paper-hungry twentieth-century artists still had choices. Many used high-quality machine-made art paper such as that produced by the Arches company, or various handmade papers. Artists could still choose between laid and wove paper as well. When Picasso and Georges Braque were experimenting with cubism, they used laid paper. The lines of the wire seemed in keeping with the geometry. Fernand Léger preferred a vanilla-colored wove paper.

SUDDENLY, IN THE early twentieth century, wood blocks were popular as book illustrations again, and the "wordless book" came into fashion. These book-length stories told completely through woodcuts are often described as the origin of the graphic novel. But both wordless books and graphic novels descend from fifteenth-century block books. Cartoons were also one of the inspirations for wordless books. Another may have been silent movies, which were enjoying popularity at the time.

When German novelist Thomas Mann was asked what film most moved him, he replied, *Passionate Journey*. But *Passionate Journey*, or *Mein Studenbuch* in German, is not a film. It's wordless novel told in 167 woodcuts by Belgian artist Frans Masereel. Published in Germany in 1919, it is the story of a man who goes to a city and learns about life.

Masereel was one of the few twentieth-century artists whose primary medium was woodcuts. In addition to his prints, he created more than fifty wordless novels in woodcuts. They sold thousands of copies, partly

Woodcut from
Passionate Journey
by Frans Masereel,
1919.

because his savvy publisher, Kurt Wolff, had seen their potential not as art-market books but as inexpensive books for working-class people who were not great readers; in other words, the cartoon market. Wolff nevertheless sought out distinguished writers such as Thomas Mann and Hermann Hesse to write the books' introductions.

The American artist Lynd Ward discovered Masereel while in Germany studying wood engraving. Ward's fine-lined prints are engravings, not woodcuts. His first wordless novel, *Gods' Man*, published in 1929, sold 20,000 copies and is still in print. It is the story of an artist who comes to the big city, signs a contract with a masked man, and is awash in the corruption of big money until he escapes to a quiet country life.

Wordless novels were usually created with woodcuts, but occasionally with wood engravings, such as those by Lynd Ward, linoleum cuts, or some other medium. Otto Nückel, a German artist, originally preferred woodcuts, but during World War I had difficulty finding suitable wood and so turned to carving lead, a technique he invented. But none of the other wordless novels ever achieved the fame and popularity of Masereel's and Ward's.

———

FINE HANDMADE PAPER is not always used for art. Over the years, the Japanese had become experts at making thin, light paper with long fibers, which made it extremely strong. During World War II, the Japanese military came up with an unusual use for such paper.

In the 1940s, airpower was still new, and all sides who had an air force believed that aerial bombardment could break the enemies' will. But in no case did this actually ever work. In 1942 the United States sent sixteen B-25 bombers, led by US Army Air Corps lieutenant colonel James Doolittle, over Japan. The bombers killed some fifty people and wounded about four hundred others, military and civilians included. But far from breaking the spirit of the Japanese, the bombings made them search for a means of retaliation. Their unpredictable response was to send armed paper balloons across the Pacific to bomb the United States. They knew that these balloons could do only limited damage, but they reasoned that such a bizarre and unprecedented attack might destroy American morale.

The Japanese took two years to develop and test their new weapon, its design based on an eighteenth-century balloon. During the Italian War of Independence in 1848, an Austrian officer had developed the idea of using thin paper balloons to drop bombs. He calculated that a balloon could stay aloft for a half hour with a thirty-pound bomb that would then explode with a timed fuse when it landed. These balloon bombs were used in the siege of Venice, but to no real effect, although one did manage to land in the Piazza San Marco and explode. A wind shift also caused a number of the balloons to float back toward the soldiers who had launched them. The attackers lost enthusiasm for their new weapon and the idea lay dormant until 1933, when Japanese lieutenant general Reikichi Tada was assigned to a research laboratory to develop new weapons.

Under the lieutenant's direction, the Japanese developed various weapons. There was the "death ray" gun that killed soldiers at close range with a jolt of electricity. And the "Ro-Go" weapon, which was a rocket propellant launched by unmanned tanks against enemy pillboxes, or guard posts. But the Japanese team was most excited about the

"Fu-Go" weapon, a paper balloon thirteen feet in diameter that carried a bomb with a timed fuse.

The Japanese estimated that it would take such a balloon an average of sixty hours to cross the Pacific and reach the US mainland 6,200 miles away. It could arrive in as little as thirty hours, or in as many as one hundred. In the winter of 1943–44, the Japanese launched about two hundred paper balloons to test the air currents, and found that the hot temperatures of strong sunlight could cause the gas in the balloons to expand, causing them to burst, while the cold temperatures of darkness could cause the balloons to deflate. So the Japanese built a valve that would automatically release gas as needed to keep the balloons at a fairly constant altitude.

The Japanese experimented with silk balloons, but found that paper, being lighter, could deliver a heavier bomb farther. They also found that the best paper for the balloons was made out of kozo, a mulberry bark fiber used by handmade-paper artisans.

The balloons were equipped with sandbags that were released by an automatic mechanism triggered by a descent in altitude. It was calculated that there would be enough bags to get the balloons over the Pacific, and when all the sandbags were gone, the same technology would release a 15-kilogram antipersonnel bomb and two 5-kilogram incendiary bombs.

In 1944, West Coast residents started observing strange things. A father and son out fishing saw a parachute or balloon noiselessly drift by and then explode over the next rise. When they got there, all they found were scraps of paper. Other people witnessed harmless, unexplained explosions. On November 4, a balloon was seen in the air sixty-six miles southwest of San Pedro, California. Reports then came in of other balloons in western states, and the army started using aircraft to shoot down the balloons wherever they appeared. The US government understood that the purpose of the Japanese balloon attacks was to sow panic and so, according to military historian Robert C. Mikesh, the Office of Censorship requested that no news media carry any stories about them. The journalists complied and the public knew nothing about the Japanese balloon attacks.

According to Mikesh, about 9,000 paper balloons were launched, with as many as 1,000 arriving in the United States, though there were only 285 official sightings. Two made it as far as Michigan, but most landed in western states. The only known property damage that the balloons caused were two small brush fires in the state of Washington. Six Americans were also killed mishandling a balloon with an unexploded bomb that they happened across near Bly, Oregon. Ironically the incident occurred on land owned by the Weyerhaeuser Company, a large papermaker.

BECAUSE IT IS lightweight, paper has often been thought of in connection with flight. The first kites, used in China about 400 BCE, possibly even earlier, were made of light wood. In the Tang dynasty, 618–907 CE, people started to use silk, but like the Japanese balloon builders, they soon switched to paper because it was light. In the nineteenth century, before real airplanes had been invented, paper airplanes were known as paper darts. In 1881, the New York Stock Exchange declared it would impose a dollar fine on anyone caught throwing a paper dart at a member while the exchange was in session.

In 2014, the world's largest paper airplane at the time, Arturo's Desert Eagle, forty-five feet long by twenty-five feet wide, was taken up in the air by a Sikorsky military helicopter. The airplane's owner was hoping to release it at 5,000 feet, but at half that altitude, 2,700 feet, it was severely buffeted by air currents and so they released it early. It flew at about 100 miles per hour for roughly ten seconds before breaking up and crashing.

Because it is light and cheap, the idea of paper clothes, a completely impractical and nonviable notion, keeps resurfacing. In the 1960s, the US military considered making disposable paper combat uniforms; they also thought of making paper pup tents for soldiers in the field who needed a quick shelter and paper parachutes that could be easily destroyed upon landing. The Scott Paper Company got interested in paper clothes as well and in 1966 came out with a shapeless paper shift that cost $1—an even better deal than the 15-cent petticoat of 1870. Scott had a coupon program and the paper dress was designed as a promotional gimmick for the coupons.

Women liked the paper dresses far more than Scott had imagined, and Scott sold half a million in eight months, despite the fact that the dresses tore, were not washable, and were highly flammable: also, when wet, their colors ran. But who could resist a dress for only one dollar? Soon paper dresses were a fashion craze and several designers jumped on the trend. The Campbell's Soup Company produced a paper dress that took advantage of the fact that Andy Warhol's paintings had made their trademark can a Pop Art icon. In 1967, the Mars Manufacturing Company in Asheville, North Carolina, became the nation's leading manufacturer of paper clothes, selling 80,000 paper dresses a week. The price of paper clothing was rising, but it was still inexpensive. A basic A-line shift cost $1.75. Bell-bottom jumpsuits, a popular '60s style, cost $4. Aprons were $1.35 and paper vests for men, $1.99. For women who wanted to splurge, there was a paper evening gown for $5. Another company, Sterling Paper Products, made a $7.50 zebra-print pantsuit, an $8 maternity dress, and even a $15 bridal gown. There were also little girls' dresses for sale for 40 cents.

For the big department stores such as Lord & Taylor and Bonwit Teller, designers created water-resistant paper raincoats and paper bikinis that could hold together in the water (if you were brave enough to wear one). Formfit Rogers produced paper lingerie, and Hallmark Cards, a "party kit" consisting of a floral-print shift dress and matching plates, cups, napkins, and invitations. The paper-clothes fad required some innovative work at the paper mills; a new paper called Kaycel, made of 7 percent nylon, was developed. It was flame resistant unless washed. But no one washed paper clothes—the whole point of paper clothes was to throw them out. It was part of a growing movement toward disposable products.

"Paper clothing," reported *Time* magazine in March 1967, "apparently, is here to stay." It wasn't. The whole paper-dress fad vanished by the end of the '60s, although every now and then someone still designs one. Paper wedding dresses are still turned out from time to time. After all, that is a dress that, theoretically, is worn only once.

Chapter 17

TO DIE LIKE GENTLEMEN

||||||||||||||||||

*I'm not going to pretend the machine isn't turning out some
properly wonderful papers; and I'm not going to say it isn't
doing far better things than ever I thought it would do. I don't
laugh at it as my grandfather did, or shake my head at it as
my father used. I recognize our craft is going down hill. But
we ain't at the bottom by a long way; and when we get there
will go game and die like gentlemen.*

—EDEN PHILLPOTTS, *Storm in a Teacup*

EW TECHNOLOGY SELDOM ELIMINATES OLD TECHNOL-
ogy. It only creates another alternative. When paper became an industrial product, it was not the end of handmade paper. Handmade paper
is still being made, because there are still people who want it, even if
it costs considerably more. There are also people who will pay more
for linen, rather than wood, paper. But most paper today is made from
wood on huge machines.

Early in the twentieth century, when there was a tremendous nos-
talgia for the old preindustrial trades, an English writer named Eden

Phillpotts wrote a series of novels romanticizing these trades. His 1919 *Storm in a Teacup* is set in a nineteenth-century English paper mill. The papermakers know that the Industrial Revolution is overtaking them. One papermaker says, "Hand-made paper is battling for its life in one sense—like a good many other hand-made things. But the machine hasn't caught us yet and it will be a devil of a long time before it does, I hope."

To Phillpotts, these nineteenth-century papermakers did not recognize the enormity of the time bomb they were sitting on. He himself probably thought that handmade paper was done for, that the world in which papermakers were valued for their very distinct handicraft, a world where the vatman "knew his worth," as he put it, and could find work anywhere because of his skill, was finished.

Today, a paper mill is no longer a small place with a vat or two, a rag room and a drying loft, employing 30 to 150 workers, each with a very specific and demanding skill. A paper mill is, first of all, no longer a mill at all. It does not derive its power from a paddle wheel in an adjacent river, though it is still always located by a river because it needs water for papermaking. The Fourdrinier machine conceived of in the eighteenth century is still in use, but now it is powered by electricity and very large and very fast. Papermaking skill lies more in the mill's machine than in the workers who maintain it and keep it running twenty-four hours a day, seven days a week.

The Glatfelter mill, still located in the same small town, now called Spring Grove, a short ride from Gettysburg, is neither a small paper mill nor an industrial giant. But in an industry where size has become a crucial advantage, as it always is for fairly low-priced products, Glatfelter is big enough. Today's giant companies, such as International Paper, were created by merging numerous smaller companies together, many of which had already acquired several even smaller companies. International Paper started in 1898, when it combined eighteen different papermaking companies.

The same process of merging smaller paper mills together into a number of larger mills has taken place all over the world. In Fabriano,

Italy, the process began with the Milani family in the eighteenth century. Pietro Milani dreamed of buying out other small Fabriano mills to create one big one, and started by acquiring the Cartiere Milani Fabriano in 1782, to form the Milani Fabriano Paper Company. The Milani family continued making acquisitions whenever there were opportunities, and by the twentieth century, they were the only papermaker in Fabriano. They called themselves Fabriano Mills. In their advertising, they played on the confusion between the name of their town and the name of their mill, claiming that Fabriano Mills had been making paper since 1264. That was not exactly the case; it was true of the town, but not of the Fabriano Mills.

In 2002 the Fedrigoni Group of Verona, which owns three other large Italian mills, bought Fabriano. Today, they make 20 percent of Italian copy paper, the drawing paper used by most Italian school-children, and fine-art paper. They also have a division that makes the fine paper needed for the Euro currency, assuring its security with a series of complicated watermarks. For paper-history buffs, it is nice to know that this is being done in the same town where the watermark was invented.

EVERY DAY, 150 tractor-trailers loaded with both hard- and softwood logs arrive at the Glatfelter mill. Each log is gobbled up and churned into a pile of chips in seconds. These chips then become pulp for the 1,000 tons of different kinds of paper that the mill produces daily. Diversity of product is the key to success in the modern paper industry, which is one of the reasons why paper companies keep trying to expand.

Over the centuries, the Crane Company has succeeded in finding new products every time there has been a downturn in the economy. In the depression following the Civil War, the Crane mill remained prosperous by making the cardboard men's shirt collars that had become fashionable; since the collars were made of thin cardboard, men needed a new one every day, resulting in huge quantities of sales. Then in 1873, the Winchester Arms Company in New Haven, Connecticut, was trying to perfect the repeating rifle—a rapid-fire weapon introduced in the Civil War, for which shell wrappers of a very thin and highly flammable paper were needed. Crane developed this paper and prospered throughout the 1870s, when other mills were going bankrupt in a difficult economy. Six years later, in 1879, Crane obtained a contract from the US Treasury to make dollars.

The Curtis Company, founded in Delaware in 1789, survived the Great Depression with a special all-rag paper that they first developed for *Fortune* magazine—although in time the magazine decided to return to using less-expensive wood-chip paper. Curtis got through World War II by manufacturing fiber paper, which they made by treating cotton paper with zinc chloride. Fiber paper was used for insulated boxes. Then, at the end of the twentieth century, a time of consolidation in many industries, Curtis, the oldest operating paper mill in America, went out of business.

By then, everyone in the papermaking industry was scrambling to find a niche, ideally one of low tonnage and high price. And there are a lot of peculiar niches in the paper business; finding one to excel at is one key to success. Circuit boards have foundations made of paper; paper is used in artificial flooring; fast-food restaurants need thin paper for wrapping. One company tried to save itself with the "leather" labels on blue jeans, which are actually made from paper.

The Glatfelter mill is still known for book paper, which is how they started. But now, what is called "communication paper"—that is, paper for writing and printing—is only about half of their output. They also make the paper for US postage stamps, wallpaper, diapers, paper towels, teabags, bottle labels, greeting cards, and envelopes. Their teabag paper is not made from wood pulp but from the stalk of abaca, a banana-like plant grown in the Philippines. Abaca was first used as a paper source at the beginning of the nineteenth century.

Successful paper mills emphasize efficiency and try not to produce waste. The considerable quantities of water they use are cleaned of impurities and put back into the river; the impurities can then be processed for reuse. Any paper scraps or defective paper is re-pulped to make new paper. Like almost all modern paper mills, Glatfelter runs on electricity, which they supply with their own coal-fired power plant. The plant provides 130 percent of their needs and they sell the extra energy to the town, meaning that they also operate as a power utility.

IN A MODERN paper mill, logs are quickly stripped of bark and chipped, and the chips are reduced to mush by the chemicals in the digester. Dyes are added at this stage of the process. At Glatfelter, there are seventy-eight shades of white alone. Chemicals are also added to make some kinds of paper more compatible with certain kinds of printing and to make paper more opaque. Georgia clay is one of the common additives used.

The modern Fourdrinier is basically the same machine as the one Robert invented at the end of the eighteenth century, but now it is powered by electricity, two stories high, and as long as a football field. Glatfelter has five of them, and each of its machines is newer, faster, and larger than the one previously installed. Larger plants sometimes have fewer but even larger machines.

The oldest machine at Glatfelter dates from 1907, and it was a state-of-the-art model when it came out—a beautiful creation with swirls and curlicues of green cast-iron grill work on one side, resembling a miniature fin de siècle Parisian bridge. It produces three tons of paper an hour, which was a dizzying amount in 1907. But between 1920 and 1923, the mill installed two new machines, each producing seven tons an hour, and in 1956, it installed a machine that makes fifteen tons an hour. Yet another machine was added in 1965; it also produces fifteen tons an hour.

Paper production begins at the wet end of the machine, where pulp and water are poured in the "head box" at a concentration of about .5 percent pulp and 99.5 percent water. The width of the opening that releases the pulp onto the moving screen below determines the thickness of the paper. This moving screen is no longer made of wire, as it was in previous centuries, but of monofilament, a kind of thin plastic that is used for fishing line. Because of this, machine-made paper resembles wove paper; laid paper remains a handmade product. This has caused the two to switch places on the ladder of status. With its ribbing caused by wire molds, laid paper has the handmade look that is preferred for high-end products such as stationery or art paper. The paper appears handmade but can be made much more inexpensively.

On the moving screen of the modern Fourdrinier machines, the long, wet pulp passes from the head box through a roller of wire known as the dandy roll. Here, the fibers are made to change direction so that rather than all lying the same way, they become randomly interwoven. Watermarks can also be added on the dandy roll. The pulp then passes three suction boxes that suck out the water. This is the most magical part of the process: a belt covered with translucent slush approaches the suction boxes and within the space of a yard, this thin, wet film visibly turns into paper. Then it is pressed and snaked up and down through a series of heated rollers. These dry the paper. From there, it moves through heated vertical rollers to give it a finish. Last, a starch sizing is added if the paper is intended to be used for writing or printing. The finished paper is still 5 percent water.

The two newest machines at Glatfelter, both already more than a half century old, don't have dandy rolls. Dandy rolls cause clay and other powders in the pulp to sink to the bottom, giving the paper two distinct sides, similar to the felt and wire sides of old, with the wire side being preferable for printing and some artists preferring the felt side. Glatfelter's newer machines have a top wire former instead of a dandy roll. It sucks the water up instead of down. The solids rise and then start to sink, ending up in the middle of the pulp, so that both sides of the paper are the same.

The noise these machines make is a deafening hum—it is a very even sound, but so loud that it is difficult to hear someone shouting. The huge rooms look empty. Occasionally someone is seen passing through. But there is no proud vatman or coucher plying their demanding craft, no busy room of fleet-fingered rag sorters. Instead, there is a soundproof room with computers that monitor the machines and workers who monitor the computers. If something were to go awry with a machine, workers would suddenly swarm into the once-empty papermaking room.

Working in a paper mill, as the nineteenth-century novelist Eden

Phillpotts understood, has always been demanding labor. The machines never stop running, but are in operation seven days a week, twenty-four hours a day, because the only way to make them profitable is to produce as much paper as possible. Spring Grove is a mill town and the 1,000 workers employed by Glatfelter work seven days a week. They don't complain because they consider themselves to be well paid. Their Saturday shift pays time and a half, and Sunday is double-time, so they earn almost a second week's salary on the weekends. They alternate shifts at different times of day and night to arrange time with their families.

THE PAPER INDUSTRY has always caused people a considerable amount of discomfort. When paper was made from rags and mills were close to population centers, there was anger about the noise and the smell, fear of spreading disease, and some worry about what was happening to the water supply. But as soon as paper started to be made from trees, concern shifted to the destruction of the forests. The 150 truckloads of large tree trunks being gobbled up every single day at the Glatfelter mill is worrisome enough, but the supersized paper mills gobble up far more.

Back in 1923, International Paper had fifty-three mills and was the largest paper producer in the world. They had bought up huge tracts of forest in New York state, northern New England, and Canada, and had leased still more; that year, they had the rights to 4,460,080 acres of forest in the United States and in Canada. Most of that property was in eastern Canada; as American paper companies grew, more and more paper was being made from Canadian trees.

International Paper chopped down hemlock, fir, spruce, and a small number of poplar trees, and was focused on the newsprint business, which had become a very lucrative trade because its paper could be made inexpensively in tremendous quantities. The preferable wood for this trade was spruce. According to the company, it turned 7 million cords of pulpwood into paper in 1923. An acre of land grew an estimated five cords of pulpwood, so the company had consumed the wood of 140,000 acres, or 220 square miles, of forestland in a single year.

International Paper and other companies that were harvesting Canadian trees were stripping the country of a valuable resource while not
even providing many jobs. In 1923, International Paper estimated that a
lumber camp needed only forty to fifty men to harvest between 2,500
and 3,500 cords of wood in a season. Paper harvesting usually began on
May 1 and ended in mid-August; this was the period when the sap was
running, which made the bark easy to strip from trunks. Stripping the
bark reduced the weight of the logs and thus lowered shipping costs.
Some accused the paper companies of clear-cutting—indiscriminately
stripping miles of forestland bare. These accusations weren't always fair,
because paper companies were selective about which trees they wanted
to harvest. But with or without clear-cutting, hundreds of thousands of
acres were being destroyed.

Canadians, as well as US conservationists, were growing angry. Was
Canada to lose its forests just because Americans wanted to read a lot of
newspapers cheaply? In November 1899, J. R. Stratton, a new minister
in the Ontario government, started getting coverage in *The Paper Mill*,
an industry newspaper, for expressing such a view. He also wanted to
make certain, he said, to "secure for the Province of Ontario the largest share of profits accruing from the conversion of raw material into
finished products."

The paper industry, both in the United States and worldwide, continues to be pressured on this environmental issue. Consumers do not want
paper made from clear-cutting rain forests or other ecologically unique
virgin forests. There have been successful campaigns to get consumers
to avoid such papers or even to avoid paper entirely by switching to electronic alternatives. Some have even called for a boycott of toilet paper,
although this is not likely to catch on since, so far, no one has found an
electronic alternative to toilet paper.

Thanks to a hard-fought battle, there is now fairly broad acceptance
of tree farming, in which harvested areas are replanted to keep the forest sustainable. The US paper industry is quick to point out that there
are more trees growing in the United States today than there were one
hundred years ago. While this is undoubtedly true, it is also true that a

high percentage of these trees were planted to replace harvested trees and that wild virgin forestland has been considerably reduced. Since any species, plant or animal, depends on numerous other species to flourish, the loss of old-growth forests is not simply a loss of trees. In the American South, as recently as the 1930s, flying squirrels were so common that there were recipes for them—they were a favorite local dish. But today, flying squirrels are a scarcity because they live only in old-growth forests.

Most wood-chip paper in the world today is made from sustainable tree plantations. In Brazil, where a highly publicized fight between environmentalists and paper companies over the destruction of the rain forest took place, papermakers are now making paper from eucalyptus trees grown on plantations. A native of Australia, eucalyptus was brought to Brazil in the early twentieth century for use in the construction and charcoal businesses. It has short, exceptionally sturdy fibers that make its paper opaque, which is good for printing. Its fibers are also soft, making it good for tissue. Eucalyptus is an excellent plantation crop because it grows quickly and does not drain the soil of minerals.

Eucalyptus has changed Brazilian papermaking. Once dependent on imports for 75 percent of its pulp, Brazil is now an exporter of paper pulp. Two eucalyptus-based paper mills have also opened in Uruguay, which previously had no papermaking industry. Millions of acres of eucalyptus have been planted in Brazil, which has led some environmentalists to worry about the repercussions of introducing a non-native species on such a large scale. But no one argues that cutting down rain forests would be better.

One of the most recent fights involving the paper industry occurred in Indonesia, where Asia Pulp & Paper (APP), one of the largest paper companies in the world, is based. It was the last place on Earth where a virgin rain forest was still being clear-cut for paper. But due to an international outcry against the practice, APP began planting acacia trees to use for making paper pulp instead. Like eucalyptus trees, acacia trees can be farmed. The international outcry had yielded results.

Emmanuelle Neyroumande, the Paris-based pulp and paper global manager for the World Wildlife Fund International, said of the paper industry: "It is an industry that has found that being environmentally friendly positions them well in the market. The big players tend to take the matter seriously." She cited Brazil as an example. "In Brazil the industry has tried to take environmentalism as a marketing tool. They are trying to restore forest."

Many campaigns continue to advise people to shun paper and turn to electronics to "save a tree." But doing so does not always save a tree, and when it does, the tree it saves may have been farmed sustainably. Company pleas to accept electronic billing rather than bills sent through the mail are not so much about saving trees as they are about saving the company billing expenses. Neyroumande said that she does not favor such messages. "Electronics has an environmental impact too," she pointed out. "I am pushing that we avoid simplistic messages. . . . You have to decide what you are using the paper for, how long will you keep it, is it necessary. You should avoid wastefulness."

What worries the World Wildlife Fund is that the amount of land available for tree farming might not be able to keep up with the demand for paper. "There is a growing population," said Neyroumande. "Where are we going to grow our crop? The planet is not big enough. We need a circular economy so that we use everything. If we made all our paper from forest the planet is not big enough." According to a World Wildlife Fund study, paper use will triple by the year 2050 because of increasing population. Most people in the paper industry, however, do not find this statistic credible. It could happen, but there is no way to know.

Nevertheless the concept of "saving a tree" remains a potent marketing plea and an incentive for reviving some old ideas about papermaking sources. One old idea that has gained new acceptance is making paper out of the scrap from sugarcane, called bagasse.

SUGARCANE IS A very thick grass that when squeezed through rollers produces a juice that can be cooked down to sugar and molasses. What remains is a dry, flattened stalk. Like most grass, a great deal of this stalk is cellulose fibers. Most cane is about 53 percent cellulose and only between 2 and 3 percent lignin, making it a better source for paper than most wood if its fibers are broken down efficiently. The sugar mill has little use for this waste, the bagasse, other than to burn it; sugar mills need constant fires to cook the sugarcane juice.

Since the late nineteenth century, when it was becoming apparent that forests were not limitless, there has been interest in making bagasse paper. Many of the sugar-producing areas of the world need paper but do not have forests, in some cases because the land was cleared centuries ago to plant sugar. In 1917, paper was made in New Iberia, Louisiana, with a mixture of bagasse and rice straw, both readily available in the area. Other places made it with cornhusks, and some places added in wood chips. In 1944 a mill opened in Puerto Rico that made paper from bagasse in combination with local scrap paper. In 1951 a paper mill started in Monte Alegre, Brazil, that made high-quality paper from a combination of bagasse, eucalyptus, and rags.

Among the places that have either experimented with or gone into full commercial production of bagasse paper are Florida, Louisiana, Hawaii, Cuba, Mexico, Colombia, Peru, Argentina, Nigeria, and India. In the first half of the twentieth century, patents for bagasse paper processes were regularly submitted. In 1915, the *Weekly Bulletin of the Canadian Department of Trade and Commerce* reported that a good quality of bagasse was being made in Preston, Cuba (a town today called Guatemala), named after an executive of the United Fruit Company, which made sugar there. In 1928, Celulosa Cubana, S.A., founded by sugar tycoon Manuel Rionda, began making bagasse paper in Tuinucu, Cuba. Paper shortages during World War II gave new importance to bagasse paper. In 1943 a mill in Santa Fe, Argentina, started producing bagasse paper. Two new bagasse paper mills were installed in the cane fields of Cuba.

The manufacture of bagasse pulp in Peru increased every year between 1940, with 800 tons, and 1945, with almost 5,000 tons. By 1950, Peru's Grace & Company had built a bagasse paper mill in Paramonga. Grace was named for its founder, an Irishman, William Russell Grace, who made his fortune in Peru on bird droppings, or guano, which is rich in nitrogen and phosphorus and valuable for making fertilizer and gunpowder. The company then branched out into shipping, sugar refining, and bagasse paper. It made very light airmail paper, a new product at the time, paper for bags, wrapping paper, and corrugated cardboard for boxes. According to a 1951 *Business Week* article, Grace saved several Peruvian newspapers from closing by providing them with bagasse newsprint.

But there was a problem with bagasse: It is 60 percent fiber and 40 percent pith, a soft, non-fibrous matter. The pith clings to the fiber and the fiber must be separated from it. This takes a good deal of time and costs money; in fact, most of the cost of making bagasse paper lies in this separation problem. There are British patents for ways of dealing with this problem dating back to 1907 and 1908. But Grace had a better idea. In 1953 his company hired Clarence Birdseye, famous for developing commercial frozen food. Birdseye was a restless genius with some three hundred patents to his credit on everything from packaging to lightbulbs, and had recently come up with a faster, more efficient way to process bagasse.

In Florida and Louisiana, sugar mills were using a cold-water separation process for bagasse; Birdseye's process involved using hot water in a confined tube under pressure. The Birdseye method was implemented in Peru. But then Birdseye himself dropped dead from a heart attack while at the Gramercy Hotel in New York City and Grace left the Paramonga mill.

Grace went on to start a paper mill in the sugar-growing region of Colombia near Cali in partnership with International Paper. But soon Grace sold its share to International Paper and decided to get out of the paper business altogether. The Colombian government started a second bagasse mill and believing, as many did, that bagasse was only good for low-grade paper, focused on newsprint, a product that was in precipitous decline. Failing, they sold their mill to International Paper. In 1997, International Paper decided to leave Colombia, thus leaving Cali with two abandoned paper mills.

———

THOSE WHO HAVE never seen a sugar plantation, an industry associated with hardship and suffering, are not prepared for how beautiful sugarcane fields can be. They look like a vast, rolling green-and-silver sea, heaving and rippling in the wind. If there are mountains on the distant horizon, as in the Cauca valley, Colombia, where the high and rugged cordilleras appear as a distant rocky coastline, the landscape is especially stunning.

Unlike almost all the sugar plantations in the Caribbean and elsewhere, the plantations of the Cauca valley are not mired in poverty. The difference can be quickly spotted. In most cane-growing areas, all the cane is in the same stage of development—small seedlings or mid-growth plants or tall plants with feathery sprouts on top ready to harvest. But here, the plantations are divided into separate rectangular plots about the size of a football field—each one called a *suerte*, which means "luck"—and the suertes are in different stages of development. The biggest economic problem with sugar production in most places is that it is seasonal and there is no work half the year, "the dead season." But in the Cauca valley, there is no dead season because in 1985 a Colombian laboratory developed a strain of sugarcane, prosaically named CC 85-92, that can be grown and harvested any time of year.

This has made it possible for the Incauca mill, owned by a Colombian multinational corporation, to employ 8,000 sugar workers year-round. Incauca's two crushing machines process 1,400 metric tons of cane a day. The cane is crushed and juice extracted. Some of that juice is cooked into sugar crystals, and some is processed into ethanol, a sellable energy source. Incauca produces 360,000 liters of ethanol every day. Then the cane that has been crushed is crushed yet more to extract even more juice, leaving behind bagasse, which by this point is nothing but a fibrous brown powder. This is blown into machines with three-foot-high steel screens. The screens block the fiber, but the dried pith blows through.

The pith powder is burned to produce energy both for the plant and to sell. The sugar mill produces 10 megawatts of electricity from bagasse every hour and operates twenty-four hours a day, seven days a week. The energy that the plant does not use is sold to the national electric grid, and the leftover fiber bagasse is sold to Carvajal Pulp & Paper, one of the largest family-owned companies in Colombia. Since cane is 30 percent bagasse, selling it rather than throwing it away is commercially important for the sugar plant. Incauca is the largest sugar mill in Colombia, but there are twelve others, all of them located in the Cauca valley. A number of them also sell bagasse to Carvajal. Some do not separate out the pith, but what they may save in not performing that process, they lose in not having the pith to burn for energy. Carvajal buys unseparated bagasse and separates it themselves, deriving energy for their paper mill.

Like Incauca and the valley's other sugar mills, Carvajal operates seven days a week, and every day thirty large triple-trailer trucks hauling 25 metric tons of bagasse per truck, packed in tightly pressed bails, arrive at its doors. And that is the delivery just from Incauca. Alongside Carvajal rises a brown badlands of mountains and buttes of bagasse waiting to be processed. Fiber that has been separated from pith is washed in water two times, then put in a digester and cooked with caustic soda. Bagasse contains much less lignin than wood pulp and does not require as much cooking or as many chemicals. When the bagasse is finished cooking, the toxic by-product of caustic soda left at the bottom of the digester is reduced to a chemical compound that can be used to remake caustic soda. The water used in the papermaking is also treated and restored before being pumped back into the river.

The bagasse pulp is bleached with chloride dioxide and hydrogen. Processed wood pulp is naturally dark brown in color, but processed bagasse is a cream color, so it needs much less bleaching. From there, the bagasse pulp is processed much like wood pulp, in large Fourdrinier machines, with water pumped from the adjacent Rio Palo. The main mill produces 400 metric tons of paper every day, 80 percent of which is photocopy paper. A second mill nearby produces magazine paper that a US company sells under the brand name Treefrog, suggesting that if you use bagasse paper, tree frogs won't be harmed.

There are other bagasse paper mills in the world, but Carvajal claims to be the only one that makes 100 percent bagasse paper. In 2000, the Quenu Newsprint Paper Company of Cairo started producing newsprint and graphic paper that was 75 percent bagasse. Tamil Nadu Newsprint and Papers Limited in southern India claims that it also has been making 100 percent bagasse paper since 1996 and also claims to be one of the most environmentally compliant paper mills in the world. The environmental advantages of bagasse paper are almost always central to its marketing. In 1972, Wells Fargo bank was flooded with letters and messages of support when they started making checks from bagasse paper.

IN AN AGE of climate change, making paper uses far too much energy, regardless of whether it is made from wood or bagasse. Large paper mills usually produce their own energy and in too many cases, that energy is coal fired and therefore a major source of carbon emissions. Pollution is the other big issue with the paper industry. Carvajal, Glatfelter, and many of the large mills now reprocess their water before putting it back in the river. But this is occurring only after a long fight. For centuries, paper mills took river water, infused it with toxic chemicals to break down fibers, and then just dumped it back in, literally turning the rivers black.

The public and government complained. In the early centuries of papermaking, their complaint was with the by-product of rags, which sometimes contained tar from old ship ropes. The rags carried a terrible smell, which they passed on to the rivers. Then, once mills switched to using wood chips, complaints died down. A 1917 letter from an official at Oxford University, which had once complained about the nearby Wolvercote Mill, said that it was good the mill had switched to wood because "it was feared that the mill would have to close because no solution to the problem [of water pollution] could be found."

But ultimately, switching to wood was not a solution; the pulp was being treated with caustic soda and a toxic cocktail was being pumped back into the river. The paper industry did not have the sensitivity to environmental concerns that it does today, because it had little awareness of how strongly the public felt about the issue. The great contribution of environmental movements is that they have made industry, or at least some industries, aware that good environmental policy is good for business.

One of the first paper mills to realize this was Crane in Dalton, Massachusetts, which gained a great deal of public support in 1952 when they started spending $100,000 a year to clean up the Housatonic River. By then, they had been polluting that river for a century and a half. Crane began sending their water through miles of pipe—with equipment they called a "flocculator" and a "clarifier"—into ponds where the impurities settled out. The water then reentered the river. Crane also used a local sewage treatment plant for particularly difficult waters. In the mid-1950s, the Curtis Paper Company in Delaware devised a similar system for flowing the water through "settling ponds."

Treating water—and boasting of it to the public—was becoming the new way for modern paper mills to operate. By the 1950s, what was called "soda recovery" had become mandatory in Britain, the United States, and many other countries. Or at least, it had become illegal to dump untreated waters into rivers and streams. The wastewater from papermaking contains caustic alkali, some fibers, and some chemical impurities from the wood itself, as well as sulfite and sulfate, which are contributed by the digesters. These contaminated waters can be cooked down to a syrup and burned. The resulting ash is largely made up of sodium carbonate, which can then be converted to sodium hydrate and reused in the digester.

In this manner, between 80 and 90 percent of the sodium carbonate, or soda, is recovered for reuse. This is not only of environmental value but of economic value. But it takes a considerable investment to implement it. So it becomes something that is easily done by large companies, corporations, and multinationals, but is almost impossible to do for small operations. And thus, it is one more factor that favors the large over the small in modern papermaking.

THOUGH ONE OF the attractions of paper has been that it was cheap and easy to throw away, it has long seemed to some that it was wasteful to throw out huge amounts of paper. In 1870, a French inventor claimed he could clean the ink off of paper so that it could be reused as new paper, but no one seemed to believe him.

On April 28, 1800, Matthias Koops was granted an English patent for "Extracting Ink from Paper and Converting Such Paper into Pulp." In the patent, Koops described his process as "An invention made by me of extracting printing and writing ink from printed and written paper, and converting the paper from which the ink is extracted into pulp, and making thereof paper fit for writing, printing, and other purposes." In the second edition of Koops's book on alternative sources for paper pulp, he used recycled paper for some of the pages. That was probably the first time anything was printed on recycled paper in the West, though Japan had been recycling paper since the eleventh century and the Indians, even earlier. Over time Koops's recycled paper pages have held up better than his wood-chip pages.

It took a long time for Koops's idea regarding ink removal from paper to be embraced. But finally, in 1939, the Wolvercote Mill in Oxford became one of the first mills in England to build a plant for "de-inking" paper. Koops's process is similar to what is done today, though the quality of the resulting recycled paper has steadily improved over the decades. Printed paper is chopped up and washed with soaps and chemicals to remove the ink. Recycled paper is very popular with consumers, and that makes it popular with papermakers. In the United States today, about three-quarters of paper mills do some recycling, and 113 mills out of about 500 work exclusively on recycled paper.

But there is a problem. Although all environmental groups and the Environmental Protection Agency support recycling paper, the environmental benefits are not clear. The chemicals and inks that are left from the process are highly toxic, and some papermakers find that it takes more energy to make recycled paper than it does to make wood-chip paper. Recycled paper is most cost- and energy-efficient, and therefore most environmentally beneficial, when it is used to make cardboard and other low-quality paper. But consumers like to have their printer paper, and even their checks, made of recycled paper. So what is the benefit of recycled paper? Perhaps it is simply that because we live in a world over-run with garbage, it is gratifying to see used paper going into making something useful rather than ending up in a landfill.

Chapter 18

RETURN TO ASIA

||||||||||||||||||

IN THE FIRST CENTURY CE, THE CHINESE BEGAN MAKING paper, and it remained an exclusively Asian product for a number of centuries to come. In time, it was embraced so universally that few thought of it as Asian anymore. But now in the twenty-first century, two thousand years later, China is again the world's leading paper producer, and the Japanese are the acknowledged masters of handmade paper.

Modern China very much wanted to be the largest paper producer in the world. It was not only that they wanted to produce a great deal of paper, they also wanted the title of "biggest." Aside from a certain desire for a verisimilitude of history, the reason why China would want such a thing baffles the world's paper industry. Centuries ago, in the time of the Han, China was a society perfectly suited for paper. But today's China is so ill-suited for modern papermaking that the industry is bemused by China's ambition. Mark Wilde, formerly of Deutsche Bank and now of the Bank of Montreal, is the leading—in fact, the last—market analyst focused exclusively on the paper industry. He said of China, "I don't think anyone is making money. Why they have been so aggressive in communication paper is a mystery. They have to import the pulp and the energy."

Although it is the fourth-largest country in the world in terms of landmass, China does not have a lot of trees and can ill afford to chop down the ones it has. The country has a long history of disastrous flooding, and trees help stave off floods and landslides. In the late 1990s, the tragic flooding of the Yangtze and other major river valleys was blamed, in part, on deforestation, which has led to an interdiction on cutting down trees. More than half of the wood pulp used to make wood-based paper in China is imported in the form of pressed board that turns back to pulp when soaked.

One alternative to importing pulp is importing used paper for recycling. China is the largest importer of used paper and the largest maker of recycled paper in the world. About half of the used paper for recycling sold in the world is bought by China, and about 40 percent of the paper made in China is recycled. On any day, ship after ship lines up in the

Workers at the Finnish-owned UPM Changshu Paper Mill in Changshu, Jiangsu Province, China, on July 23, 2012.

South China port of Ningbo, all filled with thousands of bales of used paper from all over the world, though most of it comes from Japan and the United States. Much of this paper is taken to a nearby paper mill owned by the Indonesian giant Asia Pulp & Paper.

The paper is used to make cartons and boxes, including shoeboxes. A man in Kansas City might read the *Kansas City Star* and then toss it in a recycle bin. It is baled and shipped to Ningbo, where it is made into shoeboxes that are sold to Italy and used for a pair of Italian shoes in a Florentine boutique where a vacationing American buys a pair of shoes, takes it back to New York, and throws out the box. Then it is off to Ningbo again.

PAPERMAKING REQUIRES A tremendous expenditure of energy, and while China is the world's largest coal producer, it is also a net importer of coal, oil, and natural gas. Until the early 1990s, China exported oil, but it is now the second-largest importer of oil in the world, just behind and close to surpassing the United States. It is also the largest coal consumer in the world, and as such, is under international pressure to burn less coal because of the role that carbon emissions play in causing climate change.

Even though China's per capita consumption of paper is not high by Western standards, its huge population—the largest in the world—uses a significant amount of it: some 60 million tons a year, a figure that is growing at about 15 percent annually. Even newsprint consumption, something that is rapidly fading in most of the world, was, until recently, growing in China.

But this is not to say that China's enormous paper production is for domestic use. China is so aggressively selling inexpensive, reasonable-quality paper around the world that the United States, the European Union, and Brazil have all put trade barriers in place to prevent entry of too much Chinese paper. But since the tariff is on sheets of paper, not rolls, the Chinese are starting to bring rolls and cutting equipment into the United States to cut the rolls into sheets here. In time, there will be trade restrictions on that too. As of 2014, China was selling the United States 20 percent of its copy paper.

SOUTH CHINA, WHICH includes the ports of Ningbo and Shanghai, and the provinces of Anhui, Zhejiang, Suzhou, and Hangzhou, is historically the rich part of the country. This is the region from which food comes. The soil is fertile, the climate wet. There is rain, or at least mist, much of the time, and water is everywhere—in rivers, lakes, streams, canals, and flooded rice fields. Thus, the region has two of the prerequisites for papermaking—lots of water and good transportation.

South China has the look celebrated in classical Chinese paintings of the mountain and river school—steep, green, mist-blurred mountains and winding silver rivers. Once it was a region of beautiful country villages centuries old, but most of them have been torn down in recent decades to build large high-rise buildings that are seldom filled. The cities, too, have been ruined. There is construction everywhere, which creates whole villages of blue-roofed white trailers that serve as dormitories for construction workers from other parts of the country. The workers rarely get to see their families and struggle to save their meager wages.

Of late, the Chinese have been thinking about what they have lost. The newest trend in architecture is *fanggu*, meaning "rebuilding the old." It originally referred to the practice of copying old painting masters but now also refers to the new reproductions of old houses and other traditional structures.

The city of Suzhou, a beautiful metropolis of canals and gardens, is one of the few towns in China that was never destroyed. Centuries ago, officials of the Ming dynasty built private gardens along the canals, with artificial lakes, flowers, trees, and huge wind-carved rocks that look like statues. Large red carp were farmed for the garden ponds—the world's first farmed fish. Suzhou's humid, rainy, warm climate is ideal for gardening. Its most spectacular garden is called the Humble Administrator's Garden, but the site creates the suspicion that the administrator wasn't all that humble.

Chinese gardens are all about the interplay of textures and colors. Water, rocks, and plants are their principal components. The wind-carved rocks of South China are treasured as natural pieces of art. The Chinese collect rocks—sometimes worn smooth in rivers, sometimes sculpted into wild shapes with tunnels and swirls—and these rocks decorate their homes and gardens. Tang Guo, a Suzhou artist who has a spectacular naturally carved rock in his studio and often paints rocks, said, "It is useless to talk to Western artists about rocks. They cannot understand our connection with rocks."

In 1996 the paper giant APP, with some twenty mills in China, many in South China, opened the Gold HuaSheng Paper Mill in an industrial park outside Suzhou. The city's good transportation and the Wu Song River drew them. Next to the paper mill, in Suzhou tradition, they started a garden with local plants. The area had been wild and natural before it became an industrial park, and today the mill's garden is filled with white and pink oleander and a great variety of local trees and vines. The garden lake, fed by the mill's water retreatment plant, is flush with local fish—black fish, carp, and whitefish—along with soft-shelled turtles. The garden is inhabited by local bird species native to the area when it was wild—egrets; pheasants; magpies; and the common kingfisher, a funny, stubby, long-beaked blue bird whose Latin name is *Alcedo atthis*. The park also has four ponds and a canal that carries water to the wide, brown Wu Song River. In the background, you can hear the hum of the pipes and ponds of the mill's water-treatment plant. For an industrial park, it is a successful imitation of the traditional Suzhou gardens.

Like many modern paper mills, Gold HuaSheng boasts of its environmental efforts—of its $10 million waste treatment plant that recycles all chemicals and of the $100 million that APP claims to have spent on environmental protection in China. But the Chinese people are used to paper mills polluting their environment and have grown cynical about such claims. One local said, "If they weren't polluting, they wouldn't have built a garden." And it is true that rising above the green canopy of the garden are the tall, white-and-red smokestacks of the mill's power plant, alternately fired by coal, gas, and oil.

Gold HuaSheng is the third-largest paper mill in China, thereby making it one of the largest in the world. It has four machines operating twenty-four hours a day, seven days a week. Together, they produce 600,000 tons of paper a year. Typical of China's import-based paper industry, none of the machines is Chinese-made; the largest is made in Japan and produces 1,300 tons of paper a day in rolls 8 meters wide by 200 meters long. Sixty percent of Gold HuaSheng's paper is exported to North America, South America, Europe, and Africa. They produce a range of paper products, but they are especially proud of their fine paper for art books.

Chinese paper operates on a strange economic model: it is made primarily from imports but its products are for export. The Chinese are currently trying to change this by producing some of their own pulp. Two huge APP mills, one on Hainan Island, off the southern and most tropical part of China, and one in Guangxi Province on the Vietnam border, have planted fast-growing, easy-to-farm acacia trees.

BETWEEN THE ESTABLISHMENT of the Communist state in 1949 and 1979, two years after Mao Zedong's death, there was no private enterprise in China. This meant no private paper mills, printers, or publishers. The most successful book was *Máo zhǔxí yǔlù* (Quotations from Chairman Mao Tse-tung [Zedong]), which may be the most printed book in history. It is certainly the most printed book in the twelve-year period between 1964 and the chairman's death in 1976.

The book originally included two hundred quotes from Mao; later, it was expanded to include 267 quotes. The Chinese government claimed that 6.5 billion copies of the book were printed, though some historians believe it was less. Billions were printed in thirty-seven foreign languages and in Braille. More than a billion copies were printed of the bilingual English-Chinese edition alone. The book came out in various versions, the most popular of which was palm-sized in a red plastic cover with a small, coin-shaped portrait of Mao. Westerners dubbed it the Little Red Book. The paper was of good quality and has not discolored over time.

The quotations have proven less durable. After the death of Mao, many of the Little Red Books ended up as kitschy, inexpensive souvenirs for tourists. Another popular item for tourists was an alarm clock that when wound showed a revolutionary waving a Little Red Book.

In 1979 the Chinese government broke with their previous policy of only state-run enterprise and allowed, even encouraged, Chinese people to establish their own businesses. Among those businesses were paper mills. It had been more than a generation since anyone had run a private paper mill in China, but there were still people who knew how to do it and people who thought it would be a good business to be in.

In modern Japan, Korea, and much of the rest of the world, men and women who produce handmade paper want to continue an old tradition that they fear might disappear. In Japan, small handmade paper operations are found in rural villages, and in Korea, the practice is centered around Jeonju, a city known as a center for Korean culture. Handmade paper is low-technology and requires very little investment. The papermaker simply has to buy some beaters, build a few vats, and find someone to make the molds.

In China, however, people wanting to have their own company started hundreds and hundreds of paper mills, many in South China. They would have gladly made industrial paper, but they could never get the capital investment to buy all the necessary foreign-made equipment. So they built some vats and turned out handmade paper. Many companies try to boost production by operating ten or a dozen vats or more so they can produce a large quantity of paper but it is still infinitesimal compared to the output of big industrial mills. Among the equipment that the new Chinese papermakers couldn't afford were treatment plants for contaminated water. They just poured the contaminated water back into the rivers, and soon the rivers and streams near paper mills ran black and foul-smelling. The Chinese government, newly attuned to environmental concerns, began issuing an annual list of polluting small paper mills that had to be shut down. They have already closed hundreds.

The most valued handmade paper in China comes from Jinxian County in South China's Jiangxi Province. After 1979, about three hundred paper mills were started up here, in the valleys between the county's steamy green mountains, along beautiful curving streams—beautiful, that is, before they all started turning black. By the twenty-first century, only two hundred mills were still allowed to work in the area.

Ever since the Ming dynasty, Jinxian has been famous for its paper. It is the home of *xuan zhi*, China's most valued handmade paper. White, thin, and strong, *xuan zhi* is both delicate and durable. The name derives from Duanzhou, which is what the area was called during the Tang dynasty. Many Chinese artists say they would not work on anything but *xuan zhi*.

Tang Guo, an artist from nearby Nanjing, is one of them. He works with black ink on paper, as do many contemporary Chinese artists, and is always looking for new forms of expression while remaining rooted in traditional materials. "Ink to me is like green tea," he said. "Sometimes I might want black tea. Sometimes I might even want a cup of coffee. But I always go back to green tea." For paper, he insists on *xuan zhi*.

A great deal of fake *xuan zhi* is sold, but real *xuan zhi* is made with *qing tanpi*, the bark of a blue sandalwood tree (*Pteroceltis tatarinowii*). This small round tree grows all over China, to no more than sixty feet high. But only in Jinxian is the tree's bark of high enough quality for papermaking. To make *xuan zhi*, a grass that grows around the rice fields of Shatian in nearby Anhui Province is also required. Guo said, "It is not difficult to learn how to make paper. It is difficult to get the right ingredients."

Traditionally, it takes almost a year to prepare the pulp for *xuan zhi*. The ancients used to say that the paper took three hundred days to make. The bark is soaked for two days to a week in lime. (Today the process is sometimes speeded up with the use of caustic soda; Guo denounces such "chemical" paper, however.) Then it is washed over and over again for a few months, left on a hillside for a month, and periodically turned. There used to be bark turners who did nothing but this. The grass used in the making of *xuan zhi* is also dried on the hillside for ten months.

Next, the bark and grass are chopped and pounded by stone mortar and a pestle driven by a levered pole—originally, this work was done by hand, and today, a water-powered machine is sometimes used. Seeds of the paulownia tree are broiled to ashes and added to the mix, followed by gooey syrup made by boiling roots from starfruit trees.

The Zai Yuan Tang Mill in Anhui Province, just north of Jinxian, was founded along a peaceful stretch of river in 1988 with thirty-seven employees. Among China's new handmade paper mills, this one is medium-sized. There are six vatmen working the molds used for most papers; in another room, two men work one large mold for larger paper. They all work six days a week, making 600 to 700 sheets per day, but as industrial jobs go, these are considered good ones. At least the workers are able to live at home with their families and not in dormitory trailers in far-away provinces.

The mill uses a chemical imported from Japan instead of starfruit root juice, and caustic soda instead of lime. Since the all-natural process for turning pulp white takes a long time, they also sometimes use bleach. For some orders, they don't even use blue sandalwood bark, because there is not enough; they substitute with other types of bark—sometimes even using imported pressed spruce pulp from Canada. Nonetheless, the mill follows other very exacting rules for *xuan zhi*: 100 sheets of paper measuring 70 x 138 centimeters should weigh exactly 2.8 kilos. The real stuff costs 8–9 yuan per sheet, or US $1.30 to $1.50. A more ordinary sheet of paper costs 1–2 yuan a sheet.

The Zai Yuan Tang Mill also makes other products, such as the long, bright-red banners that people buy for New Year's; their customers then hire a calligrapher to paint the banners with messages of good luck and paste them vertically on their front doors. The banners are sold mostly to poor, rural people, so they are made of less-expensive paper, though the mill also produces high-quality, expensive banners to sell to Taiwan. Whatever the quality, this is all handmade paper; the mill cannot afford machines.

Another paper based on local pulp is made in the neighboring province to the southwest, Zhejiang, where some of the most appreciated green tea in the world is grown on terraces gracefully carved into green mountainsides, blue mist-shrouded peaks behind them. The area is known for its bamboo forests, and along its Fuchun River are small, family-owned paper mills that make bamboo paper. Bamboo paper dates back to ancient times in China.

The mills make their paper only from the current year's bamboo stalk, so the forest is left intact. There will be new stalks the following year. The bamboo's green outside skin is peeled off and the white flesh is removed from the joints. The poles are then split and cut into one-foot pieces, which are bundled together and boiled in water and lime for twenty-four hours. Then they are left in a big pot with water and lime for six months, washed in fresh water, and beaten into pulp. In most cases, this paper is neither fine nor white. It is used for such ritual purposes as burning at funerals.

ONE OLD TRADITION that has remained in modern China, as well as in Japan and Korea, is calligraphy. Under Mao's rule, it was used for propaganda. Today, it is deployed in commercial advertising. But it has always been primarily an art form.

According to Sun Xiaoyun, a leading Chinese calligrapher, calligraphy has changed over the centuries with technology. Up until 400 CE, paper was very rough and so characters were not very precise. Brush-strokes were made while rolling the brush between the thumb and forefinger, as had also been the case when writing on tortoise shells in ancient times.

Then, larger molds were made. Paper became larger and thinner and had to be laid on a tabletop. This required a significant change in posture, considered an essential element in calligraphy. Still, calligraphers rolled the brush up until the Ming dynasty. "Gradually," said Sun Xiaoyun, "writing changed, though you have to be an expert to see the difference. It used to be about the techniques of movements that made stroke marks. These techniques became lost and it became about slowly making stroke marks that looked that way without having the movements. Instead of one fast stroke it became the careful painting of stroke

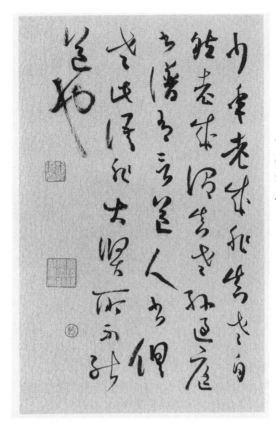

Calligraphy by Sun Xiaoyun in the cursive style.

marks. It became about the way you wrote and not finger movement. No one knows the old stroke movements anymore."

Another huge change was the adaptation of what is called "raw paper." Artists had traditionally used sized paper, which was treated with alum and wax; it held the ink and took a clear, thin line. But during the Ming dynasty, calligraphers and watercolor artists began using unsized paper—or raw paper—previously utilized mostly for wrapping or burning at funerals. This inexpensive paper is very absorbent, can blot or spread ink or watercolors, and make thick fuzzy lines. Raw paper has been the paper of choice for calligraphers and watercolor artists ever since.

Sun Xiaoyun recalled, "It used to be children were taught to write [with a brush] in school and most anyone could be a calligrapher. Applicants were tested and had to have especially beautiful calligraphy to qualify for a position as an official in the imperial court." But that all

Calligraphy by Sun Xiaoyun with the regular style of letters in a passage from Xiao Yi, 小乙, a Shang dynasty ruler.

changed when schoolchildren were taught to write with a pen instead of a brush. Born in 1959, Sun Xiaoyun grew up writing with a brush, but the generation after her was given pens, and the art of calligraphy started to fade. It was no longer taught in mainstream schools; those who were interested had to go to art school. But now, Sun said, "The government has realized that this was a mistake and they have announced that they are going back to teaching with a brush in schools."

SUN XIAOYUN WHISPERED, "Sometimes I use Japanese paper. It is better." Then she giggled. "They make us lose face."

The Chinese recognize that although they have retaken their place as the biggest papermakers in the world, they have lost their place as the best. Gong Bin, an artist and a papermaker in his forties, is particularly bitter about this. He lives and works in one of Beijing's newly bohemian neighborhoods, where brick workshops have given way to art and architecture studios, a café, a flower shop. Gong Bin is one of a new breed of papermakers popping up all over the world. He has a small, one-vat operation that makes paper to order for artists. He gets his pulp—blue sandalwood or mulberry bark—from Anhui Province. He doesn't use bleach because he believes the bark's natural vanilla color was the original color of Chinese paper. One of his customers is the China National Library, which uses his paper to repair ancient books.

On Gong Bin's right cheek are thin scars from when he deliberately cut his face in November 2014 because UNESCO had added Japanese handmade paper to its List of Intangible Cultural Heritage in Need of Urgent Safeguarding. According to Gong Bin, that was a "day of humiliation for China." He cut the lines on his cheek not because he thought the Japanese didn't deserve the honor, but because, in his words, "We lost face."

IN NINETEENTH-CENTURY JAPAN, there was a growing demand for paper and papermakers. Answering that demand, perhaps unfortunately, was the Yukosha Company, which introduced machine-made paper in Tokyo in 1874. Six other companies followed suit, establishing operations in Osaka, Kobe, and Kyoto. And from that time on, though the paper companies were not Western, handmade paper was known as *washi,* Japanese paper, and machine-made paper was *yoshi,* Western paper.

Koreans also call machine-made paper "Western." Their handmade paper is called *hanji,* which means Korean paper. "Western" is not a particularly endearing term in Asia, but the Asians do make and use a lot of Western paper. In 1880, the Japanese were using mainly *washi,* but by 1910, they had switched to mostly *yoshi.*

In Korea today, the small surviving companies that still produce *hanji* are being consolidated. Three larger multi-vat companies, including the giant Andong Hanji, which produces paper year-round and has its own

Korean calligraphy, which reads hanji, by Oh Sang Youl, a popular calligrapher known for a contemporary style used in advertising, movie posters,
and signs for stores and restaurants.

water-treatment plant, are replacing the many one-vat family operations
that run only in the winter. In 1910, there were 8,000 *hanji* makers. In
2009, there were twenty-six. But these figures are somewhat deceptive
because Korea was not divided in 1910, and 2009 figures for North Korea
are unavailable. But there is only one well-known mold maker left in
South Korea, living in the traditional town of Jeonju.

Hanji is still used for traditional objects such as lamps, umbrellas,
boxes, fans, and masks. *Hanji* strips are twisted into cords and woven
into baskets, shoes, and hats. It is used for the floor covering known as
jangpanji, found in traditional homes, which have become increasingly
rare in the past forty years. Korean red clay is believed to have health
benefits, and it is used to make a soft-rose colored *hanji* that is used for
wall coverings.

Hanji is made from *dak,* the bark of the paper mulberry, or sometimes
from *Broussonetia kazinoki,* a tree celebrated in Japan, where it is called
kozo. The bark is mixed with hibiscus root which, when beaten and
cooked, becomes the mucilage that holds the fibers of the paper together.
Koreans say that their bark is tougher than that of Japan because their
weather is more extreme and this makes their paper stronger. The Japanese, understandably, are uncertain about this claim.

IN THE EARLY twentieth century, there were 68,000 *washi* makers in Japan, which was a high point. By the second decade of the century, the number started dropping off. Now there are slightly fewer than 450, and according to some estimates, as few as 300. Still, they are almost all extremely high-quality operations, and that is enough to ensure Japan's status as the mecca of handmade paper.

Satsuya Matsulira, a gray-haired gentlemanly fellow often dressed in a blue kimono with matching pants, the traditional style worn by Japanese men in studios and ateliers, is the curator of the Ozu Shoten paper museum in eastern Tokyo, originally a paper store, founded in 1653. According to him, the biggest threat to *washi* is the fact that Western paper manufacturers have learned how to make imitation handmade paper at a fraction of the price. "It looks like *washi* and if it is made in accordance with the Japanese taste, most Japanese people don't know the difference. It's made in Japan by Japanese," he said.

In Eden Phillpotts's novel set in a nineteenth-century English paper mill, the papermakers say that the biggest threat to their livelihood is the fact that machine-made paper has gotten too good: "The public doesn't know hand made paper from machine-made." Now, Satsuya fears that the same is happening in Japan, where a good factory can make one ton of imitation *washi* in eight hours. They have even learned how to use traditional kozo bark in a Fourdrinier machine.

Yet of late, there has been a tremendous concern in Japan about preserving *washi*. Schoolchildren are brought to the Ozo Shoten museum and taught to make it. In the Tokyo school system, learning about *washi* is a standard part of a child's education. Satsuya said, "*Washi* is part of Japan."

A huge change took place in Japan after an earthquake destroyed Tokyo in 1923. The little shops where transactions were recorded with brushes on *washi* were replaced with modern stores where bills were written with a pen on pads of industrial paper. "When I was growing up, my umbrella was made of paper, the walls of my room were paper, kimonos had paper woven in them," Satsuya said. "Paper was a part of regular life but we don't use it anymore."

That is somewhat of an exaggeration. Artists still always use *washi* for wood blocks, watercolors, ink drawings, paintings, and calligraphy, and many traditional Japanese goods still come wrapped in *washi*— among them new kimonos and sweets such as mochi, a dumpling made from pounded rice, filled with fruit or sweets. The Japanese emperor, the symbolic but official head of state, uses *washi* almost exclusively. Tea ceremonies, which last for hours and involve drinking an intense, shade-grown green tea called matcha, use only *washi*. Little snacks and brightly colored sugar candies are served on *washi*, and the hefty bill delivered after the snacks is written on *washi*.

Gohei paper, folded into complex rectangles and hung from rice straw rope to mark sacred areas, is still in use and is always made from *washi*. Some sake factories still hang *gohei* in their fermentation rooms even though they now understand that fermentation is not caused by magic. And at Shinto shrines, messages of good fortune are still written on little strips of *washi* and sold for a coin in a *washi* envelope, to be tied to a nearby tree.

Traditional houses of *washi* paneling, shoji, have become rare. But some houses set aside one traditional shoji room, not only out of a sense of heritage, but for the pleasure of soft natural light. Today, most shoji paneling is at least partially machine-made and often contains some wood pulp because pure *washi* sheets of that size are extremely expensive. *Washi* absorbs humidity. In winter it holds in heat, and in summer, the panels slide open. *Karakami*, sliding *washi* room dividers, are still popular. Lamps and lighting fixtures are also still shaded with *washi*.

Ayako Kohno's family has owned the leading *karakami* company in Tokyo, Tokyo Matsuya, since 1690. Traditionally, the *karakami* are decorated with wood-block prints, and occasionally with gold or silver leaf. The Kohno family often works with a type of *washi* called *torinoko*, which means "child of a bird" and is eggshell-colored. *Karakami* paper is hard to make, because the panel is a single sheet the height of a short seventeenth-century man, which means that the man at the vat, or two men, must wield a mold this size. There are not many *washi* makers doing this kind of work anymore. Ayako Kohno said, "Yes, there is less *washi* available but there is also less demand so it balances out, but there is some fear that it will one day be gone."

The Yamastaya paper shop in Tokyo has been selling *washi* to the imperial household since the late nineteenth century. There is a tradition that states whenever the emperor has his hair cut, it can't just be thrown away. It must be wrapped in *washi*. No one seems to know what happens to it after that. The emperor is fond of parties at which the guests have a Haiku writing contest. Haiku is a traditional form of poetry from the seventeenth century. It is a seventeen-syllable verse form with three units of 5, 7, and 5 syllables. At the imperial palace, Haiku is written in a single vertical line with a brush on *washi*.

NEITHER THE TECHNIQUES and the equipment nor the material for handmade Japanese paper have changed greatly in the past thousand years. A thousand years ago, papermakers used the inner bark of mulberry bushes and cooked down the juice of the *tororo aie*, a relative to okra, just as they do today. But now the papermakers often grow their own mulberry bushes because the wild mulberry bushes are gone. The wild plants began disappearing at the beginning of the twentieth century.

The Saga prefecture on Kyushu, the southernmost of the four main islands of Japan, is the only place in Japan that still makes paper from *kajo* mulberry, which was once one of the country's principal bushes for papermaking. Kozo is a cultivated plant developed to resemble kajo, but it is now getting difficult to find even enough kozo, and so the Japanese are importing it from Korea. The other bark that papermakers use is mitsumata, which is of the *junchoge* family of East Asian flowering evergreens. But these are shrubs, not trees; a ten-foot-high mitsumata would be unusually tall.

Another problem facing the *washi* industry is that only about thirty people in Japan know how to make *washi* molds and other *washi* equipment, and almost none of these artisans are young. Washi makers are

not only traditionalists, they are a stubborn, rugged breed of individual-
ists who do hard physical labor for a small profit, spending their winters
dipped in cold water most of the day.

Shimizu Tadao, born December 8, 1937, and living in the village of
Kawai-cho, part of the town of Hida, high in snowcapped mountains, is
such an individualist. He is a tough old farmer who built his own house
on the snow flats so that he could collect the run-off from a mountain
stream in a concrete tank for *washi* making.

One papermaker in Gokayama, a very traditional area northwest of
Tokyo, rubs the kozo he uses in snow because he believes this makes its
paper whiter. This may seem unscientific, but his paper is indeed very
white. But when Tadao lays the scraped-off bark that he uses on the
snow to bleach, he *is* being scientific. If there are enough sunny days,
the bright sunlight reflected off the white snow will bleach the bark. It
is what people all over the world once did, and in some places still do,
with clothes before bleach was invented.

Tadao grows his own kozo and his own rice and pickle vegetables,
and from January to April he makes *washi*. He does everything himself
with only an occasional helping hand from his wife or a caring neighbor.
When Tadao's son was in junior high school, he wrote an essay about
why he wanted to become a *washi* maker like his dad. But the school
told him that that would be impossible and directed him to a regular
high school. Now he works for the prefecture. "He would like to be a
washi maker," said Tadao, "but I don't think it will be possible. He can't
earn a living." Then he proudly held up a sheet of white paper and said,
"But look what I made from that black bark."

Tadao and his wife make 100 sheets in a good day. In earlier years, he
used to have helpers, and together they would make 250 sheets in a day.
"Also, my back is hurting," he said, explaining the reason for the reduced
amount. But Tadao has traditions to uphold. His mother stripped bark
until she was ninety-two. "If you do everything right on a January day,
when you dip your hands in that cold mountain water you know you
are doing something good," he said.

Tadao is bothered by the way the branches stripped for *washi* making are just burned or thrown away. "People need to find a use for them," he said. "Wood ought to be used." He has tried selling them as hiking sticks to tourists who come to the mountains. He has tied *washi* strips on the end and tried selling them as feather dusters. So far these ideas have not taken off.

ABOUT FORTY-FIVE MILES north of Tokyo, in the Dohira Mountains, is the town of Ogama-Machi, famous for making *washi* for the past 1,200 years. Before World War II, the town had eighty papermakers. After the war, that number dropped to only three, but it is now back up to ten. Some people have taken up the practice and some have gone back to it. Teizou Takano, a fourth-generation papermaker, is one who went back. He said, "I hated it. Especially in the winter. All that cold water." He quit for fifteen years and then an American who wanted to know about *washi* came through town and was so interested and enthusiastic and appreciative of the paper that Teizou felt shamed into continuing the tradition.

His shop is not picturesque. His next-store neighbor, who also makes paper in the winter and farms the rest of the year, lives in a 1750 thatch-roofed house with a Japanese garden, complete with a cherry tree and carp pond. But Teizou Takano toils in a one-room shop with two women who work for him, making paper the old-fashioned way. They begin by cooking the kozo with lye to make it soft. After three hours, it is a silky mush and is poured into a big rectangular vat, along with a little slimy tororo aie pulp to make it stickier. They stir it well and lower a wooden mold—not wire, but an old bamboo strainer—into it. The size of a door, the mold is hard to handle. It makes two sheets. Teizou swishes it around in the vat and, with remarkable skill, shifts, shakes, and sifts until in a matter of seconds he has created a barely visible film of fibers. This he carefully turns out as a wet sheet of paper. He and his helpers leave the sheets in a stack for about twelve hours, then press the water out, and lay them flat one by one on a steam-heated metal wall to dry. The use of the wall is the only change in process from that used during medieval times.

The people of Ogama-Machi started making *washi* in the ninth century because so much mulberry grew there. Now, only a small amount
can be found wild in the area. Teizou uses kozo, which he buys from
places all over Japan, though he prefers the denser bark from colder
regions. Colder weather is also why Korea claims to have better bark.
Teizou is now seventy-eight and says of his craft, "I get easily sick of it."
It does not seem that there will be a fifth generation of papermakers in
this family. His son, who sells motorcycles, has made it clear that he
wants nothing to do with papermaking. And his daughter is not interested either. One of his workers, Tamara Satoni, has said she will stay
with Teizou Takano as long as he is working. Then she plans to leave
and form her own *washi* company.

There was a time when *washi* makers were part of rural life. It was
a winter activity for farmers. Children would volunteer to strip bark so
they could keep the sticks for firewood. But houses are not heated with
wood fires anymore and there are few farmers.

The Japanese government subsidizes the studies of young people
interested in learning how to make *washi*. But it takes many years to
learn how to make it well, and the government will only pay for two
years of training.

There are a few young *washi* makers, such as Tange Naoke, born in
1980, who learned the trade from his grandfather. He lives in the picturesque tile-roofed town of Kurashiki, along the beautiful Seto Inland Sea.
He grows mitsumata and kozo on a small lot in front of his studio, but
he also buys some; shoots that are less than an inch thick, which have
soft bark, are best for papermaking. He also gets people in the area to
pick wild *gampi*, a bush that has been used for making paper since ancient
times. He makes 200 sheets of paper in an eight-hour day; his grandfather, he says, could make twice that amount in the same time period.

Both in Asia and the West, the image of the vatman has an element
of machismo to it. It takes someone large and strong to wield the big
molds. But then there is Kachiwagi Kazue, born in 1936. She is a tiny
woman barely over four feet tall. The widow of a *washi* maker, she
decided to make *washi* herself after his death and learned the craft

from her forty-three-year-old son. He and his wife have given up *washi* making, but Kazue is determined "to carry on." She stands on a step to dip the large mold into the vat and quickly shake it into a perfect, even sheet.

THERE IS ONE kind of papermaking that gets more and more popular every year in Japan: nori, the thin sheets of seaweed used to wrap sushi or to wrap around rice if your chopstick skills are up to it. Nori is made exactly like paper. In fact, it fits the definition of paper—randomly woven fibers.

Nori production begins with nets that are stretched out horizontally at the low-tide level between bamboo poles. Barely visible seaweed seeds are planted on the nets. Then, for forty days, nori growers take boats out at low tide every day to check on the plants. They remove other types of seaweed and other matter that gets caught in the nets, while leaving the nori to grow—in effect, weeding their nets.

Several varieties of red algae of the genus *Porphyra*, common along the Japanese coastline, serve for making nori. They have local names such as *asukusa* and *susabi*.

In the past, nori was made like *washi*. It was chopped by hand, mixed with water, and sifted by hand on screens. Then about fifty years ago, machines were introduced and hand-made nori started to disappear. The nori machine resembles a Fourdrinier, complete with a continuous belt. The machine chops the seaweed, mixes it with water, and runs the solution over plastic screens so that the water drains through. The nori is then pressed to squeeze out any remaining water, and dried.

Some *washi* makers are switching to making nori, because, it is said, they can make better money. But not everyone, including nori maker Norio Kinman, agrees that making nori is necessarily more profitable than making *washi*. Some older people who remember handmade nori complain about the machine-made product. Machine-made nori is heated to make it crisper, which also makes it greener, less black. The connoisseurs say that handmade nori was not only blacker, but also thicker, softer, and more flavorful. Today, high-priced nori still has those characteristics.

Pegasus, a South Korean multinational, has gone one step further than both *washi* and nori to make real paper out of red algae. The product is a smooth, very white paper that has gone through a double bleaching process. Pegasus claims that making red-algae paper uses less energy than making paper from wood pulp because there is no need to remove lignin. They also say that ethanol is a by-product of the algae papermaking process. Their paper tastes like—paper.

IN EAST ASIA, the paper arts—calligraphy, watercolor, and ink on paper—remain popular. The 2000, Nobel Prize winner Gao Xingjian, author of the novel *Soul Mountain*, about a man in search of the mountain spirit, is also known for his ambiguous and evocative black-ink paintings on paper. Like the poet-artists of the classical period, he uses both writing and painting to express similar ideas linked through the theme of landscape.

Other popular Chinese artists, such as Arnold Chang and Peng Wei, are still painting watercolor landscapes in the classical tradition. Still others, such as Tang Guo, use traditional inks. Calligrapher Wang Dongling uses his training to paint abstract scrolls with huge black ink brush strokes.

Japanese paper art has had an influence on contemporary architecture. Architect Shigeru Ban, who has built museums, mansions, and corporate headquarters, is also famous for his $50 paper tube tents. He originally designed them for the aftermath to the Rwandan Civil War, and they have since been used in many other crisis situations. But much of his work is not inexpensive, such as his Aspen Art Museum, a largely glass structure in which he uses resin-infused paper.

In a very chic Kyoto studio, Eriko Horiki is redefining the role of *washi* in interior design. "I was originally a banker," she recalled. "I worked four years for a bank, and through the bank, I ended up administrating a *washi* company. I was invited to watch the *washi* making and I thought it

Wang Dongling, Open and Empty, *2005. This abstract
painting was influenced by years of training as a calligrapher.*

would be fun. I saw the artisans in that cold, cold air, their arms turning
purple in cold, cold water. I was impressed with the dedication of these
craftsmen in a tradition that went back fifteen hundred years."

Starting when she was twenty-four, it took years for Horiki to per-
suade experienced *washi* makers to work with her. She wanted to do
seemingly impossible things. "The important thing," she said, "is to
produce something that is useful. What did handmade *washi* have to

offer? It doesn't weaken over time. It improves with age. But they were making things that you only used once, like stationery and wrapping. What could this *washi* that lasted a long time be used for? Architecture."

Along with five or six papermakers working one giant mold, Horiki makes sheets of washi that are eighteen feet by forty-eight feet. She creates panels that look completely different with front lighting from how they look with back lighting, so that they change in appearance as the day progresses. Sometimes she embeds bits of silver foil, which reflect light when the panel is front-lit, but look black and opaque when it is back-lit. Sometimes she weaves in long strips of kozo. Sometimes she splashes the wet sheet with water to create random holes—like the European papermakers used to do by accident. Sometimes she adds chemical dyes. Some panels are two- and three-ply, with a different pattern on each layer. In short, the studio reinvents shoji, in ways never thought of before.

Horiki also creates large *washi* objects by molding kozo paper into shapes—spheres, cylinders, gourds, bones—and lighting them from the inside. She has made panels for the prime minister's residence, light fixtures for Tokyo's Narita Airport, and a backdrop for cellist Yo-Yo Ma.

THROUGHOUT PAPER HISTORY, there has always been a dialogue between papermakers and artists. English papermaker James Whatman consulted with J. M. W. Turner; Japanese papermakers made paper for specific artists and labeled it accordingly—for example, "Gahoo-shi," Gahoo's paper, which was made for the artist Gahō. But with less and less commercial use for handmade paper today, artisans in small Japanese shops are working even more closely with artists. An artist can now tell a papermaker exactly what he or she desires, and the papermaker responds with a custom-made product. This is what papermaker Gong Bin does in Beijing, and what many similar artisans all over the world are doing.

In the steep, velvet-green Basque hills above the port of Hondarribia, within walking distance from the French border, is a home with a flat-roofed, one-story, glassed-in studio. Here, Kikis Alamo and her husband José Ramon Alejandre make paper by hand. If you look out their windows in one direction, you see the Basque mountains, green from rain, with white-walled red-roofed houses on distant slopes. If you look in the other direction, you see the lush tropical forest of Vera Cruz state on Mexico's Caribbean coast. The couple have planted their garden with plantain bushes and agave, tamarind, and lavender-flowering jacaranda trees from their native state. They are Mexican-born Basques, the children of Spanish Civil War refugees, who moved back to this spot in the Basque Province of Gipuzkoa in 1982.

Kikis's fascination with papermaking stemmed from her interest in Mexican basket making. There are two connections. Straw is a material that is used for papermaking. More important, paper molds are woven, like baskets. It was the molds that first attracted her interest.

The place that Kikis and José chose to live, though a lovely spot, is completely unsuited to papermaking. There is no natural water source and so they use tap water, which they treat with chemicals to counteract the ones in the municipal water supply. The water also has to be filtered because it has too much metal content. Then it is kept in a large tank. The water is not recycled, and so a great deal of tap water is used. In addition, the fibers that they utilize for papermaking—raw cotton, linen, and abaca—are not native to the area.

Artists come to the studio and specify the type of paper they want. A few sample sheets are made until just the right weight, texture, and sizing is determined. "The watercolorists are the worst," Kikis joked. Turner's papermakers would have agreed. Watercolor, more than any other art form, is dependent upon the absorbency, sizing, and texture of the paper used. The same brushstroke will look entirely different on different papers.

The studio's customers range from King Juan Carlos of Spain, who requested a lightly textured thick paper, to internationally famous Basque abstract sculptor Eduardo Chillida, celebrated for his drawings, etchings, and lithographs. Chillida, who died in 2002, requested a somewhat greasy paper surface for his etchings, which the studio created by using polymer sizing on well-textured paper.

A small woman, Kikis makes small sheets of paper on small molds. Some is thick and highly textured, some is as smooth as fine Japanese paper, and some is so heavily textured it is almost three-dimensional. Asked if her paper is expensive, she said that it was, and added: "A sheet of paper is a work of art, but it is thought of as nothing. Someone draws a line on it and it is twenty times more valuable."

IN THE LATE twentieth and twenty-first centuries, artists have been using paper not only to create art on it, but to create art from it. This was probably first popularized in the West by cubists Picasso and Braque, who glued painted paper, oil cloth, rope, and other material to their work, inventing the term *collage,* meaning "glued." Toward the end of his life, French painter Henri Matisse turned from painting to making collages with colorful paper. His technique suited the physical restraints that age was imposing on him, but it also satisfied the direction in which his painting had been heading all his life as he searched for ways to strip down figurative images to their bare essence.

Matisse was not a restless connoisseur of handmade paper. He used machine-made French paper produced for artists. In particular, he liked Arches paper, made on a cylinder sheet by sheet, with deckle edges and a smooth wove surface. He also used paper manufactured on Fourdrinier machines by Barjon and by Canson & Montgolfier, another very old French company. He wanted paper that he or his assistants could paint with saturated colors.

But since Matisse's time, artists have become much more involved in the making of the paper with which they work. Kikis Alamo's artists ask her not just for various colors of paper but for various textures—some with long fibers, some with short fibers, and some with different lengths of fibers in different parts of the same sheet. Artists will even sometimes lick a corner of a piece of paper to test its sizing. If it is sticky, it means the paper is heavily sized.

Upon his return from World War II, Douglas Howell, inspired by paper historian and papermaker Dard Hunter, built his own mill for handmade paper on Grand Street in Manhattan. He had learned how to make paper in France after being discharged from the army. In New York he developed techniques for a wide variety of colors and textures, working with everything from the flax he grew in his backyard on Long Island to blue jeans. He even designed and built his own pulp beater. He made paper for many prominent artists, including Jackson Pollock, Lee Krasner, Jasper Johns, Larry Rivers, and Robert Rauschenberg. Although his own work is in major collections, he is most remembered for reviving the craft of papermaking in America and inspiring numerous other papermakers and departments of papermaking in art schools.

In 1974, Susan Gosin and Bruce Wineberg at the University of Wisconsin started the Dieu Donné Press. Their original project was to handprint a book of Bruce's poems on handmade paper. Two years later, they started their own paper mill on Crosby Street in Manhattan, a short distance from where Douglas Howell's press had been. Later, they moved to various other Manhattan locations, and are now a busy shop where artists come to invent with paper.

Most of the paper that Gosin and Wineberg produce is made from cotton, from a pressed board of semiprocessed fiber that they buy, or from abaca imported from the Philippines. But sometimes they purchase linen scraps, as in earlier eras, and beat them for ten hours in a modern Hollander beater. Sometimes they make paper with gampi. It all depends on what the artist is trying to do. Artist Saul Melman puts pigment in water, which he freezes into ice cubes. He then places the cubes on paper, and as they melt, they leave cube designs with drip marks. Do Ho Suh makes drawings with thread and presses them into paper. Roxy Paine creates sculpture out of molding pulp. Other artists paint with different colored pulp using brushes or squeeze bottles.

There are such papermakers and paper artists in many places. Matthew Shlian is a Michigan-based industrial designer who works with companies such as Apple and Procter & Gamble. These companies have become increasingly interested in how their products are packaged; there is a growing belief that opening a purchased product should be a positive experience, like opening a present.

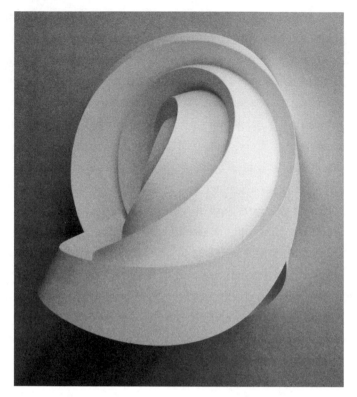

Matthew Shlian, We Are Building This Ship
as We Sail It, *paper sculpture.*

While working in the corporate world, Shlian became increasingly interested in creating aesthetic objects out of paper and is now a respected paper sculptor. He designs huge installations for thousands of dollars, and little geometric sculptures for $300. The latter are popular for first anniversaries, which, by tradition, are commemorated with a paper present. He said, "There is a renaissance in art on paper because it is such a tactile media. It's so nice to hold things in your hand." Pixar animators, who seldom get to hold anything, told him the same when he was working with them on a project.

LIKE MOST THINGS in Japanese culture, origami first came to their islands from China, arriving around the sixth century, about the same time paper did. At first, a simple type of origami was used to wrap offerings to deities. But true origami, decorative folded paper figures, didn't begin, according to legend, until a twelfth-century nobleman named Kiyosuke folded a piece of paper into the shape of a frog.

Origami is often taught to children, who are shown how to make flowers and animals. There are rules. A piece of origami must be made by folding a single sheet of rectangular paper. There can be no cutting. Nothing can be added or subtracted. The strictest origami rules state that the folding must take place in the air and not on a table, but often this rule is not observed.

Origami became sculpture with a little-known Japanese innovator named Akira Yoshizawa, who lived from 1911 to 2005. Self-taught, he left his factory job to pursue his paper-folding passion, supporting himself with odd jobs and with selling soup door to door. He invented "wet folding," folding paper while it is wet. He also invented a form of diagraming that shows how each fold is made, which is how serious origami work is recorded today. He started by making pieces with twenty folds. By the 1980s, he was making pieces with eighty folds; his later work involved between two hundred and three hundred folds. He created figures with expressive faces and remarkable details. In his life he made about 50,000 pieces, none of which he ever sold.

Because of Akira Yoshizawa's work, serious origami makers in the United States, France, and other places all over the world started producing their own human and animal figures—even whole scenes—of dazzling complexity and detail from a single rectangular piece of paper.

Physicists, mathematicians, biologists, and computer scientists have also been inspired by Yoshizawa. They are asking what can be learned from folding paper. Mathematicians see implications for problems of geometry, number theory, and abstract algebra. Engineers see implications that could apply to such things as how to fold air bags used in automobiles so that they deploy properly, or how to fold pieces of equipment used on satellites so they unfold as desired in space.

At the MIT Computer Science and Artificial Intelligence Laboratory, Erik Demaine, who earned his PhD at age twenty and was the youngest professor ever hired at MIT, is working on folding human proteins to fight diseases. It is his belief that proteins have a shape that they fold into; if they fold the wrong way, it causes diseases. He believes that developing mathematical formulas on how proteins fold could lead to the creation of protein drugs to fight particular viruses. He also creates beautifully curved origami sculptures.

California architect Tina Hovsepian uses origami paper-folding concepts to create tents out of folded cardboard that can be used to shelter the homeless. She calls her structures "carboardigami." They fold up for easy transport and fold out where needed. She says the structures are weatherproof and insulated. A trained worker can set one up anywhere in a half hour.

In a world where inventions are replacing the use of paper, new uses of paper are also being invented all the time.

Epilogue

CHANGE

||||||||||||||||

As centuries pass by, the total quantity of works grows end-lessly, and one can foresee a time when it will be almost as difficult to educate oneself in a library, as in the universe, and almost as fast to seek a truth in nature, as lost among an immense number of books . . .

—DENIS DIDEROT, *Encyclopédie*, 1755

Wholly new forms of encyclopedias will appear, ready made with a mesh of associative trails running through them, ready to be dropped into the memex and there amplified. The law-yer has at his touch the associated opinions and decisions of his whole experience, and of the experience of friends and authorities. The patent attorney has on call the millions of issued patents, with familiar trails to every point of his cli-ent's interest. The physician, puzzled by a patient's reactions, strikes the trail established in studying an earlier similar case, and runs rapidly through analogous case histories, with side references to the classics for the pertinent anatomy and histol-ogy. The chemist, struggling with the synthesis of an organic compound, has all the chemical literature before him in his laboratory, with trails following the analogies of compounds, and side trails to their physical and chemical behavior.

—VANNEVAR BUSH, "AS WE MAY THINK,"
The Atlantic, JULY 1945

THE PROBLEM WITH THE ENDING OF HISTORY BOOKS—also the beginning—is that history, unlike books, has no beginning and no end; it keeps flowing.

With remarkable frequency, the phrase is uttered, "The world is changing." It is certainly true that the world is changing, but this sentence is often announced as though the world had never changed before. There has been no period in human history when the world was not changing. There is also a popular belief that *now* the world is changing more dramatically or more swiftly than it ever has before. That too is probably not true. During the Industrial Revolution in the nineteenth century, scarcely a year passed without at least one life-changing new invention.

The invention of the cell phone has changed our lives, but has it had as great an influence as did the invention of the telephone? Alexander Graham Bell patented his telephone in 1876, the same year that Nikolaus August Otto developed the first usable internal-combustion engine, which led the way to automobiles. The following year, Edison invented the phonograph, and Eadweard Muybridge the moving picture. The year after that, Joseph Wilson Swan built the incandescent lightbulb, the first bulb that would burn long enough for practical applications, and transparent film was invented. And it should be mentioned that yet another year later, the British Perforated Paper Company came out with the first toilet paper.

With fountain pens, barbed wire, machine guns, dishwashers, sewing machines, dynamite, radio, vacuum cleaners, air conditioners, and more, it would seem that nineteenth-century people were reeling with change. Then the twentieth century started, with the airplane, plastic, cellophane, and still more. It was all dizzying, but it must also be remembered that many of these inventions, like the inventions of today, developed over decades, even over generations.

Today's ideas, facilitated by the inventions of the Industrial Revolution, are taking as long to lead to new inventions as did the ideas of the Industrial Revolution. One of the reasons why we believe otherwise, why we imagine our times to be moving so swiftly, is that we live in an age of marketing. Electronic devices are built with planned obsolescence; that is, they are deliberately built not to last, so that everyone will have to buy another one soon. Every year new devices, only slightly different from the models that came before, come on the market and we are told that they are major new technological innovations. A similar technique was used to sell automobiles in the 1950s, before the laws of aerodynamics and fuel economy were widely understood. Each year, the car companies would introduce new cars that looked completely different from the old cars, even though in terms of technology they were pretty much the same. Such tactics are what make people buy.

WE SPEAK OF the electronic, computer, and digital "revolutions," but many historians insist that there are no revolutions. Some *evolutions* are just faster than others. Certainly the digital revolution, like the Industrial Revolution, had no year attached to it like the French Revolution had in 1789.

As with the invention of paper, it is not really possible to say who invented the computer or when, despite this being recent history. Lately, it has become popular to attribute the invention—as Walter Isaacson suggests in *The Innovators* and James Essinger affirms in *Ada's Algorithm*—to Ada Lovelace, poet Lord Byron's neglected and brilliant daughter. In the early nineteenth century, she wrote the first algorithm intended to be carried out by a machine.

The computer age does seem to have its origins in the Industrial Revolution, and Ada Lovelace was probably the first to write about a machine that could be programmed to work on any problem. But her ideas were based on those of Charles Babbage, who had built a machine, the Difference Engine, that could make calculations. Her most famous work is an 1843 treatise on the potential of Babbage's machine.

Forty years earlier, Joseph-Marie Jacquard had invented a loom that could be programmed with punch cards. Ada Lovelace was probably familiar with that machine because when the Luddites tried to smash them, her father, Lord Byron, famously spoke in the Luddites' defense. Jacquard's work probably also led Babbage to imagine his calculating machine, also programmable with punch cards.

In any event, Jacquard must be given some credit for the 1890 US Census, which Herman Hollerith was able to complete in one year instead of the estimated eight through the use of punch cards and electronics. That census marked the first time that information was processed through electronic circuits. Hollerith went on to found a company that eventually became the International Business Machines Corporation, IBM.

IN THE BEGINNING of the twenty-first century, there was a great deal of talk about the death of paper—it was going to be replaced by new technology. Few people believe that anymore, and most students of history never believed it, because in history it is rare for a new technology to completely replace an old one. Usually it just presents another valued alternative. Paper is used less today because some things are done electronically, but for some things, paper is preferred. This book was written electronically, but with the help of many paper books and numerous notebooks used while interviewing people or for jotting down observations. In the end, the book will be published both on paper and electronically.

For a time, it was thought that paper would at least disappear from offices. But this, too, is no longer expected to happen. All research shows that even as offices grow increasingly computerized, they still value paper for certain tasks. Passing out a printed report at a meeting has more impact than emailing it. People like to write down quick notes and memos on paper even if they have a cell phone with a memo function. Different people have different paper preferences and appear to enjoy having choices. The sales figures for office paper remain fairly stable. It should have been obvious that this would be the case once printers were connected to almost every computer in homes and offices. Printers remain a popular, often essential, piece of equipment.

Mitchell Kapor, whose spreadsheet program, Lotus, is only one of his many computer innovations, said, "To me it's a simple-minded view that technology makes paper obsolete. . . . What I think is often underappreciated in the tech community is the virtues and properties of paper. You can take a piece and put it in your pocket. Will there ever be foldable computers?" He continued: "If you look at the history of computers, they were more conceived of as a calculating engine and filing cabinet than as literary machines." Ironically, this was also true of the written word when it was first invented and also the first uses of paper. The first function was for facilitating calculations, and the second for storing information. It seems to be the order in which people think or possibly how they prioritize.

Vannevar Bush, an engineer born in the nineteenth century, was one of the early geniuses of electronics, and was in charge of US military research during World War II. He shaped the thinking of many others, including Kapor, with a 1945 essay in *The Atlantic* entitled "As We May Think." Essentially, he was addressing the same issue that Diderot had addressed 190 years earlier: as the accumulated knowledge of humans gets ever greater, won't we reach a point where it is too much to access, too much to sift through?

In 1755, Diderot foresaw the future need for a data bank even though he did not know what it would look like or what to call it. Similarly, in 1945, after the explosion of information created by the war, Vannevar Bush realized that computers were needed. Society creates the technology that it needs. This urgent issue regarding information storage, first expressed by Diderot, is what drove computer technology forward. Computers were not developed to replace books or paper; they were developed to be a better way to store and access information.

Will computers or some other form of technology ever actually replace paper? It can safely be said that this will not happen for a long time. But will it ever? It's hard to say. As Kapor put it, "We don't really know what paper is going to be up against."

Many experiments with artificial intelligence are under way. In 2014, for the first time, two people, one in India and one in France, exchanged thoughts without using words. Is wordless communication the way of the future? If it is, there will certainly be people ready to tell us that this is the end of civilization as we know it, or at least that all grace and beauty will vanish, that life will be diminished.

There is a popular assumption that technology is limitless. Computers have advanced because other inventions—in particular, microchips— have advanced them. But it isn't necessarily true that technology has no limits, as has recently been demonstrated by what is called Moore's Law.

Gordon Moore was a chip maker and one of the founders of Intel. In 1965 he wrote an article, "Cramming More Components onto Integrated Circuits," for *Electronics* magazine. In it, he discussed how every new chip had more transistors than the one developed before it, and the more transistors a chip had, the faster, more powerful, smaller, and cheaper a computer could be. Computers could be—and have been—built the size of a fingernail. In 1965 the number of transistor chips had been doubling every year, so Moore predicted that in ten years, chips would have 60,000 transistors. But then a few years later, he backed off from his "law" and said that the number of chips might double only every two years. Today, there are chips with 8 billion transistors. But the chip industry is uncertain how much longer they can keep increasing that number, or at least, how much longer they can keep increasing it so quickly. Moore thinks that the increase will continue, but not necessarily at the current rate. At some point, an idea reaches its full potential.

On the other hand, some other completely new idea may come along.

ANOTHER POPULAR PREDICTION in the early twenty-first century was that electronic books—ebooks—would replace printed books. But it turns out that people like printed books. Even computer people enjoy printed books. Young people in particular enjoy printed books over ebooks. In the early 2000s, the ebooks industry grew at a rapid rate. But people always forget, as Moore forgot with his "law," that growth is greatest when you start at zero. If you sold one ebook last year and two this year, that is a 100 percent growth rate. But as the numbers grow higher, the growth-rate percentage slows. By the second decade of the century, it seemed that ebooks were well established but not growing. This actually came as a disappointment to book publishers, who had been counting on growth in ebook sales to counter the declining sales in other formats—for example, the paperback.

There are some kinds of books that work well as ebooks and other books that people want to have in their physical library. This has actually made books better. Before ebooks, publishers, feeling cost pressures, had started to lower expenses by using lesser-quality paper; paper usually represents one-third or somewhat less of the publisher's cost of producing a book. Attempts were made to use a white coating on paper that had too much lignin, but the browning from lignin leaked out of the cut edges, producing pages that were white in the middle but brown around the edges. Today, most publishers believe that for a printed book to compete with an ebook, it needs to be a better-quality object, and so they make a great effort, at some expense, to make their product handsome.

A noticeable change that the digital age has made in the book industry is that books are being published in smaller first printings. This is not because publishers are selling fewer books, but because they are able to reduce warehousing costs; a new printing can now be ordered up in two weeks or less. The technology of printing books has completely changed, but as is so often the case, this "new technology" is really about recycling old technology. Books used to be printed through photography, laser impressions on film. Now they are printed on aluminum plates with oil- and water-resistant materials—in effect, a lithograph. Modern bookbinders use hot glue and then cool the books on revolving carousels, the idea copied from bakeries, which use them to cool cakes. Why not? Gutenberg copied a wine press.

In 1965, J.C.R. Licklider, one of the original creators of the Internet, wrote a report on the future of libraries. He concluded that works of art and literature were unsuited to electronics, that books were needed. Like Vannevar Bush, he believed that computers best served for storage, sorting, and accessing pure information. Electronics were never supposed to be a substitute for books.

THE MOST RAPIDLY declining type of paper being used in this century is newsprint, the least expensive category of communication paper. The sale of newsprint in the twenty-first century has been dropping at a rate of about 10 percent a year. This is not only due to the decline of newspapers. Newsprint is also used for telephone books and catalogues, trades that have been nearly killed by electronics. If accessing information is what computers do best, publications that are so purely informational are doomed.

Unquestionably, newspapers are in trouble too. It is not that people don't want to read them anymore; it is that they were built from their beginnings on an economic model that is no longer working. As was distinctly stated by Roy Howard, one of the founders of the Scripps-Howard newspaper chain, in Detroit in 1921, "We come here simply as news merchants. We are here to sell advertising and sell it at a rate profitable to those who buy it. But first we must produce a newspaper with news appeal that will result in a circulation and make the advertising effective."

The formula was always to sell as many newspapers as possible and sell them for cheap and make money on the advertisers who would pay more for higher circulation. Newspapers are so tied to selling ads that the number of pages of news is determined not by what is going on in the world or the town but by the amount of advertising that has been sold. A reporter knows that the least-favored features have a chance to run on holidays because of the extra pages created by holiday advertising.

Today the problem is that advertisers would rather spend their money on electronic advertising than on print newspapers. Ad revenue is steadily evaporating from print media. By 2014 more than half of the revenue earned by the *New York Times* came from selling newspapers themselves, rather than from advertising, representing a historic shift in the company's finances. The only bright spot in their faltering ad revenues came from the circulation of their online newspaper, which was steadily attracting more advertisers.

According to Ken Doctor, a longtime newspaper editor who now runs a company called Newsonomics, which monitors the newspaper industry, "Sixty-two percent of the *New York Times* is reader revenue. It used to be 80 percent advertising revenue."

The same thing is happening all over the world. The decline in advertising revenue has been devastating for British newspapers. According to Doctor, the *Daily Telegraph*, which derives an unusually high percentage of its earnings from paid subscribers, is the only paper in London showing a significant profit. "All over the world there is the same problem for newspapers. India is a little more stable than others because India has a steady growth of the middle class. Also the *Times of India* and other newspapers are companies with wide commercial interest. So they can survive difficulties in their newspaper division."

In the United States, newspapers are charging readers more to boost circulation revenue. Readers have generally accepted the hikes without complaint. The papers also try to earn more from advertising on their online editions. The *New York Times* and *Financial Times* both now have more online subscribers than print subscribers. But online newspapers and magazines have not been attracting as much advertising as companies with a larger Internet presence and vastly greater resources, such as Google and Facebook.

Some newspapers have folded, but not a huge number. Doctor estimates that about 1,450 daily newspapers were published in the United States in 2000, and 1,389 in 2014, a decline of only about 60. But the real loss, according to Doctor, is not newspaper closings, it is newspapers shrinking their operations and staff. There are 30 percent fewer newspaper journalists today than there were in 2000. And the papers, having less advertising, have become noticeably smaller.

Doctor guesses that eventually print newspapers will disappear and all move online because it is a better economic model. They can charge readers as much as they have in the past for a print paper and deliver it for much less money. Their profits will increase substantially. That is, unless advertisers rebel.

JERRY DELLA FEMINA is a longtime advertising man, said to be an inspiration for the popular television series about advertising, *Mad Men*, and famous for successful campaigns, such as his first in 1970, when he made the mediocre German wine Blue Nun a household name in America. He advertises online because his clients want him to.

The first tenet of advertising is that you must know your market. You are appealing to a specific gender of a certain age bracket and a certain income and a certain level of education. You identify those people with a particular newspaper or a particular television show—television is generally thought to be the best way to advertise—and that is where you place the ad.

But about online advertising, Della Femina says, "No one really knows how good digital advertising is. You reach a zillion people, but do any of them buy the product? No one knows what happens on Facebook. There are no success stories. . . . With print ads, I see results, sales jump 5 percent the following day or week. You don't see that with digital. There is no proof that it is working. But you will die if you go into a meeting with a client and don't talk about how great your digital group is going to be."

David Remnick, the editor of *The New Yorker,* said that this was old thinking. "My job is to get it to readers the way they want to read it. I can't insist on one technology. Go online and subscribe in one click and save on subscription or you can read it on a phone. I am in the wine business, not the bottle business." *The New Yorker* has been changing not only their bottle, but also how they pay for it. The magazine was never focused on advertising. They earned 80 percent of their revenue from the price of the magazine itself. But now they earn half of their revenue from advertising, in part because of their digital presence.

Remnick's experience with NewYorker.com supports Della Femina's argument, however. The print magazine has 1,050,000 subscribers, and the magazine's staff knows a great deal about who these people are. They know, for example, that the average magazine is passed on to four people, meaning that their circulation is actually about 4 million. Their website gets 10 million visits a month, but they don't know as much about these readers. They don't know if they are one-time visitors, or if they are a totally different group of visitors every month, or if the same readers habitually visit month after month. They might have 10 million online readers or they might have 120 million. They don't know their reading habits, let alone their spending habits, or if they are serious consumers at all.

Remnick has a bright, airy corner office with a view of both the old copper-roofed *New York Times* building with its stone masonry and the glass high-rise next to it where the *Times* lives today. From this perch, he told me that he spends a great deal of time pondering what he should be doing about the digital age. He said, "I cannot afford to be sentimental about paper. J. D. Salinger defined sentimental as when you love something more than God does. I cannot afford to love paper more than God does."

AS IS ALWAYS true with change, there are some winners, some losers, and some who are not affected at all. Fashion magazines remain a lucrative draw for advertisers and are unaffected by the problems of the twenty-first-century press. But the paper business is getting tougher, due to fewer people demanding paper, and stiffer competition.

Harry Gould, who has been trading and distributing paper since 1969, said about the future, "There will be far fewer players, but when you are in the commodity business like steel or aluminum, if you are one of the five left standing, you will make a pretty good buck." He also had a number of other predictions to share about the paper industry, including that some small paper mills will survive and that the sales of art paper will remain stable. "Office paper sales will drop about 3 percent a year, but that is not a serious amount, and with less competition the prices can go up." Sales of business letterhead will decline, but personal stationery, especially that made of high-quality linen, will do well. "Diapers and paper bags," according to Gould, "are recession-proof."

One of the bigger winners of the digital age is boxes and cardboard for packaging, both white and brown. With online shopping, packaging has become a booming industry and is one of the reasons why, for the first time in history, less than half the paper made in the world is "communication" paper. Actually, now is the second time in history that this has happened. In ancient China before Cai Lun, paper was used mostly for wrapping.

ONE FINAL PREDICTION from Harry Gould: "Paper will probably never disappear."

Certainly for the time being, paper has a solid, even if slightly diminished, place in our culture. Mitchell Kapor said, "At the moment, paper still has some advantages over screens. Flexibility. It has more longevity because it has attributes for which there are no substitutes. I think we will have paper for a long time, which does not mean forever."

There is another advantage of paper. To use electronic terminology, it is very "secure." Electronic messages can be hacked, accessed, reconstructed. Paper cannot. When National Security Agency (NSA) whistleblower Edward Snowden started revealing to journalist Glenn Greenwald the extent of the surveillance on the public by the NSA, they feared government interception of their communication, and with good reason. They could talk, but the room might be bugged. They could send highly sophisticated encrypted electronic messages, but even that might not be safe. In the end, they sat together and passed notes handwritten on pieces of paper that could be torn up and burned. Another advantage of paper is that it is easy to destroy—much easier than electronic information.

Ironically, many books on paper are being published about the ruinous effect that digital communication is having on human beings and civilization. We are told that we will lose our memory, our ability to sustain a thought, our ability to think and truly find our way through an idea. Those same warnings were made when communication changed from oral to written. There was some truth to it when Plato and Socrates were debating the notion and there is some truth to it today. It is very easy, when in a conversation with an annoying interlocutor with a cell phone in hand, who repeatedly Googles every subject for factoids, to understand what Socrates was saying in Plato's *Phaedrus*: "It will implant forgetfulness in their souls: they will cease to exercise memory because they rely on that which is written, calling things to remembrance no longer from within themselves. . . . And it is no true wisdom."

It is no true wisdom. How often do we think this thought about people who spew facts from the Internet? Don't Plato's words about people who rely on writing resonate when observing people who rely so much on search engines? "They seem to know much, while for the most part they know nothing." And yet, even with the establishment of written language, human discourse and intellectual pursuits continued. The written word proved useful. In the words of the first-century BCE poet Horace, *"Littera scripta manet."* The written word remains.

Before predicting all the things that will disappear in the digital age, it is worth remembering that orality still survives. The first step in promoting a new book is having the author read it in public, because when people hear it, it tends to make them want to read it. Recordings of books have also become tremendously popular.

There are still many oral traditions—African storytellers, calypso musicians in Trinidad engaged in improvisational contests with a very specific rhythm and rhyme, ancient Jewish prayers such as the Kaddish recited for the dead in an unmistakable and easy-to-remember cadence. In oral traditions, rhythm and rhyme are essential memory aids.

The Basques have a tradition called *bertsolari*, which is a contest between oral poetry improvisers. The poems are highly rhythmic and rhymed. In Basque country, 1,400 people will attend a *bertsolari* and it will be broadcast on television. And for that matter, poetry itself, from any culture, is an example of oral literature that has continued in written form. Anyone who doubts the oral nature of written poetry should listen to old recordings of Irish Poet William Butler Yeats chanting his poems.

It is apparent that human beings have an innate desire for connection. There is a part of the brain that makes human beings, the most social of animals, want to connect with one another. Our brains have evolved this way; it is in our genetic coding and it is likely to grow stronger as humans further evolve because it is a trait that benefits survival. It is why humans invented a spoken language, then a written language, then paper, then printing, then electronics. This is evolution, not revolution.

And written language itself has been returning to its early development, to pictographs and hieroglyphics. There are the signs by the side of the road, the signs denoting women's and men's bathrooms, and the growth of the use of emoticons—which stands for "emotion icon"—in digital communication. Why are we revisiting early writing forms? Why are these pictographs conveying feelings, such as ☺, meaning "happy," increasingly becoming part of the digital vocabulary of the twenty-first century? It is because change and the resistance to change always work hand in hand.

TIMELINE

IIIIIIIIIIIIIIIIIIIIIIIIIIIIIIIIIIIIIIIIIIIIIIIIIIIIIIIIIIIIIII

38,000 BCE	A red dot painted on the El Castillo cave in Northern Spain is thought to be the oldest image drawn by man.
3500 BCE	Oldest writing ever found in Mesopotamia on limestone.
3300 BCE	Oldest writing on clay tablet found in Uruk, southern Babylonia (Iraq), the beginning of cuneiform.
3000 BCE	Date of oldest papyrus, a blank scroll in the tomb of Saqqara, near Cairo.
3000 BCE	Beginning of Egyptian Hieroglyphic writing.
2500 BCE	First script in the Indus valley.
2400 BCE	Oldest known Egyptian book, written on woven linen.
2200 BCE	Writing on copper and pottery in the Indus valley.
2100 BCE	Date of the oldest piece of tapa, a fragment found in Peru.
1850 BCE	Date of the oldest-known document written on leather, an Egyptian scroll.
18TH CENTURY BCE	First writing system in Crete.
1400 BCE	Writing on bones in China.
1300 BCE	Writing on bronze, jade, and tortoise shell in China.
1200 BCE	Characters for Chinese language developed.
1100 BCE	Egyptians begin exporting papyrus, first to Phoenicians.

1000 BCE	Phoenician alphabet begins.
600 BCE	Zapotec/Mixtec writing in Mexico.
600 BCE	Accounts written on wooden tablets in China and Greece.
5TH CENTURY BCE	Chinese write on silk.
400 BCE	The Ionian alphabet becomes standard in Greece.
400 BCE	True ink from lampblack invented in China.
300 BCE	King Eumenes II of Pergamum, barred from importing papyrus, builds a library of 200,000 volumes in parchment.
3RD CENTURY BCE	Library at Alexandria.
255 BCE	First mention of seals in China but used without ink in clay.
252 BCE	The dating of the oldest piece of paper ever found in Lu Lan, China.
250 BCE	In China Meng Tian invents the camel's hair brush for calligraphy.
250 BCE	Mayan hieroglyphic writing.
207 BCE	Beginning of the Chinese Han dynasty, in which paper is developed.
63 BCE	Strabo, the Greek geographer, writes of marveling at a watermill in the palace of Mithridates, King of Pontus, along the Black Sea.
31 BCE	The earliest known Olmec glyph writing.
30 BCE	Romans conquer Egypt and spread papyrus in the Mediterranean world.
1ST CENTURY CE	Wax tablets used for temporary writing in Rome.
75 CE	The last inscription written in cuneiform.
105 CE	The eunuch Cai Lun of the Chinese Han court is credited with inventing paper.
2ND CENTURY CE	Runic alphabet created in Scandinavia.
250–300	Approximate date of paper found in Turkestan.
256	First known book on paper, the *Phi Yu Ching,* produced in China.
297	Earliest known Mayan calendar, carved in stone.

394	Last inscription written in Egyptian hieroglyphics.
5TH CENTURY	Japanese develop their own alphabet.
450	Date of earliest known writing on palm-leaf fragments of a manuscript found in northwestern China.
476	Official end of classical antiquity as the last Western Roman emperor, Romulus Augustus, is overthrown.
500	Mayans begin writing on amate.
500–600	Mayans develop bark paper.
548	The king of Paekche (Korea) sends sutra and statues made of paper to Japan.
610	Korean monk Dancho takes papermaking to Japan.
630	Muhammad conquers Mecca.
651	Paper is made in Samarkand.
673	Monks at the temple of Kawahara begin copying Buddhist scriptures, which soon became a major activity in Japan.
8TH CENTURY	China starts printing.
706	Arabs bring paper to Mecca
711	An Arab-led Berber army crosses the Straits of Gibraltar from Morocco into Spain.
712	Earliest known piece of Japanese literature, *Kojiki*, is written in Chinese.
720	Use of paper in Japan greatly expands as Japan becomes Buddhist.
751	Papermaking in Samarkand begins.
762–66	Baghdad founded.
770	Japanese empress Shōtoku orders the first known printing on paper, 1 million copies of a prayer to drive away disease.
795	Rag paper mill opened in Baghdad.
800	Paper first used in Egypt.
832	Muslim conquest of Sicily.
848	Date of the oldest-known complete book in Arabic on paper.

850	Estimated date of earliest known version of *One Thousand and One Nights*.
868	The Diamond Sutra, the oldest printed book ever, is found.
889	Mayans begin writing all their records on paper rather than stone.

LATE 9TH CENTURY Baghdad becomes an important papermaking center.

900	Egyptians begin making paper.
969	Earliest known use of playing cards in China.
1041–48	Date of earliest known moveable type in China made of earthenware set in an iron form.
900–1100	Mayans write the Dresden Codex.
1140	Papermaking begins in Muslim Spain in Xátiva.
1143	The Qur'an is translated into Latin.
1264	First record of papermaking in Fabriano, Italy.
1282	First watermarks, in Fabriano, Italy.
1308	Dante begins writing *The Divine Comedy*.
1309	Paper first used in England.
1332	Paper first used in Holland.
1338	Papermaking starts in Troyes.
1353	Boccaccio writes *The Decameron*.
1387	Chaucer starts writing *Canterbury Tales*.
1389	German papermaking begins in Nuremberg.
1403	King Taejong of Korea orders bronze type.
1411	Papermaking begins in Switzerland.
1423	Earliest known European block prints.
1440–50	First European block books.
1456	Gutenberg completes printing his first Bible with moveable type.
1462	Mainz is destroyed and its printers disperse.

1463	Ulrich Zell starts the Cologne printing industry.
1464	The Subiaco Monastery near Rome becomes the first print house in Italy.
1469	*Epistolae ad Familiares* by Cicero is the first book printed in Venice.
1473	Lucas Brandis establishes first printing press in Lübeck.
1475 OR 1476	*Le livre de merveilles du monde* becomes the first book printed in the French language.
1477	William Caxton opens Britain's first printing press
1494	Aldus Manutius starts the Aldine Press in Venice.
1495	John Tate establishes the first paper mill in England in Hertfordshire.
1502–20	Aztec tribute book lists forty-two papermaking centers. Some villages produce half a million sheets of paper annually.
1515	Albrecht Dürer starts etching.
1519	Hernán Cortés lands near Vera Cruz and begins the destruction of Aztec culture.
1520	Martin Luther's *To the Christian Nobility of the German Nation* is printed and 50,000 copies are distributed in two years.
1528	Fr. Juan de Zumárraga arrives in Mexico as protector of the Indians, and burns books.
1539	Spanish begin first printing press in Mexico to make books for the indigenous people.
1549	Mayan library burned by the Spanish.
1575	Spanish build the first paper mill in Mexico.
1576	Russians begin papermaking.
1586	A decree authorizing papermaking in Dordrecht is earliest record of Dutch papermaking.
1605	Publication of Cervantes's *Don Quixote*.
1609	The world's first newspaper, *Avisa Relation oder Zeitung*, published in Strasbourg.

1627	The Catholic siege of La Rochelle in France drives Huguenot papermakers to England.
1635	Papermaking begins in Denmark.
1638	First English printing press is brought to America.
1672	With invention of the Hollander beater, Holland becomes a net exporter rather than importer of fine white paper.
1690	William Rittenhouse establishes first paper mill in America.
1690	America's first newspaper, *Publick Occurrences Both Forreign and Domestick*, published in Boston.
1690	First paper money in the American colonies issued in Massachusetts.
1698	Thomas Savery designs the first steam engine to pump out mines.
1702	*The Daily Courant* in London, the first daily newspaper, begins publishing.
1719	René Antoine Ferchault de Réaumur describes how wasps make paper from wood.
1728	Papermaking in Massachusetts begins.
1744	*A Little Pretty Pocket Book*, the first illustrated children's book, is published in England
1744	Papermaking in Virginia begins.
1767	Papermaking in Connecticut commences.
1768	Abel Buell is the first to cut and cast type in the American colonies.
1769	First manufacturer of printing presses in the British American colonies, Isaac Doolittle begins in New Haven.
1773	Papermaking in New York begins.
1774	The Swedish apothecary Carl Scheel discovers chlorine, which eventually leads to bleach.
1785	An independent London newspaper, *The Daily Universal Register*, begins publishing. Three years later it changes its name to *The Times*.

1790	Thomas Bewick becomes the most sought-after illustrator in Britain.
1798	Nicolas-Louis Robert applies for a patent for his continuous-paper machine.
1798	Artist J. M. W. Turner begins his experiments with watercolors.
1799	Alois Senefelder invents the lithograph.
1800	Lord Stanhope invents a cast iron printer.
1801	Joseph-Marie Jacquard invents the automatic loom, operated by punch cards.
1804	Bryan Donkin builds the first working Fourdrinier machine.
1809	John Dickinson patents his cylinder papermaking machine.
1810	Friedrich Koenig invents a steam-powered printer.
1811	The Luddites start smashing automatic looms in England.
1814	*The Times* of London uses Koenig's steam-powered printer.
1818	Joshua Gilpin builds the first continuous-paper machine in America.
1820	More than 29 million newspapers are sold in Britain this year.
1825	Joseph Nicéphore Niépce makes the first photograph.
1830	New bleaching process makes white paper from colored rags possible.
1833	An English patent is granted for making paper from wood.
1840	William Henry Fox Talbot makes first permanent photo on paper.
1841	Ebenezer Landells starts the London satirical magazine *Punch*.
1843	American Richard M. Hoe invents the steam-powered rotary printing press.
1863	American papermakers start using wood pulp.
1867	English wood pulp grinder exhibited in Paris.
1867	Wood pulp for paper first ground in the United States in Stockbridge, Massachusetts.

1867	Typewriter invented.
1872	United States surpasses Britain and Germany to become the largest paper producer in the world.
1874	Yukosha Company begins making machine-made paper in Tokyo, and six other companies follow in Osaka, Kyoto, and Kobe.
1890	US census tabulated by punch-card machines.
1899	Swedish explorer Sven Hedin, while excavating the ruins of the vanished city of Lu Lan, finds paper from 252 BCE, completely upsetting the history of paper.
1931	Vannevar Bush builds an analog electromechanical computer.
1945	John von Neumann publishes a paper on using binary numbers to program electronic memory.
1947	Transistor invented at Bell Labs.
1951	Remington Rand produces forty-six UNIVAC I computers with memory storage and output on magnetic tape.
1958	Microchip invented.

ACKNOWLEDGMENTS

||||||||||||||||||||||||||||||||||||||||||||||||||||||||||||||||||||

MY FIRST THANK-YOU IS TO KERMIT HUMMEL, WHO CAME TO ME out of the blue and convinced me that paper was the subject on which I ought to be writing. He got me started with books from his love of antiquarian book shopping and some good discussions about ideas. I also want to thank Nancy Miller for her advice and being a friend, and most especially want to thank Christiane Bird for her many thoughtful suggestions and careful guidance that was pivotal in shaping this book. Next, my thanks go to my editor, John Glusman, for skillfully and enthusiastically guiding it through. I also want to thank Susan Birnbaum Fisher.

I am extremely grateful for the generous assistance of Mike Foster in both Colombia and Italy, and the kind and helpful assistance of Marco Bocci in Italy. Also thanks to historians Franco Mariani and Giorgio Pellegrini for their insights on the town of Fabriano.

In China, great and warm thanks to Laura Trombetta, my guide, translator, and friend, and to Tang Guo for his help and hospitality. I also want to thank Maya Wang for her artful translation of some difficult Mandarin writing.

Thank you to Yoko Clark, Louisa Rubinfien, Satoru Urabe, and Kikuo Yamamoto in Japan.

Thanks to Karen Cooperstein and Herman Barten for their help in Holland, and thanks to Aizpea Goenaga and Walter Kruse for help in the Basque Country.

Thank you to Allesandro Vettori and Wayne Storey for their insights into the life and work of Dante.

A big thank-you to Janet McCarthy Grimm at Lindenmeyer for her generous assistance.

Although I include a detailed bibliography of books that have helped me, I wanted to give special thanks to a few scholars whose work has been invaluable. First of all to Jérôme de Lalande, the first historian of Western papermaking; to Dard Hunter, one of the pioneers of paper history; to Oriol Valls i Subirá, the Catalan historian who spent his life studying the paper of Spain; to Tsien Tsuen-Hsuin, who died at the age of 105 while I was writing this book, for his brilliant studies of the Chinese language; to Henri-Jean Martin, the great French scholar of the history of books; to Jonathan M. Bloom for his brilliant history of Islamic paper; to the great Canadian scholar Harold Innis, whose work has guided me in a number of my books; and to John Bidwell for his remarkable history of American paper mills.

Thanks to my good friend and wonderful agent, Charlotte Sheedy, for her help and to my good friend and wonderful wife, Marian Mass, for working so hard to help me.

BIBLIOGRAPHY

|||||||||||||||||||||||||||||||||||||||||||||||||||||||||||||||||

Allen, Danielle. *Our Declaration: A Reading of the Declaration of Independence in Defense of Equality.* New York: Liveright Publishing Corporation, 2014.

Anderson, James L., ed. *The Paper Maker: Vol. 29, Number One.* Wilmington, DE: Hercules Powder Company, 1960.

Appelbaum, Stanley. *The Triumph of Maximilian I: 137 Woodcuts by Hans Burgkmair and Others.* New York: Dover Publications, 1964.

Bacon, Francis. *Advancement of Learning, Novum Organum, New Atlantis.* Chicago: Encyclopædia Britannica, 1952.

Baker, Nicholson. *Double Fold: Libraries and the Assault on Paper.* New York: Random House, 2001.

Balston, J. N. *The Elder James Whatman: England's Greatest Paper Maker.* Vols. 1 and 2. West Farleigh, Kent: J. N. Balston, 1992.

Bambach, Carmen C., ed. *Leonardo da Vinci: Master Draftsman.* New York: The Metropolitan Museum of Art, 2003.

Barkan, Leonard. *Michelangelo: A Life on Paper.* Princeton, NJ: Princeton University Press, 2011.

Barnes, Julian, *A Life with Books.* London: Jonathan Cape, 2012.

Becker, Jörg, ed. *Small Pulp and Paper Mills in Developing Countries.* Frankfurt: KomTech GmbH, 1991.

Bell, Lilian A. *Papyrus, Tapa, Amate & Rice Paper: Papermaking in Africa, the Pacific, Latin America & Southeast Asia.* McMinville, OR: Lillaceae Press, 1992.

Benjamin of Tudela. *The Itinerary of Benjamin of Tudela: Travels in the Middle Ages.* Malibu, CA: Pangloss Press, 1993.

Benson, Richard. *The Printed Picture.* New York: Museum of Modern Art, 2009.

Bentley, Kyle, ed. *Gauguin, Metamorphoses*. New York: Museum of Modern Art, 2014.

Bidwell, John. *American Paper Mills: 1690–1832*. Hanover, NH: Dartmouth College Press, 2013.

Birkerts, Sven. *The Gutenberg Elegies: The Fate of Reading in an Electronic Age*. Boston: Faber and Faber, 2001.

Bishop, Nathaniel H. *Voyage of the Paper Canoe*. Boston: Lee and Shepard Publishers, 1878.

Bland, David. *A History of Book Illustration: The Illuminated Manuscript and the Printed Book*. Cleveland: The World Publishing Company, 1958.

Bliss, Douglas Percy. A *History of Wood Engraving*. London: Spring Books, 1964.

Bloom, Jonathan M. *Paper Before Print: The History and Impact of Paper in the Islamic World*. New Haven, CT: Yale University Press, 2001.

Blum, André. *On the Origin of Paper*. New York: R. R. Bowker Company, 1934.

Blumenthal. Joseph. *The Printed Book in America*. Hanover, NH: University Press of New England, 1989.

Boise Paper Holdings, *The Mill at the Falls: 100 Years of Papermaking on the Border*. International Falls, MN: North Star Publishing, 2010.

Bolam, Francis, ed. *Paper Making: A General Account of its History, Processes and Applications*. London: Technical Section of the British Paper and Board Makers Association, 1965.

Borges, Jorge Luis. *Seven Nights*, translated by Eliot Weinberger. New York: New Directions, 1984.

Bower, Peter. *Turner's Papers: A Study of the Manufacture, Selection and Use of His Drawing Papers*. Vol. 1 *(1787–1820)*; Vol. 2 *(1820–1851)*. London Tate Gallery Publications, 1991.

Bowie, Henry P. *On the Laws of Japanese Painting: An Introduction to the Study of the Art of Japan*. New York: Dover Publications, 1911.

Brotherston, Gordon. *Painted Books from Mexico*. London, British Museum Press, 1995.

Buchberg, Karl, Nicholas Cullinan, Jodi Hauptman, and Nicholas Serota, eds. *Henri Matisse: The Cut-Outs*. New York: Museum of Modern Art, 2014.

Carr, Nicholas. *The Shallows: What the Internet Is Doing to Our Brains*. New York: W. W. Norton & Company, 2010.

Carruthers, Mary. *The Book of Memory: A Study of Memory in Medieval Culture*. Cambridge: Cambridge University Press, 2008.

Carter, Harry. *Wolvercote Mill: A Study in Paper-Making at Oxford*. Oxford: Oxford at Clarendon Press, 1974.

Carter, Thomas Francis. *The Invention of Printing in China: And its Spread Westward.* New York: Columbia University Press, 1931.

Chappell, Warren. *A Short History of the Written Word.* New York: Alfred A. Knopf, 1970.

Clanchy, M. T. *From Memory to Written Record: England 1066–1307.* Oxford: Blackwell Publishing, 1993.

Coleman, D. C. *The British Paper Industry: 1495–1860.* London: Oxford University Press, 1958.

Coleman, Matt. *Trains, Tracks & Tall Timber: The History, Making and Modeling of Lumber and Paper.* Milwaukee, WI: Wm K. Walthers, 1996.

Cooper, Constance J. *The Curtis Paper Company: From Thomas Meeteer to the James River Corporation.* Wilmington, DE: The Cedar Tree Press, Inc., 1991.

Corinaldesi, Giuseppina. *Fabriano Paper and Paper Mills from Its Origins to Modern Day.* Fabriano, Italy: Museo della Carta e della Filigrana, 1948.

Cortés, Hernán. *Letters from Mexico,* translated by Anthony Pagden. New Haven, CT: Yale University Press, 1986.

Crosby, Alfred W. *The Measure of Reality: Quantification and Western Society, 1250–1600.* Cambridge: Cambridge University Press, 1997.

Darnton, Robert, and Daniel Roche, eds. *Revolution in Print: The Press in France 1775–1800.* Berkeley: University of California Press, 1989.

De Cervantes, Miguel. *Don Quijote de La Mancha.* New York: Vintage Español, 2010.

de Lalande, Jérôme. *Art de faire le papier.* Paris: J. Moronval, 1820.

Derby, E. H. *The History of Paper Money in the Province of Massachusetts Before the Revolution.* Boston: The New England News Company, 1874.

Desgraves, Louis. *Etudes sur l'imprimerie dans le sud-ouest de la France: aux XVe, XVIe et XVIIe siècles.* Amsterdam: Erasmus, 1968.

De Vinne, Theodore Low. *The Invention of Printing: A Collection of Facts and Opinions.* New York: Francis Hart & Co., 1876.

Diderot, Denis. *A Diderot Pictorial Encyclopedia of Trades and Industry.* 2 vols. New York: Dover Publications, 1959.

Du Halde, Jean-Baptiste. *The General History of China.* 4 volumes. London: Watts, 1736.

Ebrey, Patricia Buckley. *Cambridge Illustrated History of China.* Cambridge: Cambridge University Press, 1996.

Eisenstein, Elizabeth L. *The Printing Revolution in Early Modern Europe.* New York: Cambridge University Press, 1983.

Febvre, Lucien, and Henri-Jean Martin. *L'Apparition du livre.* Paris: Editions Albin Michel, 1958.

Fenollosa, Ernest F. *Epochs of Chinese and Japanese Art*. 2 vols. Berkeley, CA: Stone Bridge Press, 2007.

Ferdowsi, Abolqasem. *Shahnameh: The Persian Book of Kings*, translated by Dick Davis. New York: Penguin Books, 2004.

Fischer, Steven Roger. *A History of Writing*. London: Reaktion Books, 2001.

Fletcher, Richard. *Moorish Spain*. Berkeley: University of California Press, 1993.

Fu Shen C. Y. *Traces of the Brush: Studies in Chinese Calligraphy*. New Haven, CT: Yale University Press, 1977.

Fukushima, K., trans. *Handbook of the Art of Washi*. Tokyo: Wagami-do K. K., 2007.

Gaur, Albertine. *A History of Writing*. New York: Charles Scribner's Sons, 1984.

Geck, Elisabeth. *Johannes Gutenberg: 1468–1968*. Bad Godesberg, Germany: Inter Nationes, 1968.

Goff, Frederick R. *The John Dunlap Broadside: The First Printing of the Declaration of Independence*. Washington, DC: Library of Congress, 1976.

Goodyear, Dana. "Paper Palaces: The Shigera Ban Phenomenon." *The New Yorker*, August 11–18, 2014.

Greenleaf, Richard E. *Zumárraga and the Mexican Inquisition 1536–1543*. Washington, DC: Academy of American Franciscan History, 1961.

Hackforth, R., trans. *Plato's Phaedrus*. Cambridge: Cambridge University Press 1972.

Haggith, Mandy. *Paper Trails: From Trees to Trash—the True Cost of Paper*. London: Virgin Books, 2008.

Hargrave, Catherine Perry. *A History of Playing Cards*. New York: Dover Publications, 1966.

Haskell, W. E. *News Print: The Origin of Paper Making and the Manufacturing of News Print*. New York: International Paper Company, 1921.

Havelock, Eric A. *The Muse Learns to Write: Reflections on Orality and Literacy from Antiquity to the Present*. New Haven, CT: Yale University Press, 1986.

Healy, John F., trans. *Pliny the Elder: Natural History, a Selection*. London: Penguin Books, 1991.

Heidegger, Martin. *The Question Concerning Technology and Other Essays*, translated by William Lovitt. New York: Harper Perennial, 1977.

Heijnen, Henk. *The Zaan Mills: A Unique Story*. Zaanstad, Netherlands: Society of Zaan Mills, 2014.

Hill, Donald R. *Islamic Science and Engineering*. Edinburgh: Edinburgh University Press, 1993.

Hind, Arthur M. *A History of Engraving & Etching: From the 15th Century to the Year 1914*. New York: Houghton Mifflin Company, 1923.

———. *An Introduction to a History of Woodcut*. 2 vols. New York: Houghton Mifflin Company, 1935.

Hinton, David, trans. *The Selected Poems of Li Po*. New York: A New Directions Book, 1996.

———. *The Selected Poems of Po Chü-I,* New York: A New Directions Book, 1999.

———. *The Selected Poems of Tu Fu*. New York: A New Directions Book, 1989.

———. *The Selected Poems of Wang Wei*. New York: A New Directions Book, 2006.

Holcomb, Melanie. *Pen and Parchment: Drawing in the Middle Ages*. New Haven, CT: Yale University Press, 2009.

Horiki, Eriko. *Architectural Spaces with Washi*. Tokyo: A+u Publishing, 2007.

Hsi, Kuo. *An Essay on Landscape Painting*, translated by Shio Sakanishi. London: John Murray. 1935.

Hunter, Dard. *My Life with Paper: An Autobiography*. New York: Alfred A. Knopf, 1958.

———. *Papermaking*. New York: Alfred A. Knopf, 1943.

———. *Papermaking in Pioneer America*. Philadelphia: University of Pennsylvania Press, 1952.

Innis, Harold A. *The Bias of Communication*. Toronto: University of Toronto Press, 1951.

Irwin, Robert. *The Arabian Nights: A Companion*. London: Penguin Books, 1995.

Isaacson, Walter. *The Innovators: How a Group of Hackers, Geniuses, and Geeks Created the Digital Revolution*. New York: Simon & Schuster, 2014.

Knight, Michael, and Joseph Z. Chang, eds. *Out of Character: Decoding Chinese Calligraphy*. Los Altos Hills, CA: Guanyuan Shanzhuang Press, 2014.

Kouris, Michael, ed. *The Dictionary of Paper*. New York: American Pulp and Paper Association, 1940.

Krill, John. *English Artists' Paper: Renaissance to Regency*. New Castle, DE: Oak Knoll Press, 2002.

Kurth, Willi. *The Complete Woodcuts of Albrecht Dürer*. New York: Dover Publications, 1963.

Latham, Ronald, trans. *Marco Polo: The Travels*. London: Penguin Books, 1958.

Lee, Aimee. *Hanji Unfurled: One Journey into Korean Papermaking*. Ann Arbor, MI: The Legacy Press, 2012.

Lee, Samuel, ed. and trans. *The Travels of Ibn Battuta in Near Asia and Africa 1325–1354*. Mineola, NY: Dover Publications, 2004.

Lemonedes, Heather, Belinda Thompson, and Agnieszka Juszczak. *Paul Gauguin: The Breakthrough into Modernity*. Ostfildern, Germany: Hatje Cantz, 2009.

Lenz, Hans. *El Papel Indígena Mexicano*. Mexico City: SepSetentas, 1973.

Licklider, J.C.R. *Libraries of the Future*. Cambridge, MA: The MIT Press, 1965.

Lowney, Chris. *A Vanished World: Medieval Spain's Golden Age of Enlightenment.* New York: Free Press, 2005.

Maddox, Harry Alfred. *Paper, Its History, Sources, and Manufacture.* Bath, England: Sir Isaac Pitman and Sons, 1916.

Martin, Henri-Jean. *The History and Power of Writing.* Chicago: University of Chicago Press, 1994.

Mandl, G. T. *Three Hundred Years in Paper.* London: Butler & Tanner Ltd., 1985.

Manguel, Alberto. *A History of Reading.* Toronto: Alfred A. Knopf, 1996.

———. *The Library at Night.* Toronto, Alfred A. Knopf, 2006.

McLuhan, Marshall. *The Gutenberg Galaxy: The Making of Topographic Man.* Toronto: The University of Toronto, 1965.

Mikesh, Robert C. *Balloon Bomb Attacks on North America: Japan's World War II Assaults.* Fallbrook, CA: Aero Publishers, Inc., 1982.

Mingus Sr., Scott L. *Human Interest Stories of the Gettysburg Campaign.* Vol. 1. Orrtanna, PA: Colecraft Books, 2006.

Nicolson, Adam. *Why Homer Matters.* New York: A John Macrae Book, 2014.

Nodier, Charles. *Critiques de l'imprimerie par le docteur Neophobus.* Paris: Édition des Cendres, 1989.

Ong, Walter J. *Orality and Literacy.* London: Routledge, 2012 (1982).

Paludan, Ann. *Chronicles of the Chinese Emperors: The Reign-by-Reign Record of the Rulers of Imperial China.* London: Thames & Hudson, 1998.

Panofsky, Erwin. *The Life and Art of Albrecht Dürer.* Princeton, NJ: Princeton University Press, 1955.

The Paper Mill and Wood Pulp News, vol. 22, June 29–December 7, 1899.

Peters, Charles M., Joshua Rosenthal, and Teodile Urbana. "Otomi Bark Paper in Mexico: Commercialization of a Pre-Hispanic Technology. *Economic Botany* 41, no. 3: 423–32.

Petroski, Henry. *The Pencil: A History of Design and Circumstance.* New York: Alfred A. Knopf, 1993.

Phillpots, Eden. *Storm in a Teacup.* London: Hutchinson & Co., 1919.

Pierce, Wadsworth R. *The First 175 Years of Crane Papermaking.* North Adams, MA: Excelsior Printing Company, 1977.

Ranc, Robert. *Le siècle d'or de l'imprimerie Lyonnaise.* Paris: Editions du Chêne, 1972.

Reynolds, John. *Windmills & Watermills.* New York: Praeger Publishers, 1970.

Roberts, J. A. G. *A Concise History of China.* Cambridge: Harvard University Press, 1999.

Robinson, Andrew. *The Story of Writing: Alphabets, Hieroglyphs and Pictograms.* New York: Thames & Hudson, 1995.

Rockhill, William Woodville. *The Journey of William of Rubruck to the Eastern Parts of the World, 1253–55*. London: Hakluyt Society, 1900.

Rodinon, Maxime, A. J. Arberry, and Charles Perry. *Medieval Arab Cookery*. Totnes, Devon, England: Prospect Books 2001.

Rosenband, Leonard N. *Papermaking in Eighteenth-Century France: Management, Labor, and Revolution at the Montgolfier Mill 1761–1805*. Baltimore: Johns Hopkins University Press, 2000.

Sakanishi, Shio, trans. *The Spirit of the Brush: Being the Outlook of Chinese Painters on Nature from Eastern Chin to Five Dynasties A.D. 317–960*. London: John Murray, 1939.

Schlesinger, Arthur M. *Prelude to Independence: The Newspaper War on Britain, 1764–1776*. New York: Alfred A. Knopf, 1971.

Seldes, George, *Lords of the Press*. New York: Julian Messner, 1939.

Sellen, Abigail J., and Richard H. R. Harper. *The Myth of the Paperless Office*. Cambridge, MA: The MIT Press, 2002.

Shorter, Alfred H. *Paper Making in the British Isles: An Historical and Geographical Study*. London: David & Charles Newton Abbot, 1971.

St. Clair, William. *The Reading Nation in the Romantic Period*. Cambridge: Cambridge University Press, 2004.

Stephenson, J. Newell, ed. *The Manufacture of Pulp and Paper*. Vol. 3. London: McGraw-Hill Book Company, 1922. Vol. 4, 1924; Vol. 5, 1925.

Takaki, Masayoshi. *The History of Japanese Paper Currency (1868–1890)*. Baltimore: Johns Hopkins University Press, 1903.

Thomas, Alan G. *Great Books and Book Collectors*. New York, Excalibur Books, 1975.

Time, "Real Live Paper Dolls." *Time*, March 17, 1967, 52.

Tooze, Adam. *The Deluge: The Great War, America, and the Remaking of the Global Order 1916–1931*. New York: Viking, 2014.

Toribio de Benavente Motolinía. *Historia de los Indios de la Nueva España*. Barcelona: Herederos de Juan Gili, 1914.

Tsien, Tsuen-Hsuin, *Paper and Printing, Science and Civilization in China*, edited by Joseph Needham. Volume 5, *Chemistry and Chemical Technology*, part 1. Cambridge: Cambridge University Press, 1985.

———. *Written on Bamboo and Silk: The Beginnings of Chinese Books and Inscriptions*. Chicago: University of Chicago Press, 1962.

Valentini, J. J. *Mexican Paper: An Article of Tribute; Its Manufacture, Varieties, Employment and Uses*. Worcester, MA: Press of Chas. Hamilton, 1881.

Valls i Subirá, Oriol. *La Historia del Papel en España*. Vols. 1–3. Madrid: Empreso Nacional Celulosas, 1978.

————. *A Lively Look at Papermaking.* North Hills, PA: Bird & Bull Press, 1980.

van Roojen, Pepin. *Marbled Paper Design.* Amsterdam: The Pepin Press, 2007.

Victoria & Albert Museum. *Masterpieces of Chinese Painting.* London: V & A Publishing, 2013.

von Hagen, Victor Wolfgang. *The Aztec and Maya Papermakers.* New York: Hacker Art Books, 1977.

von Karabacek, Joseph. *Arab Paper.* London: Architype Publications, 1991.

Walton, Perry. *Two Related Industries: An Account of Paper-Making and of Paper-Makers' Felts as Manufactured at the Kenwood Mills Rensselaer, New York, U.S.A., and Arnprior, Ontario, Canada, the Two Plants of F. C Huyck & Sons, Albany, New York.* Albany: F. C. Huyck & Sons, 1920.

Ward, Gerald W. R., ed. *The Grove Encyclopedia of Materials and Techniques in Art.* Oxford: Oxford University Press, 2008.

Weeks, Lyman Horace. *A History of Paper-Manufacturing in the United States, 1690–1916.* New York: B. Franklin, 1916.

West, Clarence J. *The Utilization of Sugar Cane Bagasse for Paper, Board, Plastics, and Chemicals.* New York: Sugar Research Foundation, Inc. 1952.

West, M. L. *The East Face of Helicon.* Oxford: Oxford University Press, 1999.

Wilcox, Scott. *British Watercolors: Drawings of the 18th and 19th Century from the Yale Center for British Art.* New York: Hudson Hills Press, 1985.

Wolf, Richard J. *The Mysterious Marbler: James Sumner (1854).* New Castle, DE: Oak Knoll Press, 2009.

Woll, Gerd. *Edvard Munch: A Genius of Print Making.* Ostfildern, Germany: Hatje Cantz, 2014.

Wood, Frances, and Mark Barnard. *The Diamond Sutra: The Story of the World's Earliest Dated Printed Book.* London: the British Library, 2010.

Wye, Deborah. *The Picasso Portfolio: Prints from the Museum of Modern Art.* New York: Museum of Modern Art, 2010.

Xiaoyun, Sun. 書法有法 (The Techniques of Chinese Calligraphy). Nan Jing: Jiang Su Province Publishing House, 2014.

Yee, Chiang. *Chinese Calligraphy: An Introduction to Its Aesthetic and Technique.* Cambridge, MA: Harvard University Press, 2002 (first printing 1938).

INDEX

IIIIIIIIIIIIIIIIIIIIIIIIIIIIIIIIIIIIIIIIIIIIIIIIIIIIIIIIIIIIIIIIIIIIIIIIII

Page numbers in *italics* refer to illustrations.

abaca, 278, 317, 319

abacus, 87

'Abbas ibn 'Abd al-Muttalib, Al-, 50

Abbasid Caliphate, 50, 52–53, 57–60, 62–65

Abd al-Mu'min, 71

Abd al-Quddus, 62–63

Abd al-Rahman III, emir of Córdoba, 70

acacia trees, 283, 298

accounting, written records and, 91

Ackermann, Rudolph, 198

Ackermann's Repository of Arts, 198

Adams, John, 217, 223

Adams, Peter, 244

Ada's Algorithm (Essinger), 325

"Address to the People of Great Britain, An" (Fox), 203

Adelaide, countess of Sicily, 78

advertising, 330–32

Aelst, Hans van, 88

Aesop's Fables, 134, 201

Affaire des Placards, 166

Afghanistan, 50, 57

Africa, 73–74

   see also North Africa

agave, 154–55, 248

agriculture, Arab knowledge of, 69

Aigues-Mortes, France, 73

Aimes, Thomas, 225

Alamo, Kikis, 316–18

al-Andalus, xix, 339

   architecture of, 70, 75

   Christian reconquest of, 74–75, 142, 157

   Christians in, 68, 86

   culture of, 68–70

   Jews in, 68, 69, 71, 73, 75

   paper in, 70

   papermaking in, 71–74, 78, 340

Albaida River, 71

alchemy, 52, 59

alcohol, Arabs' distillation of, 59

Aldine Press, 135, 137, 138, 341

Aldus in His Printing Establishment in Venice Showing Grolier Some Book Bindings (Flameng), 138
Aldus Manutius, 135–38, 140, 147, 341
Alejandre, José Ramon, 316–18
Alexander the Great, 9, 49
algebra, 58, 89
Algeria, 89
Algonquin language, 207
Alice in Wonderland (Carroll), 261
Almanack for 1639, calculated for New England by Mr. William Pierce, mariner, An, 206
almanacs, 215–16
Almanzor, 86
Almohad dynasty, 74
Almoravid dynasty, 74
Alphabet, An, 262
Alphabet of Children (Holbein), 116
alphabets, xiv, 15
    development of, 6–7
    moveable type and, 113–14
    see also writing; *specific alphabets*
Altamira, Spain, cave art in, 3
Altdorfer, Albrecht, 130
Amalfi, Italy, 78, 82
amate (Aztec writing surface), 152–54, 160–61
American colonies:
    first paper money in, 211, 342
    newspapers in, 211–13, 342
    papermaking in, 208–10, 212, 213–15, 342
    printing in, 206, 207–8, 209, 211–13, 215–17, 342
American Indians, 207
American Revolution, 202, 208, 232
    Continental currency in, 209
    papermaking in, 218–25

Ames' Almanack, 216
Amman, Jost, 188
Amsterdam, Netherlands, 176
Amu Darya River, 50
Ancona, Italy, 78
Andong Hanji, 305–6
Andreä, Hieronymus, 125, 126, 130
Anglicus, Robert, 89
Anhui Province, China, 305
anti-Semitism, 85
Anti-Slavery Society, 203
Antwerp, Belgium, 172
Apicius, 63
Apparition du livre, L' (Febvre and Martin), 162
Appert, Nicolas, 241–42
Apuleius Barbarus, 194
aquatint, 174
Arabs, 176
    bureaucracy of, 52
    calligraphy of, 51, 52, 55, 60, 106
    distillation of alcohol by, 59
    European culture influenced by, 77
    food writing by, 62–65
    Greek manuscripts translated by, 57–58
    libraries of, 53, 58, 59–60, 69
    literature of, 61–62
    oral literature of, 51, 60
    papermaking by, xiii, xv, xix, 48–49, 52, 53, 54–55, 97, 339
    papyrus and, 53
    parchment and, 53, 54
    philosophy and theology under, 69–70
    pre-Islamic writing of, 51
    scientific knowledge of, xv, 52, 57–59, 69, 85, 86

scribes of, 51–52, 53–54, 55, 56–57, 60, 105–6

use of term, 49–50

writing as primary visual art of, 60

see also Muslims, Islam

Arches, 265, 318

Archestratus, 63

Archimedes, 58

architecture:

Andalusian, 70, 75

paper in, 308–9, 314–15, 322

Aristotle, 19, 194

armillary sphere, 87

art:

affordable, woodcuts as, 123–24, 128

from paper, 318, 320–21

artificial intelligence, 328

artists:

papermaking and, 198–202, 318–19

Art of Paper Making, The (Lalande), 169–70

Art of Preserving All Kinds of Animal and Vegetable Substances for Several Years, The (Appert), 241–42

art paper, machine-made, 265, 269, 280

Arts and Craft movement, 256–57

Arturo's Desert Eagle, 273

asbestos paper, 249

Asia:

European trade with, 176–77

expanding European knowledge of, 87–88

Asia Pulp & Paper (APP), 283, 295, 297, 298

Aspen Art Museum, 314

Assyrians, xix–xx, 12, 108

"As We May Think" (Bush), 323, 327

Atlantic, 259, 327

Atogi, Korean prince, 44

Atuona, French Polynesia, 266

Augsburg, Germany, 125

Australian aborigines, 4

authors, impact of printing on, 196

Auvergne, France, 83

Averroes, 69

Avignon, France, 111, 115

Avisa Relation oder Zeitung, 203, 341

Aztecs, xviii, 28, 150–51, 248, 341

calendar of, 151–52

codices of, 152, 159, 341

number system of, 152–53

paper-like material of (*amate*), 152–54, 156–57, 160–61, 341

possible true papermaking by, 154–55

scribes of, 151–52

writing of, 148, 151–52

Babbage, Charles, 325, 326

Babylon, 6, 13

Bacon, Francis, 191, 194, 195, 231

Bacon, Roger, 88, 90

bagasse, papermaking with, 284–88

Baghdad, 50, 58, 65, 339

paper mill in, 54–55

Baghdad paper, 55, 56

Balearic Islands, 73

Balkh, Afghanistan, 57

Bally, Ellen and Steart, 199

Bamberg, Germany, 125, 133

bamboo:

paper from, 33, 302

as writing surface, 26, 27–28, 32

Bambyx, Syria, 55

Ban, Shigeru, 314

Banbury, Oxfordshire, 242

Bantu, 5

Barcelona, Spain, 86, 141

Barjon, 318

Barmak, Khalid, 53–57

Barmak family, 57

Bart, Italy, 50

Bartholomaeus Anglicus, 181

baseball cards, 261

Basel, Switzerland, printing in, 163

Baskerville, John, 197

basket making, 317

Basque language, 5

Basques, 68, 77, 316–18, 335

Basra, 60

Bay Psalm Book, The, 206–7

Bayt al-Hikma, 58

Beilby, Ralph, 201

Belgium, 171

Bellaert, Jacob, 172

Bell Labs, 344

Bembo, Pietro, 137

Bembo (typeface), 137

Bentley, Richard, 261

Bentley's Miscellany, 261

Berbers, 50, 66–67, 74, 339

Berlin, Germany, 267

bertsolari, 335

"Betrayed Inhabitants of the City and Colony of New York, The," 216

Bewick, Thomas, 200–201, *201,* 213, 239, 258, 343

Bible:
    of Gutenberg, 114, 340
    of Luther, 164
    Massachusetts language edition of, 208
    Polyglot, 172–73
    of Quentell, 122

Bibliothèque Nationale, Paris, 150

Bicknores, Dartford, England, 183

Bilbao, Spain, 77

binderies, 172

Binns, John, 225

Birdseye, Clarence, 286

Birn, Raymond, 230

Bi Sheng, 104, 111

Bishop, Nathaniel, 253

Black River, Wis., 246

Blake, William, 238

Blauw, Dirk and Cornelius, 224

bleach, 171, 239, 288, 301, 342, 343

Bloom, Jonathan, 52, 60

Bly, Oreg., 273

Boccaccio, Giovanni, 95, 340

Bodleian Library, 152

Bologna, Italy, 82, 111

Bonnard, Pierre, 257

bookbinders, 193

Book of Curious and Entertaining Information (Al-Tha'ilibi), 48

Book of Martyrs (Foxe), 164, 221

Book of Perfume Chemistry and Distillation (Al-Kindt), 59

Book of Songs, The, 20, 39

books:
    in American colonies, 215
    block-printed, 124, 125, 263, 269
    burning of, 146, 147
    in China, 26, 105–6, *107*
    and cost of paper, 230
    covers of, 191
    endpapers of, 191
    French Revolution and, 233
    future of, 328–30
    and growth of private reading, 94–95, 237, 238
    handmade, 257–58
    illuminated, 93, 95
    illustrated, for children, 202, 32
    initial capitals in, 116
    in Korea, *106*

limited-edition, 257
parchment as medium of choice
    for, 97
popular demand for, 226
printed vs. handwritten, 116–17
remaindering of, 238
Renaissance demand for, 110–11
science and, 194, 195
as status symbols, 84
woodcuts in, *see* woodcut
    illustrations
see also codex, codices
bookselling, growth of, 110
Bordeaux, France, 73, 141
Borges, Jorge Luis, 20
Borrell II, count of Barcelona, 86
Boston, Mass., 212, 213, 253, 257, 342
Boston News-Letter, 212
Boston Public Library, 257
Boston Society of Arts and Crafts, 257
Bower, Peter, 264–65
boxwood, 200
Boyle, Robert, 191, 194, 195
Bracquemond, Félix, 263
Bradford, William, 209–10
Bradshaw, Md., 221
Brahmagupta, 57–58
Brandis, Lucas, 341
Brandywine, Battle of (1777), 221
Brandywine Creek, 225
Brandywine Mill, 243
Braque, Georges, 269, 318
Brazil, papermaking in, 283
Breslau, 133
Breydenbach, Bernhard von, 126
British Museum, 102
Brito, Johannes, 115
broadsides, 216, 223, 226, 228
Broich, Germany, 208

Brown, Thomas, 209
Brückmann, Franz Ernst, 249
Bruegel, Pieter, 172
Bruges, Belgium, 111, 115, 180
brushes, 16, 26, 27, 37, 338
Budapest, Library of, 159
Buddhism, 44
    printing and, 99–103
    and spread of papermaking, xv,
        xviii, 42, 44, 49, 98, 339
Buell, Abel, 218, 342
Bulmer, William, 239
bureaucracy:
    in Muslim world, 52
    paper and, 32, 44–45, 52
Burgkmair, Hans, 128, *129*
Burgundy, France, 128–229, 167
burin, 131, 200
Burnet, William, 210
Burton, Richard, 61
Bush, Vannevar, 323, 327, 344
Business Week, 286
Buyer, Bathélemy, 140
Byron, Lord, 326

Cadart, Alfred, 263
Cade, Jack, 185–86
Cai Lun, xviii, 29–31, 38, 114, 177, 334
Caine, Hugh, 210
Cairo, Egypt, 56, 289
calculations, paper and, *119*
Calderón, Diego de Landa, 159
Cali, Colombia, 286
calligraphy, 195–96
    Arabic, 51, 52, 55, 60, 106
    Japanese, 44
    Korean, *306*
calligraphy, Chinese, 35–38, 106, 301,
    303, *303, 304*, 314

calligraphy, Chinese (continued)
  brush styles in, 35–36, 37–38, 302–3
  painting and, 39
Calvin, John, 165
Cambridge, England, 183
Cameron, Robert, 242–43
Campbell, John, 212
Campbell's Soup Company, 274
Canada, 253, 281–82, 301
Cangjie, 23, 24
Canson & Montgolfier, 318
Canterbury Tales, The (Chaucer), 340
carbon emissions, 289, 295
cardboard, 286, 322, 334
Cartiere Milani Fabriano, 277
cartoons, 259, 260–61, 263
Carvajal Pulp & Paper, 288–89
Caslon, William, 257, 258
Caspian Sea, 87
Castaldi, Panfilo, 115
Castellano (Giano) River, 78
Castile, 73
Castro, Fidel, 145
Catalonia, 77
Catania, Sicily, 73
Catherine of Aragon, queen of Eng-
    land, 182
Cauca valley, Colombia, 287
caustic soda, 288, 289, 300, 301
cave art, 3–4, 337
Caxton, William, 179–81, 341
cellulose, 28–29, 251, 252, 285
Celulosa Cubana, S.A., 285
Census, US, of 1890, 326, 344
Central Asia, 31, 50, 100, 148
  papermaking in, 49, 52
Cervantes, Miguel de, 132, 143, 147,
    186, 238, 341
Cézanne, Paul, 264

Champagne, France, 83
Chancery Standard, 182
Chang, Arnold, 314
Chang'an, China, 32
change, 323–36
  Diderot on, 323, 327
  paper and, 326–36
  technological, see technological
    change
  Vannevar Bush on, 323, 327
Changshu, China, 294
Charivari, Le, 260
Charlemagne, 59, 76, 90, 130
Charles II, king of England, 211
Charles V, Holy Roman Emperor,
    147, 156
Charles V, king of France, 89–90
Charlie Hebdo, 233
charta bambycina (cotton paper), 55
charta damascena (Damascus paper), 55
Chaucer, Geoffrey, 181, 340
  Kelmscott Press edition of, 257
Chemnitz, Germany, 83
Cherokee, 5
Chester Creek, 209
Chiang Chung, 32
Chiang Yee, 37–38
chiaroscuro, 128
children's books, illustrated, 202, 342
Chillida, Eduardo, 317
China, 5, 10, 168, 294
  books in, 26, 105–6, 107
  bureaucracy in, xviii, 24, 25–26, 32
  clocks in, 89
  Communism in, 298–99
  compass invented in, 92
  deforestation in, 294
  divination in, 23, 24–25, 92
  energy consumption in, 295

Europeans' knowledge of, 176
gardens in, 296–97
handmade paper in, 299–305
High Tang period in, 40–63
kites in, 273
literacy in, 26, 31–32
modern paper industry in, 293–305
moveable type invented in, xix,
    104–5, 340
oral literature in, 39
painting in, 38–39, *41*
papermaking in, xiv–xv, xviii, 23,
    28–35, 38, 49, 101, 105, 176, 178,
    188, 249, 293–305, 338, 344
poetry in, 39, 40, 41
pre-paper writing materials in, 24,
    25, 26, 27–28, 32
printing invented in, 99, 107, 339
private businesses in, 299
seals in, 99, 338
South, 296
tree farms in, 298
used paper imports of, 294
woodblock printing in, 99
wood pulp imports of, 294
writing in, *see* Chinese writing
    system
China National Library, 305
Chinese writing system, 4, 31, 114,
    337, 339
brushes and, 27, 338
calligraphy and, *see* calligraphy,
    Chinese
divination and, 23, 24–25
ink and, 26–27
Japan and, 43–44
Korea and, 43
legendary origin of, 22–24
Mao's simplification of, 35

moveable type and, 104–5
Shang period, 25
vertical direction of, 27–28
Zhou period, 26
ch'in (qin), 39
chlorine, 239, 342
chloride dioxide, 288
Cholula, Mexico, 150
Christians, in al-Andalus, 68, 86
Church of England, 182, 206, 207
Churchyard, Thomas, 186–87
Cicero, 108, 110, 340
civilization, paper as mark of, xviii–xix
Civil War, Rwandan, 314
Civil War, US, 245–46, 258, 259, 278
clay, as writing surface, 7, 9, 11
Clemente VIII, Pope, 82
Cleveland Museum, 264–65
climate change, 289, 295
clocks, 89–90
clothing, of paper, 273–74
Cluny monastery, 60
coal, Chinese consumption of, 295
Cobb, Thomas, 242
Cock, Jerôme, 172, 173
codex, codices, 53
    Aztec, 152, 159, 341
    as forerunner of books, 13
    Mayan, 149, 150, 154, 159, 340, 341
    parchment and, 14
Codex Dresdensis, 150, 340
Codex Mendoza, 152
Codex Peresianus, 150
Codex Troano-Cortés, 150
Codorus Creek, 245–46
coins, 210, 211
coke, 238
Cologne, 122, 133, 180
    printing in, 133–34, 341

Colombia, 286, 287

Colonna, Francesco de, 135–36

colophon, 126

color, Newton's experiments with, 194–95

commerce:
Phoenician alphabet and, 15
writing as response to needs of, 5–6

Common Sense (Paine), 202–3, 216–17

communication, as primal urge, 4

compass, 92–93, 97, 176

computers, development of, 325, 327, 344

Confucius, Confucianism, 26, 31, 44, 104

Connecticut, 211

Constitution, US, 224

Continental Army, 214

Continental Congress, 222

Continental currency, 209, 222

Conwell, Clarke, 256, 258

Cook, Henry, 191

copper-plate etching, 130, 173–74, 176, 187, 201–2

Coptic Christians, parchment used by, 56

Córdoba, Spain, 69, 70, 74

Cornejo, Juan, 160

Cornelilus (Dutch bookseller), 115

Corot, Jean-Baptiste-Camille, 263

Corporation for Promoting and Propagating the Gospel of Jesus Christ in New England, A, 207, 208

Cortés, Hernán, xviii, 147, 150, 155–57, 158, 341

Coster, Laurens Janszoon, 114–15

cotton, 187, 213, 214, 250, 251, 252, 254, 265, 317, 319

coucher, 188–89, 280

couch rolls, 240

counterfeiting, of paper money, 222

craftsmanship, return to, 256–57

"Cramming More Components into Integrated Circuits" (Moore), 328

Cranach, Lucas, the Elder, 128

Crane, Walter, 256

Crane Company, 254, 277–78, 290

Crantz, Martin, 139

Crete, 4, 109, 337

Crimean War, 258

Cromberger, Juan, 159, 160

Cromwell, Oliver, 175, 207

Cromwell, Thomas, 182

Cruikshank, George, 261

Cuba, 285

Cuenca, Spain, 142

Cuesta, Juan de la, 143, 144

Cumberland, England, 193

cuneiform, 6–7, 8, 9, 11, 23, 25, 337

Curtis Paper Company, 278, 290

Curtisville, Mass., 252

Cyprus, 50

Cyrenaica, 50

Daguerre, Louis-Jacques-Mandé, 236

daguerreotypes, 236

Daily Courant, 204, 342

Daily Telegraph, 331

Daily Universal Register, 204, 343

Dalton, Mass., 254, 290

Damascus, Syria, 55, 59

Damascus paper (*charta damascena*), 55

Dance of Death, The (Holbein), 116

Dancho, 44, 339

dandy rolls, 240, 280

Dante Alighieri, 20, 76, 84, 115, 340

Darly, Scotland, 183

Daumier, Honoré, 260, *260*

Dauphiné, France, 229

Day, Matthew, 206, 207, 215

Daye, Stephen, 206

Dead Sea Scrolls, 12

Decameron, The (Boccaccio), 95, 340

deckle edges, 187–88, 258, 318

Declaration of Independence, 202,
    257
  imported paper used for, 224
  parchment copy of, 223
  printing of, 223–25

Defoe, Daniel, 163, 196, 203

deforestation:
  in China, 294
  papermaking and, 281–84

Degas, Edgar, 264

Delacroix, Eugène, 236

Delft, Netherlands, 172

Della Femina, Jerry, 332

Del Tuppo, Francesco, 134

Demaine, Erik, 321–22

Demarest, Nicolas, 232

Denmark, papermaking in, 342

De proprietatibus rerum (Bartholo-
    maeus), 181

"Description and playne discourse of
    paper, A" (Churchyard), 186–87

De Vinne, Theodore Low, 108–9

*"Dialogues sur la Peinture dans la Ville
    de Rome"* (Francis of Holland), 118

Dialogus creaturarum moralizatus
    (Leeu), 172

Diamond Sutra, 100, 102–3, *103*, 107,
    340

Díaz del Castillo, Bernal, 155

Dickens, Charles, 258, 261

Dickinson, John, 242, 243, 343

Dickinson foundry, 257

Dictes and Sayings of the Philosophers,
    180

Diderot, Denis, *112*, *170*, 226, 227, 228,
    230–31, 233, 235, 237–38, 241, 244,
    256, 323, 327

Didot, Pierre-François, 240

Didot family, 226–27, 240

Didot typeface, 240

Dieu Donné Press, 319

Difference Engine, 325

digesters, 252–53, 279, 288

digital age, fears about, 334–36

diptychs, 13

divination, 23, 24–25, 92

Divine Comedy (Dante), 20, 340

Doctor, Ken, 331–32

Domesday Book, 90

Donkin, Bryan, 241, 242, 243, 343

Don Quixote (Cervantes), 132, 143–44,
    144, 145–46, 196, 341

Doolittle, Isaac, 218, 342

Doolittle, James, 271

Dorchester, Mass., 207

Doré, Gustave, 263

Doubleday, 137

drawing, xiv, 2
  paper as superior medium for,
    118–19
  as primal human urge, 3, 4, 118, 337

Dresden, fire-bombing of, 150

Dresden Codex, 154, 340

drop hammers, 80, 83

Ducrest, Charles-Louis, 191

Dufy, Raoul, 257

Dunhuang, China, cave temples at,
101–2, 104

Dunlap, John, 223–24

Dünne, Hans, 111, 113

Durand, Peter, 242

Dürer, Albrecht, 119, 120, 123, 125, 130,
147, 172, 174, 190, 265, 266, 268
etchings of, 130, 341
goldsmith training of, 126
woodcuts of, 127–28, 127

Dutch East India Company, 176

Dymott, Richard, 192

East Asia:
paper arts in, 314–16
papermaking in, 42, 47

ebooks, 328–29

Edict of Nantes (1598), 184

Edison, Thomas, xvi, xviii

Edward IV, king of England, 180

Egypt, 50, 52, 73, 339
Arab conquest of, 53
papermaking in, 56, 289, 340

Egypt, pharoanic, 5, 9
writing in, xix, 4, 9–10, 11–12, 24,
336, 337, 339

Eisenstein, Elizabeth L., 164

El Castillo cave, 337

Electronics, 328

electronic word processors, xiv

Elements, The (Euclid), 58

Eliot, John, 207–8

Elizabeth I, queen of England, 183–
84, 186

Elizabethtown, N.J., 210

El Paular monastery, Segovia, 143–44

Elston Press, 258

emoticons, 336

Encyclopédie (Diderot), 226, 231, 323

England, 73
newspapers in, 204
paper as used in, 189–91, 340
papermaking in, 179, 181–93, 197–
98, 199, 250, 341, 342
paper marbling in, 191–93
printing in, 179–82, 341
printmaking in, 201–2
written law in, 90–91
see also Great Britain

English language, standardization
of, 181, 182

engravings, wood, 200–202

environmentalism, papermaking and, 282–84, 289–92, 297,
299–300

Environmental Protection Agency,
291

Epistolae ad Familiares (Cicero), 340

Epistolae Gasparini (Gasparinus de
Bergamo), 139

Erasmus, Desiderius, 163

escapements, 89

esparto grass, 250, 265

Espinosa, Antonio de, 160

Essay for the month of December 1716
. . . . , 248

Essinger, James, 325

Estates-General, 234

etchings, 130–31, 200, 201, 263, 269, 341
copper-plate, 130, 173–74, 176, 187,
201–2

ethanol, 287

Etruscan alphabet, 16

eucalyptus, 283, 285

Euclid, 58
Eumenes II, king of Pergamum,
    13–14, 338
Euphrates River, 6, 7, 50, 53, 54, 55
Euro currency, 277
Europe, Europeans:
    carved-block printing in, 110–11,
        340
    compass adopted by, 92–93
    explosion of literacy in, 110
    increased knowledge of Asia in,
        87–88
    influence of Arab culture on, 77
    intellectual backwardness of, xix,
        85
    Japanese paper imported by,
        177–78
    libraries in, 94, 116
    Middle Ages in, 76–77, 90–95
    oral tradition in, 94–95
    papermaking in, 87, 96–97
    Renaissance in, 110–11, 117, 118–22
    scientific discoveries in, 88–89
    as slow in adopting paper, xv, xix,
        73, 77, 83, 85
Evelyn, John, 191
Examination of the Rights of the Colo-
    nies upon Principles of Law, An
    (Dymott), 192
experimental method, 194–95
Exposition Universelle (1889), Paris,
    264

Faber, Jakob, 163
Fabriano, Italy, 276–77
    papermaking n, 78–83, 87, 120, 340
Fabriano Mills, 277
Fadl al-Yahyā, Al-, 53, 58

fanggu, 41, 296
Fantin-Latour, Henri, 263
Faust (Goethe), 236
Fauvism, 264
Febvre, Lucien, 162
Federalist Papers, 224
Federico of Urbino, 116
Fedrigoni Group, 277
felt, 79, 189, 228
felting, 29
felting mills, 79
Feltre, Itlay, 85, 115
Feng Dao, 104
Ferdinand, king of Spain, 157
Ferdowsi, Abolqasem, 60–61
Fez, Morocco, 71
fiber paper, 278
Fibonacci (Leonardo Pisano), 89
Fibonacci series, 89
Fichet, Guillaume, 138–39, 140
fig trees, 10, 153–54, 161
Financial Times, 331
firearm cartridges, 189, 190
Flameng, Léopold, 138
Flanders, Belgium, 232
flax, 56, 71, 83, 187, 209, 250, 251, 252,
    265
Florence, Italy, 82, 84, 121, 134
Flugschriften (pamphlets), 165
Foligno, Italy, 82
food writing, 62–65
Ford, Jazaniah, 214
Formfit Rogers, 274
Formschneiders (wood-block carvers),
    125, 128, 129, 130, 188, 259
Fortune, 278
Four Books on Human Proportion
    (Dürer), 120

Fourdrinier, Henry, 241, 243

Fourdrinier, Sealy, 241

Fourdrinier machines, 241, 243, 244,
        245, 255, 276, 279–81, 288, 318, 343

Four Horsemen of the Apocalypse, The
        (Dürer), 127

Fox, William, 203

Foxe, John, 164, 221

Frame Breaking Act (1812), xvi

France, 73, 167, 184, 226
    literacy in, 230
    oral culture in, 234
    papermaking in, 83, 228–29, 231–32,
        340
    printing in, 134, 138–41, 165, 227–28

Franche-Comté, 234

Francis of Holland, 118

Franco of Cologne, 92

François I, king of France, 166

Frankfurt, Germany, 111, 133, 141, 165

Franklin, Benjamin, 197, 198, 215, 222,
        223
    currency printing and, 192
    in newspaper business, 212
    paper mills of, 209, 212

Franklin, James, 214

"Freeman's Oath, The," 206

French Revolution, 202, 228, 244
    printing and, 232–35

Friburger, Michael, 139

Froben, Johann, 163

Fuchun River, 302

fulling mills, 184

Fulton, Robert, xviii

funerals, Chinese, burning of paper
        at, 34–35

Fust, Johann, 114, 117, 124, 132, 133

Fu Xi, legendary Chinese emperor,
        22–23

Gainsborough, Thomas, 189

Galen, 63

Gamble, John, 240

gampi, 45, 312, 319

Gandhi, Mohandas, 224

Gao Lin, 37

Gao Xianzhi, 48

Gao Xingjian, 314

Gart der Gesundheit, 194

Gasparinus de Bergamo, 139

Gauguin, Paul, 264–66, 267

Gazette Universelle, 233

Gela, Sicily, 63

General History of Air, The (Boyle),
        195

General History of China, The (Halde),
        177

General History of Quadrupeds, A
        (Beilby), 201

*General History of the Things in New
        Spain* (Sahagún), 153

Genesis, book of, 6, 7

Geneva, Switzerland, 165

Genoa, Italy, 73, 82

George III, king of England, 217, 250

Gering, Ulrich, 139

German Expressionists, 264, 266–68

German Peasant War (1524–25), 166

Germantown, Pa., 208–9

Germany:
    papermaking in, 83, 122, 340
    as printing industry center, 122–23,
        132–33, 162, 183, 184, 341

Gesner, Konrad, 193

Gettysburg, Battle of (1863), 245, 246

Gibraltar, Strait of, 67, 339
Gilpin, Joshua, 222, 225, 239, 243, 343
Gilpin, Thomas, 243–44
Giunta, Lucantonio, 135
Glatfelter, Philip Henry, 246
Glatfelter Company, 246, 254, 255, 276, 277, 278–81, 289
Glover, Elizabeth, 206
Glover, John, 206, 215
God's Man (Ward), 270
Gogh, Vincent van, 265
gohei paper, 308
Gokayama, Japan, 310
Gold HuaSheng Paper Mill, 297–98
Goltzius, Hendrick, *173*
Gong Bin, 304–5, 316
Gosin, Susan, 319
Gouda, Netherlands, 172
Gould, Harry, 333–34
Goya, Francisco, *174*
Grace, William Russell, 285–86
Grace & Company, 285–86
Grainsborough, Thomas, 189
Granada, Spain, 70, 75
graphic novels, 269
graphite, 193
Great Britain:
    newspapers in, 331, 343
    wood pulp imported by, 253
    see also England
Great Depression, 278
Great Exhibition of 1851, London, 261
Great Gunpowder Falls, 221
Greatrake, Lawrence, 243–44
Great Wall of China, 27
Great Wave of Kanagawa, The (Hokusai), 266
Greece, ancient, 4, 5, 12, 14

engraved maps of, 108
food writing in, 63
hydraulic engineering by, 52, 54
science in, 86
transition from oral to written culture, 17–18
writing in, 2, 8, 338
Greek alphabet, 15–16, 338
Green, Bartholomew, 212
Green, Samuel, 207–8
Greene, Robert, 196
Greenwald, Glenn, 334
Gregorius, *136*
Gregory IX, Pope, 157
Griffo, Francesco, 137
Grolier de Servières, Jean, *138*
Guadalete, Battle of, 68
Guangxi Province, China, 298
Guatemala, 148
Guernica (Picasso), 268
Guido of Arezzo, 91
Gu Kaizhi, 39–40
Gulliver's Travels (Swift), 196
gunpowder, 88, 97, 148, 190
guns and ammunition, paper for, 190, 220–21, 242, 278
Guo, 39
Gutenberg, Johannes Gensfleisch, xviii, 111, 116, 132, 133, 329
    Bible of, 114, 340
    as goldsmith, 111, 123–24
    innovations of, 113
    printing experiments of, 111, 113–14, 340

Haarlem, Netherlands, 114–15, 172
hafiz, 51
Hahn, Ulrich, 134

Hainan Island, 298

Halde, Jean-Baptiste du, 177

Hallmark Cards, 274

halwa, 65

Hamdani, 63

Hamilton, Alexander, 224, 225

Hancock, John, 208, 223

Hancock, Thomas, 208

Han dynasty, 29–30, 35, 39, 43–44, 101, 293

Hangul (Korean writing system), 105

hanji (handmade paper), 305–6, *306*

Hapsburg dynasty, 167

Harijan, 224

Harper & Brothers, 258–59

Harper's Weekly, 258–59, *259*

Harris, Benjaminm, 212

Harun al-Rashid, Caliph, 53, 58, 59, 62

Harvard University, 206, 207, 257

Hauer, Jacob, 245

Hebrew alphabet, 15

Hedin, Sven, 344

Heidegger, Martin, xx

heliographs, 236

hemp, 30, 43, 45, 55–56, 73, 82, 83, 187, 214, 248, 251, 252, 254

Hempstead, Long Island, 210

Henry VI Part 2 (Shakespeare), 179, 185–86

Henry VIII, king of England, 181, 182

Herbal (Apuleius Barbarus), 194

Hercules, 263

Hesse, Hermann, 270

Heynlin, Johann, 138–39, 140

Hida, Japan, 310

hieroglyphics, *336*, 337, *338*, *339*

High Wycombe, England, 244

Historia de Los Indios de la Nueva España (Mololinía), 158

Historical Account of the Substances which Have Been Used to Describe Events (Koops), 250, 254, 291

Hoe, Richard M., 239, 343

Hoffman, William, 221

Hoffmann, François-Ignace-Joseph, 227–28

Hokusai, Katsushika, 266

Holbein, Hans, the Younger, 116, 163

Holland, 340

  Japanese paper imported by, 177

  maritime trade of, 176

  papermaking in, 167–71, 231–32, 258, 341, 342

  printing industry in, 134, 167

  see also Lowlands

Hollander beaters, 169–70, 214, 228, 232, 319, 342

Hollerith, Herman, 326

Holy Roman Empire, 130

Homer, 17–18, 20

Homer, Winslow, 259, *259*

Hondarribia, Spain, 316–17

Honig, Jan Simonz, 168

Honig family, 224

Hopfer, Daniel, 130

Horace, 335

Horiki, Eriko, 314–16

Housatonic River, 290

House of Commons, British, 244

House of Representatives, Massachusetts, 219

Hovsepian, Tina, 322

Howard, Roy, 330

Howell, Douglas, 318–19

Huangdi, legendary Chinese
    emperor, 23
Huécar River, 142
Huematzin, 150
Hugo, Victor, 98, 117
Huguenots, 184–85, 342
Hu Han Shu, 30
Huizong, Chinese emperor, 37–38
Hull, John, 211
Humanism, 110, 165
humans:
    brain size of, 2
    drawing as primal urge of, 3, 4, 118,
        337
    recording as unique trait of, 1–2
    tool use by, 2
Humble Administrator's Garden, 296
hummādiya, 64
Hunchback of Notre Dame, The (Hugo),
    98
Hunter, Dard, 2, 147–48, 221, 250, 318
Hunter, William, 215
Hurus, Paulus, 141
Husz, Martin, 141
huun (Mayan writing surface), 149–
    50, 339
Hypnerotomachia (Colonna), 135–36

Ibadis, 60
Iberia:
    Muslim conquest of, 67–68
    Visigoths in, 67–68
IBM, 326
Ibn al-Bawwab, 55
Ibn al-Hasan, Muhammad, 63–64
Ibn Arabi, 69
Ibn Battuta, 32, 34
ibn Salih, Ziyad, 48

I Ching (*Book of Changes*), 25
ideas, spread of, printing and, 163,
    164, 165, 182, 204, 216–17, 232
Idrisi, al-, 72
Île de la Cité, 89
Iliad (Homer), 17
Illustrated Newspaper, 258
Impressionism, 264
Incas, 4, 5–6
Incauca sugar mill, 287–88
India, 50
    mathematical knowledge of, 57, 58
    newspapers in, 331
    papermaking in, 42, 289, 291
Indonesia, 283
Industrial Revolution, 231, 238, 244,
    246, 276, 324, 325
Indus valley, 4, 9, 337
Inferno (Dante), 76, 84
information, explosion of, 323, 327
initial capitals, 116, 124
ink:
    acid content of, 53
    from lampblack, 26–27, 37, 53, 105,
        338
    Korean, 105
Innovators, The (Isaacson), 325
Inquisition, 157–59
intaglio printing, 131
Intel, 328
internal combustion engine, 236
International Paper, 276, 281–82, 286
Internet, 329, 335
IQ tests, 21
Iraq, 50
Irish Paper Company, 185
irrigation, 69
Isaacson, Walter, 325

Isabella, queen of Spain, 74, 157
Islam, *see* Muslims, Islam
Italian language, 84
Italian War of Independence (1848), 271
italic typeface, 136–37, 160
Italy, 73, 277
 papermaking in, 77, 78–83, 276–77, 340
 printing in, 134–38, 340
Itsama (Mayan god), xx
Ivan V, tsar of Russia, 134
Ivy mill, 222

Jacob Hauer paper mill, 245–46
Jacquard, Joseph-Marie, 241, 326, 343
Jaime I, king of Aragon, 74, 77
James I, king of England, 184
Japan, 176, 265–66, 295
 armed paper balloons of, 271–73
 bureaucracy in, 44–45
 calligraphy in, 44
 carved-block printing in, 99–100, 339
 Chinese writing system introduced in, 43–44
 Doolittle raid on, 271
 as handmade paper center, 299, 307–13
 Heian period of, 44, 45
 houses in, 46, 308–9
 papermaking in, 44, 45, 177, 258, 265, 293, 299, 305, 307–16, 339, 344
 paper uses in, 46–47, 307–8, 314–16
 recycled paper in, 45, 291
Jay, John, 224
Jefferson, Thomas, 223, 224
Jensen, Peter, 252

Jews, 15
 in al-Andalus, 68, 69, 71, 73, 75
 intellectual achievements of, xix
 paper adopted by, xiii
 papermaking and, 71
 parchment used by, 56–57
 Spanish persecution of, 157–58
Jinxian County, China, 299–300
joglar, 94
John, king of England, 90
John Clark & Company, 246–47
Johnson, Marmaduke, 208
journalism, *see* magazines; newspapers
Juan Carlos, king of Spain, 317
Judeo-Arab, 15
Judeo-Persian, 15
Junius, Hadrianus, 114–15
jute, 214

Kahnweiler, Daniel-Henry, 268
Kapital, Das (Marx), xvii
Kapor, Mitchell, 327, 334
karakami (paper panels), 46, 308–9
Kaycel, 274
Kaysere, Pierre de, 139
Kazue, Kachiwagi, 312–13
Keith, George, 209
Keller, F. G., 251
Keller-Voelter wood grinders, 252
Kelmscott Press, 257, 258
keyboards, 261–62
Khalid ibn Barmak, 53, 57
Khizanat al-Hikma, 58
Khwārizmī, Muhammad ibn Musa al-, 58
Kibi-no-mabi, 99
Killingworth, Conn., 218

Kindt, Al-, 59
Kinman, Norio, 313
kites, 273
Kiyosuke, 321
knotters, 214
Koberger, Anton, 122–23
Koenig, Friedrich, 239, 343
Kohno, Ayako, 308, 309
Kojiki, 339
Kollwitz, Käthe, *267*, 268
Koops, Matthias, 250, 254, 291
Korea:
    books in, *106*
    calligraphy in, *306*
    Chinese writing system in, 43
    Hungul writing system of, 105
    ink in, 105
    Japanese invasion of (370), 44
    papermaking in, xv, 43, 105, 299,
        305–6, 339
    printing in, 104, 105
kozo trees, 306, 309, 310, 311, 312
kraft process, 254
Kufa, 50, 59
Kurashiki, Japan, 312
kutab (writers), 54
kutub al-bah, 62

Ladino language, 15, 75
La Huerta, 69
laid paper, 197, 269, 279–80
Lalande, Jérôme de, 169–70
Landells, Ebenezer, 260, 343
Laozi, 31
La Rochelle, France, 165, 184, 341
Lascaux, France, cave art in, 3
Latin language, 84, 90
laws, written vs. oral, 90–91

Leeu, Gerard, 172
Lefèvre, Raoul, 180
Léger, Fernand, 269
Legros, Alphonse, 263
Lely, Peter (Pieter van der Faes), 169
Leo X, Pope, 121
León, Moses de, 69
Leonardo da Vinci, 91, *119*, 120, 121,
    121, 122
Le Roy, Guillaume, 140
Leslie, Frank, 258
letter writing, paper and, 120
Lettou, John, 181
Ley, Pieter Janz van der, 168
Liberty Paper Mill, 208
libraries:
    in ancient world, 13, 31–32
    of Arabs, 53, 58, 59–60, 69
    in China, 31–32
    in Europe, 94, 116
    future of, 329–30
Library of Congress, 255
Libya, 50
Licklider, J.C.R., 329–30
Life of Luxury, The (Archestratus), 63
lignin, 254, 285, 288
Lima, Peru, 160
linen, 49, 55, 56, 71, 73, 82, 83, 187,
    209, 213, 214, 249, 250, 254, 275,
    317, 319
linoleum cuts, 269
linotype machines, 262
Li Po, 39, 40–41
literacy:
    European explosion of, 110
    in France, 230
    in Muslim world, 52
    reservations about, xvii, 18, 19

literature:
    Arabic, 61–62
    popular, printing and, 196
    vernacular, growth of, 84, 95
lithography, 235, 237, 260, 260, 262, 263, 269
    printmaking and, 235–36
    Senefelder's invention of, 235, 343
Little Pretty Pocket Book, A, 342
Liu Pin, 104
Lives of the Most Eminent Painters, Sculptors, and Architects (Vasari), 120
Livre des merveilles du monde, 141, 341
Lloyd, Mary, 199
logograms, 11–12
Lombardy, Italy, 82
London, England, 182, 184, 198, 261
London Chronicle, 205
Longfellow, Henry Wadsworth, 84
looms, punch-card, 241, 326, 343
López de Gómara, Francisco, 155
Lotther, Melchior, 164
Louis XIV, king of France, 184
Louvain, Belgium, 180
Lovelace, Ada, 325–26
Lowlands, 171, 179–80
Lübeck, Germany, 341
Lü Buwei, 26
Lucca, Italy, 82
Luddites, xvi–xvii, 326, 343
Luipart, Jan, 168
Lu Lan, China, 338, 344
Lünenburg, 133
Luoyang, China, 32
lute, 75
Luther, Martin, 162, 163
    German Bible of, 164
    printing and, 163–65, 341

L. V. Gerrevinck, 224
Lyon, France, 124, 139–40, 165

Maasbüll, Germany, 252
Machlinia, William de, 182
Madison, James, 224
Madrid, 151
magazines, 230
    future of, 332–33
    illustrated, 258–61
Maghreb, 66–67
Magna Carta, 90
Mahdi, al-, caliph, 62
Maidstone, England, 244
Maimonides, Moses, 69
Mainz, Germany, 111, 113, 126
    sack of (1462), 133, 340
Malinche, 156
Mallermi, Niccolo de, 135
Ma'mun, Caliph, 58
Manet, Édouard, 263–64
Mann, Thomas, 269, 270
Mansion, Colard, 172
Mansur, Al-, 50
Manutius, Aldus, 254
Mao Zedong, 15, 298, 302
    Little Red Book of, 298–99
    simplified writing system of, 35
maps, mapmaking, 70, 176
marbling, 191–93
Marcourt, Antoine de, 166
Margaret, duchess of Burgundy, 180
Mariani, Franco, 79
Marie Antoinette, queen of France, printed attacks on, 233
Marinoni, Hippolyte, 263, 264
maritime republics, 82
Marquesas Islands, 266

Marranos, 157
"Marseillaise, La," 234
Marseilles, France, 73
Mars Manufacturing Company, 274
Martin, Henri-Jean, 162, 164, 229
Marx, Karl, xvii
Maryland, 221
Mary of Burgundy, 128–29
Masanobu, Okumura, 266
Masereel, Frans, 269–70, 270
Masha'allah, 50
Massachusetts colony, 210, 211
    British settlers in, 205–8
    first mint in, 211
    first paper mill in, 208
    first print shop in, 206, 207–8, 215
    papermaking in, 219–20
Massachusetts House of Representatives, 219
Massachusetts language, 207, 208
Master of Jacob Bellaert, 172
Masudi, 85
mathematics:
    Arabs' knowledge of, 52, 57–59, 85
    European discoveries in, 88–89
    Mayan knowledge of, 149
Mather, Cotton, 207
Mather, Increase, 207
Mather, Richard, 206–7
Matisse, Henri, 265, 318
Matlock, Timothy, 223
matrix, matrices, 113, 227–28, 262
Matsulira, Satsuya, 307–8
Maximilian I, Holy Roman Emperor, 128–29, 190
Mayan language, 156
Mayans, xx, 4, 28
    calendar of, 149

codices of, 149, 150, 154, 159, 340, 341
libraries of, 149, 341
mathematical knowledge of, 149
paper-like material (*huun*) of, 148–50, 339, 340
possible true papermaking by, 154, 339
writing of, 148–49
McLuhan, Marshall, 117
Mecca, 32, 50, 70, 339
medicine, books and paper in, 194
Medina, 49
Melman, Saul, 319
memory:
    digital age and, 334–36
    writing and, xvii, 18–19, 62, 335
Ménagier de Paris, Le (anonymous), 95
Menasseh Ben Israel, Samuel, 175
Meng Tian, xiv, 3, 27, 338
Mennonites, 208
Mercator, Gerardus, 176
Mercure de France, 233
Mesoamerica, 147–48
    paper-like material in, xiv, 148–50, 152–54, 156–57
    papermaking in, xix, 154–55
    Spanish conquest of, 150–51, 155–57, 341
    writing in, 148–49, 151–52
    see also Aztecs; Mayans; Mexico
Mesopotamia, 4, 5, 24, 25, 50, 337
Messina, Sicily, 73
Metamorphoses (Ovid), 172
Mexico, xix, 4, 147, 148, 150–51
    basket making in, 317
    Inquisition in, 157, 158–59
    papermaking in, 160, 341

Mexico (*continued*)
   printing in, 159–60, 341
   Spanish conquest of, 155–57, 341
Mexico City, Mexico, 160
mezzotints, 174, 200, 201
Michelangelo, 118, 120, 147
Michelet, Jules, 241
microchips, 344
Middle Ages, 76–77
   laws in, 90–91
   scribes in, 93–94, 95
   writing in, 90–92
Middle East, xv, 50
mi hsiang zhi, 42
Mikesh, Robert C., 272–73
Milani, Pietro, 277
Milani Fabriano Paper Company, 277
Milani family, 277
Milne, A. A., 261
Milton, Mass., 213–14
Ming dynasty, 296, 300, 302, 303
Minoans, as possible inventors of
   moveable type, 109–10
Miró, Joan, 268
mitsumata, 309, 312
Moche, 4
molds, 33, 187–88, 221–22, 301, 302,
   308–9, 311, 312, 317
   wire, 72, 80–81, 83, 228
Moll Flanders (Defoe), 196
monasteries, 93–94
money, paper, *see* paper money
Mongolia, Mongols, 27, 65, 87
Moniteur, 233
Monmouth, Battle of (1778), 221
Monte Alegre, Brazil, 285
Montecuçoma (Montezuma), 155–57,
   161

Montoya, Diego de, 160
Moon Ik-jeom, *106*
Moore, Gordon, 328
Moore's Law, 328
Moriscos, 157
Morning Chronicle, 204
Morning Post, 204
Moronobu, Hishikawa, 265–66
Morris, William, 256–57
Moses (prophet), 9
Mosher, Thomas Bird, 257–58
mosques, 60
Motolinía (Toribio de Benavente),
   155, 158
moveable type, *see* printing, with
   moveable type
Mozi, 26
Mubashshir ibn Fatiq, al-, 180
Muhammad (prophet), 49, 51–52, 339
Muhammad VIII, sultan of Granada,
   73
Mukhtar al-hikam wa mahasin al-
   kalim (al-Mubashshir ibn Fatiq),
   180
mulberry, 10, 11, 33, 43, 45, 88, 99, 104,
   149, 161, 272, 305, 306, 309, 312
Munch, Edvard, 267
Mūsá bin Nuṣayr, 67
music, 70, 91–92, 196
Muslims, Islam:
   calligraphy of, 52, 55
   spread of, 49–51
   Iberia conquered by, 67–68
   intellectual achievements of, xix
   literacy of, 52
   parchment used by, 56–57
   Spanish persecution of, 157–58
   Sunni–Shi'a schism and, 51, 60, 74

Nabu (Assyrian god), xx
Nahuatl, 153, 156
Naoke, Tange, 312
Naples, Italy, 73, 134
Napoleonic Wars, 245
Nassau, Adolf von, archbishop of
    Mainz, 133
Nast, Thomas, 259
National Security Agency (NSA), 334
Navigation Act of 1663, 210
navigational charts, 93
Nawbakht, 50, 58
Near East, 13
Negker, Jost de, 128
Neponset River, 208
Netherlands, *see* Holland; Lowlands
Neuchatel, 231
Newberry, John, 202
Newcomen, Thomas, 238
New England, 206, 281
New Hampshire, 211
New Haven, Conn., 218, 277
New Iberia, La., 285
New Jersey, 211
New Rochelle, N.Y., 185, 258
Newsonomics, 331
newspapers, 262, 342
    advertising and, 330–31
    in American colonies, 211–13, 220,
        342
    cartoons in, 263
    in French Revolution, 233
    future of, 331–32
    in Great Britian, 331, 343
    growing readership of, 226, 237,
        247–48
    in India, 331
    paper and, 202–4

    photography in, 258
    Stamp Act and, 217
    in US, 330–31
newsprint, 252, 254, 281, 286, 289, 295
    declining sales of, 330
Newton, Isaac, 194–95, 231
New York, N.Y., 209–10
New York Assembly, 220
New York colony, 210, 211, 216,
New Yorker, 332–33
New York Gazette, 210
New York Public Library, 255
New York state, 281
New York Times, 330–31
New York Tribune, 247
Neyroumande, Emmanuelle, 283–84
Niaux, France, cave art in, 3
Nicolson, William, *262*
Niépce, Claude, 236
Niépce, Joseph Nicéphore, 236–37, 343
Nile River, 9, 12
"Ninety-Five Theses on the Power
    and Efficacy of Indulgences,
    The" (Luther), 163
Ningbo, China, 295, 296
Nolde, Emil, 267–68
Norfolk, England, 191
nori, 313–14
North Africa, xv, 52, 74
    papermaking in, 71, 73–74
North Carolina, 220
Northern Renaissance, 163
North Newington Mill, 242
Norton, Charles Eliot, 257
novels, wordless, 269–70
numerals:
    Aztec, 152–53
    base-ten system of, 58, 86

numerals (*continued*)
  Hindu-Arabic, 58, 70, 86, 87, 89, 91
  Mayan, 149
  Roman, 58, 77, 84, 87, 91
Nuremberg, Germany, 83, 111, 125, 126
  papermaking in, 122, 340
  printing industry in, 122–23
Nuremberg Chronicle (Die Schedelsche
    Weltchronik) (Schedel), 123

Odyssey (Homer), 17
offset printing, 263
Ogama-Machi, Japan, 311–12
Oh Sang Youl, *306*
O'Kane, Helen M., 258
okra, 250
Old Man with Noose (Kollwitz), 267
Oliver Twist (Dickens), 261
Olmecs, 148
Onderdonk, Hendrick, 210
One Thousand and One Nights, 61–62,
  95, 340
Ontario, Canada, 282
Open and Empty (Wang), *315*
oral literature, 20–21, 60
  in China, 39
  in France, 234
  rhythmic nature of, 17, 335
  survival of, 335–36
origami, 320–21
Ortelius, Abraham, 176
Otomi people, 160
Ottoman Empire, 50
Ovid, 172
Ozu Shoten paper museum, 307

Pacioli, Luca, 91
packaging, paper for, 334

Padua, Italy, 82
Pagenstecher, Albrecht and Rudolf,
  252
Paine, Roxy, 319
Paine, Thomas, 202–3, 216–17
Pakistan, 50
Palazzo Medici, 120
pamphleteering, 202–3
pamphlets, 217, 228, 230
Panckoucke, Charles-Joseph, 233
Paoli (Pablo), Giovanni, 159–60
paper, 204, 241
  acid content of, 45
  acid-free, 255
  advantages of, over earlier record-
    ing media, 2
  in architecture, 308–9, 314–15, 322
  art, machine-made, 265, 269, 280
  art from, 318, 320–21
  blue, 190, 199
  brown, 72, 121, 169, 184, 187, 189,
    190–91
  bureaucracy and, 32, 44–45, 52
  calculations and, 119
  Chinese invention of, xiv, xviii, 23,
    28–31, 178, 338, 344
  colored, 42, 45, 72–73, 214, 232, 264
  cost of, 80, 229–30
  deckle edge, 187, 258
  drawing, 197
  Europeans as slow to adopt, xv,
    xix, 73, 77, 78, 83, 85
  exploding demand for, 226
  fiber, 278
  for guns and ammunition, 190,
    220–21, 242, 278
  journalism and, 202–4
  laid, 197, 269, 279–80

marbling of, 191–93

as mark of civilization, xviii–xix

for packaging, 334

predicted "death" of, 326–27

printing and, *see* printing

raw (unsized), 303

recycled, 45, 291–92, 294–95

Renaissance and, 117, 118–22

science and, 194

security of, vs. online communication, 334

shortages of, 231, 285

silk-thread, 242

specialized uses of, 34, 46–47, 57,
189–91, 199, 232, 253, 271–74

as superior medium for drawing,
118–19

as superior medium for printing,
108–9, 117

US tariffs on imports of, 224–25

white, 56, 72, 137, 140, 169, 171, 183,
184, 187, 189, 199, 232, 254, 279,
342, 343

wove, 197, 222, 264, 269, 279–80, 318

paper, forerunners of:

in Mesoamerica, xiv, 148–50, 152–
54, 156–57

tapa, 10–11, 149, 153–54, 337

see also papyrus; parchment

paper, handmade (modern), 257–58,
269, 272, 275, 293

in China, 299–305

in Japan, 299, 305, 306–13, 314–16

in Korea, 305–6

in Spain, 316–18

in US, 318–19

paper airplanes, 273

paperboard, 191, 242

papermaking, xv–xvi

with bagasse, 284–88

bleaching and, 171, 239, 288, 301,
342, 343

Buddhism and, xv, xviii, 42, 44, 49,
98, 339

continuous-roll machines for,
240–41, 242, 243–44, 245–46, 255,
276, 279–84, 288, 318, 343

controversies over, 185–86, 281,
289

drop hammers in, 80, 83

energy demands of, 289, 295

environmentalism and, 282–84,
289–92, 297, 299–300

with esparto grass, 250

felting mills and, 79

impact on artists of, 198–202

Jews and, 71

with mill sweepings, 250

molds in, 33, 72, 80–81, 83, 187–88,
221–22, 228, 301, 302, 308–9, 311,
312, 317

rags in, *see* rags, in papermaking

with red algae, 314

Schäffer's experiments with,
249–50

single-sheet machines in, 242–43

sizing in, 33, 83, 169

specialized, 189–91, 197–98, 199,
201–2, 277–78, 286

stampers in, 142, 169–70, 214

steam power and, 239

with straw, 250

by wasps, 248–49, 343

watermarks in, 72, 81, 83, 222, 240,
277, 280, 340

waterwheels and, 55, 80, 83

papermaking (*continued*)
  wood pulp in, *see* wood pulp, in
    papermaking
  see also specific countries and regions
Paper Mill, 282
paper money, 88, 240, 255, 277, 278
  in American colonies, 209, 211, 222,
    341
  in China, 34, 87, 192
  counterfeiting of, 222
  Franklin and, 192
  watermarks of, 222
paper workers:
  in France, 228–29
  guilds of, 96, 241, 244
  industrialization and, 241, 244
  life expectancy of, 96, 142
papier-mâché, 190
Papyrer, Der (Amman), *188*
papyrus (plant), 9, 12
papyrus (writing surface), xvi, 9–10,
  12, 56, 109, 176, 337
  Arabs and, 53
  export of, 11, 14, 337
  parchment vs., 14
  scrolls of, 10
  sizing on, 11
Paradiso (Dante), 84, 115
Paramonga, Peru, 285
parchment, xvi, xx, 78, 84, 93, 97, 116,
  197, 226
  Arabs and, 53, 54
  codex and, 14
  cost of, vs. paper, 80
  Dante's use of, 84
  European preference for, xv, 223
  invention of, 14
  in North Africa, 71

  papyrus vs., 14
  as poor medium for printing, 117
  sacred texts and, 56
Paris, France, 83, 89–90, 141, 150
  book trade in, 138–39
  rue Saint-Jacques in, 139
Paris World's Fair (1937), 268
Parliament, British, 203, 204, 244
Passionate Journey (Masereel), 269, *270*
pasteboard, 189–90
Payen, Anselme, 29, 252
Peasant Alphabet (Halbein), 116
pencils, 193–94
Peng Wei, 314
Pennsylvania:
  Council of Public Safety in, 220
  German-language newspapers in,
    217
  as papermaking center, 208–9, 213
Pennsylvania Gazette, 212, 215
Périgueux, 141
Pérotin, 92
Pergamum, 13–14, 338
Perry, James, 204
Persia, Persians, 50, 60–61, 168, 191
Persian Gulf, 6
Peru, 4, 10, 153, 160, 285, 337
Peter the Venerable, xiii, 73, 85
Petrarch, 93, 137
Petroski, Henry, 193
Pfister, Albrecht, 125
Phaedrus (Plato), 18–19, 335
Phaistos Disc, 109–10, *109*
Philadelphia, Pa., 209, 225
Philip II, king of Spain, 172–73
Philip IV, king of Spain, 142
Phillpotts, Eden, 275–76, 280–81, 307
Philo of Byzantium, 54

Phoenician alphabet, 15–16, 338
Phoenician language, 51
Phoenicians, 4, 7, 337
phoneticism, xiv, 6–7, 9, 15
phonograms, 11
photography:
  invention of, 236–37, 343
  in newspapers and magazines,
    258
Piazza San Marco, Venice, 271
Picasso, Pablo, 128, 257, 318
  printmaking by, 268–69
Pico, Giovanni, count of Mirandula,
    135
pictograms, 6
pictographs, xiv, 3, 12, 336
*Piedra Gloriosa o de la Estatua de Nebu-
    chadnesar, La* (Menasseh Ben
    Israel), 175
pine tree shilling, 211
Pisa, Italy, 82
Pissarro, Camille, 264
plague, 185
planned obsolescence, 325
Planter (ship), 206
Plantin, Christophe, 172–73, *173*, 174
Platner & Smith, 252
Plato, 18–19, 110, 180, 335
playing cards, 124, 141, 213–14, 232,
    261, 340
Pleistocene Age, 2
Pleyden, Wilhelm, 123
Pliny the Elder, 1, 14
Poe, Edgar Allan, 264
poetry:
  Andalusian, 70
  in Arab culture, 61
  in China, 39, 40–41

oral nature of, 335
  Persian, 60–61
Pollock, Jackson, 36
pollution, from papermaking, 289–
    90, 297, 299–300
Polo, Marco, 88
Polyglot Bible, 172–73
Pompeii, 20
Poor Richard's Almanack, 215
Portland, Maine, 257
Pound, Ezra, 40
Prague, 133
Preston, Cuba, 285
Prince, Edward, 257
printing, xiv, xvii, 2
  Buddhism and, 99–103
  Chinese invention of, 99, 107, 339
  early near-misses in development
    of, 108
  etching and, 130–31
  in French Revolution, 232–35
  growth of reading and, 237
  impact on authors of, 196
  intaglio, 131
  in Korea, 104
  lithographic, *see* lithography
  paper as superior medium for,
    108–9, 117
  Stamp Act and, 217
printing, carved-block, 134
  books of, 125, 263, 269
  in China, 99
  in Europe, 110–11, 340
  in Japan, 99–100, 339
  paper and, 99
  playing cards and, 124, 141
  on textiles, 124
  see also woodcut illustrations

printing, with moveable type, xiv
  in American colonies, 206, 207–8,
    209, 211–13, 216–17, 342
  Chinese invention of, xix, 104–5, 340
  Chinese writing system and, 104–5
  copper-plate etching and, 173–74
  in England, 179–82
  European alphabet and, 113–14
  in France, 134, 138–41, 165
  Germany as center of, 122–23,
    132–33, 162, 183, 184
  Gutenberg's experiments with, 111,
    113–14, 340
  handwritten manuscripts imitated
    by, 115–16
  in Holland, 167
  in Italy, 134–38, 140, 147, 340, 341
  in Korea, 105, 340
  in Lowlands, 171–72
  Luther and, 163–65
  matrices for, 227–28
  in Mexico, 159–60
  Minoans as possible inventors of,
    109–10
  popular literature and, 196
  Protestant Reformation and,
    162–66
  rivals of Gutenberg, 114–15
  in Spain, 134, 141–46
  and spread of ideas, 163, 164, 165,
    182, 204, 216–17, 232
  spread of, 133–34
  woodcuts and, 125–26, 135–36, 141,
    160, 171–72, 174
printing presses, xviii, 227
  American-made, 218
  of iron, 238–39, 343
  limited-edition books and, 257

  linotype, 262
  offset, 263
  rotary, 239, 343
  steam-powered, 239, 343
printmaking:
  as affordable art, 268–69
  in England, 201–2
  etchings, 130–31, 173–74, 176, 187,
    200, 201–2, 263, 341
  lithography and, 235–36, 260,
    263–64
  mezzotints, 174, 200, 201
  nineteenth-century revival of,
    263–64
  in twentieth century, 268
  Protestant Reformation, xvii, 182,
    184, 232
  printing and, 162–66
Ptolemy I, king of Egypt, 13–14
Publick Occurences Both Foreign and
  Domestic, 211–12, 342
Puebla, Mexico, 160
Puerto Rico, 285
Punch, 260, 343
punches, 112, 113, 133, 257
Puritans, 206–7, 211
Pynson, Richard, 182
Pyrenees, 50

qaliya al-shiwa, 64–65
Qian Fo Dong (Caves of the Thou-
  sand Buddhas), 101–2
Qin dynasty, 27
Quentell, Heinrich, 122
Quenu Newsprint Paper Company,
  289
Question Concerning Technology, The
  (Heidegger), xx

Quevedo, Francisco de, 142
Quotations from Chairman Mao Tse-tung (*Máo zhǔxi yǔlù*), 298–99
Qur'an, 51, 53, 55, 56–57, 59, 60, 63, 340

Racine, Jean, 227–28
Ragazzo, Giovanni, 135
ragmen, 245–46
rags, in papermaking, 55–56, 73, 83, 96, 189, 190, 209, 228, 285, 289
  in American Revolution, 218, 219–20
  Arabs' use of, 49, 54, 55–56, 339
  bleaching of, 239, 343
  Chinese as first to use, 30, 49, 177
  Franklin and, 212
  growing demand for, 82, 142, 167, 183
  Italian use of, 74, 77, 80, 82
  pulping of, 169–70, 187
  quality and, xiii, 97, 137
  shortage of, in American colonies, 214
  shortages of, 213, 246–48, 249
  sorting of, 170–71, 170, 280
  "souring" of, 171
  trade in, 82, 142, 183
  from uniforms of dead soldiers, 245
  US imports of, 247
  wood pulp vs., 251–52, 254–55
rag sorters, 280
rain forest, destruction of, 283
Raleigh, Walter, 186
"Raven, The" (Poe), 264
Ravensburg, Germany, 83
Ravensburg-Constance, 141

raw cotton, 317
reading:
  fear of, 238
  growth of, 94–95, 237
  and improvements in printing, 237
reams, 79
Réaumur, René Antoine Ferchault de, 245, 248, 342
recording, as uniquely human trait, 1–2
Recuyell of the Historyes of Troye (Lefèvre), 180
recycled paper, 250
red algae, 313–14
Redon, Odilon, 264
Red Sea, 55
Rembrandt van Rijn, 174–76, *175*, 177
Remington, 261
Remington Rand, 344
Remnick, David, 332–33
Remsen, Henry, 210
Renaissance:
  demand for books in, 110–11
  paper and, 117, 118–22
Report on Manufacturers (Hamilton), 225
Reuwich, Erhard, 126
Revelation of Saint John, The (Dürer), 127
Revere, Paul, 212, 214
Rhau-Grunenberg, Johann, 163
Rhode Island, 211
Rhône River, 139
Ribot, Théodule-Armand, 263
Richelieu, Cardinal, 184
Riessinger, Sextus, 134
Rights of Man, The (Paine), 203
Rionda, Manuel, 285

Rio Palo, 288
risma (ream), 79
Rittenhouse, Claus, 209
Rittenhouse, William, 208–9, 214, 342
River Darent, 183
Robert, Nicolas-Louis, 240–41, 279, 343
Robinson Crusoe (Defoe), 196
Robles, Francisco de, 143–44
Roderic, Visigoth king, 67–68
Roger I, count of Sicily, 78
Roger II, count of Sicily, 78
Roger of Sicily (textile printer), 124
Roman alphabet, 16
Roman Catholic Church, 182
Roman type, 182
Rome, 134
Rome, ancient, 12, 14
  engineering skill of, 52, 69
  fall of, 87
  potters' stamps in, 108
  scribes in, 109
  writing in, 19–20
Rosenbach, Johann, 141
Rosenband, Leonard N., 229
rosin paper, 191
Rouault, Georges, 257
Rouget de Lisle, Claude Joseph, 234
Rousseau, Jean-Jacques, 202, 231
Royal Academy, French, 249
Royal Navy, 238
Royal Society, 191, 194, 201, 236
Rubens, Peter Paul, 173–74
Rundi, Abi Sharif al-, 66, 74
Ruskin, John, 256
Russia, 134, 341
Rustichello of Pisa, 88
Rwandan Civil War, 314

sabots, 190
Ṣabūr, Iran, 59
Sachs, Hans, *188*
Saga prefecture, Japan, 309
Sahagún, Father, 153
St. Clair, William, 203, 220–21, 237
Saint-Cloud, France, 83
Saint Gall, Abbey of, 60
Salem witch trials, 207
Salinger, J. D., 333
Salisbury, Marquis of, 250
Samarkand, 48, 49, 55
Samarkand paper, 49, 56
Samuel ibn Nagrella, 70
Sánchez de Muñón, Hernán, 160
Sanctae Peregrinationes (Breydenbach), 126
sandalwood trees, 300, 305
Sanderson, Robert, 211
San Pablito, Mexico, 160–61
San Pedro, Calif., 272
Santa Fe, Argentina, 285
Santiago de Compostela, Spain, 180
Saône River, 139, 140
Satoni, Tamara, 312
Saugerties, N.Y., 244
Savery, Thomas, 238, 342
Scandinavia, 4–5
Sceptical Chemist (Boyle), 195
Schäffer, Jacob Christian, 249–50
Schäufelein, Hans, 128
Schedel, Hartmann, 123
Scheele, Carl, 239, 342
Schöffer, Peter, 124, 132, 133, 194
Schuyler, Philip, 219
Schuylkill River, 208–9
science, books and paper in, 194, 195
scientific method, 194–95

Scotland, 183, 185
Scott Paper Company, 273–74
scribes:
    Arabic, 51–52, 53–54, 55, 56–57, 60,
      105–6
    Aztec, 151–52
    as calligraphers, 195–96
    Egyptian, 12
    Mayan, 149
    in Medieval Europe, 85, 93–94, 95
    printing and, 116, 195
    Roman, 109
    Sumerian, 7
seals and stamps, 99, 338
Seba, Albertus, 249
Seesaw—Gloucester, Massachusetts
    (Homer), *259*
Sele Mill, 179, 183
Self-Portrait Leaning on a Stone Sill
    (Rembrandt), *175*
Sellers, Nathan, 221
Senate, US, 224
Senefelder, Alois, 235, 343
Seville, Spain, 74, 151
shabti (Xátiva paper), 71–72
Shahnameh (Ferdowsi), 61
Shakespeare, William, 179, 185–86,
    196
shamans, 24, 25
Shang dynasty, 25, 27
Shanghai, China, 296
Shelley, Percy Bysshe, 238
Shennong, legendary Chinese
    emperor, 23
Shepard, Ernest, 261
shi (poetry), 40
Shi'as, Sunnis vs., 51, 60, 74
Shinto religion, 46

shirt collars, 277
Shlian, Matthew, 319–20, *320*
shoji (paper windows), 46
Shotoku, empress of Japan, 99, 339
shu-ssu (bookshop), 31–32
Sicily, 50, 52, 73, 339
Siegen, Ludwig von, 174
silk:
    Chinese painting on, 38
    as writing surface, 28, 32, 35, 338
silk industry, in Lyon, 139–40
Silk Road, 31, 49, 59, 100–101
Sixtus IV, Pope, 157
sizing, 11, 33, 169, 189, 199, 228, 280
    animal-based, 79–80, 83, 113
Skelton, John, 181
small presses, 257–58
Smith, Charlotte, 222
Smith Paper Company, 252
Snowden, Edward, 334
Soar River, 242
social change, technology as
    response to, xiv, xv, xvii–xviii,
    24, 106–8, 110, 193, 235
Social Contract, The (Rousseau), 202
Société des Aquafortistes, 263
Society for the Arts, 192
Socrates, 18, 180, 335
sodium carbonate, 290
sodium hydroxide, 254
sodium sulfide, 254
Song dynasty, 36, 92
"Song of the War-Carts" (Tu Fu), 41
Sonnets and Other Poems (Smith), 222
Sorbonne, 138, 140
Sotheby's, 61
Soufflet-Vert, 139
Soul Mountain (Gao), 314

South America, tapa in, 153–54
Southeast Asia, 10
Spain, xiii, 52, 167
    Inquisition in, 157–58
    paper adopted in, xv
    papermaking in, 77, 141–42, 316–18
    printing in, 134, 141–46
    Reconquista in, 74–75, 142, 157
    see also al-Andalus; Iberia
Spanish Civil War, 268
Spilman, John, 183–84, 186
Spira, Johannes de, 134–35
spoken language, xiii, xiv, 2
Spring Grove, Pa., 276, 281
Springinklee, Hans, 130
spruce, 281, 301
Stamp Act (1765), 217, 218
stampers, 142, 169–70, 214, 228
stamping mills, 228
Standard Sounds for the Instruction of
    the People, The, 105
Ständebuch, Das, 188
Stanhope, Lord Charles, 238–39, 343
stationers, 198
steam engine, 238, 342, 343
Steart, George, 199
steel, 238
Stein, Marc Aurel, 49, 100–102, 101
stereotyped printing, 227–28
Sterling Paper Products, 274
Stockbridge, Mass., 344
Stoke Holy Cross paper mill, 191
Stone Age, 4
Storm in a Teacup (Phillpotts), 275, 276
Strasbourg, Germany, 83, 111, 114, 133,
    203, 342
Stratton, J. R., 282
straw, 250, 317

Straw Paper Manufactory, 250
Stuart, Daniel, 204
styluses, 7, 12, 16
Subiaco monastery, 134, 340
Sudan, 73
Sueño y Mentira de Franco (Picasso),
    268
Sufism, 69
sugarcane, bagasse from, 284–88
sugar plantations, 287
Suh, Do Ho, 319
sulfite process, 254
sulfur-dioxide, 252
sulphite process,, 252–53, 254
Sumerian language, 9
Sumerians, 4, 11, 15, 23
    literature of, 7–9
    technology of, 7
    writing first developed by, 5–7
Sunnis, Shi'as vs., 51, 60, 74
Sun Xiaoyun, 36–37, 302, 303–4, 303,
    304
Sutton, Mass., 219–20
Suzhou, China, 296, 297
Swahili, 5
Swift, Jonathan, 196, 203
Switzerland, 165, 340
Sylvester II, Pope, 86
Symbolism, 264
Syracuse, Sicily, 56, 73
Syria, 50, 52, 55, 61, 69, 73

Tabasco, Mexico, 148
Tacitus, 19–20
Tada, Reikichi, 271
Tadao, Shimizu, 310–11
Taejong, king of Korea, 105, 340
Tahiti, 266

Taiwan, 301

Takano, Teizou, 311

Talas, battle of (751), 48

Talbot, William Henry Fox, 236, 343

Tamil Nadu Newsprint and Papers Limited, 289

Tang dynasty, 37, 40–63, 273, 300

Tang Guo, 297, 300, 314

Taoism, 31, 39–40

tapa (bark paper), 10–11, 99, 149, 153–54

Taranto, Italy, 50

Tarifa, Spain, 67

tariffs, on US imports of paper, 224–25

Tariq ibn Ziyad, 67–68

tar paper, 191

Tate, John, 179, 181, 182, 183, 341

technological change:
  fears about, xvi–xvii, 2–3, 14, 19, 256–57, 334–36
  pace of, 324–25
  and pursuit of wealth, xx

technology:
  coexistence of old and new, xv–xvi, 107, 275, 326–27, 328–29
  Diderot's belief in power of, 231, 241, 244
  as elaboration of primary ideas, xx
  fallacies about, xiii–xiv, xv–xvi, 106–7, 137, 162, 237, 328
  as practical application of knowledge, xiii–xiv, 2
  as response to social change, xiv, xv, xvii–xviii, 24, 106–8, 110, 193, 235

telegraph, 247

Tenant, Charles, 171

Tenant, Gilbert, 221

"Tenants and Landlords" (Daumier), 260

Tenniel, John, 261

Tennyson, Alfred Lord, 53

Tenochtitlán, 151, 155, 156

Teoamoxtli, 150

textile industry, 184

textiles, carved-block printing on, 124

Thackeray, William Makepeace, 258, 260–61

Tha'ilibi, Al-, 48–49

Theatrum orbis terrarium (Ortelius), 176

Theuerdank (Maximilian I), 128

Thionville, Guillaume de, 180

"Thirty-Six Views of Mount Fuji" (Hokusai), 266

Thomas, Isaiah, 222

Thomas Aquinas, Saint, 20

Thomas Reeves, 198

Thompson, Isaiah, 213

Thomson, Charles, 223

Thoth (Egyptian god), xix, 19

Tigris River, 54

Tihamah, Arabian peninsula, 55

Tilghman, Benjamin Chew, 252–53

Time, 274

Times (London), 204, 239, 253, 343

Times of India, 331

Tisha B'Av, 75

Tlaxcalteca, 155

toilet paper, Chinese invention of, 34

Tokyo, Japan, 307, 344

Tokyo Matsuya, 308

Toledo, Spain, 73, 74

Toltecs, 150
Töpffer, Rodolphe, 263
totem poles, 4
To the Christian Nobility of the German Nation (Luther), 341
Townshend, Charles, 218
Townshend Act (1767), 218
Tract Against Jews, A (Peter the Venerable), 73, 85
Trade and Industry (Diderot), *112*, *170*, *227, 228*
transistors, 344
Travaux d'Hercule (Doré), 263
Treasury, US, 278
tree farming, 282–83, 298
Treefrog, 288
Tresse, Thomas, 209
Treviso, Italy, 82
Triumph of Maximilian, The, 129–30, *129*
troubadours, 94
Troy, N.Y., 253
Troyes, France, 83, 340
Tsien Tsuen-Hsuin, 34–35, 49
tuberculosis, 142
Tu Fu, 22, 24, 41
Tuinucu, Cuba, 285
Tula, Mexico, 150
Turkestan, 31, 100–101
Turkey, 191
Turkey Mill, 197, 199
Turner, J. M. W., 194, 198–200, 316, 343
Turner, Robert, 209
Twain, Mark, 261
Tyler, Benjamin Owen, 225
type cases, 227
typefaces, *112*, *113*, *227*
    italic, 136–37, 160

typesetting:
    keyboards and, 261, 262
    linotype, 262
typewriters, xiv, 261–62, 344
typist-secretaries, 262
typography, typographers, 117, 257

Udine, Italy, 82
ukiyo-e, 266
Ulm, Germany, 125, 133
Umayyad Caliphate, 50, 66–67
UNESCO, 305
United Fruit Company, 285
United States, 295
    imports of Chinese paper in, 295–96
    Japanese paper balloon attacks on, 272–73
    newspapers in, 330–31
    papermaking in, 243–44, 245–46, 250, 251, 253, 255, 276, 277–78, 318, 343, 344
    rag shortages in, 246–48
    recycled paper in, 291
    tariffs on paper imports in, 224–25
UNIVAC I, 344
universities, 93, 94, 110
    and spread of printing, 133
UPM Changshu Paper Mill, *294*
Upper Darby, Pa., 221
Ur dynasty, 8
Uruguay, 283
Uruk, 6, *337*
Utamaro, Kitagawa, 266

Valencia, Spain, 74, 77, 141
Valentini, J. J., 152
Valley Forge, 221

Valls i Subirà, Oriol, 77, 96, 141

Vasari, Giorgio, 120

Vatican Library, 116

vatmen, 187–89, *188*, 276, 280, 301, 312

Vega, Lope de, 143

Velde, Jan van de, 174

vellum, 14, 97, 173

Venice, Italy, 73, 79, 82, 134, 140, 141, 271
    printing in, 134–35, 340, 341

Vera Cruz, Mexico, 148, 155, 341

Vernus, Michel, 234

Verona, Italy, 134, 277

Verrocchio, Andrea del, 122

Vietnam, papermaking in, 42

Villard de Honnecourt, 89

Vindication of the Rights of Woman, A (Wollstonecraft), 203

Vingle, Pierre de, 166

Virgil (Baskerville's edition), 197

Virginia Gazette, 215

Visigoths, in Iberia, 67–68

Vitruvius, 54

Vizlant, Jakob, 141

Vollard, Ambroise, 257

Voltaire, 202, 231

von Neumann, John, 344

Vosges, France, 83, 265

Waiting for Death (Bewick), *201*

Waldvogel, Prokop, 115

Walker, John, 204

wallpaper, 190

wampum, 210–11

Wang Dongling, 314, *315*

Wang Hui, *41*

Wang Yuanlu, 102

Wang Zhen, 104–5, 114

Ward, Lynd, 270

Warhol, Andy, 274

War of the Roses, 185

washi (handmade paper), 305, 307–13, 314–16

Washington, George, 221

wasps, papermaking by, 248–49, 342

water clock, 89

watercolors, 197–200, 303, 314, 343

waterleaf, 189

watermarks, 72, 81, 83, 222, 240, 277, 280, 340

Water of Leith River, 183

waterwheels, 54, 55, 69, 80, 83, 228

Watt, James, 238

wax tablets, 12–13

We Are Building This Ship as We Sail It (Shlian), *320*

weaving, wire for, 221

Wedgwood, Thomas, 236

Weedley, Yorkshire, England, 168

Weekly Bulletin of the Canadian Department of Trade and Commerce, 285

Wees, William de, 209

Weisskunig (Maximilian I), 128

Wells Fargo, 289

West, M. I., 9

West Africa, 73

Whatman, James, 197, 199, 202, 222, 224, 316

Whigs, 204

Wilcox, Thomas, 209

Wilde, Mark, 293–94

William I, king of England, 90

William II, king of England, 210

William of Rubruck, 87–88

Winchester Arms Company, 277–78

windmills, 168

Wineberg, Bruce, 319

Winnie the Pooh (Milne), 261

Wissahickon Creek, 208, 209

Wittenberg, Germany, 163, 164

Wohlgemut, Michael, 123

Wolff, Kurt, 270

Wollstonecraft, Mary, 203

Wolvercote Mill, 289, 291

wood, as writing surface, 26, 28, 32, 338

wood chippers, 252

woodcut illustrations, 100, 102, *106, 107,* 122–23, 124–25, 134, 171–72, 174, 200, 202, *262,* 264, *270*
    as affordable art, 123–24, 128
    of Burgkmair, 128, *129*
    of Dürer, 127–28, *127*
    German Expressionists and, 266–68
    in Japan, 265–66
    Maximilian I and, 128–29
    moveable type and, 125–26, 135–36, 141
    in twentieth century, 269–70

wood engraving, 200–202, 258, *259,* 260, 270

wood pulp, in papermaking, 251, 275, 277, 343–44
    acid and, 255
    China as importer of, 294
    as counter intuitive, 251
    deforestation and, 281–84
    digesters in, 252–53, 279
    early experiments with, 251
    kraft process for, 254
    rags vs., 252, 254–55
    sulphite process for, 252–53, 254
    in US, 252–55

Woodville, Anthony, 2nd Earl Rivers, 180

Worde, Wynkyn de, 181

wordless novels, 269–70

World War I, 268

World War II, 271, 278, 285

World Wildlife Fund International, 284

wove paper, 197, 222, 264, 269, 279–80, 318

writing, xiv
    casual vs. permanent, 12–13
    direction of, 27–28
    early systems of, xix–xx, 4–9, 10–11, 337
    fears about, 18–20, 335
    in medieval Europe, 90–92
    memory and, xvii, 18–19, 62, 335
    phonetic, 6–7, 9, 15
    as response to needs of commerce, 5–6
    see also specific countries and regions

Wudi, Chinese emperor, 31

Wu Song River, 297

Xátiva, Spain, 71, 74, 77, 340

Xia dynasty, 23

Xiao Yi, *304*

Xiongnu, 27

xuan zhi, 300–301

Xuanzong, Chinese emperor, 40

Xylographer (Nicolson), *262*

Yamastaya paper shop, 309

Yangtze River, 294

Yeats, William Butler, 335

Yellow Kid, The, 263

Yellow River, 24

Yemen, 55

Yiddish, 15
Yoruba of Nigeria, 4
yoshi (machine-made paper), 305
Yoshizawa, Akira, 321
Yu, Chinese emperor, 23
Yukosha Company, 305, 344
Yzamatitlan, 152

Zaanland, Netherlands, 168–69, 171
Zainer, Gunter, 125
Zainer, Johann, 125

Zai Yuan Tang Mill, 301
Zapotec/Mixtec culture, 4, 338
Zaragoza, Spain, 141
Zell, Ulrich, 133, 180, 340
zero, concept of, 58, 86, 87
Zhang Heng, 38
Zhejiang Province, China, 301–2
zhi (paper), 32
Zhou dynasty, 25–26
zincographs, 264–65
Zumárraga, Juan de, 158–59, 341

A NOTE ON THE
PAPER AND TYPE

||||||||||||||||||||||||||||||||||||||||||||||||||||||||||||||||||||||

This book was printed on Sebago paper, an acid-free sheet manufactured by Glatfelter, a prominent American paper maker founded in 1864. Each chapter of this book opens with a capital letter based on the alphabet designed by Albrecht Dürer in 1525 and cut in linoleum by the author. The text was set in Dante, a serif face designed by Giovanni Mardersteig in 1954 and influenced by the Renaissance-era typefaces of Francesco Griffo. Dante was first used in 1955 for Boccaccio's *Trattatello in Laude di Dante*, for which it is named.

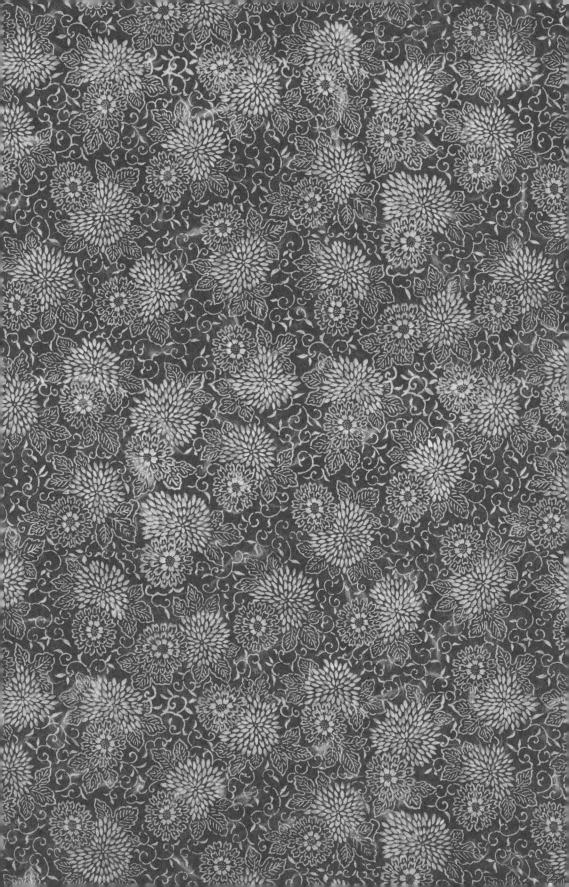